EDWIN FORREST

*First Star
of the American Stage*

EDWIN FORREST

FIRST STAR
OF THE AMERICAN STAGE

BY

RICHARD MOODY

1960
ALFRED · A · KNOPF   NEW YORK

L. C. catalog card number: 60–6648

© RICHARD MOODY, 1960

THIS IS A BORZOI BOOK,
PUBLISHED BY ALFRED A. KNOPF, INC.

FIRST EDITION

TO

Past, Present, and Future

GUESTS

OF

THE EDWIN FORREST HOME

FOREWORD

In our present era of abundant entertainment when television fills every half-hour piece of the day with another glamorous personality, and Hollywood is swarming with stars and starlets, it is hard to realize that the country was not always so richly endowed. Yet, Americans have been passionately devoted to the theatre for well over a century.

A hundred years ago they battled snow and hail and cheerfully endured hard seats, cold feet, dim lights, and noisy neighbors to escape for an evening from the dreary monotony of their daily lives and into the magical world of the theatre. Not only in the metropolitan centers, but also in Albany, Pittsburgh, Lexington, Cincinnati, St. Louis, and New Orleans they jammed the theatres whenever their favorite actors appeared, and for fifty years Edwin Forrest was their first favorite. No other actor could churn up their emotions as Forrest did with his stormy renderings of Shakespeare's tragic heroes or with his passionately patriotic impersonation of any one of a half-dozen freedom-loving zealots struggling against tyrannical oppression.

Edwin Forrest was the first native-born, native-trained actor to become a star. He was the first actor who refused to subscribe to the nation's cultural inferiority complex.

Even after America's Puritan conscience had been dulled—from overwork if from no other cause—and after the new Republic had asserted its political independence a second time in 1812, pitifully few cultural heretics dared to suggest that the new country was prepared to claim independence in art and literature. An American play might occasionally reach the stage if the author remained anonymous or if he was known to have enjoyed the advantage of study and training abroad. An

American actor might capture the seal of approval by spending a season or two on the London stage.

Forrest broke the pattern with a vengeance. He never appeared in England until he was ready to appear as an "American star." He passionately believed that a native son, imbued with patriotic zeal, committed to the cause of the common man, burning with inner fire, and blessed with natural perseverance and devotion, could shape a repertoire of stage heroes that would overshadow the effete creations of his British brothers. Forrest struck for complete independence. In 1828, just two years after he had made his sensational New York debut as Othello—he was then twenty—he challenged American writers to turn their talents to the stage and submit their manuscripts to his playwriting contest.

The country was ripe for Forrest's declaration of independence. Andrew Jackson showed the world that a rugged son of the frontier could capture the White House from a New England Adams. James Fenimore Cooper had proved that novels could be written about the new land, novels that would be avidly read even in London. And in his Phi Beta Kappa address at Harvard in 1837, Ralph Waldo Emerson insisted that Americans had "listened too long to the courtly muses of Europe"; they must learn to walk on their own feet, work with their own hands, and speak their own minds.

In the long history of the theatre few actors have matched Forrest's mighty power over an audience, few have led such a turbulent personal life, and fewer still have been so handsomely rewarded at the box office. If the Federal tax men ever regretfully reflect on what they missed a century ago, Forrest must trouble them.

CONTENTS

ILLUSTRATIONS

xi

Illustrations

EDWIN FORREST

First Star
of the American Stage

CHAPTER *i*

Twelve Happy Heirs

One morning late in March 1866, Edwin Forrest sat in the library of his town house in Philadelphia working through the final revision of his last will and testament. "To take and hold," it read, "all said property and estate in trust for an institution, which they will call 'THE EDWIN FORREST HOME,' to embrace the purposes of which I hereinafter give the outlines: . . ." The charge to his executors must be clear and precise, permitting no misunderstanding, offering no possibility of escape from his final command:

The said institution shall be for the support and maintenance of actors and actresses, decayed by age, or disabled by infirmity, who if natives of the United States shall have served at least five years in the theatrical profession; and if of foreign birth shall have served in that profession at least ten years, whereof three years, next previous to the application, shall have been in the United States; . . .

The number of inmates in the Home shall never exceed the annual net rent and revenue of the Institution; and after the number of inmates therein shall exceed twelve, others to be admitted shall be such as shall receive the approval of the majority of the inmates as well as the Managers. . . .

The purposes of the said institution are intended to be partly educational and self-sustaining, as well as eleemosynary, and never to encourage idleness or thriftlessness in any who are capable of any useful exertion. My library shall be placed therein in precise manner as now it exists in my house in Broad Street. . . . The Edwin Forrest Home shall also be made to promote the love

3

of liberty, our country and her institutions, to hold in honor the name of the great dramatic Bard, as well as to cultivate a taste and afford opportunity for the enjoyment of social rural pleasures; therefore, there shall be read therein to the inmates and public, by an inmate or pupil thereof, the immortal Declaration of Independence, as written by Thomas Jefferson, without expurgation, on every Fourth Day of July, to be followed by an oration under the folds of our national flag; there shall be prepared and read therein before the like assemblage, on the birthday of Shakespeare, the twenty-third day of April, in every year, an eulogy upon his character and writings, and one of his plays, or scenes from his plays, shall on that day be represented.

From the moment the first guest, William B. Lomas, entered the Edwin Forrest Home on November 7, 1876, to the present day, Forrest's directions have been scrupulously observed. Each year the old actors gather on the lawn to listen to the reading of the Declaration of Independence; each year they resurrect their old costumes and brush up their Shakespeare. In April 1955, Michael Moss, an Uncle Tom actor who had just passed his ninetieth birthday, introduced some non-Shakespearean verse into the celebration of the bard's birthday. Moss recited a poem of his own composition called "My Gratitude."

Of all the actors on the stage
Who have gained renown and fame
There is one I'll mention
You will know his name.
He was a leader in society
None with him could compare,
His kindness flowed as freely as water —
His talents were rare,
To describe his personality
Would require a mighty pen
Such a Shakespearean tragedian
We ne'er shall see again.
He gave me a home (and a good one too)
And no longer need I roam!
God Bless Edwin Forrest,
AND MAY HEAVEN BE HIS HOME!

Mike Moss echoed the sentiments of the twelve heirs of Forrest who were at that moment enjoying his bounty and of the hundred guests who had preceded them. For more than three quarters of a century retired actors have found peace and security for their final years among the antique treasures of the Edwin Forrest Home.

Men have sought to perpetuate their memories with hospitals, libraries, schools, and statues; few have achieved the kind of living immortality, an unbroken link with the past, a daily reminder of the benefactor's generosity, that Edwin Forrest achieved in the creation of his Home for "decayed actors."

Forrest's mark is on the Philadelphia landscape at several points. During his final season he appeared at the Academy of Music. The Moore Institute of Art at the corner of Broad and Master is the mansion in which he composed his will. In its heyday in the 1860's, this establishment housed its own theatre, a private art gallery, and a library then unsurpassed by any in this country.

However well-informed Philadelphians may be about the historic monuments within their city, few of them now know the monument that still perpetuates the memory of Edwin Forrest. Sunday strollers who have wandered to the far end of Fairmount Park, where Parkside Avenue runs into Belmont Drive, may have admired the Elizabethan manor house at 4849 Parkside Avenue. Few could identify the elegant baronial structure as the present Edwin Forrest Home.

Here a dozen actors who have passed beyond the days of professional usefulness delight in a daily living more serene than they had ever anticipated; the first real home for many of them. In the theatre of their day every actor was an itinerant; home was a dismal dressing room or a cramped bedroom in a flea-ridden hotel. Fortunately, the actor is blessed with a facility for assuming new roles. In spite of the itchiness cultivated by professional habit, he submits to the pleasures of retirement in this luxurious retreat with the greatest ease.

When he enters the Home, all worries about the future are quickly forgotten. Without turning a hand, he can enjoy a life of solid comfort for the rest of his days. The Board of Managers—the Mayor of Philadelphia is an ex officio member of the Board—the resident supervisor, a staff of cooks, a gardener, a chauffeur, upstairs maids, and downstairs maids attend his needs and whims. The twelve guests are substantially outnumbered by the group that serves them.

Each actor regards the house as his own, each day as his own. Except at mealtimes, he goes his own way. He may wander about in Fairmount Park, stroll down the back lawn and onto the golf course of the Bala Country Club, cat nap in the "Great Room," in one of the sitting rooms, or on the back terrace. If he insists on an uninterrupted siesta, he retires to his private quarters on the second floor. Each actor's room carries its own aura of past theatrical glory. Each displays the name of an illustrious actor on the door: Lawrence Barrett, Otis Skinner, E. H. Sothern. Inside, the walls are covered with pictures, programs, and other mementos testifying to the past triumphs of the present occupant.

Forrest often grieved because natural paternity had been denied to him, yet his name has been more firmly perpetuated by this posthumous brood of dependents than it could have been by natural heirs subjected to the vagaries of filial devotion and genetic accident. Forrest would delight in his elderly children, in seeing the players so well bestowed. He might be shaken to see his coveted books and paintings that were his constant and most intimate companions so shamelessly ignored by the old actors. He insisted that his possessions be maintained as he left them "to improve the taste and to promote the health and happiness of the inmates" of the Home.

Forrest's treasures may no longer serve the purpose that he intended. They do serve the visitor who seeks the acquaintance of the great actor at first-hand, or as close to first-hand as is now possible.

From the third-floor passage, through the hallways and living rooms of the second floor, down to the "Great Room" and the sitting rooms of the ground floor, and into the large storage compartment of the basement, the house bulges with his treasures.

The larger-than-life white marble statue of Forrest as Coriolanus surveys the main hallway. In a way it dominates the entire household. The walls of the "Great Room" are hung with solemn portraits of Forrest, of his mother and father, and of his brother William. In one corner of the room is a cabinet containing Forrest's rosewood make-up box. Under a glass bell jar in another corner are the charred remains of the "First Folio of the Works of William Shakespeare," one of Forrest's prized possessions. Another pedestal holds a hoof and the sterling silver mounts from Forrest's favorite trotting horse.

A ceiling-high glass case in the main corridor contains a rich display of swords, rapiers, dirks, and daggers. Not all of these heroic implements were Forrest's; some bear the faded fingerprints of other great tragedians: John Philip Kemble, Edmund Kean, and Talma. Bookcases are squeezed into every available wall space throughout the three floors of the house. In the basement some four thousand additional volumes are packed in wooden crates, and a ten-by-twelve-foot enclosure is stacked to the ceiling with paintings: "Edwin Forrest with Side Burns," "Edwin Forrest in Winter Attire," and "The Side-Wheeler, Edwin Forrest." Even the "ladies room" on the first floor yields its bit of Forrestiana. A heavy gray safe buried behind the vacuum cleaner and brooms contains a box of jewelry, a brace of dueling pistols, the manuscripts of several plays by Robert Montgomery Bird and one of the two known fragments of *Metamora*, Forrest's famous Indian play.

The Forrest collection has not had a regular custodian since Charles J. Fyffe died in 1910. During his eighteen years as a guest in the Home, Fyffe was its self-appointed librarian. From time to time since his death the books and paintings have been scanned by professional appraisers for insurance purposes. In February 1955, they estimated that the collection was worth $74,704.56, a price considerably below the true market value. Except for the legalistic necessity, ascribing a monetary value to these treasures is a kind of impertinence. Their value is incalculable.

A quick tour through the Home immediately reveals that Forrest, though a mere actor, competed with the financial wizards of his day in building an extraordinary private library and art gallery. Thumbing through a few volumes, the visitor soon discovers from the ruffled pages and the marginal notes that Forrest was not a dilettante. He employed these resources to further his education, the formal aspects of which had been almost totally neglected.

Forrest sailed through a wide ocean of human experience with a landlubber's perverse disregard for stormy and uncharted waters. He was continually battling the vicissitudes common to all strolling players. His temperamental juices were perpetually erupting, tossing him into one stormy adventure after another. Wandering among the subdued surroundings of the Home, one may not immediately perceive this side of Forrest's nature; yet like a death mask that in its tranquillity hides the tortures of the living, the scrapbooks, account books, diary jottings, and miscellaneous letters conceal hints of the living adventures of a rebellious and impatient spirit.

Two crumbling notebooks wedged into the case at the head of the stairs on the third floor demand first attention: young Edwin's geography exercise book and his father's receipt book, with entries dating back to 1794.

The geography lessons, written in a strong, well-embroidered hand when he was ten, reveal that not all his attention was given to peninsulas, isthmuses, and bays. The book is filled with extracurricular notations. The name "June Harvy" appears in a bold script on one page; on another, the three words: "Money! Money! Money!" The stream of consciousness of a ten year old? Prophetic of Forrest's later preoccupation?

The yellowed pages of the other volume, his father's receipt book, disclose the aggravating financial struggles of the head of the house, perpetually skirting the fringe of disaster while fighting to maintain a show of respectability: always months behind on the house rent, borrowing to pay the $45 yearly tuition for his sons' schooling.

These touching tokens of his childhood, perpetual reminders of the lowly station from which he had begun his long climb, were preserved by Forrest with the same loving care that he gave to his most valued books and paintings. They were his constant guardians against false pride. Forrest's contemporaries might have understood him better if they could have first made his acquaintance through these little books.

Although the faded pages illuminate details of Forrest's early years that might otherwise elude discovery and provide a backdrop against which to view his fierce ambition and passion for wealth, they reveal no hints of his youthful yearning to be an actor. That story must be pieced together from the contemporary accounts of others and from what Forrest wrote and said in later years.

CHAPTER *ii*

"The Germ of Tragic Greatness"

Forrest made his theatrical debut as an ingénue. He may not have been the first actor to inaugurate his career in a female role, nor the first to begin so young—he was eleven; he may well have been the first to interrupt a Saturday-afternoon game of marbles to step directly into the candlelight magic of the theatre.

One sunny spring afternoon in 1817, when Forrest and his companions had gathered for their regular game outside the stage door of the South Street Theatre, Charles Porter, the theatre manager, called Edwin aside and inquired if he was Ned Forrest, the "spouting school boy." If he was, Porter had a proposition. *Rudolph; or, the Robber of Calabria* [1] was billed for the evening; the actress who was to play Rosalia was ill. Would Forrest attempt the part? He would not need to memorize the lines; Rosalia was captive in a Turkish prison and reclined on a divan throughout the play. Ned could have the book safely by his side.

Forrest agreed immediately, raced home to announce his good fortune and to solicit the assistance of his mother and sisters in preparing a costume. It never occurred to him to question the advisability of appearing in female garb. Enough to know that he was to tread the boards of the famous Southwark Theatre (sometimes known as the South Street Theatre).

[1] An adaptation by John D. Turnbull of a French melodrama by Loaisel de Tréogate which in turn was based on Schiller's *Robbers.*

"The Germ of Tragic Greatness"

Erected in 1766, this was the first permanent theatre in Philadelphia. During the Revolutionary War it had been used for soldier theatricals by General Howe's officers, under the guidance of Major André. After the war, Washington had been a regular patron, and his box, in the middle of the first tier, still carried its eagle insignia. Although in 1817 it had been superseded as the principal Philadelphia theatre, it still retained the magic of its former years, particularly for a youngster about to receive his theatrical baptism.

For the remainder of the afternoon domestic tasks were forgotten while Forrest's three sisters prepared a disguise. The only silk dress large enough to encompass his sturdy frame reached just to his knees; they decided that his lower extremities could be covered with a shawl. For his female tresses they denuded an old cavalry helmet of its long black horsehair tail. One of the windows was stripped of its curtain to supply turban and veil.

When Edwin crawled into position on his prison couch, lounging in the dim glow of the stage candles, the deception was complete. A few of the spectators detected an occasional huskiness in the voice, which, fortunately, aroused further pity for the sad beauty. Rosalia's first speech was a soliloquy, and though Edwin had some difficulty keeping with the text, his book being hidden from the direct rays of the footlights, he, carried through. When the Governor entered and poor Rosalia was obliged to follow the book for appropriate answers, the footlights proved totally inadequate. Observing that the light from the side candles was brighter, Forrest climbed out of bed. This was a mistake. He had not changed his boots or his blue Germantown wool stockings. He delivered the first speech and was studying through his next when a raucous shout rose from the pit. One of his friends had recognized him.

The audience broke completely and joined in the clamor, laughing, hissing, and applauding. Realizing that Rosalia's time was up, Forrest threw down his book, stamped to the footlights, shook his fist at the traitor and assured him that he would suffer for his folly.

Burning with humiliation and yet glowing under the spell of his initiation, Forrest hitched up his skirt and ran for home. By the time he had torn off his female disguise, he had determined his course. He substituted a Harlequin costume that his sisters had made for his parlor recitations and headed back toward the site of his debacle. He was sufficiently up on theatrical matters to know that there would be an interval between the main play and the farce. He timed his return to coincide with this recess.

Before sneaking through the stage door he peeked into the beer shop next door to make sure that Mr. Porter and the prompter were nestled over their mid-evening glasses of grog. The stage was completely deserted, as he had known it would be. Beyond the curtain the screeching strings of the orchestra were trying to work up a tune. Forrest stationed himself at the curtain pull waiting for the musicians to conclude their number. When they finished, he yanked the curtain open, and jumping to center stage recited David Garrick's "The Harlequinade." The rendition provoked a round of applause. Warmed by the hearty response, he proceeded with his customary acrobatic encore: a series of somersaults and twice around the stage with cartwheels. This brought more applause. He was just going back on stage, walking on his hands, when Porter returned from the grog shop. Forrest ran out the stage door, Porter's curses following him down the street. Recalling the incident in later years, Forrest wrote to a friend: "From that moment my destiny was sealed. I felt that I was to be an actor, and an actor I would be, come what may!"

Unlike so many of his immediate predecessors, contemporaries, and successors in the acting profession, Forrest was not born into a theatrical family. Whether genes or the ubiquitous theatrical trunk controlled the destinies of the Booths, Jeffersons, and Davenports, Forrest had neither heredity nor environment to direct his attention to the stage.

His father, William Forrest, had been brought up in the easy, genteel atmosphere of Grandfather Forrest's country seat at Cooniston, Midlothian, Edinburgh County, Scotland. In his early twenties William abandoned the security of his home to find the rainbow's end in the new Republic across the waters. His purse was light and his baggage contained little more than a few samples of Scotch cloth with which he proposed to set up a mercantile importing business.

Rebecca Lauman, Edwin's mother, was born in Philadelphia. Her parents were German immigrants who had come to the Colonies and settled in Philadelphia around the middle of the eighteenth century.

When the couple met and married in 1795—he was thirty-seven and she thirty-two—William was not a prize catch. His first business venture in Trenton, New Jersey, had failed, and when he moved to Philadelphia, he was hopelessly in debt. Rebecca was sure that together they could change his fortune. She was a remarkable woman: gentle and cheerful, yet endowed with pioneer-like fortitude.

After their marriage William turned to banking, not as a professional banker, but as a runner, first for the United States Bank, later for the bank of Stephen Girard. Somehow he had struck up a friendship with Girard, the millionaire who had gone to sea as a cabin boy and who now owned his own bank and who, when he died in 1831, left an estate of seven million dollars, six million of which went into the founding of Girard College. In spite of William's honest efforts, he was less fortunate than Girard; each year took him a step further away from solvency. At his death in 1819 he left a burden of debts which Edwin carried on his conscience until he finally cleared his father's name some ten years later.

If Rebecca and William had been allowed a longer interval of honeymoon bliss, the later years might have been less rigorous. Young Forrests made an early entry. Lorman, the first child, was born in 1796, just a year after the marriage, and from then until 1808 a new addition arrived every second year. In the order of their appearance after Loman they were Henrietta, William, Caroline, an unnamed boy who died at birth, Edwin, and Eleanora. On November 13, 1813, after a wait of five years to allow for any possible delayed entries, the group was taken en masse to the Episcopal Church of Saint Paul on Third Street to be baptized by the Reverend Doctor Pilmore. It was cheaper by the half-dozen.

Rebecca and William felt strongly that their children's appetites for learning must be whetted by formal education. Even the girls were allowed brief periods of instruction, and this at a time when the female mind was regarded neither as susceptible to nor worthy of cultivation. None of the children was given a full program, but Edwin came off better than the rest. He had eight years of spasmodic instruction from the time he was five until he was thirteen.

The Forrest household never bubbled with free and easy gaiety, yet all the children developed an enduring love for their home and for each other. Any intra-family strife there may have been faded before it left a mark. With this initiation to domestic bliss one might expect that each of the young Forrests would march to the altar upon reaching an eligible age. None of them did. Only Edwin ever married—at thirty, and then disastrously. Either Rebecca and William had drawn their offspring so tightly to them that the thought of introducing an outsider was repulsive, or the struggle for domestic felicity made matrimony seem not worth the price.

The boys went to work as soon as they were able. Lorman began as a tanner and currier; William as a printer's devil; and Edwin as a clerk in Baker and Sons' importing house. When their father died and the boys saw the rewards of his conscientious service, they lost their enthusiasm for steady work. In fact, they became so intent on escaping the trap of steady servitude that they jumped into the most precarious pursuits: Edwin and William to the theatre, Lorman to plain, unadulterated adventure.

When the boys left home, they did their best to keep their mother free of anxiety, often shielding her from the unpleasant details of their undertakings. When, for example, Lorman set out for South America in 1822, Edwin wrote from Philadelphia to William in Sheperdstown, Virginia, urging him not to tell their mother of the adventure. Nothing more was ever heard of Lorman.

Edwin was only thirteen when his father died; yet he assumed his share of the family burden by intermittent jobs: at Baker and Sons, at the printing office of the *Aurora*, at a cooper shop on the wharf, and at a ship-chandlery store on Race Street.

As the youngest son and the frailest, Edwin received the constant loving care of his mother. In later years when questioned by a newspaper reporter about his mother and his early years, he said: "She was extremely pious. I was not a strong child. I often heard the old people say: 'Ned is a weak child; we fear she shall never be able to raise him.' I wondered why I should not live like the rest of our children. Early in life I took a great deal of exercise and made myself what I am, a Hercules."

The first ten years of his life seem to have been occupied with a continuous fight for survival. He was pale and thin, and his sunken chest and the forward stoop of his shoulders marked him as a consumptive and a likely candidate for an early grave. (His father died of consumption.) Yet he possessed nervous fire that often drove him beyond the limits of his physical capacities and to a state of collapse, frequently accompanied by crying spasms.

Before he was ten he became fascinated with the circus and with the muscular development and control demonstrated by circus performers. He adopted a regimen of imitating their gymnastics: climbing ropes, leaping bars, walking on his hands, standing on his head, throwing somersaults, balancing, and wrestling. Forrest recalled that by the time he reached his teens he had deepened his breathing, invigorated the circulation of his blood, and improved his posture. This attention to body culture, adopted out of sheer necessity at the beginning, developed into a ruling passion in later years.

Most of all, he nursed an uncontrollable ambition to be an actor. He sought every opportunity to train and exhibit his talent. One evening, shortly after the escapade at the South

Street Theatre, Forrest attended a lecture on nitrous oxide at the Tivoli Garden. When the "Professor" called for volunteers, Forrest climbed to the rostrum, inhaled a few puffs of the laughing gas and began to recite. Colonel John Swift, an alderman and later a three-term mayor of Philadelphia, was in the audience. At a dinner in Forrest's honor twenty years later Mayor Swift recalled that he had put his arm around the boy when he stepped down from the platform in Tivoli Garden and announced to the crowd: "This lad has the germ of tragic greatness in him."

Forrest's father recognized Edwin's elocutionary inclinations and provided lessons for him with Alexander Wilson [2] and with Professor Lemuel G. White, the Philadelphia elocutionist.

Edwin arranged his own extracurricular enterprises. He recited for his brother Lorman's fellow workers at the tannery. He and brother William organized a Thespian Club; in order to entice more members they called it a secret club for "young men of spirit and daring." For two years Edwin served a vigorous thespian apprenticeship. His group frequently joined forces with the Mortonians, another dramatic society, for evenings of declamations and scenes from Shakespeare at the Southwark Theatre.

Forrest's first real chance to test his amateur training with professionals came on Monday, November 27, 1820, when he made his formal debut at the Walnut Street Theatre in the part of young Norval in James Home's *Douglas*.[3] This role had be-

[2] Wilson was better known as an ornithologist than as an elocutionist. As a result of the publication of his *American Ornithology*, in 1810, he became known as the "father of American ornithology."

[3] First performed in Edinburgh in 1756, *Douglas* was written by the Reverend James Home, a Scotch clergyman, who was expelled from the church for trafficking with the theatre. The play tells the story of the foundling young Norval—"stamp'd a hero by the sovereign hand of nature!"—who is revealed to be the long-lost son of Lady Randolph. Glenalvon, the villain, poisons the mind of Lady Randolph's second husband against the boy and Lord Randolph and Glenalvon kill him. In a final touching scene Douglas (young Norval) dies in the arms of his mother.

come the accepted vehicle for young actors, and Forrest must have had it well in hand before the opening.

Although shrouded in anonymity—he was billed as "a young man of this city"—Forrest received one flattering notice on his debut performance. William Duane [4] wrote in his Jeffersonian paper, the *Aurora*: "Of the part of Norval, we must say that we were much surprised at the excellence of his elocution, his self-possession in speech and gesture, and a voice that, without straining, was of such volume and fine tenor as to carry every tone and articulation to the remotest corner of the theatre." Fearing that he had gone overboard in praise of the novice, Duane also noted "some occasional stiffness in the moments of passive action," and that Forrest, like all young performers, had difficulty controlling his hands.

Impressed by Duane's notice, managers William Warren and William Wood gave Forrest three additional performances: on December 2 (*Douglas*), December 29 (*Lovers' Vows*),[5] and January 6 (*The Mountaineers*).[6] For all this furious beginning —four performances in a little over one month, thirty-nine dollars for his efforts, and extravagant praise in the press—he was disappointed to find that his fourth performance was his last, at least for the moment. William Wood admitted that "Forrest was a well grown young man, with a noble figure, unusually developed for his age," and that his performances "were considered by all the principal actors, as far beyond any they had ever witnessed from a novice," yet he did not detect sufficient public enthusiasm to keep him.

Forrest returned to pedestrian occupations for his livelihood and to amateur activities for theatrical nourishment, working up *Richard III* with the Mortonians. In his first attempt at Shakespeare he performed triple duty. He staged the production, played Richard, rented the Prune Street Theatre for the

---

[4] Duane became Secretary of the Treasury under President Jackson.

[5] An adaptation by John Howard Payne based on Mrs. Inchbald's and Benjamin Thompson's translations of Kotzebue's play *Das Kind der Liebe*.

[6] A melodrama by George Colman, Jr., frequently played by Edmund Kean.

performance, and if his report to brother William can be accepted, succeeded in all departments: *"Richard III* drew a good house, came off with a liberal quantity of applause and a small pecuniary gain." Thus he closed his first theatrical season.

Even with his limited appearances he had drawn considerable attention in the press. The Honorable Joseph R. Chandler, editor of the *United States Gazette*, later a congressman, and President Buchanan's minister to Naples, composed a twenty-six-line verse extolling the young actor. A few lines will give the tone; more might discredit Chandler:

> *Cooper's our Sun, his orbit is our stage,*
> *Long may he shine, by sense and taste approved,*
> *By fancy reverenced, and by genius loved!*
> *And when retiring, mourned by every grace,*
> *May Forrest rise to fill his envied place!*
> *Dear child of genius! round thy youthful brow*
> *Taste, wit, and beauty bind the laurel now.*

Forrest was delighted with the suggestion that he might be a likely candidate to succeed Thomas Abthorpe Cooper. Cooper had come to America from England in 1796 when he was twenty, had rapidly climbed to the top of his profession, and was now the wealthiest actor in America, traveling from one engagement to another in his own private coach. Responding immediately to Chandler's flattering hint, Forrest secured an interview with the old actor. Cooper cautioned him against putting too much stock in his first flashes of success; a young actor must learn his art step by step. The old man may have been alerting him to the need for diligent and devoted study; Forrest thought that he was advising him to backtrack and begin as a super. He could not endure such nonsense. He got up and walked out.

This episode notwithstanding, Forrest was not unwilling to learn from his superiors. When Edmund Kean, the great English actor, appeared at the Walnut Street Theatre in January 1821, Forrest attended every performance, his attention riveted on Kean as he roared through his Shakespearean repertoire.

Forrest did not meet the great man on this occasion, yet the results of his observation soon became apparent. Some of his friends reported that he quickly out-Keaned Kean.

However strongly Forrest impressed his friends, when the 1821 fall season began he was still unable to get a solid footing in the Philadelphia theatre. Finally, in December, he wearied of marking time and applied to James H. Caldwell, manager of the New Orleans Theatre. His first professional solicitation was not a humble entreaty. Informing the manager that he desired to perform in his company for "six or eight nights, in such parts as I shall name," he gave Caldwell no hint of his fledgling status. "I acted last season in Messrs. Warren and Wood's Theatre for a few nights," he wrote, "and drew respectable and profitable houses, which is a difficult matter to do at this season in Philadelphia." To keep his intentions secret from his mother and sisters, Forrest requested the manager to answer in care of John R. Baker and Sons, 61 Race Street. Caldwell never replied.

Happily his Philadelphia fortunes improved, and he could ignore the New Orleans rebuff. He was engaged to play the part of Zaphna in *Mahomet* [7] at the Walnut Street Theatre on Saturday, January 31. Two days after the performance he wrote a detailed account of his success to his brother William in Harrisburg. "I played better than ever I did before. The curtain fell amidst bravos that kept up till the beginning of the farce which was forced to be suspended. Mr. Wood called me to his apartment, and told me to go on, they were calling for me." On the strength of his strong performance, Wood re-engaged him. Forrest was certain that he was finally on his way. However, when he appeared at the theatre on the designated night the following week, Wood had changed his mind. Again he was thrown on his own resources.

Discounting two nights of *Richard III* with the Mortonians in April, his *Mahomet* was his first and last performance of the 1821–2 season. The managers' perversities did not diminish his

[7] Adapted by John Howard Payne from the Reverend James Miller's translation of Voltaire's *Mahomet.*

determination to become an actor. In fact, he was so determined that he quit his job at Baker and Sons—a foolhardy decision. In June he was obliged to write to his brother William: "When you can spare from your salary the sum of $5, I wish you would send it to me, as I at present stand in much need, and ere long I will transmit it to you again." If Forrest had been a little older in the profession, he would have realized that such letters to older brothers, fathers, and rich uncles constituted the principal correspondence of young actors.

Late in the summer he made another futile attempt to secure an engagement away from home. He wrote to James Hewett, manager of the Charleston Theatre. Again, as in the letter to Caldwell, he did not write in humble supplication. He outlined his sterling qualifications and requested an immediate reply "so that in case you decline my services I may be enabled to make arrangements elsewhere." Hewitt never answered.

Having passed his sixteenth birthday the previous spring, Forrest felt compelled to get on with his profession. Just before the end of September, opportunity opened up right under his nose. Joshua Collins and William Jones, proprietors of theatres in Pittsburgh, Lexington, and Cincinnati, arrived in Philadelphia to recruit a company. Edwin presented himself at their hotel and was given an interview. Jones recalled later that he was impressed with "this fine specimen of manly youth, his free open bearing, his steadily-confronting eyes, and his clear, deep voice." He also recalled that the youngster was inclined to overrate his capabilities. Jones made it clear that for eight dollars per week Forrest was "to play, without question, whatever parts he was cast in, no matter how high or how low." Forrest accepted the terms. He was confident that his talents would be recognized and that he would not be limited to inferior roles.

Leaving his family on short notice—the company was to depart within the week—was not easy. He had never been away from home, and had not the vision of his impending adventure appeared so irresistible, he might have backed down when faced with tearful farewells.

Much as his mother and sisters fussed over the packing, it could all have been done in an hour. One small trunk held his meager wardrobe, the Bible his mother had given him, a one-volume edition of Shakespeare, Walker's *Classical Pronouncing Dictionary*, and a few paper-bound playscripts that he had used during his apprenticeship. With this small burden, he reported to the stagecoach.

Except for Mrs. Riddle, whom he had known at the Prune Street Theatre, and her two daughters, Eliza and Sallie, Forrest had only a nodding acquaintance with the five women and six men whom Collins and Jones had recruited. Most of them were as new to the profession as he was. Yet when the coach pulled out into the open country headed for Pittsburgh, the dozen actors were drawn together by that inexplicable magnetism that invariably seems to be generated when a group of strolling players is embarked on a theatrical mission.

CHAPTER *iii*

On the Western Circuit

The bedraggled company arrived in Pittsburgh on Wednesday, October 9, 1822. The journey had been exhausting and the reward they now received seemed hardly worth the price. After the cleanliness of Philadelphia they were depressed to find Pittsburgh buried under a filthy black cover, and, being accustomed to the varied theatrical establishments of the Quaker City, were shocked by the bleak and dilapidated playhouse in which their talents were to be exhibited.

Edwin's first thoughts turned toward home, as they did throughout his life. He wrote immediately to his mother:

> Dear Mother,—I arrived here yesterday at about eleven o'clock, and am much pleased with the place and its inhabitants. I was quite out of patience riding so long in the stage over such tremendous mountains, but was greatly delighted, on reaching the summit of them, to view the surrounding country,—so vast and varied a landscape.
>
> Pittsburgh is three hundred miles from Philadelphia. It is a sort of London in miniature, very black and smoky. The Allegheny River and Mountains surround it. The theatre is very old.
>
> This, you know, is the first time I have ever been away from you. I have felt many qualms of homesickness, and I miss you, dear, dear mother, more than words can give out. Has William gone to Petersburg? The long ride in the stage has made my hurdies so callous that they would ward off a cannon-ball.
>
> Give my respects to all my friends, and write as early as pos-

sible, and pray pay the postage, as I am out of funds. I expect the managers by the next stage.

> Your affectionate son,
> Edwin Forrest

The engagement began on Monday, October 14, with the old stand-by *Douglas*, with Forrest as Norval. Two years had passed since he had made his debut in the same part, and as he looked about the decaying structure—on rainy nights the audience in the pit held up umbrellas—he must have wondered how far he had advanced in those two years.

The small and solemn houses in Pittsburgh did not provide an auspicious beginning. For a week the troupe battled fruitlessly to arouse attention; one night the total receipts dropped to seven dollars, not a cheering recompense for an evening's labor. Still the company had no thought of turning back. Their itinerary was fixed, and Collins and Jones assured them that the strong towns on the Western circuit were down the river: Cincinnati, Lexington, and Louisville. Pittsburgh was always a questionable prelude.

The company collected its stage and personal properties, pitched them onto an Ohio River flatboat, and was soon floating serenely downstream toward the centers of frontier culture. After the jostling stage journey from Philadelphia, gliding along on the gentle waters of the Ohio was like floating on a cloud.

A warm Indian-summer sun bathed the deck for the full five days; the nights were crisp and clear, with occasional sharp cuts of breeze to warn them that November was almost here. This lazy carefree living was a new experience for Forrest, as for most of the company. Swapping anecdotes of stage misfortunes, extravagant stories of Cooke, Cooper, and Kean—generously interlarded with recitations and imitations—they filled the days with vicarious theatrical delight. Forrest spent most of his time on deck, studying his parts and soaking in the glories of the countryside. Even with the leisurely progress of the flatboat, the three hundred and fifty miles of frontier panorama passed with amazing rapidity, or so it seemed to a youngster who had never before set foot outside of Philadelphia.

When the boat tied up at Maysville, Kentucky, Collins and Jones announced that after the five days of inactivity the company needed a few warmup nights before proceeding to Lexington. If the rustic theatre in Maysville appeared no more inviting than that in Pittsburgh, the audiences were markedly improved both in quantity and quality. The local citizenry augmented by the entire population of the surrounding countryside streamed in every night and gave them a roaring reception. When the players moved on to Lexington, they were convinced that the backwoods lovers of the drama were eager to reward their efforts.

The seventy-five miles to Lexington appeared a short journey when compared with their first overland ordeal, yet after the feathery smoothness of the river, the jarring and banging of the coach was like a nightmare. If the roadbed from Philadelphia to Pittsburgh was rough, this was no road at all. The two indistinct ribbons stretching across open country were planted with boulders to make them firm under the sogging rain; these gave the passengers a perpetual banging, as if a sledge hammer was at work on the underside of the coach. In some places the ruts were reported "deep enough to bury a horse."

Lexington, then the most important town in the state, was to give the company its first real test. Collins and Jones decided not to open the theatre until the plays were well rehearsed, the stage accoutrements and the theatre itself in good shape. Situated at the corner of Spring and Vine, Usher's Theatre was actually a long narrow (eighty by thirty foot) second-story room of an old brewery which had been converted to a theatre by Luke Usher in 1816.

On December 16, 1822, the *Lexington Reporter* announced that the company was ready. The doors would open at five and "the Curtain will rise at a quarter past 6 o'clock. We hope the patronage bestowed, will be sufficient to reward the efforts of those who 'live to please, and please to live.'" The repertoire would include a hodgepodge of sparkling entertainments: *Broken Sword; A Russian Waltz; Laugh When You Can.* Out

24

of fear that such stage gaieties might induce undue levity among the patrons, the gentlemen in the audience were respectfully requested "not to smoke segars in the Theatre."

Settling down to a two months' engagement was an encouraging experience for Forrest and the troupe, though not devoid of assorted aggravations. Merely combatting the unsympathetic impositions of nature required hardihood and stamina. The weather was as cold as it had ever been known to be in Kentucky, and the theatre offered little defense against the assaults of winter. One reporter noted that they were also assaulted by "noise and vulgarity from within."

For the first month, Collins and Jones concentrated on minor farces, then in quick succession brought out *Hamlet*, *The Merchant of Venice*, and *King Lear*. Forrest's name appeared in none of the early advertisements; only when they turned to their major pieces did his name sneak into the bills, as Bassanio in *The Merchant of Venice* and as Edmund in *King Lear*.

In later years when Forrest reminisced about his Lexington sojourn, he invariably spoke of the strong impression made on him by the performance of M. M. Noah's patriotic Revolutionary War drama, *Marion; or, the Hero of Lake George*. *Marion* was one of the first plays to commemorate the glories of the nation's past. Forrest's parents had instilled in him a fervent love for his native land. Here for the first time he was alerted to the challenging prospect of combining his natural patriotism with his love for the stage.

When the company moved from Lexington to Cincinnati, they found no public conveyance available—in fact, not even a regular road. They hired their own horses and market wagons, bundled the ladies and stage properties onto the wagons, the men mounted the horses, and the caravan set off cross-country.

News of their impending arrival preceded them. On February 26 the *Cincinnati Advertiser* "perceived with pleasure" that the Lexington engagement had been concluded, and that "many rich theatrical repasts" were in store for Cincinnati. Word that the company had a "comer" by the name of Forrest may also have reached the city. At any rate Collins and Jones had been sufficiently impressed by the young man's progress to increase his salary to twelve dollars per week, to list his name at the head of the company in the initial notice in the *Advertiser,* and to allow him a benefit [1] for which Forrest chose *Richard III.*

The Columbia Street Theatre, located on the south side of Columbia between Main and Sycamore, had been opened just two years earlier and boasted a pit, two tiers of boxes, and a "spacious gallery," providing places for eight hundred patrons. In addition it had "commodious lobbies, punch rooms, etc.," all crowded into an area measuring forty by one hundred feet. Even if the theatre was less grand than the advertisements led one to believe, it was a marked improvement over Usher's.

Other marked improvements were evident in Cincinnati. The press noticed Forrest immediately. Moses Dawson, editor of the *Advertiser* and "leading Democrat of the West," observed that in the afterpieces Forrest "gave strong indications of his capacity in comedy," and that in *Richard III* he demonstrated that he possessed a genius in tragedy "in a degree inferior to no tragic actor on the American stage except Cooper."

Sol Smith, editor of the *Independent Press,* wrote on March 27, 1823: "We are told that when Mr. Kean, the celebrated English tragedian, saw Mr. Forrest play Richard in New York or Philadelphia [Forrest's performance at the Prune Street Theatre in Philadelphia] he was heard to say 'that young man never ought to stay in this country—he ought to go to England.' But we do hope it will not be necessary for him to leave his native country to have his talents acknowledged— that the time will come ere long, when native talent will be permitted to live at home." Smith was an amateur actor and printer who had just started his weekly paper. When it failed a year later, he returned to the cultivation of his talents as actor, play-

---

[1] It was a common practice in the nineteenth century to give the principal actors a benefit performance during each engagement. On his benefit nights the actor usually received either the entire net profits or one half of the gross receipts.

wright, and theatrical manager, and eventually became the leading impresario of the Western circuit.

Dawson's and Smith's judgments were corroborated by a series of "Letters to the Editor," one of which particularly excited Forrest: "It is seldom, Mr. Editor, in our power to admire and reward genuine native talent, as on the present occasion. Let us, then, show that we can discriminate between boisterous presuming arrogance and modest retiring worth, whether the possessor be nurtured in the polished cities of Europe, or among our own rude mountains." Forrest was beginning to sense that the nativist badge might become a kind of professional trademark.

Unfortunately, the company could not subsist on glowing press notices unaccompanied by cash at the box office. On April 12, 1823, the engagement terminated. According to one reporter: "the house closed for want of an exhaling public spirit to draw off the vapor."

Regardless of the lack of financial success, Forrest had a fine time in Cincinnati. During the month-and-a-half he spent there he boarded at the home of Widow Bryson on Main Street, quarters that had been secured with the help of General (later Senator and President) William Henry Harrison. The old Indian fighter had apparently taken a fancy to Forrest and, feeling that "if the youth boarded with the other players, he might form bad habits," had persuaded Mrs. Bryson to take him in.

Forrest's stay with Mrs. Bryson was peaceful and happy except for one incident. When Forrest detected what he thought was indecent behavior on the part of one of the female boarders, he chastised her with hell-fire insults and added some peripheral reflections on the character of her (and his) landlady. Mrs. Bryson was furious with the young upstart. She called in General Harrison, and the General called Forrest.

"Sir, the father of this lady was a Revolutionary soldier; her husband was one of my trusty officers in the late war; and she is a lady whom I highly esteem. When I introduced you into her family, I did not suppose you would treat her with disrespect; and I now ask you to make her a humble apology." These

27

were the General's words as Mrs. Bryson recalled them fifty years later. Forrest apologized, Mrs. Bryson forgave him, and the household was back on keel.

Abandoning the comforts of Mrs. Bryson's home for the rigors of the open road was not an inviting prospect. After the final performance Collins and Jones shut up the theatre and disbanded the company. Like endless troupes of strolling players before them who had been forsaken by their managers, the actors did the only thing they knew how to do, pooled their resources and took to the road.

The vagrant company appropriated two rickety wagons and two emaciated horses, which also had been abandoned by their masters, and set their caravan in the direction of Hamilton, Ohio, some twenty-five miles north. In Hamilton they found that the second story of a "venerable barn" had already been christened a theatre by the local thespian society. They moved in.

The citizenry gave the players a warm welcome, and on the occasion of their opening night, C. R. Smith, one of the local thespians, recited an address written for the event by the Hamilton poet and doctor, John C. Dunlevy.

From Hamilton they moved on to Lebanon for a week's stand, and then to Dayton. They encountered no overwhelming enthusiasm, just enough attention to nurse their egos and enough cash to keep them alive. With the closing night in Dayton, the members of the company decided that they would not stretch their luck by pushing deeper into the wilderness. They turned the wagons back to Cincinnati.

When Forrest and his companions discovered that Cincinnati had been deprived of theatrical entertainment since their departure, they rented the Globe Theatre for a summer season. The Globe had only recently been rechristened a theatre. Archibald Woodruff, proprietor of the Globe Inn, had cleaned out the barn adjoining his Inn and relabeled it. The company was well conditioned to such hasty transformations. On June 2 they gave their initial performance of *Douglas*—Forrest was becoming well seasoned in the part of Norval—and for the next month-

and-a-half paced through a dozen plays; remarkable training for a fledgling actor. Luckily, Forrest was blessed with an extraordinary memory and, according to one old actor, also with an uncommon compulsion to stick to the author's text, particularly with Shakespeare. Most of his colleagues regarded this as ridiculous fanaticism which they tolerated only so long as the young actor did not try to impose his notions on them.

In mid-July, just as the company was ready to disband, Sol Smith, having relinquished his editorial enterprise in favor of the theatre, arranged to rent the Globe for one night and to engage the services of the company. Ostensibly Smith's reason for the venture was to get a hearing for a new play by his brother Martin, though other items were added to fill out the evening. For the actors it must have been a labor of love; each received a token two dollars for his services. And what an evening's work! Forrest appeared as a dandy in *Modern Fashions,* the comedy by Sol's brother; as a Negro in a farce concoction by Sol himself called *Tailor in Distress;* and also participated in the concluding pantomime, *Sancho Panza.*

On July 16, the day before the Smith evening, Forrest's attention had been aroused by an item in the *Cincinnati Adververtiser* announcing a poetry contest. Caldwell was opening the new American Theatre in New Orleans and was offering a prize of one hundred dollars for the best dedicatory poem. The opening of this new theatre was to be a major theatrical event. According to one report, Caldwell even planned to install gas lighting. In fact, as it turned out, he built his own gas works, and for many years received sufficient revenue from supplying gas to New Orleans homes to keep his theatre solvent.

Forrest had no poem; instead he sent a letter requesting a place in the company. Remembering his previous experience with Caldwell, he held little hope of being accepted. He posted the letter and forgot it.

Having once explored the surrounding countryside with no ill effects, Forrest and his fellows decided to try the same circuit again. The summer tour was less successful. Among the few papers Forrest retained from this period was a small note dated Hamilton, August 6, 1823: "Due Wm. Cooper on order one dollar and fifty cents for value rec'd. Edwin Forrest." When the company broke up in Dayton, according to Sol Smith's recollection, Forrest was obliged to leave his stage wardrobe as security for his board bill before he set out on foot for Cincinnati.

When he finally reached Cincinnati after a hot forty-mile walk in mid-August along the banks of the Miami River, his clothes were dirty and torn and his feet covered with blisters. Although it hurt his pride to sponge on his friends, he had no choice. The most likely prospect was Mrs. Riddle whom he had known in Philadelphia and who had been with the company up until their barnstorming venture. She had always treated him like a son, and when he knocked on the door of her cottage in Newport, she gladly agreed to revamp the sleeping arrangements for herself and her two daughters and give him a bed.

Cincinnati theatricals were in the doldrums. Forrest worried over his poverty, yet with the help of Mrs. Riddle, her daughter Sallie, and a neighbor, James Taylor, whom he had met in Lexington, he kept up his spirits. One night he filled in at an amateur performance in Newport for an actor too drunk to play, collecting five dollars for his last-minute services and practically ruining the thespian society—the total proceeds for the evening having been seven dollars.

Most of his acting that summer was on a strictly amateur basis in what was known locally as Taylor's Barracks. General James Taylor had gone to Kentucky from Virginia in 1792, had made a fortune on land warrants, in 1804 had built the barracks and arsenal at Newport and during the War of 1812 had pledged his funds and facilities to the army. Now he was in command of the Point of Licking (Newport) army post and gave his son and Forrest permission to fix up a small theatre in one of the barracks to put on plays for the soldiers. Young James Taylor, Forrest's companion, had just graduated from law school at Transylvania. This friendship with Taylor endured throughout Forrest's life. Writing to a friend just after

Forrest's death, Taylor vividly recalled their summer performances, the many nights when they had sat up until early morning in his father's old office, and particularly Forrest's great delight in "sailing for hours on the river when the wind was high."

Many of the patterns of personal and professional behavior later so strongly identified with Forrest evolved during the summer. He began a rigid program of self-discipline, studying and experimenting with parts out of earshot of an audience. He found Sallie (Sarah) Riddle a willing companion in his unorthodox rehearsals. Day after day they tramped in the woods, reciting scenes from Shakespeare interspersed with a few tender lines of their own invention.

Having recovered from the soreness and distemper brought on by the hike from Dayton, and with a pretty girl beside him, he again opened his eyes to the beauty of the countryside. Together they strolled along the Ohio and the Licking, climbed the steep banks and looked down at the busy Cincinnati waterfront on the opposite shore.

In later years Forrest often recalled the August day on which he had crossed the Licking River, from Newport to Covington, and climbed alone up the western hills. As he sat looking out over the two Kentucky towns, Cincinnati, and the winding rims of the Ohio, he unconsciously tugged at the tough grapevines on the ground beside him; they had held on in spite of the giant oaks which had tried to uproot them. Forrest recalled that he found here a lesson in tenacity that was to sustain him through many periods of uncertainty. Less than twenty years later he purchased sixty acres of this hillside, pruned and nursed the vines back to their former glory, and christened the plot Forrest Hill.

During the summer Forrest's ambition took on a clearer purpose and direction. To be a "walking gentleman," a run-of-the-mill actor, would never satisfy him. He must become a serious tragedian, an actor whose physical power would reflect the sublime sweep of his native land, whose spirit would be imbued with the fresh, free air of the young democracy. The

American stage had been overrun with effete copyists of the British. It was time a home-grown, able-bodied, high-spirited American actor took over.

When he heard that the Lexington Theatre had opened for the season on August 27, he persuaded Mrs. Riddle to let Sallie go with him to Lexington. Together they would enchant the management.

Collins and Jones were no longer in charge. The former masters of the Western circuit, Mr. and Mrs. Samuel Drake, had again taken over. The Drakes with their three children were pioneers in this area. They had abandoned the unrewarding comforts of the Albany Theatre in 1815 to open up the Western regions and were now considered the first-rank entrepreneurs outside the Philadelphia-New York orbit.

The Drakes had met neither Sallie nor Forrest, but whether they were impressed with the praise they had heard in Lexington of the young actor, intrigued by the young couple out on their own, or simply unable to brush Forrest aside, they agreed to add them to the company.

If Forrest expected to step into the strong parts he had been preparing, his initial evening must have been discouraging. He opened on September 22 in *Everyone Has His Fault* and *Sprigs of Laurel*, and soon discovered that the selections with which the Drakes were trying to lure the Lexington citizenry were all of this "catch-house" variety: *To Marry; Wheel of Fortune;* and a "laughable farce" concoction with the intriguing title, *Prize; or, 2 5 3 8*.

It was not a good season. Discouraged by the response, the Drakes gave up, turned the theatre back to Collins and Jones, and moved on to Frankfort, taking part of the group with them. Forrest and Sallie Riddle stayed in Lexington. The promise of a chance at *Othello* led Forrest to remain.

No eye-witness accounts of the seventeen-year-old actor's first attempt at *Othello*, on November 4, have been preserved, if indeed there were any. No Moses Dawson was keeping tab on Lexington theatricals. If Forrest missed the encouragement from the press, he cherished the helpful advice of President

Horace Holley of Transylvania College. Holley had taken Forrest under his wing during the previous winter's engagement, and he and his students had become regular patrons. Holley was a minister as well as a college president, and was said to possess remarkable oratorical gifts. Unlike most ministers and college presidents of his time, he held strikingly liberal attitudes toward the stage. In fact, his liberality extended to all branches of human behavior and learning, and his insistence that medical science be taught on a strictly scientific basis without regard to church doctrine finally led to his dismissal. Some educators have speculated that if Holley's spirit of free inquiry had been allowed to persist at Transylvania, the institution would have become the Harvard of the Middle West.

Forrest had never encountered Holley's brand of serious talk on the art of the actor. The minister advised him to quit comic and farcical parts and devote himself exclusively to serious tragedy in which characters were embued with lofty motives and audiences embroiled in the living moral lessons that the life of the tragic hero revealed. Minor *divertissements*, though perhaps necessary to the theatre's economic survival, were unworthy of Forrest's attention. Having been newly aroused to nature's inspiration, Forrest listened avidly to Holley's discourses. In later years he insisted that these sessions with Holley "marked an epoch" in his early training.

One day in mid-November Forrest unexpectedly received a reply to the letter to Caldwell that he had posted five months earlier. Perhaps his brother William, who was now in the New Orleans company, had persuaded the manager to risk an offer. If Forrest considered that possibility, it did not disturb him. Overjoyed with the prospect of eighteen dollars per week in the Crescent City and the chance for better parts, he immediately quit the Lexington company.

A week later he had a change of heart and pleaded to be reinstated. According to Sol Smith, who had now taken over the management, Forrest insisted that he would rather stay in territory where he was known at ten dollars per week than go to Caldwell at eighteen. When Smith refused, insisting that the

33

actor must accept the New Orleans offer, Forrest signed up with a Lexington circus.

Not believing that the young actor really meant to pass up this opportunity with Caldwell, Smith went to the circus one evening to see for himself. "Sure enough," he reported in his *Theatrical Management*, "there was Ned in all his glory, surrounded by riders, tumblers, and grooms. To convince me of his ability to sustain his new line of business, he turned a couple of flip-flaps on the spot." After the performance, "I asked him to walk with me to my lodgings, where, by dint of hard lecturing and strong argument, I prevailed on him to abandon his new profession, and commence his journey to New Orleans immediately." Forrest finally agreed.

Before he left for Louisville, where he was to board the boat for the journey down the river, Forrest's Lexington friends gave him a send-off dinner at the Ayres Hotel on New Year's Day, 1824. James Taylor, Tom Clay, and a half-dozen of his Transylvania pals were on hand for the dinner. By the time the festive farewell turned to the speeches and recitations, the dining room was overflowing with well-wishers.

At the behest of Tom Clay, son of Henry Clay, Forrest had been a frequent visitor at the Clay mansion. The senator was in Washington, so Forrest did not meet him until several years later. At "Ashland" Forrest got his first intimate glimpse of domestic affluence, yet he was less intrigued by that than by Tom's brother Theodore. Theodore suffered from a mental derangement which, according to Forrest, led him to think that he was George Washington. Whenever Theodore was taken with one of his spells, Forrest followed him with a clinical eye. At the time, simple curiosity prompted him to observe the boy. In later years he admitted that Theodore had served as the model on which he built his interpretation of Lear. Gruesome recompense for family hospitality, but Forrest never allowed sentimental inhibitions to deter him from carrying out his appointed task.

Lexington and Cincinnati gave Forrest many happy moments and many friends: Dawson, Clay, Holley, and Taylor.

To abandon them, to increase his distance from his mother, and to expose himself to new risks and uncertainties, even in view of a prospective reunion with his brother, seemed a foolhardy course; yet the teasing thought that New Orleans might enlarge his professional fortunes overrode his fears.

CHAPTER *iv*

New Orleans:
Crinoline and Linsey-woolsey

In 1824 Louisville was the division point for steamboat traffic. The falls there, a drop of some twenty-five feet in a distance of two miles, had not yet been circumvented by a canal, so river traffic from both directions halted at Louisville.

Forrest must have felt some qualms in boarding the precarious steam-propelled contraption. Each year ten out of every hundred steam vessels on the river blew up, burned, or were abandoned on sand bars. To pay twenty-one dollars, two weeks of his Lexington salary, for the privilege of exposing himself to this jeopardy must have struck Forrest as a ridiculous investment.

Of the seven-day voyage over the 1,350 miles from Louisville to New Orleans, Forrest left no account, except to note in a letter to his mother that "Old Fuss and Feathers," General Winfield Scott, was a passenger, and that they held many conversations on deck that were "entertaining and lastingly instructive and useful." Scott could not have been too gay. He had just come from Washington where at a party that Secretary of State Adams had given in his honor his pocket had been picked of six hundred dollars.

Theatrical activity, though by no means a novelty in New Orleans, had been rejuvenated by the opening of Caldwell's new theatre. Performances in French had been done as early as 1791, and by 1809 three French theatres were in operation.

Noah Ludlow, who had gone from Albany to Lexington with the Drakes in 1815, had drawn off part of their group in 1817 and brought the first regular American company to New Orleans. James H. Caldwell, now in control of the theatre, was an English actor who had first played in this country with the Charleston company in 1816. In 1820 he had induced the Petersburg, Virginia, company to risk the ravages of yellow fever in New Orleans, and from then until 1841 he was the principal Southern impresario.

The theatre had become so much a part of the cultural life of the city, even as early as 1816, that the Municipal Council had passed strict regulations governing its operation. All scripts had to be submitted to the mayor for approval. Actors were to be fined from five to fifty dollars for failing to appear on stage at the time called. No spectator could enter "by means of cunning" nor carry a stick, cane, sword, or saber. To be certain that all regulations were observed, the mayor or one of his representatives was to be on hand at all performances.

Caldwell's new American Theatre on Camp Street, three blocks above Canal and just below Poydras, was the first substantial structure to be be built in the newly developing American quarter. The handsome brick edifice had a flight of marble steps running the width of the building. On the entry porch four marble piers topped by cast-iron tripods held four gas torches, the fuel supplied by Caldwell's new gas works. The building was 60 feet wide and 160 feet deep, with a proscenium opening of 38 feet and seat accommodations for 1,100, distributed among pit, parquet, and three galleries. The parquet was divided into forty-two boxes, each supplied with five mahogany chairs with stuffed seats and crimson coverings.

After the primitive makeshift theatres that Forrest had encountered, he was unprepared for such elegance and at the same time surprised to find the building so inaccessible. Built on marshy ground, it had to be reached by planks laid on flat-boat gunwales. In bad weather the mud was often knee deep and performances had to be suspended.

Forrest opened in grand style on February 4, playing Jaffier to Caldwell's Pierre in *Venice Preserved*.[1] After this auspicious beginning he slipped into "walking-gentlemen" parts in a collection of pedestrian pieces and when he was finally given a chance to demonstrate his powers in *Richard III*, he found that Caldwell had so brutally altered and amended the text that it bore little resemblance to the play as he knew it. The only delight he found in the performance was in having the beautiful and gracious Jane Placide as the Queen.

Except for the accumulation of more acting experience, the New Orleans season added little to his stature as a performer. It did, however, offer social opportunities he had never encountered before.

New Orleans, fashion and commercial capital of the South, was alive with all modes of society. Its inhabitants—at that time just under 30,000—carried a vast assortment of bloodlines and cultural backgrounds. Nowhere else in the country were the Old World and the New combined with such striking results. The light and fashionable gaiety of France, the dark, voluptuous intoxication of Spain (more properly of Spanish America), the chivalrous gentility of the slave-holding Southern planters and their decorative ladies—the refined living associated with the ante-bellum South just then gaining a foothold. Coexisting with these mannered drawing-room and grillwork-balcony creatures in their satins and crinolines, were rough-and-ready linsey-woolsey characters from up the river. Every flatboat, keelboat, raft, or river packet that withstood the hazards of the Mississippi disgorged a fresh group of ragged and rebellious Ohioans or Kentuckians. Wealth, leisure, and gracious living existed on one side, hand-to-mouth battling for food and shelter on the other. Drawing-room ripostes and duels vied with street fights and saloon brawls for popularity.

The slender, sinewy form of the young actor and his handsome dark face topped with a voluminous growth of black hair undulating in Byronic waves provided an inviting showpiece

[1] *Venice Preserved* by Thomas Otway is a heroic tragedy dealing with the ill-fated conspiracy of Jaffier and Pierre against the state of Venice.

for Caldwell to exhibit to his friends. Three years as purveyor of theatrical culture had established the manager's social respectability. Recognizing Forrest's decorative values for the drawing room, he steered the young man into high society.

Flattered as he was to be lionized by the first families, Forrest had a deep-rooted distate for fashionable living. Burdening the natural man with social schemes to inhibit his free spirit offended the democratic impulses that charged every fiber of his body. He refused to appear as Caldwell's protégé. Instead he sought companionship in the streets, the gaming houses, and along the river, where, though rough and untutored, a man might be known for what he was.

A gambler and duelist, a steamer captain, an Indian chief, and a frontier desperado—each about ten years his senior—became his closest friends. In speaking of this quartet years later, whether not remembering or wishing to hide their identities, Forrest attached fictitious names to all but the Indian and the frontiersman, Chief Push-ma-ta-ha and James Bowie, the inventor of the bowie knife.

Forrest admired Bowie's fearless courage, and delighted in hearing the bloody details of his many duels. His famous knife, sometimes called the "Arkansas toothpick," was designed for hand-to-hand combat. Two duelists were bound side by side on a bench with only their right hands free to manipulate the knife. Again and again Bowie had daringly placed his life in jeopardy; each time he had either killed his opponent or slashed him into submission.

The boatman—Captain Graham, as Forrest called him— epitomized the hard-living, hard-drinking riverman. Forrest first made his acquaintance when the Captain and fifty of his fellow boatmen came to the theatre. Forrest discovered that these ruddy characters, freshly released from their own precarious exploits, were gullible devotees of bold, violent stage effects. Playing up—later critics labeled it playing down—to the unrefined tastes of these river ruffians taught Forrest that roars from this herd and their constancy at the box office could be very satisfying to an actor. Here was an audience that his more genteel colleagues had not yet tapped, and sometimes as many as five thousand of them were in New Orleans at one time.

Graham's anecdotes of the river provided Forrest with his principal entertainment on many off-nights. One story that Forrest frequently repeated dealt with Graham's allegiance to his comrades. A friend of Graham's had been abused by one of the levee madams. The next day Graham hitched a towline to the pilings that supported her pleasure palace, ordered full steam ahead, and pulled the entire establishment out into the stream. Sinners and innocents alike were bathed in the muddy waters of the Mississippi.

For his excursions among the iniquitous dens of the city, Forrest chose an expert guide—Monsieur Gazonac, Forrest called him. In the saloons, in the purple salons, at the race-courses and the cockpits, this sleek gambler and duelist was well known and could command immediate attention for his protégé, and Gazonac, like Graham, had a rich store of weird tales.

For a youngster of eighteen to absorb a steady stream of horror stories and to have his social education directed by this trio of rousers would seem to be excellent training for a life of crime. Forrest, however fascinated with these exploits, was far more interested in bottling their essences for future stage use.

Whatever evil influence Bowie, Gazonac, and Graham may have exerted on him was counteracted by Chief Push-ma-ta-ha, Forrest's fourth companion. The Choctaw chief turned his attention to moral and spiritual matters. From him Forrest learned the simple values that governed the life of the red man: swift, stern revenge on the marauder, steady devotion to anyone who offered kindness and love.

Forrest found greater intimacy with the Chief than with his other companions. When his spirits were low or he felt the fever about to strike (a constant threat in New Orleans at that time), he sought the ministrations of Push-ma-ta-ha. The Chief's extensive repertoire of cures both for mind and body provided something for every need.

New Orleans: Crinoline and Linsey-woolsey

As the end of the season approached and Forrest surveyed the engagement, he found little in the professional line to encourage him. Caldwell had not allowed him to demonstrate his full capacities. When he had rebelled at Caldwell's assignments of Romeo and Hamlet—Forrest did not think he was ready for either part—and had rebuffed the manager's social sponsorship, his chances of getting parts of his choosing became more remote.

Other misfortunes were heaped on him through no fault of his own. One evening late in the season, his performance aroused a burst of applause and huzzas. Intent on joining one of his companions, he left the theatre not realizing the cheers were for him. Before his benefit a few nights later Forrest learned that the audience did not intend to allow him to appear unless he apologized. To knuckle under in this fashion was beneath his youthful dignity; he refused.

Captain Graham enlisted a group of his rivermen to be at the theatre on the benefit night "to put him through," as Graham expressed it. With these husky sympathizers in the audience, Forrest waited impatiently in the wings, eager to challenge his detractors. When his cue came—his audience knew it as well as he—an explosion of hisses and shouts of "Apology! Apology!" enveloped the stage. Forrest circled down to the gaslights at the foot of the stage, stretched his shoulders to their full height, and fixed the audience with a glare. The shouting stopped. He waited a moment, surveying the crowd, and then told them that he had nothing to apologize for. He had simply left the theatre and had not heard their applause. According to one eye-witness account, "A perfect hush followed, and in a moment the changed temper of the audience declared itself in a unanimous cheer, and the play went swimmingly on to the close."

The New Orleans season closed in the middle of June. Half the company under Ludlow's guidance was scheduled to invade the river towns to the north, the other half, with Caldwell, to undertake the long sea voyage back to Virginia. Forrest was chosen to join the Caldwell contingent.

Before the season was concluded, Forrest came down with malaria. In spite of his hygienic efforts, once the dreaded swamp fever attacked his system he had to let it run its course. Every summer it descended on New Orleans like a plague, and everyone unlucky enough to stay in the city was almost certain to be caught in its path.

Forrest suffered through the sweating delirium, calling for his mother while Captain Graham sponged him with cold water and poured whiskey down his throat. For two days Forrest tossed and struggled to expel the fever through his streaming pores. Finally it was gone, almost as suddenly as it had come on. In his weakened state he was happy to have before him the long voyage to Virginia to recover his strength.

During the trip Forrest could not get the delirious dreams of his mother out of his head, and when they finally tied up at the City Point Wharf and he settled into his boarding house in Petersburg, he wrote to her immediately.

Petersburg, July 26th, 1824

Beloved Mother,—I must indeed beg ten thousand pardons for not writing to you earlier. Although we are separated, think not you are forgotten by me. Oh, no, dear mother, you are ever in my memory, and your happiness is my greatest wish. I hope, my dear mother, in the course of three or four weeks, to be with you on a visit of a fortnight or so, but must then return here to perform at Richmond and Norfolk. I sincerely desire that this vacation may occur. Then I shall see you; and I assure you such a meeting will be as great a happiness as I can possess in this world. . . .

Forrest and his mother were both to be disappointed; he did not get home. At the end of September, he wrote to her from Fredericksburg explaining that they had been acting every night in Richmond, Norfolk, and Washington and that he saw little prospect of a vacation before the end of their Northern tour.

With no opportunity to talk with her, he wrote of the aggravations and delights of the summer season. " I performed Pythias for my opening here [Fredericksburg], and have succeeded to the delight of all the inhabitants. I had some difficulty with the manager [Caldwell] again. He cast me, as an opening part, in Mortimer in the comedy of *Laugh When You Can*. I refused to play it, and left the theatre. However, in two days I saw my name in the bill for Pythias and resumed my situation. All has gone on smoothly since, and I have triumphed over him as a tragedian in the opinions of those who recently esteemed him above praise or censure." Forrest's estimate of his success undoubtedly had some foundation in fact. The *Richmond Compiler* noted that Forrest was "appreciated by those who prefered excellence in a subordinate character to mediocrity in a higher. If he will be persevering, public opinion must sooner or later lift him into that sphere, where he will not be fettered by the restraint of managerial authority." Certainly Caldwell would not have tolerated Forrest's insubordination if he had not detected compensations at the box office.

Forrest recalled few details of this Virginia tour. The Richmond engagement alone stood out in his memory. There on successive nights he had played before Chief Justice John Marshall, the grand old man who had established the supremacy of the Supreme Court, and the Marquis de Lafayette, then on his triumphal tour of the country.

At the end of November the company returned to City Point, sailed for New Orleans on December 1, and on January 8, 1825, reopened the American Theatre. Forrest must have had a strong hold on the New Orleans audience, for his popularity increased in spite of his running battle with Caldwell. The manager reserved the best parts for himself, forcing Forrest into inferior and repulsive characters whenever he could. Caldwell found, however, that this maneuver did not work as easily this season as it had the year before. The young man's demands were backed by the public, and Caldwell's professional schizophrenia compelled him to respect his managerial responsibilities even when they struck at his actor's pride.

On the whole, Forrest got along much better than he had previously. He did Iago in *Othello* and Malcolm in *Macbeth*. Early in May *King Lear*, for "the first time in New Orleans," was announced for Forrest's benefit. Bad weather forced the postponement of this performance and when the benefit finally took place, Forrest appeared as Octavian in Colman's *The Mountaineers*, not as Lear. No explanation was given for the shift in plans.

Caldwell's annoyance with Forrest was not limited to professional jealousy. He might be forced to endure the young man's growing favor with the audience, but he could not tolerate Forrest's blossoming infatuation with Jane Placide, the sparkling young leading lady of the troupe.

When the first spark had been struck the season before, Forrest's shyness and ignorance of the ways of women had restrained him from any demonstration of his affection. He knew his own weakness: a pathological inability to accept defeat. If he risked his chances in a bumbling and unrewarded advance, he would be unable to renew the attack at a later time; better to postpone his overtures until he had more confidence. His knowledge of women was limited. He had tried a little fumbling love talk with Sallie Riddle. He had on occasion, with his friend Gazonac, enjoyed the nocturnal delights of female companionship on a temporary, anonymous basis. What he had learned from these hasty encounters was not applicable to Jane Placide. She was on another plane. In fact, her status in the company—she had been with Caldwell since the 1823 season—and the professional standing she automatically acquired from her theatrical family placed her somewhat outside the reach of a novice like Forrest.

Jane had gone to New Orleans from Georgia, where her family lived after her father's death. Her father, Alexander Placide, had arrived in this country in 1801 and had taken over the Charleston (South Carolina) Theatre. From there he went to Richmond, where he had the misfortune to be in command at the time of the calamitous Richmond Theatre fire in 1811. Jane had begun her career as a singer and dancer; now she was described as "the *beau ideal* of youthful tragedy," the "Queen of the Drama in New Orleans." One critic remarked that she had a single fault: her shrieks of horror were too loud.

New Orleans: Crinoline and Linsey-woolsey

During the first season, Forrest contented himself with meeting Jane Placide in the presence of an audience. During the second season the role of silent lover became intolerable. Unable to steel himself to a direct attack, he struck an opening wedge with the time-honored tool of shy lovers, poetry. He did not hand over his compositions directly, plant them in the wings of the stage, or slip them under her dressing-room door; instead, he persuaded the editor of the *Louisiana Advertiser* to let him display his amatory effusions in a small box in the newspaper. As poems they do not warrant a second printing—if indeed they deserved the first—but selected snatches will reveal the tone of Forrest's infatuation:

> *Thy spell, O Love, is elysium to my soul;*
> *Freely I yield me to thy sweet control;*
>
> . . . .
>
> *For her I'd yield whole worlds of richest ore,—*
> *Possessed of her, the gods could give no more.*
> *For her, though Paradise itself were given*
> *I'd love her still, nor seek another heaven.*

Such love-sick verses from an adolescent usually indicate that their author has spent his days in melancholy moping and his nights committing his depression to paper. Forrest did not allow his mooning over Jane to interfere with his acting.

As he was threading his way through his first experience with the prickly heat of adolescent love, he was also getting his first major lesson in stage deportment from a professional master, William Augustus Conway. His previous tutors—Wilson, White, Dawson, and Holley—helpful as their advice had been, could not speak with Conway's authority. In 1825 Conway, along with Cooper and Kean, occupied the top rung of the theatrical ladder in America.

Conway had acquired a solid reputation in England before he made his American debut in New York in 1824. He possessed a commanding stage presence, being tall and handsomely proportioned. Much as Forrest admired the sheer physical figure of the man, he was more intrigued with studying the inner

45

force and passion that he released through his powerful frame. Performing Malcom to Conway's Macbeth, and Iago to his Othello gave Forrest the chance to probe every volcanic burst, to study each turn of the head, each unfurling of a gesture, each rumbling accumulation of vocal force from a gentle dripping pianissimo until he raised the roof with a tremendous crash.

In his second New Orleans season, Forrest pushed resolutely into the ranks of the professionals. In spite of his continuing feud with Caldwell, he progressed as an actor if not as a lover.

During the entire spring he vied with the manager for the attentions of Jane Placide. The inevitable explosion occurred just before the end of the season. Caldwell announced a performance of *Twelfth Night* with himself as the Duke and Jane Placide as Olivia. To stand by on the stage and hear the pair speak Shakespeare's mellifluous love music, to see Caldwell take her hand and say: "You shall from this time be your master's mistress," was more than Forrest could endure. He quit the company.

When he walked out, he had no plan of action. The next day he realized that he had to do something. He hastily composed his sentiments into a brief sentence that he filed with the editor of the *Advertiser*. In the next issue of the paper the public was notified of the outrage.

> Whereas James H. Caldwell has wronged and insulted me and refused me the satisfaction of a gentleman, I hereby denounce him as a scoundrel and post him as a coward.
>
> —Edwin Forrest

In recalling the eposide, Forrest never made it clear that he had actually invited Caldwell to settle their differences with a duel. Certainly the notice in the *Advertiser* gave that impression.

When he deserted the company so precipitously, he relinquished his chances of joining it for the summer tour and his chances of forwarding his romance with Jane Placide. He did not see her again for four years.

Forrest discovered that he had thrown himself upon his own resources, which at that moment were in no condition to bear the burden. When his anger subsided, his spirits drooped even lower. He realized that the explosion he had engineered had, when it reached Caldwell, been reduced to an insignificant puff of ill wind.

Pushed into a corner, he sought the aid of Chief Push-ma-ta-ha. The Chief was preparing to depart for the summer, to camp with his tribe a hundred miles north of the city, and Forrest asked to join them as a lay brother. At first the Chief was reluctant to introduce a white man into the tribe. He finally consented when he saw the anguished loneliness in the young man's eyes.

For almost two months Forrest cast aside all connections with civilization. He dressed like the Indians. He smoked with them, danced with them, sang their songs, followed them in their hunts. In this fresh atmosphere he found it easy to rid himself of the bitter taste of his quarrel with Caldwell. The long evenings by the fire, listening to Push-ma-ta-ha spin out stories of the adventures of his ancestors, brought back a serenity of spirit he had not felt since the days he had wandered along the banks of the Ohio.

The Chief was just six years his senior, still the grandeur of his manner and bearing constrained Forrest to worship him as a kind of natural god rather than to treat him like a fellow human. When he spoke of this sojourn in the wilderness in later years, his most vivid recollection centered on the symmetry and grace of the young Indian's figure. The story he recalled most frequently he might have hesitated to repeat today.

Forrest shared the ancient Greeks' delight in the beauty of the naked human form. He maintained that fashionable clothes degraded and obscured the beauty that God had created. One evening he asked the Chief to strip and walk back and forth before him between the moonlight and the firelight so that he might feast his eyes and soul on so complete a physical type of what man should be. The Chief obliged. Forrest said that it was as if a living statue of Apollo in glowing bronze had come to life.

With this weird exhibition in his mind, it is not surprising that Forrest concluded his recollection of the episode by writing in his notebook: "My God, what a contrast he was to some fashionable men I have since seen, half made up of false teeth, false hair, padding, gloves, and spectacles!" Forrest's fascination with the natural man and his distrust of bedecked and mannered society creatures persisted throughout his life.

Much as he reveled in the free pastoral enchantments of the Indian's paradise, he was impatient to get back to the theatre, once he recovered his peace of mind. He had destroyed his local prospects and must seek an engagement in other quarters. With two years' experience, he might be ready for the Eastern managers. At least he would try.

In the middle of July he and the Chief held their farewell fireside session. Forrest returned to New Orleans and took passage on a "coasting-vessel" bound for Philadelphia.

CHAPTER v

Meeting Kean in Albany

The homeward voyage was uneventful except for one frightening moment. On the third day out the boat was becalmed. The weather was scorching. Forrest disrobed and jumped over the side for a swim. After circling the sloop several times, he heard frantic shouts from the deck above. Treading water for a moment, he discovered that someone had spotted a shark trailing in his wake. Forrest swam madly for the anchor chain and swung on board just before the shark caught up with him. Exhausted from the chase, he lay on deck surrounded by his fellow passengers. Everyone was breathing sighs of relief and thanking God for his miraculous escape, that is everyone except Forrest. He was taking inventory of the emotional reactions that he had experienced while the bloodthirsty devil had been hot on his trail. A hundred years later this "memory-of-emotion" system, which Forrest adopted intuitively, became one of the principles on which Stanislavsky built his method for actors.

The vessel tied up at the Philadelphia waterfront in the middle of August. Forrest had not told his mother that he was coming, yet the homecoming on Cedar Street was just what he had anticipated. His mother wept. His sisters wept. Edwin wept. For three years the family had been living on a starvation diet of fraternal affection; now they made up for it.

For a month Forrest luxuriated in the comforts of home, living the life of a potentate. He had left as a boy, returned as a man. Three years earlier he had tolerated being babied by the four females. Now he relished their solicitous attention. When he occasionally roused himself from the languorous luxury, he tramped around his old haunts. He called on Colonel Swift to report on his successes on the Western circuit. He attended Cowell's circus at the Walnut Street Theatre. The new Chestnut Street Theatre, where he had thought he might secure an engagement, was dark. Warren and Wood were on the point of dissolving their partnership; the playhouse might not even reopen for the season. Faced with these dim prospects in Philadelphia, Forrest applied to managers in other cities and to actors he had met along the way.

Only one petition received a reply and that came indirectly. He had written to William Conway, the actor who had inspired and instructed him in New Orleans. The response came in the form of an offer from Charles Gilfert, the eccentric Dutchman who managed the Albany Theatre. Conway must have convinced Gilfert of Forrest's accomplishments, for he was engaged to play leading parts in the Albany stock company and second parts to visiting stars. Conway was scheduled to be the first visiting star.

Albany was an old theatre town. As early as 1759 British officers had performed plays there. *Venice Preserved* was acted by a group of comedians from New York at the Albany hospital in 1769. By the turn of the century a regular company was in residence every season, though no proper theatre was available until the Green Street was opened in 1813. Noah Ludlow, Sol Smith, and the Drakes had all started their theatrical careers in this establishment. Six years before Forrest arrived, this theatre had been converted into a Baptist church.

In Albany, as in New Orleans, Forrest was to appear in a new playhouse. The Pearl Street Theatre had been dedicated the previous May with Stephen Van Rensselaer, the last of the Dutch patroons, heading the list of stockholders. Van Rensselaer was the fifth direct descendant of the first Dutch patroon, Kiliaen Van Rensselaer, and in 1825 was Albany's, if not the state's, first citizen. The theatre had been designed by Philip

Ib The comfort and happiness of his mother, Rebecca Lauman Forrest, was Edwin's constant concern. When she died, he wrote: "My mother is dead. That little sentence speaks all I can say, and more — much more."

Ia Samuel Lawrence's portrait of Forrest was painted shortly after his triumphant New York debut in 1826, at the age of twenty. Such a dashing, Byronic-looking hero was bound to capture the American audiences.

*II John Neagle's 1826 portrait of Forrest as the fierce
Peruvian rebel in* PIZARRO IN PERU *was the first picture of
the actor to be reproduced and widely circulated.*

*III Thomas Sully's portrait of Forrest was begun in 1837,
shortly after Forrest's marriage, and when completed in
1839 was presented to the Garrick Club in London, where
it still hangs.*

VI Jack Cade was another role in which Forrest glorified
the cause of the common man. One critic called the play
"a battle song of liberty."

VIIb Forrest as Virginius. The scene in which Virginius kills his own daughter to save her from the tyrant Appius Claudius was one of the most pathetically moving scenes in Forrest's repertoire.

VIIa Forrest first performed RICHARD III when he was fifteen. Contrary to the custom of his contemporaries, Forrest played the part without a noticeable physical deformity; the "mountain on his back' was a mere mole-hill."

VIII *Forrest in* KING LEAR *announced on the billboards of the Broadway Theatre, the "theatre of stars," as it became known after its opening in 1847.*

Hooker, who had also planned the State Capitol and the Albany City Hall. In keeping with the fashion of the period, Hooker had constructed an elegant Greek Revival building which became known as one of the handsomest theatres in the country. Included in the building—one is continually amazed at the facilities crowded inside these small playhouses—were a "spacious refreshment room," an "elaborately furnished ladies' *boudoir*," and a "large Punch Room" extending the entire width of the building.

In his first attempt at management—he had previously been director of the orchestra at the Charleston (South Carolina) Theatre—Gilfert was determined to give the Albany Theatre high-quality talent for its first season. J. B. Booth had appeared in May; Conway was to initiate the fall season: Hamblin and Kean were to follow. And if Conway's recommendation could be trusted, Gilfert had picked good support in young Forrest.

The season began on October 5 with *Macbeth*, Conway in the title part and Forrest as Macduff. This was a step up for Forrest; in New Orleans he had done Malcolm to Conway's Macbeth. The big parts came in rapid succession. Before the end of October, he played Michael to Conway's William Tell; [1] Mark Antony to his Brutus in *Julius Caesar*; Jaffier to his Pierre in *Venice Preserved*. He also got his first chance to use his aboriginal training as the Indian in Noah's *She Would Be a Soldier*.[2]

Forrest apparently carried the burden without betraying his inexperience. One reviewer commented that in *Julius Caesar* he produced "such grand effect as to cause great chagrin to the star, if it did not make him positively jealous." Forrest

---

[1] *William Tell*, by John Sheridan Knowles, was based in the story of the Swiss peasant hero. After shooting the apple from the head of his son, Tell slays the tyrant Gessler and shouts: "Let no sword be sheathed/ Until our land, from cliff to lake, is free!"

[2] Noah's play was based on the battle of Chippewa, July 5, 1814, in which the American Army, under Generals Jacob Brown and Winfield Scott, redeemed the earlier defeats of the Canadian campaign. Though a subordinate character in the play, the Indian was endowed with the red man's conventional distrust of and hatred for the white man.

was delighted to be back in civilized territory where the newspapers took serious account of the actor.

The *Advertiser* (October 25, 1825) was positively rhapsodic:

> Mr. Forrest is a stranger to us; we are ignorant whether he be a native of this country or of England; upon himself it depends to do honor to the country which gave him birth. Nature has been bountiful to him. His face and figure are such as to prepossess an audience in his favor—his voice (with the single exception of Mr. Cooper's) is, we think superior to any we have ever heard. If this young gentleman will listen to the voice of truth and avoid the destructive school of vanity (which has ruined so many who promised greatly) few, aye, a very few years, will place him in the rank with our own Cooper, and with those highly gifted strangers, Conway, Booth, and Kean, who have of late thrown a halo over the American stage.

Undoubtedly these remarks were from the pen of the editor, James Hunter, for he, like Dawson in Cincinnati, became patron and tutor to the young player. "I would seat myself in the box nearest the stage in the Pearl Street Theatre," Hunter wrote, "and watch, as a cat would a mouse, Forrest's every movement, action, and utterance. Later I would communicate these points to him."

When Conway completed his engagement at the end of October, Forrest took over as leading man. However, in the absence of a star, Gilfert abandoned the heavy repertoire for a series of frothy farces. In a way, Forrest enjoyed settling back into the stock routine he knew so well.

Gilfert had an additional reason for adopting the lighter program. It seemed more appropriate to the festivities that were to mark the opening of the Erie Canal. On Wednesday, November 2, Gilfert closed the theatre, knowing that it was futile to compete with the show at the landing and at the Capitol. Everyone was out to greet the *Seneca Chief* and the *Young Lion of the West*, the first boats to arrive from Buffalo. The Gilfert company did not get back to normal operation for a week.

On November 7 Lydia Kelly arrived from the Park Theatre in New York for a two-week engagement. Forrest was annoyed to return to playing second fiddle, particularly to a female like Miss Kelly, who insisted that the manager appear on stage after the final curtain and deliver, in cash, her percentage of the receipts for the evening.

Even had Miss Kelly been more agreeable, Forrest would not have liked her. Stage females, especially those with star ratings, were anathema to him. He recognized that the dramatis personae could not be filled without women; but he thought that to elevate them to stardom, or even to regard them as more than feeders to the male actor, dishonored a noble calling. Forrest persisted in this view throughout his career.

On November 21 he was delighted to welcome Thomas Sowerby Hamblin, especially since his arrival signaled Miss Kelly's departure. Hamblin was six years Forrest's senior, had just completed his first engagement in this country—he had followed Miss Kelly at the Park—yet he had made an immediate impression with his handsome bearing and his skillful renderings of tragic heroes. In later years some critics insisted that he never sustained the promise he had shown as an actor in London, yet he made his mark as the affluent manager of the Bowery Theatre in New York, and when he died in 1853, he left an estate of $100,000. He also achieved a minor reputation for his marital prowess: four ladies went to the altar with him; numerous others were said to have shared his favors on a less formal basis.

The Albany engagement gave Forrest a kind of post-graduate course in acting. The sessions with Conway and then with Hamblin were, however, a prelude to the master class with Edmund Kean. On Monday evening, December 5, Forrest appeared as Richmond to the Richard III of Kean. Five years earlier, a wide-eyed youngster of fifteen, he had sat in the Walnut Street Theatre observing for the first time the magnificent power of this stage giant. Kean revealed to him the emotional combustion that could be ignited by a great actor. The image of Kean had lain at the back of his head as a model with which to compare his own histrionic efforts. Seeing the man in action was an inspiring lesson for a young actor; appearing in a supporting role with him opened unequaled opportunities to discover, if it could be discovered, the alchemy, the incantations, the psychic manipulations, or whatever it was, that gave him such irresistible authority.

Forrest felt again, as he had five years earlier, an affinity with Kean's style. The great actor seemed indeed to penetrate the inner life of the characters he portrayed, to possess them so completely that they in turn possessed him. He brought to the audience a preternatural creation that stunned them, excited their imaginations, and chilled their blood. To Forrest, this was acting of the highest order.

As Forrest got to know Kean, he was happy to find that his path to the pinnacle had borne some resemblances to his own. Kean, like himself, had been a sickly youngster. He had been a contortionist and a tightrope dancer, and as a strolling player had played anything and everything that the program demanded. Once Kean had been permitted to show the full powers of this genius, as Shylock at Drury Lane in 1814, he had attained his star-standing almost overnight. Forrest had this last step yet to make.

Forrest insisted that meeting Kean, performing with him, listening to his advice was the most powerful directing influence on his life. In later years, one of the mementos Forrest treasured and displayed to all visitors to his home was a lock of Kean's hair.

Forrest received his first lesson on the day Kean arrived. When the actor did not appear for the Monday-morning rehearsal, Forrest asked Gilfert's permission to call on him at his hotel to receive directions for the evening's performance. Kean welcomed him, and, in answer to his questions about appropriate business, was reported to have given his stock reply to all such inquiries. "My boy, I do not care how you come on or go off, if while we are on the stage you always keep in front of me and let not your attention wander from me." Having transmitted these simple instructions, he sat down at the piano and sang Moore's "Farewell, but whenever you welcome the hour," with such teary tones that by the time he reached the last verse both he and Forrest were crying.

Kean's only previous American tour, in 1821, had begun triumphantly in Boston and had ended disastrously in the same city when he refused to appear because the house was too slim. Now, four years later, the furor created by that incident had not completely disappeared.

On the earlier visit he had not played Albany, and he was delighted to discover that Albany had no interest in Boston's quarrels. In response to the "prolonged cheers" that greeted him, he came before the curtain and assured them that "the American people have revived, resuscitated and invigorated the spirit of a poor, broken-hearted man." Kean had just struggled through an unwholesome litigation in London, involving purported intimate relations with the wife of an Alderman.

The Albany reception soothed his spirits, yet the recent ordeal and his excessive dependence on alcohol before a performance had considerably reduced his vigor. Kean at half-strength gave Forrest more than he could quickly absorb. For two weeks he scrutinized every move, every intonation, and, finding Kean so amenable to his perpetual inquiries, Forrest was emboldened to introduce some of his own special interpretations of Iago for the old actor's approval.

The traditional Iago was represented as a sullen, somber scoundrel, so oppressed with gloom that his villainy pervaded the play. Taking Shakespeare's reference to the "honest" ancient literally, Forrest created a superficially gay, dashing, and lighthearted fellow. Through this bright exterior, at appropriate moments, Iago hurled poisonous darts to infect the mind of Othello. For example, in the lines,

> *Look to your wife; observe her well with Cassio;*
> *Wear your eye thus, not jealous,—nor secure.*

every word, with the exception of the last two, was spoken in a frank and easy fashion. Suddenly, the fiery evil of his suspicion broke through, betraying his secret, as if in spite of his will. He hissed the words, "nor secure," into Othello's ear. The audience was electrified. Forrest claimed that they applauded wildly though even he seemed uncertain whether his innovation or Kean's startled expression had elicited the reaction.

According to one Albany reporter, Kean called Forrest to his dressing room after the performance and shouted: "In the name of God, boy, where did you get that?"

Forrest replied: "It is something of my own."

"Well!" Kean said. "Everybody who speaks the part hereafter must do it just so."

A standing ovation could not have pleased Forrest more. He knew that he had completed his apprenticeship. What he had borrowed from Conway and Kean could now be embroidered with his own creative handiwork.

Kean recognized in the young man a budding stage genius. At a public dinner in Philadelphia a month later he was reported to have said: "I have met one actor in this country, a young man named Edwin Forrest, who gave proofs of a decided genius for his profession and will, I believe, rise to great eminence."

Although Forrest concentrated on his professional training during his Albany stay, he enjoyed occasional moments of levity outside the theatre, even if his comrades were somewhat tamer than those in New Orleans. One escapade almost landed him in jail; another did. One evening he and his companions were rounded up by the "leather-heads" (night watchmen) for singing bawdy songs on the street after midnight. Forrest distracted the captors by reciting Shakespeare while his companions escaped. When the watchmen discovered the trick, they could not bear to take Forrest in. They thanked him for the elocutionary interlude in their dreary night and released him. On another night he was not so lucky. He was incarcerated in the Howard Street Jail. When he was released the next morning, Judge John C. Cole, not Forrest, spoke from Shakespeare. Striking a pose in imitation of Forrest, he intoned from *Othello*:

Meeting Kean in Albany

. . . what's the matter
That you unlace your reputation thus,
And spend your rich opinion for the name
Of a night brawler? Give me answer to it!

Before he left Albany, Forrest turned over a new leaf. In a sober valedictory to his nocturnal companions he explained that he was no longer going to fritter away his precious time. He had hard work to do, both mentally and physically.

Forrest's attention to cultivating his body had always been a part of his regimen. In Albany he systematized the program. Every night and morning he took a thorough sponge bath followed by "vigorous friction with coarse towels." After the morning ablutions, he devoted a half-hour to gymnastics with springs and dumbbells and to practicing postures that might be used on the stage. He concluded the drill by walking around the room two or three times on his hands.

Again, as in Philadelphia, Cincinnati, and Lexington, Forrest attracted the attention of a patron: Major Mordecai M. Noah, journalist and playwright who at various times held editorial posts on six New York papers and was for a time a highly regarded dramatic critic. More significant to his influence on Forrest, he was one of the few native playwrights whose works had been performed. He was the author of *Marion; or, the Hero of Lake George*, the patriotic drama that had made such an impression on Forrest in Lexington.

Noah had gone to Albany to supervise the production of his *She Would Be a Soldier*, a play that had been first performed at the Anthony Street Theatre in New York in 1819, and in which Forrest was now to play the Indian Chief. The night before that opening, Noah watched Conway and Forrest in *Julius Caesar*. Returning to the Congress Hall Hotel after the performance, he encountered manager Gilfert. The following is Noah's account of the evening:

Went to the theatre to see *Julius Caesar*. Forrest a young man of nineteen or twenty, thick set, athletic, stiff, and with coarse but powerful voice, played Mark Antony. In the dining room I found Gilfert rapidly eating his lunch of corned beef and horse-radish. We commenced the following dialogue; "Gilfert, who is that young man who played Mark Antony?" "His name is Forrest." "Where from?" "Philadelphia, I believe." "What's his character?" "Good." "Is he sober-steady?" "Yes." "Keeps good company?" "Why, I believe so." "Always perfect in his parts?" "Always perfect." "How long have you engaged him?" "For a year or two." "What salary?" "Very small."

I paused while Gilfert got through his supper, and after a glass of brandy and water, he looked at me across the table, over his specs, in his peculiar way, and said: "Tell me, Noah, why you asked me those questions about that young man?"

"Because he has all the material of a great actor, and if his habits are good, we would advise you to make a long engagement with him, and by all means increase his salary."

Late in the spring another Albany visitor gave a more substantial boost to Forrest's career. This was Prosper M. Wetmore, a New York dry-goods merchant who was also a contributing editor to the *New York Mirror* and later spent one session (1834–5) in the state legislature. At the moment he was a member of the Board of Directors for the new Bowery Theatre and was in Albany scouting for talent. Gilfert had already been engaged as manager of the new establishment, which was scheduled to open in the fall. After seeing Forrest perform, Wetmore insisted that Gilfert hire him for the Bowery. Forrest was elated by the proposal: twenty-eight dollars per week and a chance to play in New York. Still, he was wise to the ways of the theatre. An actor had to be leery of an engagement six months away and in a theatre not yet built.

During the spring season (1826), Gilfert abandoned his star system and shifted to the standard potpourri of fluff. Forrest was disheartened at having to slip back into feeble, nonsensical parts, even reverting occasionally to his circus tricks: jumping through a barrel of fire and walking on stilts; he was even more discouraged to see his finances deteriorate.

By closing date, May 2, box-office returns were down to a

trickle and Gilfert could no longer pay the company. When it disbanded, Forrest was forced to leave his meager wardrobe and trunk as security for his room and board. He was not yet initiated into the tricks that strolling players have developed to escape the grasping fingers of sheriffs, bailiffs, and land-ladies.

With no immediate prospect for a summer engagement, he went home to Philadelphia. Forrest thought that he might per-suade Warren and Wood to give him a few fill-in parts, their Chestnut Street Theatre having not yet closed its season. He had not had an opportunity to play in this elegant new marble palace at the corner of Sixth and Chestnut, which had opened in December 1822 while he had been in Kentucky.

According to the description in the opening night program, the theatre boasted places for 2,000 people in its three circles of boxes, and with no spectator more than thirty-five feet from the stage. Hanging from the center dome was "an elegant chandelier, nine feet in diameter, containing sixty patent lamps enriched with appropriate ornaments." The front of the theatre on Chestnut Street was built of "marble in the Italian style; the leading features of which were an Arcade supporting a skreen [*sic*] of composite columns and a plain entablature, flanked by two wings and decorated with niches and basso relievo's rep-resenting the Tragic and Comic masks [3] with the attributes of Appolo [*sic*]." Even with the apparent extravagance of the building, not everything had come off as anticipated. The plan for gas lighting had been abandoned because of lack of money and some skepticism regarding its practicability.

Forrest hoped that Kean's praise and some word of his Al-bany reception had reached Warren and Wood. He soon dis-covered that the partners were completely at loggerheads and had no other thought than to terminate their intolerable asso-ciation as quickly as possible. However, through the interces-sion of Charles Porter, who had given him his first chance at the old Southwark, they consented to Forrest's appearance.

[3] When the theatre was torn down in 1855, Forrest bought these masks and set them up in front of his house at Holmesburg.

The playbill for Porter's benefit performance of *Venice Preserved* on Monday, May 15, announced Forrest as "From the theatre at Albany, his first appearance these 4 years." He could not have asked for a more triumphant reception in his home town. As he read the newspaper report to his mother the following morning, tears of pride poured down her cheeks: "He left us a boy, and has returned a man. The talents he then exhibited, improved by attention and study, now display themselves in the excellence of his delineation. He is by no means what he was when he left us. Just in his conception of his part, clear and correct in his utterance, graceful in his action, he never offends us by unmeaning rant. On the dropping of the curtain at the end of the fourth act, he was rewarded with nine rounds of cheers."

With such a clear sign that the Philadelphians wished to honor their native son, and with box-office proceeds of $410, well above the season's average, Warren and Wood readjusted their remaining week's schedule to feature Forrest. Two performances of *Pizarro*,[4] William Dunlap's thriller, were announced for the final dates, Friday and Saturday, May 19 and 20.

Forrest's star was ascending rapidly. The accumulating interest from diverse sources which goes into the building of an actor's reputation was beginning to operate. F. C. Wemyss, the English actor, then a member of the Philadelphia company, wrote: "When I first met Edwin Forrest behind the scenes of the Chestnut Street Theatre in the month of May, 1826, he was a modest, unassuming young man, who scarcely mustered courage sufficient to enter the Green Room. Charles Porter introduced me to him. I saw him act and was much pleased. I suggested to Frederick Huber that he publish a picture of him in 'Acting American Theatre' which he did. This engraved por-

---

[4] Dunlap's *Pizarro in Peru; or, the Death of Rolla*, like Richard Brinsley Sheridan's *Pizarro*, was adapted from Kotzebue's play, *The Spaniards in Peru*. The principal character, Rolla, another of nature's noblemen, struggles against the Peruvian tyrant Pizarro.

trait of Forrest as Rolla was the first picture of him to appear before the public."

When the curtain was rung down for the season, Forrest's spirits were riding high. Acclaim in his native city, with his mother and sisters on hand to share his triumph, set him on top of the world. Unfortunately, the fever pitch of this exciting week did not hold up. The theatre was closed for the season after his Saturday-night performance.

For a few days he tried to relax and enjoy the comforts of home, but he was depressed and impatient to be about his business. He decided to go to New York, inspect the progress of the Bowery Theatre, get acquainted with the city, and perhaps find some spot he might fill for the summer. After a frustrating week he became more gloomy than ever. No engagement was to be had; the Bowery Theatre construction was moving at a snail's pace, with little chance that it would be ready before November. The prospect of five idle months, worse than that, five months of solitude, brought his spirits to a new low. Now just past his twentieth birthday, and with four years in the profession, he had not yet adjusted to the occupational hazard of his calling, riding with the applause at one moment and wandering lonely and aimless the next. As he brooded on his dark prospects, he decided that suicide offered the only escape. "I was thoroughly disgusted with the world," Forrest later wrote to a friend, "and resolved to kill myself. I was without a dollar. I did not have two shirts in the world. I went to the drug store and bought some arsenic. I told the apothecary I wanted to kill rats." Unfortunately, he did not have the *Book on Suicide* by Reverend Solomon Piggott, which he later bought for his library, and which contained "suggestions on mental distress" and a list of antidotes for various poisons.

Before Forrest administered the lethal application, a chance theatrical opening—the hope that perpetually keeps actors from being submerged in their gloom—constrained him to discard the rat poison. He was asked to appear at the Park Theatre in a benefit for Jacob Woodhull.

61

As was usual at the end of the Park season, when the hot weather reduced the patronage, the actors in the stock company were each allowed a benefit performance. Woodhull was at a loss to contrive an attraction that would coax the public into the theatre. One evening when he and Charles Durang, an actor who later gained a reputation as a chronicler of the Philadelphia stage, were walking up Broadway on their way to dinner, Durang reported that they spied Forrest lounging on a chair on the front porch of Washington Hall on the corner of Broadway and Reed Street.

Durang pointed out the young man and remarked: "Woodhull, if I were you, I would get Forrest to volunteer for your benefit. There he sits; let us go over and ask him if he is at liberty to do so."

Woodhull, however, was not convinced. "What kind of an attraction would he be? He has never played New York; his name is not known here in any way."

They went in to dinner, and while they ate, Durang explained that Gilfert had engaged Forrest for the new Bowery. The Albany manager had a sharp eye for theatrical talent. He would not have risked his fortunes on Forrest if he were not convinced of his abilities. Woodhull was still skeptical, but having nothing better in the offing, he agreed. Naturally, Forrest grasped at the opportunity.

When Gilfert heard of the Woodhull benefit, he refused to let Forrest appear. If he should fail in this absurd premature venture, he would automatically be eliminated from the Bowery. With the prevailing prejudice against native players, Gilfert was already assuming a foolhardy risk. He had bowed to Wetmore's demands that he engage the young actor; aggravating the situation further was sheer nonsense.

Forrest settled the matter. He would stake his success at the Park against his fall engagement even without Gilfert's approval; so on Friday, June 23, 1826, the twenty-year-old actor made his New York debut, playing Othello to Woodhull's Iago. Such a risky venture could have sent him back to the rat poison. Instead, it threw him into the forefront as the most promising young actor of the day.

Durang wrote a detailed account of the momentous evening:

Feeling some interest in the matter, first for my friend Woodhull and then for the honor of our Quaker City (although Forrest was not announced from there), I took a seat in the pit near the orchestra. Gilfert on the tenter hooks of anxiety for the result, ensconced himself in a corner of the orchestra plying his nasal organ with huge quantities of snuff as the performance progressed. The task was perilous and daring, much to Gilfert's discomfort.

Forrest entered with a calm mien and a dignified manner and took the center of the stage. His figure and manner elicited hearty applause at once. His youthful manly form—symmetrical as the Apollo Belvidere with all that figure's repose—devoid of all superfluous flesh—an expressive youthful face, rather thin in its outline —a flashing hazel eye that foreshadowed vivid intellect—deportment and action naturally graceful and well costumed, made a *tout-ensemble* that at once struck like an electrical chord of harmony from the actor to the audience as he bowed to their warm greetings. The ladies especially threw up their white cambrics in token of heartfelt admiration.

His great future depended on this appearance. It was Forrest's first essay before the then advancing critical metropolitan audience of the United States, and, therefore, if he failed in this entree, his professional aspirations might receive in their opening bud a blight, an eternal quietus.

I can only say that Forrest came upon us with all the genius— the spirit and power of the great Edmund Kean. He came—we saw,—and he conquered! Mr. Lewis Godey [the founder of *Godey's Lady's Book*] then a resident of New York, but now an honored citizen of Philadelphia—sat on the same bench with me, witnessing, with intense interest Forrest's Othello. When the curtain fell on the tumultuous applause and silence again restored we arose to make our exit, Mr. Godey inquired of me who he was and whence he came. I replied he was a young man of Philadelphia, native of Southwark, with some little listing of his stage novitiate when a boy at our city. Then said Godey, he is an honor to his native place, and will become one of the first tragedians that ever trod our stage. Godey was prophetic. His prophecy was in less than three years fully realized.

After the curtain, Gilfert cried, "A hit, a hit by Jupiter," and ran up behind the scenes to congratulate his protégé.

Gilfert now said nothing of having opposed the performance. Forrest graciously did not remind him. The manager was so enthusiastic in contemplating Forrest's prospects for the fall that he volunteered to take Forrest with him to Albany the following day, pay off his bills so that he could retrieve his trunk, and give him pocket money to keep him until the Bowery opened. Forrest happily fell in with the plan.

The whole world had brightened. When he came home to Philadelphia, he found that Kean had just concluded an engagement of twelve performances at the Chestnut Street Theatre. With the theatre reopened, and with Forrest again available, Wood decided that he might as well keep the company together a while longer. He had not forgotten the enthusiasm Forrest had aroused in May, and now favorable reports were drifting in from New York. Forrest opened on Wednesday, July 5, in *Othello*, and for the first time was billed as the star. To reach stardom and in his native city could only have been a most thrilling experience. To be sure, an off-season star was not quite on a par with a regular winter-season star, yet he was moving in the right direction. During the next week-and-a-half he forgot the dejection that had hounded him the month before. Although the houses were only moderately filled, averaging $255 per night, this was just $75 under Kean. For his benefit Forrest drew a phenomenal $461, flattering evidence that he had power to override the weather. More important, it was a welcome boon to his sagging finances.

Forrest's depression had now evaporated, and except for a brief excursion to Washington, D.C., at the end of the summer, where he played Rolla in *Pizarro* for his brother William's benefit, he was content to idle in Philadelphia awaiting the fall opening of the Bowery. With his successful first appearance in New York, his star billing in Philadelphia, his trunk out of pawn, and, above all, money in his pocket, the future looked brighter than it ever had. As he remembered the summer, the happiest moment occurred when he turned over $400 to his mother. Describing the incident a few years later, he wrote: "The applause I had won before the foot-lights? Yes, it was most welcome and precious to me; but, compared with this, it was nothing, less than nothing. Her fond and approving eyes seemed to sink into my very bones."

CHAPTER *vi*

Debut at the Bowery

On Monday, October 23, 1826, the handsome new Bowery Theatre was opened. Forrest did not appear on the first bill, though he was there to enjoy the inaugural festivities. With accommodations for over three thousand, the Bowery was now the largest theatre in the country. In later years it became known as the democratic playhouse, in contrast to the aristocratic Park; initially, it drew just as much on the fashionable segment of the metropolis as did the Park.

Gilfert held Forrest back for two weeks, relying on the drawing power of the new theatre itself to fill the house. By this delay, he hoped also to intensify the interest in Forrest's official debut. The big event occurred on Monday, November 6, and as in May, Forrest chose *Othello*.

Forrest understood the importance of the occasion, facing up to the final and irrevocable judgment of the New York public. He was confident that he could win them over. However, as he stepped on the stage, the assured control over his voice and body which usually arose so automatically at a first entrance seemed to falter. According to one observer, he showed "obvious nervousness and trepidation." As he warmed up, the constrictions in his throat disappeared. The full impassioned Kean-like tones he had stored up for *Othello* floated out clear and true, and he could sense the excitement rising.

After the curtains closed on the final tragic scene, a long moment of silence was followed by a thundering burst of applause breaking against the curtain. Both Forrest and the audience knew that they were sharing a memorable event. Three hours earlier, he had been a promising and hopeful stock actor. Now he had moved into the first rank alongside Booth, Cooper, Kean, and Conway.

When the audience and actor finally struck a truce on further applause and curtain calls, Forrest was ushered into the committee room behind the scenes. He had never seen such a concentrated array of society gentlemen at close range. Prosper Wetmore was the official spokesman.

He announced that the stockholders were so impressed with Forrest's success that they wished to cancel the engagement made with him at twenty-eight dollars a week and to draw a new agreement giving him forty. When Forrest accepted the proposal, the group broke into "nine cheers." Four years earlier he had been struggling for an irregular twelve dollars per week; now he was to receive an assured forty for an entire season.

Forrest marveled at the change that a single night's performance could make. Not only did his financial fortunes assume a healthier aspect, the question of roles and plays was settled. He would perform only principal parts in major dramas. No longer would he be obliged to break his stride by stepping down to miscellaneous *divertissements* and farces. Moreover, his playing schedule was reduced to three nights a week.

On this new schedule and under the new terms, Forrest gave the New York patrons a look at the other major roles in his growing repertoire: Damon in *Damon and Pythias*; [1] Jaffier in *Venice Preserved*; Mark Antony in *Julius Caesar*; Tell in *William Tell*. For Evacuation Day, November 25, he honored Mordecai Noah by performing the Indian Chief in *She Would Be a Soldier*. He also returned to his study of *King Lear*.

---

[1] John Banim's *Damon and Pythias* relates the romantic story of the extraordinary devotion between the two ancient Greek friends. When Damon protests the election of Dionysius to the dictatorship of Syracuse, he is thrown into prison and doomed to die. Pythias volunteers to take his place while Damon is given a six-hour reprieve to visit his wife and child. Because his servant has slain his horse hoping thereby to save his life, Damon returns just in time to jump on the scaffold and rescue Pythias.

He had begun working on *Lear* in New Orleans, and in Albany he had kept a sharp eye on Kean's performance of the title role. Forrest was more fascinated by Lear than by any other Shakespeare character, and throughout his life continued to enlarge his concept of the part. Like Kean, he made a first-hand study of insanity.

His clinical examination of mental aberration had begun on his first visit to Lexington, where, as already noted, Henry Clay's son, Theodore, had served him as a model. In his mature years, Forrest unhesitatingly proclaimed that no living man could match his performance of Lear. No actor visited as many lunatic asylums throughout the world. He often insisted that he had never met a doctor who knew as much about insanity as he did. In an asylum in Paris he met an old white-haired man who believed himself to be Napoleon. Forrest unthinkingly made some uncomplimentary remark about the diminutive general, whereupon the seventy-year-old man grabbed him, and threw him into the air. Forrest used this example to silence the critics who thought that he was too loud and strong in Lear's mad scenes. In later years he said that he had found the living model closest to his conception of Lear in a Philadelphia asylum. This was John Rush, son of Dr. Benjamin Rush, the one-time surgeon-general of the Continental Army and, ironically, now known as the father of American psychiatry. Young Rush had quarreled with a friend in Canada, challenged him to a duel, killed him, and ever since had been insane. Now a sad old man, Rush was still erect and possessed of a handsome, open, manly countenance, the image of what Forrest thought Lear should be.

The Lear that the twenty-year-old Forrest brought out in New York on December 27, 1826, did not have the benefit of this later study, yet his performance contained a strong touch of the overpowering force that was to become his trade-mark.

Forrest's new professional rank effected an immediate change in his social status outside the theatre. In the past distinguished citizens had honored him with their patronage; now he was admitted to their society as an equal. Two lifelong friendships were begun after the opening night of *Othello*: with James Lawson, specialist in marine insurance, poet, editor, and would-be playwright, and with William Leggett, the oracle of radical Democrats and editorial assistant to William Cullen Bryant on the *Evening Post*, both of whom came backstage soliciting introductions to the new star.

Forrest was embarked on a new and exciting life in the theatre and out. He found it hard to believe that six months earlier, just a few blocks from the site of his present triumph, he had been tempted to ease himself out of his despondency with a dose of poison. Now, six months before his twenty-first birthday, he stepped into the elevated social and professional world he was to inhabit for the rest of his life, a world in which he was the kingpin, in which he was no longer obliged to seek friends or engagements. Both came to him. Abruptly faced with the demands of high position, anyone less firmly persuaded of his eventual destiny might have stumbled in embarrassment and uncertainty. Not Forrest. Except for the brief derangement during the previous summer, he had never questioned the inevitability of his success.

While Forrest was engrossed in his enlarged and brightened world, the appearances at the Park Theatre of a highly regarded English actor, William C. Macready, seem not to have caught his eye. It is understandable that they did not. Macready's mannered refinements, the mere fact that he held front rank in the London theatre, disqualified him as a possible model for Forrest. Macready did observe Forrest, and although "the young and awkward American was just beginning his career," Macready detected, if only faintly, that Forrest might eventually offer him dangerous competition.

Macready saw Forrest perform Mark Antony to Conway's Brutus, and on another night saw him in *William Tell*. Twenty years later he recalled the impressions of these two performances in his *Reminiscences*. "His figure was good," Macready wrote, "though, perhaps a little too heavy; his face might be considered handsome, his voice excellent; he was gifted with extraordinary strength of limb, to which he omitted no opportunity of giving prominence. He had received only the commonest education, but, in his reading of the text, he showed discernment and good sense." In his William Tell there was too much "vehemence and rude force." He undoubtedly possessed a strong natural talent that, if disciplined in the British theatre, would make him a first-rate actor, but Macready was certain that he would succumb to "injudicious and ignorant flattery" and never submit to the "severe study of his art" which he obviously needed. Forrest would have admitted to himself, if not to Macready, that he needed more study. He never would have admitted that quick success would destroy him. The two men did not meet on this occasion; nor was there at the time any hint of the animosity that flamed up later between them.

Forrest's triumph during the fall season was marred by a single incident, an inexplicable physical collapse. On Sunday, November 26, he had been dining out. He was just about to take a glass of wine when a pain shot through his heart and tumbled him to the floor. According to Forrest, he lay on the floor speechless for fifteen minutes. A doctor was called, and after a "copious bleeding" he felt better and got back to his room. After spending the next day in bed, he went to the theatre in the evening. On Thursday night, in the middle of *William Tell*, he had another attack, worse than the first: "pains in all my limbs, and my head nigh to bursting." With the "unavoidable use of brandy, ether, and hartshorn [smelling salts]," he explained in a letter to his mother, he got through the performance. The next morning he decided to take a week's rest.

Undoubtedly the strain on his heart and a mild touch of the rheumatic ailment that was to plague him in later years were brought on by the heavy repertoire he had undertaken in a single month. He had not appeared every night, yet each performance had been in a major role, and Forrest never walked through a part. Either he used full steam or he did not play. Even when he was in a weakened condition, no diminution in his power was apparent; Macready saw him in his most enfeebled state.

In view of all the attention Forrest had devoted to cultivating his bodily energies, to discover weakness where he had thought he was least vulnerable was disheartening. He wrote to his mother about his illness, explaining how depressed it had made him: "Alas! I know not how soon sickness may render me incapable of the labors of my profession; and the penury, perchance the poor-house, may ensue." Overdramatizing his gloom was symptomatic of a kind of manic-depressive compulsion, which pursued him throughout his life. Whenever he was forced to quit the stage, for whatever reason, he found life unendurable and was certain that doomsday was fast approaching.

On Thursday, December 14, Forrest returned to the Bowery and continued without a relapse until January 3, 1827. During this final stretch Hamblin replaced Conway as his chief supporting player. Just a year earlier he had been playing second fiddle to each of them.

With the commanding way in which the young man was taking his elevated status, Gilfert realized that he probably could not hold his managerial control beyond this first season; he would do better to keep Forrest occupied every possible moment. From New York, Forrest went immediately to Albany for two weeks; the *Advertiser* thought "his improvement far outstripped what his most sanguine friends had anticipated." On January 31, he was back at the Bowery for a one-night benefit, in *Damon and Pythias*, for the Greek Fund. In later years Forrest took a dim view of charity benefits; now he was happy to support the Greeks in their noble struggle for freedom. The following Monday he opened at the Federal Street Theatre in Boston, his first visit to "the literary emporium of the Western hemisphere."

Forrest was overawed to appear as a star in this theatrical landmark at the corner of Federal and Franklin streets. The Federal, or Boston Theatre as it was sometimes called, had been built in 1794 after plans by Charles Bulfinch, who later achieved fame as the architect for the Capitol in Washington. The Federal was an elegant structure with a projecting front arcade allowing carriages to drive up under cover, spacious saloons, and a vast army of Corinthian columns throughout the building.

Forrest was charmed with the Bostonians: "every attention is paid me by the young men of first respectability," he wrote to his mother. He was certain that in this environment much would be added to his reputation as well as to his purse. The refined, yet open, manner of the visitors who came backstage to greet him compelled Forrest to modify the delusions he had held about the educated aristocracy. During his Western adventures, he had cultivated the notion of a natural antagonism between honest, rough-and-ready, freedom-loving patriots and polite, city-bred, literary-infected aristocrats. In Boston he discovered that knowledge of books did not reduce one's patriotic zeal or necessarily induce an effete disposition. He became convinced that his horizon must be broadened.

Among the many Bostonians who called backstage after his opening night was James Oakes, a sturdy young man just one year Forrest's junior. Their meeting was warm and friendly. Neither of them, however, saw in the play, *Damon and Pythias*, a forecast of their later relationship. They were to become inseparable; in fact, some said, they began to look so much alike that one was frequently mistaken for the other.

Forrest arrived in Boston at a propitious time. The theatregoers still held a grudge against Kean for having walked out on them. They were ecstatic to find a native star who could match him, and the more they applauded, the farther Forrest pulled out the stops. He was riding high and gaining complete confidence in his professional position.

He became so cocksure of himself that he bypassed Gilfert in negotiating an engagement with William Warren in Philadelphia. He insisted to the Chestnut Street manager that sharing the nightly profits after $300 (the manager's calculation of his basic operating costs) was unsatisfactory. Warren, remembering the young man who had begged for a place in the company just a few years earlier, had not caught up with the new Forrest. He assumed that the actor would turn up on February 20 as originally scheduled and on Warren's terms. On the appointed day he was forced to announce in the *United States Gazette* that as Forrest was still in Boston, the *Red Rover* would be substituted; "should Mr. E. Forrest arrive, immediate notice will be given and a favorite play substituted, in which he will sustain the principal character."

Whether the Philadelphia management succumbed to Forrest's demands or Gilfert eventually figured in the negotiations is not clear. Forrest opened his homecoming engagement on Monday, the 26th, and for the next four weeks ranged through his repertoire for his old friends; he was not a prophet without honor in his own city. He closed on March 24 with a family celebration: brother William playing Pythias to his Damon.

The whirlwind pace continued without interruption: no time for rest, no time for rehearsals, no time to introduce new roles. For three weeks he was back at the Bowery, and on the first of May was again in Philadelphia to share an engagement with Cooper. He had not crossed paths with the old actor since he had sought his counsel in the spring of 1821. Meeting him now on equal terms, Forrest was not embarrassed to recall his impolite and impetuous behavior on the previous occasion. Forrest had now shared star billing with all the principal actors of the time with the exception of Junius Brutus Booth, who would be added in another year. Macready shared the stage with no one; nor did Forrest desire to identify himself with the high-hat Britisher.

Forrest returned to New York for a late May engagement and on June 6 concluded his first regular season as a star. With his steam up he was unwilling to quit, and so decided to test his popularity off the beaten path.

Having become accustomed to commodious establishments, cheering audiences, and competent support, Forrest was shocked when he opened in Providence, Rhode Island, on June 15, to find "a beggarly account of empty boxes, an old barn of a place that reminds me of my early itinerant expeditions," and a company that was "utterly wretched." He could not tolerate inadequate and undedicated actors. His summer tour was quickly terminated, though not because of the depressing conditions in Providence. One night in "one of the most impassioned scenes" of *Virginius* [2] Forrest had another attack like that of the previous November. "The blood rushed with such violence into my head," he wrote his mother, "that it was with the utmost difficulty I could complete the performance." He had never in his entire life felt "such agony and horror as in that moment." The next morning a doctor "cupped [him] on the back of the neck," and he felt better. After finishing his week he gave up and returned to Philadelphia.

Forrest was glad for a moment in which to catch his breath; however, after he had celebrated the Fourth of July—always a big holiday for him—with his mother and sisters, he was restless to get back to work. Off he went to New York.

Ordinarily New York limited itself to light refreshments for the summer. Beginning on July 7, Forrest gave the Bowery patrons three weeks of his usual heavy fare and they liked it. He even added a new role: Shylock in *The Merchant of Venice*, not a part he enjoyed and one that he rarely played thereafter.

Forrest's first season's agreement with Gilfert was now at an end. The manager had hesitated to approach Forrest about a renewal of the contract, preferring to keep the young man occupied and postpone the inevitable showdown. Now the matter had to be settled. One day late in July, Gilfert asked Forrest what terms he expected for the new season. Forrest knew that he had the upper hand. He quietly told Gilfert that he himself had fixed the price. Gilfert had been asking the theatre managers two hundred dollars a night for Forrest's services.

Risky as it was for a manager to gamble with such high stakes, Gilfert knew that he could secure Forrest on no other basis. He agreed. For eighty nights during the next season Forrest was to receive $16,000, an incredible salary for an actor who had just passed his twenty-first birthday and had just concluded his first New York season. The figure seems even more

---

[2] John Sheridan Knowles's *Virginius* was based on the old Roman story of Virginius's struggle against the tyrant Appius Claudius. Forrest relished the pathetic scene in which Virginius slays his daughter in the Forum to save her from Appius.

astonishing when translated to its present-day equivalent, somewhere in the neighborhood of $64,000. None of this was "funny money," as the Hollywood actors describe their extravagant salaries that pass, almost untouched by them, into the hands of the United States Treasury. Today several hundred entertainers boast gross, if not net, seasonal earnings beyond this figure. In 1827 no more than three or four could match Forrest's profits. None guarded his income so carefully.

With this healthy prospect for the fall, Forrest decided to allow himself a vacation. With D. P. Ingraham, the young lawyer who was later to become a distinguished Judge of the New York State Supreme Court, he headed up the Hudson, bound for Niagara.

Although he had resolved to keep off the stage, he could not resist trying a few performances for his Albany friends. This was a mistake; the engagement was tedious and unprofitable. Forrest's attention was on other matters. He was eager to get on the boat for Buffalo, to sample the newest innovation in transportation, the Erie Canal, and to see the countryside. As he wrote to his mother on August 18th, after reaching Buffalo: "I make this journey for the purpose of recreation, in viewing the romantic beauties of our country, and the developments of art and industry which are so rapidly leading to wealth and happiness. I have passed through a series of flourishing towns—Schenectady, Amsterdam, Utica, Clinton, Vernon, Auburn, Canandaigua, Rochester, and others—all of which have given me delight."

He found Buffalo "a dull situation," which he endured only long enough to transfer to the Niagara steamboat. His visit to the Falls was to be the high spot of his journey. "Before that tremendous and sublime cataract I anticipate much pleasure in the excitement of those exalted feelings in which my soul loves to luxuriate." Much to Forrest's pleasure, many later critics maintained that the roaring verbal cataracts with which he flooded the theatre were like the rushing waters of Niagara.

As frequently happened when Forrest was not occupied with the theatre, his thoughts turned toward home. He wrote from Buffalo: "I should now like to settle you and my dear sisters down in some respectable, handsome, and quiet part of Philadelphia, where you may gently pass your dear reserves of time apart from the care and toil with which you have too long been forced to struggle. I say Philadelphia, because I fear you could not be prevailed on to come to New York. And indeed I do not wonder; for, besides the numerous circle of friends you have, it is there that the sacred ashes of my father lie."

Early in September, Forrest was back in New York ready to begin a strenuous year, his first season completely free of uncertainty. Most of the year he would be occupied with the eighty performances for Gilfert at the Bowery. Whatever time was not taken up in New York he knew could be filled with engagements in Philadelphia and Boston. The critics would undoubtedly judge him more severely in 1827 than they had in 1826. If he could satisfy himself, he was certain that he would please them.

There was no cockiness in this attitude, just the natural confidence of an artist whose conscience demands undeviating devotion to his art. Other players might strut through their recitations, not Forrest. He was driven by a fanatical compulsion to give his full energies to the actor's art. A moment of the day dissipated to other purposes, or a fraction of his mental and physical resources squandered on other enterprises was simply wasteful. And unlike most of his fellow players his compulsion became more intense as his hold on the public became more secure.

During that first winter and spring in New York, he had evolved a program of self-development which now, during his second season, became fixed as a lifelong pattern.

A beautiful body was a recognized stage asset then as it is today, although tastes have changed. Where Hollywood's strong men concentrate on broad shoulders, Forrest, and apparently his audience, was fascinated by calves and biceps. Forrest's exercise program went beyond the sheer necessity of developing muscularity for his heroic roles; he was simply fascinated by physical culture. In addition to setting-up exercises, walking on his hands, and churning the air with dumbells and Indian clubs, he took up boxing under the instruction of George Hernizer, a distinguished professor of the manly art.

Under this vigorous physical regimen, Forrest developed a Herculean body. In later years his five-foot-ten frame carried a massive burden of over two hundred pounds. In 1827 he had no excess fat. His legs, arms, shoulders, and even his neck seemed a mass of muscles. When he came on stage, anyone who had not yet glimpsed the new star was immediately struck by his handsome, upright figure and the tremendous display of strength. Most of his roles permitted a free exhibition of his physique—bare legs and bare arms—which made the initial impact even more provocative. Although not of more than average height, spectators invariably were amazed at his seemingly gigantic proportions. When Fanny Kemble saw him for the first time, she exclaimed: "What a mountain of a man!" The swooning female, overcome by his sheer physical magnificence, was a common sight in Forrest's audiences. One critic wrote that Forrest played only parts especially written for "his private legs and larynx." Some said he would have pleased the eye more were he less "Samson-like." Others insisted that to see a giant move with such matchless grace gave them an uncommon thrill.

Forrest did not limit his attention to developing his anatomical attractions. He pursued a Spartan health program in conformity with the self-abusive and discomforting hygienic notions then current. His diet was simple and probably wholesome. Oatmeal, cracked wheat, corn-meal mush, and brown bread, with generous portions of cream and buttermilk were the staples. For a special feast he gorged himself on a stack of Scotch bannocks, a kind of unleavened bread made from oatmeal or barley meal baked on a griddle. Before a performance he ate sparingly; afterward he would return to his hotel, throw off his coat and boots, loosen his shirt and belt, and dive into a generous bowl of cold corn-meal mush and milk. He became an ardent devotee of the new fad for ventilation. The motto for the fresh air fiends, "the prime condition of health is to breathe pure air plentifully," compelled him to spend many uncomfortable nights with cold blasts swirling around his bed. Perhaps it was this practice that forced him regularly to nap in the daytime to supplement the insufficient repose of the night.

Each night and morning he gave himself a thorough washing followed by an energetic scrubbing with coarse towels. This routine was followed by a massaging flagellation of his back and spine with two little rubber balls fastened to the ends of small clubs. Forrest never made clear how this maneuver was accomplished. Either long elastic fastenings were employed, supplemented by considerable dexterity on his part, or a servant must have administered the massage. These regular ablutions and rubbings were said to have produced the polished marble appearance of his skin of which Forrest was so proud.

His pride and ambition exhibited themselves in other ways. His passion for success and for social acceptance could not be satisfied merely by transforming a feeble body into an Apollonian marvel. Other handicaps—inadequate formal schooling, limited acquaintance with the social graces—had to be overcome. His zeal, coupled with the conspicuous position he had achieved, made this task relatively easy. The newspaper and literary headliners—William Leggett, William Cullen Bryant, Prosper M. Wetmore, and James Lawson—had already taken him into their circle. Fitz-Greene Halleck, a leading "Knickerbocker" and the author of *Fanny*, a poetic satire on New York society, and William Dunlap, painter, art and theatre historian, and playwright, both sought his acquaintance. All of them became his tutors, opening their more abundant resources for him to feed on. They seemed as eager to share their knowledge as he was to receive it.

In this fascinating world of ideas and manners, Forrest discovered new materials for his histrionic creations. Much as he may have concentrated on showy aspects in his earlier performances, he had always carried an image of himself, at the pinnacle of his career, as an actor not only applauded for the power of his portrayals but also revered for his intelligence, understanding, and humanity. His new companions opened his eyes to the world of intellectual speculation, to the sport of enlarging on the artistic creations of others. He had always held a reverence for books, though his reading had been limited to the Bible, Shakespeare, Robert Burns, and assorted books on elocution. He now bought books freely and widely, accepting the guidance of his literary mentors, and he avidly read everything that he bought.

Forrest's leech-like feeding on the literary and artistic blood of his friends seems never to have annoyed them. To begin with, they had sought his company; and his decorative value—both his physical elegance and his vibrant personality—more than compensated for his intellectual deficiencies. Forrest was gay and lighthearted in their company; he recited humorous and pathetic poems. He could be counted on to loosen social rigidities or deflate pomposity. This was in sharp contrast to the earnest and often melancholy demeanor he maintained on stage during both rehearsal and performance. The theatre was always serious business to him: levity was just as inappropriate there as it might be at Mass. As someone said: "he knew how to act in the theatre, and to be simple and sincere in the parlor."

Few people saw, or even heard about, the light side of Forrest's nature. Many of his fellow actors found him harsh, brutal, impatient, and humorless. Some actors, particularly those who had suffered one of his tongue lashings, called him bitter and abusive. Certainly Forrest was intolerant of actors who did not share his high purpose. Carelessness, sloth, tardiness, untruthfulness, drunkenness, neglect of duty—qualities fairly common among the actors of the day—drove him to frequent tirades. The victims who squirmed under his castigations were quick to circulate revengeful stories. In 1827–8 these hot-tempered unflattering accounts made good reading and good talk. They did not reduce Forrest's popularity. He never denied these explosions; however in a letter to a friend, he insisted that he never knowingly swore "before ladies or clergymen, lest it should shock or grieve them. But at other times when it is necessary either for proper emphasis or as a vent for passion too hot and strong, why I let it rip as it will." These journeymen players may have called it rudeness; "in their hearts they knew it was provoked by some gross neglect of their professional duty."

Many of his associates were irked that Forrest refused to be drawn into backstage camaraderie. He preferred companions unconnected with the stage. This aloofness, "brusquerie," as it was frequently described, did not endear him to his fellows. In answer to this charge, Forrest invariably replied that he shrank from all familiar association with those of his profession who were not gentlemen and ladies in their personal self-respect and professional conduct. He never stooped to eccentricities or tricks to get himself talked about. He never arranged conspiracies to push his own claims or to restrain others. He was honestly resolved to resist the insidious lures of indolence, dissipation, and improvidence seemingly so enticing to many of his professional comrades. To others this might appear to be a smug, holier-than-thou posture. To Forrest, it was the natural consequence of his devotion to the theatre and his ingrained sense of duty. The journalists might make lurid copy out of his rehearsal behavior if they wished; these exhibitions were not manufactured for their benefit.

Forrest firmly believed, as he wrote in his notebook, that "in a single impersonation, a great actor will more clearly illustrate the divine mind of Shakespeare, than a thousand commentators as Johnson, Warburton, and Stevens." To prepare himself for this task, he probed the play texts, particularly those of Shakespeare, uncovering the layers of meaning, and translating each new discovery into elocutionary form. He experimented with vocal colorings and pauses until he found voice patterns that conformed to the text and magnified and enriched the author's meaning. Other actors marveled at the energy he applied to a microscopic and painstaking examination of a single phrase, or even a single word. No detail was neglected. As one writer said: "He heightened here and mellowed there, rounded this and smoothed that, long after the average actor would have ceased to see that there was room for betterment."

Forrest approached the new season of 1827–8, his first full season as an established star, firmly committed to a program of self-improvement that would enable him not only to hold the ground he had gained but also to enlarge his command. Even with his social position assured, with sufficient funds to provide for his mother and for himself, with stimulating support for his ego in the applause and cheers of his public, Forrest never coasted on his reputation. The nightly audience, whether in Cincinnati, Albany, or New York, had always commanded his full attention. Now his obligation stretched beyond the immediate performance. He was responsible to the entire American theatre. Forrest grasped at this leadership. To mold audience tastes, to direct the course of the American theatre appealed to him. He might break its bondage to England and fashion a new native American theatre. This was a fascinating challenge.

CHAPTER vii

Call to Native Playwrights

When Forrest began his second season at the Bowery on Wednesday, September 5, 1827, his professional durability was being tested. Some of those who had tentatively acclaimed him one year earlier wondered if the bright comet-like flash might have expired during the summer. A single performance of *Damon and Pythias* assured them that the new star meant to hold his ground.

A few critics thought that he "appeared too young," that his dress was "too rude and coarse," that occasional "false readings" marred his performance. Most echoed the sentiments of the *New York Mirror:* "Of Forrest's personation we cannot use language that would be thought too laudatory by those who witnessed the effort as it is scarcely credible to what a wonderful height of excellence this young tragedian has arrived." No actor could match him in shaking the rafters and lifting the spectators out of their boots. To be sure, some few genteel souls were assaulted by his violence. The majority were thrilled by the battering Forrest gave them.

Forrest had never felt more assured and pleased with his playing. Money was rolling in at a fast clip, his body was bearing the strain, his interpretations were cutting closer to his ideal, and, most of all, the audiences shouted their cheers at every performance. Complete absorption in the theatre always boosted Forrest's spirits; no time to brood on his ailments or his inadequacies, just time enough to rehearse, perform, and revel in the adulation of his admirers. There seemed to be a kind of providential concatenation in the present order. Forrest had written in his notebook just before the opening: "Circumstances make men what they are and we all contain the germ of greatness whose connection with our character is determined by events." The present circumstances were certainly nurturing his germs of greatness.

When Forrest left New York at the end of October and moved to Boston, he took his notebook with him, and, for the first time, kept an account of his nightly receipts. The pleasure he must have felt in jotting down these figures was not shared by the managers nor by the rest of the acting company. He dug too deeply into the treasury. For eleven performances during the month of November—still on his three-nights-a-week schedule—the box-office gross reached $3,893.25. Forrest pocketed $2,714.37½. Not much was left for the managers, nor for the other actors, not even an extra half cent. A story was circulated around Boston that he came back to the treasurer one night with a quarter that had worn smooth, insisting that it be replaced.

If there had been any doubt, the month in Boston made clear that the newly crowned star, now just a half-year beyond his twenty-first birthday, dominated the treasurer's office as well as the stage. Managers were faced with the tantalizing choice: they were damned if they hired him; damned if they didn't. In a way, they relinquished their managerial prerogatives. Forrest really hired them. They might scheme and connive to outwit him; they rarely succeeded, and the running battle, begun at this time in Boston, persisted to the end of his career. He was the liveliest theatrical commodity on the market. They had to accede to his demands. That the merry tune of the cashbox sang only for Forrest was one of the occupational hazards they must endure. Forrest had no sympathy for their whining. What was good for him was good for the theatre. If they wished to wallow in their penurious short-sightedness, let them. They would get no solace from him.

Forrest tripped through the season with a gay heart and an increasingly heavier purse. After a three-week return engagement at the Bowery he went home to his family for the holidays. He loaded the Christmas table and filled the Christmas stockings. For the first time Christmas gaiety in the Forrest household was more than a shield from the oppression of daily existence. To top off the season's celebration he collected six hundred dollars, which he turned over to his mother, for four performances at the Chestnut Street Theatre.

Although not scheduled to reopen at the Bowery until January 22, he went back on the 9th to give himself extra time to work up a Shakespeare festival. In light of what followed, he must have had a busy ten days. He began with *King Lear*, followed this on the 24th with *Richard III*, took a breather on the 26th with *Damon*, then continued on the 28th with *Othello*, and on the 30th with *Macbeth*. When he came back to the Bowery in April, after an interlude in Baltimore and Boston, he added *The Merchant of Venice* and *Julius Caesar*.

Only once during the spring season did he try a non-Shakespearean role. He appeared for the first time as Sir Giles Overreach in Massinger's *A New Way to Pay Old Debts*. Overreach, a memorable comic portrait, had been played by every leading actor since the seventeenth century. Both Kean and J. B. Booth did the part regularly. Forrest felt obliged to try all the standard roles of his predecessors. Two performances, April 18 and 22, convinced him that the part was not his meat. He never played Overreach again.

Othello was by far his most successful production during the season, if not entirely through his own efforts. He alternated the Iago and Othello roles with Cooper. Neither Forrest nor Cooper ordinarily shared billing with another actor; with each other they were happy to violate the rule. Forrest regarded Cooper as his master. Cooper saw Forrest as his heir apparent. Both found the joint enterprise profitable. So profitable, in fact, that after an initial engagement in Boston, they offered the program in Philadelphia, and then in New York, closing at the Bowery on May 21, five nights before the theatre burned down.

The building was said to have been insured for $50,000, but many of the actors lost their entire wardrobes, which were not insured. Forrest felt so lucky to have escaped and so sorry for the victims that he gave a benefit at the Park on the 31st, the entire proceeds going to the "sufferers of the Bowery fire."

Forrest might have been more saddened at the destruction of the theatre, the site of his first real New York triumph, had it not been announced that a new Bowery Theatre was to be constructed with all speed. With this assurance he decided to take a rest from theatrical activities for the summer. Before going home he made a quick trip to Albany to play a benefit of *Brutus* for his brother William, who was then a member of the Albany company.

With time on his hands and money in his pocket, Forrest took up a new project. The family had never possessed more than the bare household necessities. He decided to introduce more comfort and a show of elegance in keeping with his elevated station. He bought a set of silver spoons for $46.90, "cabinet furniture" for $100, and, the real mark of class, a horse and carriage. He also purchased china, glassware, and pictures, and added to his rapidly growing library.

Forrest's affluence did not go unnoticed by his friends and colleagues; his purse was raided regularly by his needy brothers. Perhaps he could not be classed as a "soft touch," for he kept meticulous notations of these outlays, loans, as he called them, but he willingly shared his good fortune with others, and he rarely was repaid.

By the middle of the summer Forrest discovered that his free lending policy and his refurnishing of the Philadelphia house had severely lightened his purse. He had not yet discovered the fascination he later found in guarding his liquid capital assets. In early August he received a request from Prosper M. Wetmore for a donation to support their dear friend William Leggett; Forrest had only fifty dollars to donate. Leggett, who was then Bryant's assistant on the *Evening Post*, was in financial trouble most of his life. At one time, some half-dozen years later, his despondency brought him almost to suicide. On that occasion Forrest saved him with a loan of six thousand dollars, which had not been repaid when Leggett died in 1839.

With the depressed state of his finances, Forrest was glad that the season at the New Bowery was about to begin. The construction had been moving along rapidly, and it promised to be a magnificent building. The façade was covered with a newly invented stucco, said to be of extraordinary durability and an excellent imitation of marble. The three entrance doors opened into a spacious vestibule, brilliantly lighted with gas. The drop curtain was discarded, being replaced with a drapery curtain of crimson damask which could be parted in the middle to drape in beautiful festoons. In point of size, the number and arrangement of its traps, grooves, and other stage accouterments, the theatre would be unequaled on this side of the Atlantic!

The dedicatory program, set for August 20, was to include Henry Wallack in *The Dramatist;* Miss Rock reciting a prize poem by Prosper Wetmore; Herr Cline "On the Elastic Cord"; the farce, *Is It a Lie?*; and to conclude with Hutin-Labasse, Rosalie, and M. Barbière dancing a *Pas de Trois.* Forrest spoke a dedicatory poem written by William Leggett, intoning the feeble iambic pentameter in his best Shakespearean manner, the least he could do to make up for his meager donation to the charity fund. Unhappily for Leggett, the arrangements committee had also honored him with a sentimental token rather than with cash. The poet found small comfort in knowing that the silver cup was valued at fifty dollars; the money would have been more welcome.

Forrest began his season on August 22 with his old stand-by, *Damon and Pythias.* For the next two months, on his customary three nights per week, he ranged through his repertoire. Only for a single performance did he experiment with a new part, that of Falconbridge in *King John.* The experiment was unprofitable; he returned to his familiar friends and on the 16th and 17th of October alternated with Junius Brutus Booth in the parts of Othello and Iago.

Forrest did not slip into the pedestrian routine he might have adopted. He continually embellished and refined his interpretations. As the *Mirror* commented: "His style is wavering with the vacillation of his own feelings, and resembles the morning light on the clouds, which eludes all the painter's endeavors to transfer it to the canvas."

With study and devotion, he knew that he could grasp the first-rank position that was already slipping away from Cooper, Booth, and Kean. He realized, however, that he could not be satisfied by merely stepping into their shoes. As the first native-born, native-trained tragedian who had ever approached within shouting distance of the top of the theatrical ladder, he must make the American theatre something more than a transplanted British enterprise. More than that, his deeply rooted patriotic fervor demanded that he force the theatre to serve the cause of democracy.

In the fall of 1828 Forrest grew increasingly eager to carry his nationalistic sympathies to the stage. To be sure, he had in many of his roles—Rolla, Tell, and Damon, for example—championed man's intrinsic nobility and demonstrated that natural instincts were superior to the compulsions imposed by society. As one reporter put it, these roles showed that "genuine virtue, power, and nobleness took the crown and sceptre away from empty prescription." Forrest had to find some means of incorporating these democratic and humanistic desires into a stage character, preferably a native American character.

That Forrest was fired up at this moment was not all his own doing. He was riding with the rising tide of democracy. The Greek fight for freedom had brought Americans to their feet to cheer that cause and to testify to a renewed faith in their own liberty. Andrew Jackson had become the political symbol around which the faithful could rally. This rugged military hero, son of the soil, was about to show the world that a common man could rise to the highest position in the land and occupy the "palace."

With this strong surge of Americanism to support him and with his professional position assured, Forrest demanded a new American drama. He had read Noah's preface to *She Would Be a Soldier*: "National drama should be encouraged. They [the plays] have done everything for the British nation, and can do much for us; they keep alive the recollections of important events, by representing them in a manner at once natural and alluring."

Forrest's plea for a new American drama went beyond the documentary reporting that Noah had in mind. He challenged the new dramatists to explore the lives and times of the first inhabitants of the continent, the American Indians.

Early in November 1828, Forrest wrote to William Leggett, who was then editing a weekly review called *The Critic:*

> Feeling extremely desirous that dramatic letters should be more cultivated in my native country, and believing that the dearth of writers in that department is rather the result of a want of the proper incentive than of any deficiency of the requisite talents, I should feel greatly obliged to you if you would communicate to the public in the next number of the "Critic," the following offer. To the author of the best Tragedy, in five acts, of which the hero or principal character shall be an aboriginal of this country, the sum of five hundred dollars, and half of the proceeds of the third representation, with my own gratuitous services on that occasion. The award to be made by a committee of literary and theatrical gentlemen.

On November 22, 1828, Leggett printed the offer in *The Critic.* Confident that the announcement would evoke an immediate response, Forrest had already enlisted his judges: William Cullen Bryant, Fitz-Greene Halleck, James Lawson, William Leggett, Prosper M. Wetmore, and J. G. Brooks, who had been literary editor of *Minerva* and was now an editor of the *Morning Courier.* To give the prospective dramatists a clearer picture of the patriotic potential in Indian dramas, and of his own capabilities as an interpreter of the aboriginal, Forrest performed the part of the Indian in Noah's *She Would Be a Soldier* at the Bowery in celebration of Evacuation Day, November 25, just two days after the announcement of the contest.

Like so many zealots, Forrest found his noble motives conveniently backed by compatible selfish desires. The prize money would be cheap payment for a role tailored to his talents and which would become his exclusive property.

That Forrest solicited an Indian drama was not surprising. He had savored the excitement implicit in the lines of the Indian Chief in Noah's play: "The Indian warrior knows no master but the Great Spirit, whose voice is heard in thunder, and whose eye is seen in the lightning's flash, free as air, we bow the knee to no man. . . . We fight for freedom, and in that cause, the great king and the poor Indian start upon equal terms." The happy days with his Indian friends in New Orleans were still vivid in his memory. Forrest visualized the noble red man, the natural man incarnate, commanding the stage with his heroic postures, his muscles shimmering with their pent-up energy, and his piercing tones rousing the spectators to cheer his noble cause. He saw the stage Indian as an almost literal embodiment of the histrionic qualities he cherished: physical vigor and passionate expression. Nor was he unaware of the fact that the colorful, yet scanty, tribal regalia would permit a provocative display of his calves and biceps.

The contest announcement did not send many wishful playwrights digging into their trunks to resurrect old scripts. Before 1828 only a handful of Americans had tried writing for the theatre: J. N. Barker, M. M. Noah, William Dunlap, Royall Tyler, Samuel Woodworth, John Howard Payne, each of whom depended on other occupations or professions for his livelihood.

If Forrest's contest was thus addressed to a limited audience of would-be playwrights, the subject-matter restriction further handicapped it. Indian characters had appeared in the American drama some half-dozen times before 1828. Barker had employed the Pocahontas story in *The Indian Princess* in 1808, and Noah used an Indian Chief as a minor figure in *She Would Be a Soldier*. None of these, however, had aroused wild enthusiasm for the stage Indian.

Forrest's contest announcement brought in fourteen plays by the following summer, and one of these, *Metamora*, later became a permanent fixture in Forrest's repertoire and his steadiest money-maker for the next thirty-five years. The success of the contest must be attributed solely to Forrest's theatrical acumen. He had not catered to a public clamor for native playwrights or for Indian drama.

In sponsoring this first playwriting contest, the first call to native writers to turn to the stage, Forrest set a milestone in American theatre history. For the next seven years, he conducted the annual competition, raising the stakes to a thousand dollars for the prize-winner and lifting the subject-matter restriction. Some of the entries continued to deal with Indians. Most of them either treated an American patriotic theme or showed an honest freedom-loving soul of some other country struggling to shake the shackles of an evil despot.

Some two hundred plays were read by Forrest and the committee. All but two of the nine prize-winners were performed by him, and four of these seven were retained in his repertoire. No twentieth-century playwriting contest can match this record.

The winners in the nine contests were:

Metamora; or, the Last of the Wampanoags by John Augustus Stone. First performed in New York at the Park Theatre, December 15, 1829.

Caius Marius by Richard Penn Smith. First performed in Philadelphia at the Arch Street Theatre, January 12, 1831. Performed again but not retained in Forrest's repertoire.

Pelopidas; or, the Fall of the Polemarchs by Robert Montgomery Bird. Never performed. In 1840, W. E. Burton announced a production that never materialized.

The Gladiator by Robert Montgomery Bird. First performed in New York at the Park Theatre, September 26, 1831.

Oralloossa, Son of the Incas by Robert Montgomery Bird. First performed in Philadelphia at the Arch Street Theatre, October 10, 1832. Occasionally this play was drawn out of Forrest's inactive file for another performance.

The Ancient Briton by John Augustus Stone. First performed in Philadelphia at the Arch Street Theatre, March 27, 1833. This single performance was enough to convince Forrest that the play had best be forgotten.

The Broker of Bogota by Robert Montgomery Bird. First

performed in New York at the Bowery Theatre, February 12, 1834.

Jack Cade by Robert T. Conrad. Performed by Forrest in New York at the Park Theatre, May 24, 1841. Under the title *Aylmere*, this play had been performed by Augustus Addams at the Walnut Street Theatre in Philadelphia on December 9, 1835.

Mohammed, the Arabian Prophet by G. H. Miles. Never performed by Forrest, although it was presented in New York on October 27, 1851.

The final competition, which yielded the unusable *Mohammed*, was held in 1847, twelve years after the spurt of successive annual contests had ended. In this final contest, the only one for which a complete record is now available, the bulk of the fifty-five manuscripts came from New York and Philadelphia, though entries came from Portland, Maine; Salem, Massachusetts; Kalamazoo, Michigan; and Harrodsburg, Kentucky.

Forrest's contests produced no Shakespeare nor Sheridan; they did, however, stimulate an interest in native drama. American playwrights might have had to wait many years to find honor in their own country had not Forrest swung the door open.

CHAPTER *viii*

Metamora and Spartacus

After the contest announcement in November 1828 and the Evacuation Day performance of *She Would Be a Soldier*, Forrest went to Boston for a December engagement, came back to the Bowery in January, and in the middle of February decided that his friends remote from the Eastern seaboard should see him in his newly acquired glory.

He took a boat for New Orleans and on April 10 opened at his old stand, the American Theatre in Camp Street. The theatre was said to have been remodeled, yet Forrest detected no change except the addition of gigantic mirrors, decorated with blue damask and topped with eagles, which hung in the back of the stage boxes. They were intended to give the occupants a panoramic view of the audience. The new reflectors had not cleared the theatre of the heavy smell of whisky and tobacco, about which the ladies regularly complained.

Everyone noticed a change in Forrest. He had taken on new authority. As a reporter from the *Courier* observed: "He has climbed the steep where Fame's proud temple shines afar." "Let us support this tender sapling," the *Advertiser* urged, "and prove to the pedants of Europe that our soil is fertile in genius and that her children know how to cherish and reward it."

Forrest loved the sweet words and the noisy applause of his old friends. Even more he loved the happy reunion with J. B. Booth and with his former sweetheart, Jane Placide. Caldwell was either too occupied with his gasworks or his new theatre in Natchez to observe the reunion. At any rate, he did not disturb them. When Forrest had closed his engagement four years earlier, he had camped out with the Indian chief; this season, when he concluded with a benefit for the "destitute orphan boys" on May 8, he stayed with Jane. Under what arrangement is not quite clear; certainly they did not scout the countryside nor sleep out as Forrest had before. Never in robust health, Jane seems to have been in particularly frail condition this season. In July, Jane and Edwin went north to share an engagement at the new theatre in Nashville.

Forrest's appearance at this frontier theatre was the headline event of the year. The manager was proud to have captured the American tragedian for six nights, though he had done so at great risk, which he beseeched the patrons to share with him. The prices were doubled: $1.50 for the first circle and pit, $1.00 for the second tier. To give equal opportunity to Nashville's first citizens, the boxes were auctioned off to the highest bidder at nine o'clock each morning.

Managers wailed whenever Forrest appeared. His big hands gathered in most of the money. They thought it better, however, to have the company paid, the house full, and a small profit than to have nothing at all.

At the end of July, Jane returned to New Orleans and Forrest went home to Philadelphia. If Forrest tried to persuade her to come East, he was unsuccessful. Her theatrical orbit was limited to New Orleans and the outlying towns of the Southern and Western circuit, and, except for a brief trip to England in 1833, she seems to have been unwilling to venture beyond this familiar territory. They never met again.

Jane died in New Orleans on May 16, 1835. Forrest learned of her death in Paris the following October. In his diary he wrote: "And so Jane Placide is dead. The theatrical people of New Orleans then have lost much. She imparted a grace and a force and dignity to her role which few actresses have been able so admirably to combine. She excelled in a profession in the arduous sphere of which even to succeed requires uncommon gifts, both mental and physical. Her disposition was as lovely as her person. Heaven lodge and rest her fair soul!"

In later years, it was rumored that Forrest erected the tombstone that marks her grave in the Girod cemetery and that he composed the inscription:

> *There's not an hour*
> *Or day or dreamy night but I am with thee;*
> *There's not a wind that whispers o'er thy name,*
> *And not a flower that sleeps beneath the moon*
> *But in its lines of fragrance tells a tale of thee.*

If true, Forrest never accepted credit for the stone or the marker.

Forrest was now accustomed to begin his fall season at the Bowery in late August or early September. This year he delayed until October 17, appeared at the Park instead of the Bowery, and cut his first engagement to two weeks. Charles Gilfert having died the previous July and a new Bowery management having not yet been established, Forrest chose the Park.

The play contest was responsible for the delay and for the short run. During his sojourn in the South, the entries had piled up—fourteen of them—and he wanted to read them carefully before becoming engrossed with an engagement. After the committees initial screening, Forrest studied the manuscripts himself and even wrote to the authors suggesting changes and commenting on their dramaturgy. When John Howard Payne, for example, sent him his play *Romulus*, Forrest pointed out that it had too much narrative and declamation: "I need not tell you that the action of passion is the secret of dramatic writing."

After his benefit night on October 30, 1829, when he played *Brutus* [1] and *Thérèse*,[2] both plays by Payne and both performed in the same evening, he took a three-week layoff to work with John Augustus Stone on the manuscript of *Metamora*, the first prize play. Stone was particularly equipped to tailor an aborigi-

---

[1] John Howard Payne's *Brutus* was not based on the Brutus of Shakespeare's *Julius Caesar* but on the half-mythical rebel patriot Lucius Junius Brutus who fought against the lust and tyranny of the Tarquins in the sixth century B.C.

[2] Payne's adaptation was derived from the French melodrama *Thérèse* by Victor H. J. B. Ducange. Contrary to his usual custom, Forrest played the villain.

nal drama for Forrest. He had acted with Forrest on many
occasions and had had a close-range view, both in New York
and Albany, of Forrest's Indian in Noah's *She Would Be a
Soldier.*

That the first prize play should come from an actor rather
than from a literary man was not surprising. First of all, Forrest
was looking for a spectacular central figure, imbued with noble
sentiments and introduced to a series of chilling escapades. He
was confident that his own theatrical magic would obscure any
literary deficiencies. When he first read Stone's description of
the Indian warrior Metamora, he knew that this was the part
for him: "the grandest model of a mighty man [who] sleeps
amidst the roar of a mighty cataract." (No doubt Stone knew
of Forrest's passion for Niagara.) Metamora loved his tribe, his
native land, his home, his wife, his child, but he had a savage
hate of the white man and a steadfast determination to see him
destroyed. He was the "natural man" incarnate, possessed of a
beautiful spirit and a beautiful body, two qualities highly favored by Forrest.

On November 24 Forrest returned to the Park for a six-night
engagement and then took another interval of ten days to rehearse the company in *Metamora.* If not a lengthy preparation
for a major opening compared to present-day New York sched-
ules, in 1829 giving up a single night of performance for the
sake of a new play was regarded as a ridiculous extravagance.

The *première* performance of *Metamora* on December 15,
1829, was framed by a prologue and an epilogue, the treatment
reserved for important theatrical events. Both the prologue by
Prosper M. Wetmore and the epilogue by James Lawson commanded the audience to heed the noble drama that had sprung
from the pen of one of their native sons:

. . . .

> *Tonight we test the strength of native powers,*
> *Subject, and bard, and actor, all are yours—*
> *'Tis yours to judge, if worthy of a name,*
> *And bid them live within the halls of fame!*

(from Wetmore's Prologue)

. . . .

A native bard—a native actor too,
Have drawn a native picture to your view;
Yet, not that they are native do I plead,
'Tis for their worth alone I ask your meed.

(from Lawson's Epilogue)

Lawson need not have pleaded for applause. The crowd that
stretched out into the lobbies—every inch of standing room was
occupied — recognized the importance of the play and of the
occasion. Never had the noble red man been so gloriously portrayed. "Forrest caught the very manner of their breathing,"
one reporter noted; it was a piece of acting that "transcended
all criticism." For sheer "destructive energy," another observed,
he had never heard anything so "tremendous in its sustained
crescendo swell and crashing force of utterance. His voice
surged and roared like the angry sea; as it reached its boiling,
seething climax, in which the serpent hiss of hate was heard, at
intervals amidst its louder, deeper, hoarser tones, it was like
the falls of Niagara, in its tremendous down-sweeping cadence;
it was a whirlwind, a tornado, a cataract of illimitable rage."
One critic objected to the panoramic display in the fourth act:
"the stale trickery of burning ships and houses and of canoes
rowed by pasteboard men" was beneath the dignity of so fine a
tragedy. Some insisted that Forrest used too much gesticulation
for an Indian. These were minority reports.

Stone's principal character had been modeled on the famous
New England Sachem, King Philip of Pokanoket, son of Massasoit. The primary plot [3] is centered on Metamora's valiant, yet
vain, attempts to repel the encroachments of the white man.
He refuses "to forsake the home of his fathers and let the
plough of strangers disturb the bones of his kindred."

Metamora also participates in the subplot, a conventional
melodramatic story involving the white characters: Mordaunt;
his daughter Oceana; Walter, the hero; and Fitzarnold, the villain. Oceana's love for the honest Walter, a young man of hum-

---

[3] No complete manuscript of the play has been preserved. One fragment
is in the Forrest Home, another in the University of Utah Library.

ble origins, is threatened by Fitzarnold, newly arrived from England. Fitzarnold has enticed her father into promising that Oceana will become his bride. Metamora is entangled with this action from the very beginning. He had once rescued Oceana from a tiger. When Metamora is bitten by a wolf, she binds his arm with her scarf. He rewards her with an eagle plume that will, and does, protect her from the Indians. When Metamora stabs the Indian traitor Annawandah and the whites level their guns at him, Metamora grabs the nearest white man as a shield. His victim, Mordaunt, is killed and Metamora escapes. When Fitzarnold is on the point of seizing Oceana, Metamora appears and kills the villain.

The play is filled with thrilling actions and spectacular scenes: Metamora poised like a bronze statue on a rocky crag, the ships on fire in the harbor, the burning of Mordaunt's house.

The tremendous impact of the play depended, however, on Metamora's noble character and noble utterances. He is a true child of nature. He tells Oceana that "the red man's heart is on the hills where his father's shafts have flown in the chase. . . . The Great Spirit hears his evening prayers, and he sleeps amidst the roar of a mighty cataract."

He reminds the white men that both he and his father, Massasoit, had been their friend. "The red man took you as a little child and opened the door of his wigwam. The keen blast of the north howled in the leafless wood, but the Indian covered you with his broad right hand and put it back." They must beware, however, for "if the flint be smitten too hard it will show that in its heart is fire."

Metamora is blessed with prophetic gifts; he foresees the gloomy destiny of the Indian: "The power of dreams has been on me," he explains to Nahmeokee, his wife, "and the shadows of things that are to be have passed before me. When our fires are no longer red, on the high places of our fathers; when the bones of our kindred make fruitful the fields of the stranger; which he has planted amidst the ashes of our wigwams; when we are hunted back like the wounded elk far toward the going down of the sun, our hatchets broken, our bows unstrung and war whoop hushed; then will the stranger spare, for we will be too small for his eye to see."

When Metamora is accused of harboring a white man who had been banished from the village, he challenges the white men's right to reject one of their own because the "Great Spirit did not speak to him as he had spoken to you? . . . If my rarest enemy had crept unarmed into my wigwam and his heart was sore, I would not have driven him from my fire. Your great book, you say, tells you to give good gifts to the stranger. The Wampanoag needs no such counselor, for the Great Spirit has with his own fingers written it upon his heart."

When he sees that a final battle is inevitable, Metamora is fierce and relentless in rallying his warriors: "Snatch your keen weapons and follow me! . . . Call on the happy spirit of the warriors dead and cry, 'Our lands! Our nation's freedom! Or the grave!' "

The play was crowded with exciting moments, yet none of them matched the final pathetic scene. Metamora's warriors have been scattered, his child has been killed, he and Nahmeokee have been driven into the woods. When he puts his ear to the ground and hears the white men approaching, he takes Nahmeokee in his arms for a final embrace and stabs her. As he lowers her body to the ground, his sadness is relieved by the thought that "she felt no white man's bondage—free as the air she lived—pure as the snow she died!" When the soldiers surround him, Metamora refuses to surrender. As they fire he shouts: "My curses on you, white men! . . . May your graves and the graves of your children be in the path the red man shall trace! And may the wolf and the panther howl o'er your flesh-less bones, fit banquet for destroyers!" Then "Drums and trumpet sound a retreat till curtain. Slow curtain!"

Forrest had poured his soul into *Metamora,* and he knew he had played it well at the opening performance. He did not realize that on that December night he had begun a lifetime occupation. On January 22, 1830, he took the play to the Arch Street Theatre in Philadelphia, and for the twenty-five years following that date only two Philadelphia seasons were without a performance of it. On April 9 he did the play in Albany "to the largest business of the engagement." Four years later, at the same theatre, the members of the orchestra had to leave their seats to accommodate the crowd, while hundreds were not able to enter the theatre. On January 5, 1842, the Bowery announced: "In consequence of the number of persons unable to gain a sight of the stage on New Year's night, to witness the Indian play, Mr. Forrest has agreed to play it one night more." The gallant Spartacus (in *The Gladiator*), the jealous Moor, the mad Lear, and the murderous Macbeth could not hold up against the noble Indian. Throughout the rest of his life, whenever Forrest or the management needed a boost at the box office they scheduled *Metamora*. However, during this first year Forrest did not overwork *Metamora*; he gave it only one or two performances wherever he played.

Forrest had a busy spring. After Albany, he made a quick Southern trip to Baltimore and Richmond. In Richmond he had difficulty holding his own, even with *Metamora*, against his alternate-night attraction: Madame DeJack, a trained elephant, appearing in *The Elephant of Siam*, a drama which had been especially written for Madame's talents.

From Richmond he returned to New York, then to Boston, and on June 23 he was back in New York to play *Metamora* for Woodhull's benefit. The choice of date was no accident. It marked the fourth anniversary of Forrest's first New York appearance when he had also appeared in a benefit for Woodhull.

At this point in his career Forrest saw no reason for venturing beyond the Eastern theatrical centers. They were treating him nobly. For the first two weeks of his new fall season at the Park he earned $3,000, more than Booth, Cooper, Kean, or any other actor had received from an American audience in a comparable period. During the fall Forrest shuttled between New York and Philadelphia. For a pre-Christmas run at the Chestnut Street Theatre he alternated with J. B. Booth in the parts of

Othello and Iago. "No two more finished artists ever came to-gether," one critic remarked. For Christmas night he was back at the Park for a performance of *Metamora*. Special occasions now demanded the Indian play.

On January 12, he was again in Philadelphia for a première of Richard Penn Smith's *Caius Marius*.[4] Smith was a fellow Philadelphian, seven years older than Forrest, a lawyer, and a son of the first Provost of the College of Philadelphia. He had not entered his play in the contest; he had merely sought Forrest's comments. Forrest liked the play, gave Smith a prize, and agreed to give it a chance on the stage. It did not meet the test. After this first performance and another at the Park on May 7, it was dropped.

During the spring Forrest discovered another Philadelphian, who had entered the contest and whose career was to be inter-twined with his for the next few years, Dr. Robert Montgomery Bird.

Medical men have frequently been drawn to the drama. The names of Dr. Morris of Brooklyn and Dr. Johnson of New York, who entered Forrest's 1847 contest, may be unfamiliar. Certainly Anton Chekhov, James Bridie, and Arthur Schnitzler are better known today as playwrights than as doctors. R. M. Bird is not in their class, yet anyone who may know of him knows him as a playwright, not as a doctor.

Bird was just one month Forrest's senior. Like Forrest, he had been raised in Philadelphia though under somewhat more affluent circumstances. He was trained in the classical and modern languages, and, even before he took his medical degree at the University of Pennsylvania in 1827, was drawn more to literature than to medicine. He maintained a perfunctory medical practice, and in 1841 became Professor of *Materia Medica* at the new Pennsylvania Medical College; but his energies were directed to dramatic writing.

Whether complying with Forrest's contest formula, or with his own natural sympathies, Bird's high-blown romantic dramas

---

[4] Smith's play was based on the life of the great Roman general Gaius Marius. No copy of the play has survived.

were bursting with just the kind of righteous struggle against tyranny and oppression that delighted Forrest. In the 1830 contest, *Pelopidas* [5] first alerted Forrest to Bird's talent, and though he did not find the central character sufficiently developed, he awarded Bird the prize just to encourage him.

When the manuscript of *The Gladiator* reached him on May 1, 1831, Forrest knew that his judgment had been confirmed. Here was a native-born dramatist who sang the song of freedom in a strong clear voice. If the Doctor could continue as he had begun, a new day was dawning for the American theatre.

Forrest was so anxious to cultivate Bird and his talent that he abandoned his usual dictatorial manner toward professional associates. He was friendly and even deferential. On May 6 he wrote to Bird: "Producing your play in June, say about the 20th, controllable entirely by your direction. *The Gladiator* must prove victorious winter or summer. To be sure he [Spartacus] would not groan and sweat quite so much in cooler weather, but that will be *his* task and not yours. Will be in Philadelphia about the close of next week. We can then discourse fully upon the subject."

Forrest was certain that he had struck a rich lode in this new prize-winner, and when they met, he was convinced that he had found a new friend. Not since his sojourn with the Chief in New Orleans had he enjoyed such easy companionship. They both agreed that the play could be improved if they spent the summer together working on it. After a week of struggling with Spartacus in the Philadelphia heat, they decided that the three of them would do better in a more favorable climate.

In mid-June they headed for Niagara Falls. Forrest believed that any vacation must begin at the Falls. For a week they climbed around and under the roaring waters, catching the sights and sounds from every angle. They then swung up through New England, pausing long enough at Portland, Maine (July 11, 1831), to give Forrest a one-night stand of *Damon and Pythias*. From Maine they traveled south, bound for the

---

[5] Bird's play is based on Plutarch's account of Pelopidas and the revolt of the Thebans against the Spartan tyrants.

Natural Bridge in Virginia; they were visiting only the most spectacular natural wonders.

Niagara and the Natural Bridge evidently provided the proper stimulation. When they returned to Philadelphia in August, they had an improved manuscript of *The Gladiator* and were certain that they had cemented a lasting friendship. For the next two years while their professional horizons broadened together and their friendship grew, they found pitifully few opportunities to share each other's company.

In its first performance at the Park Theatre on September 26, 1831, *The Gladiator*, like *Metamora*, achieved an immediate success.

Although Bird had steeped himself in Roman history, he had molded his material to conform to his dramatic purpose. In the character of Spartacus, the leader of the gladiators' insurrection, he epitomized man's eternal struggle against tyranny. When Spartacus is brought to Rome and his master asks him what he thinks of the noble city, Spartacus replies: "If Romans had not been fiends, Rome had never been great! . . . There is not a palace upon these hills that cost not the lives of a thousand innocent men; there is no deed of greatness ye can boast, but it was achieved upon the ruin of a nation; there is no joy ye can feel, but its ingredients are blood and tears."

Spartacus has been brought from Thrace to display his prowess in the arena. After he has slain a Gaul, the praetor Crassus announces that if he wins over his next opponent he and his family will be freed. Spartacus discovers that his adversary is his brother Pharsarius who had been captured some years earlier. They embrace in the arena, leaving Crassus and the spectators bewildered. During the confusion the brothers plot their rebellion. When Crassus insists that the combat continue, Pharsarius shouts: "Freedom for gladiators!" Spartacus takes up the call to arms:

> *Death to the Roman fiends, that make their mirth*
> *Out of the groans of bleeding misery!*
> *Ho, slaves, arise! it is your hour to kill!*

Metamora and Spartacus

Kill and spare not—for wrath and liberty!
Freedom for bondmen—freedom and revenge!
    (Shouts and trumpets—The guards and gladiators rush
    and engage in combat, as the curtain falls.)

After seeing this spine-tingling scene, one reporter commented that for sheer excitement it was "unsurpassed in any theatre in the world."

The noble deeds and sentiments of the succeeding three acts never reach the pitch of this Act Two finale.

After their victory the two brothers disagree about their next move. Pharsarius wants to sack Rome; Spartacus insists that they not imitate the enemy, a campaign of conquest would not serve the cause of freedom. They must advance to Sicily and rally more slaves to break the shackles. Pharsarius deserts, attacks Rome with fifty thousand men, is routed, and returns to Spartacus. His soldiers have all been crucified. Spartacus forgives him for his folly and leaves his wife and child under Pharsarius's protection while he continues his effort to reach Sicily. Before Spartacus embarks he learns that Pharsarius has again disobeyed, attacked some Roman soldiers, and his wife and child have been killed. Enraged, Spartacus storms the Roman camp, kills their general, reaches the inner sanctum of the praetorium, is stabbed by Crassus's guard, and expires in front of the praetor in the exact attitude of the dying gladiator.

Throughout the play Spartacus repeatedly asserts his faith in man's intrinsic worth and his abhorrence for the tyrant's outrages. When the Romans offer a ransom for Julia, Crassus's niece whom Spartacus had captured, claiming that Romans never war on women, Spartacus reminds them of their fearful conquests when

Fire flashed from burning villages, and famine
Shriek'd in the empty cornfields. Women and children,
Robb'd of their sires and husbands, left to starve—
These were the dwellers of the land!—Say'st thou
Rome wars not then on women?

When one of Crassus's emissaries tells Spartacus that he would have made a fine Roman general, Spartacus proudly rebukes him:

> *I thank the gods I am a barbarian;*
> *For I can better teach the grace-begot*
> *And heaven-supported masters of the earth,*
> *How a mere dweller of a desert rock*
> *Can bow their crown'd heads to his chariot wheels.*
> *Man is heaven's work, and beggar's brats may 'herit*
> *A soul to mount them up the steeps of fortune,*
> *With regal necks to be their stepping blocks.*

Forrest found the noble Thracian an ideal role. The play offered abundant opportunities for muscular exertion, ferocious passion, and reiteration of the freedom-loving sentiments he held so dear. Throughout the remainder of his career *The Gladiator* shared the position of honor in his repertoire with the Indian play.

During the 1831–2 and 1832–3 seasons, Forrest restricted himself to New York, Philadelphia, and Boston, and though he did not limit himself to his two new prize plays, they were his chief items.

On October 10, 1832, Forrest introduced another Bird play, *Oralloossa,* the story of another barbarian committed to the cause of freedom, a Peruvian barbarian who assassinates Pizarro. Forrest chose the Arch Street Theatre in Philadelphia for the *première* to give his brother William, then co-manager of the theatre, the benefit of whatever extra business might be stimulated by the event. It was a noble but unprofitable gesture. *Oralloossa* fared only slightly better than Smith's *Caius Marius.* After its initial performances in Philadelphia, Forrest tried it once in Boston, three times in New York, and then gave it up.

Forrest supported another effort to help William's business. The Arch Street was relabeled the "American" to put it into direct opposition to the Chestnut Street which at that moment was featuring the British actors Charles Kemble and his daughter Fanny. This was Forrest's first taste of the nationalistic rivalry which, in a few years, led to open warfare with Macready. On this occasion no personal animosity developed between him and Kemble. In fact, a month later they joined forces in New York in a grand dramatic festival in honor of John Howard Payne, and in February played together again at the Park, in *Venice Preserved.*

This February performance with the Kembles was Forrest's last in New York for some time. The nightly average had dropped from $621 in November to $380 in February. He decided to give Baltimore a try for a week and then go to Philadelphia to prepare for a first production of another prize play.

The single performance of Augustus Stone's *The Ancient Briton* [6] on March 27 was enough to convince him that it, too, was unworthy of further attention. Forrest must have grown a little skeptical of his contest; the last three attempts had failed. The disappointment of Stone's play and the poor business in New York convinced him that this was an appropriate time for a trip to New Orleans, particularly if he could persuade Bird to go with him.

After a performance of *King Lear* on April 2, 1833, Forrest announced his plans to the Arch Street audience. According to a newspaper report of the occasion, a see-America-firster could not have invented a more extravagant description of his forthcoming adventure. First he thanked them for their "unequivocal approbation of his efforts in establishing an American national drama." Now for awhile he was going to "forego the gratification of their smiles, to exchange the populous city for the mountain-top, the broad lake, the flowering prairie, and the solitude of the pathless wood, in the hope that, thus communing, my heart may be lifted up, and I may with more fidelity portray the lofty grandeur of the tragic muse."

He had had no difficulty in persuading Bird to accompany him. The next day they boarded a boat for Charleston. After a few days in Charleston they took the cross-country stage for

[6] Stone's story is based on Queen Boadicea's attack against the Romans in the first century A.D. The ancient Britons in the play bear a strong resemblance to the Indians in *Metamora.*

New Orleans, a fearful journey according to Bird, "enough to break the necks of half Christendom." One time the coach was stalled in a bog for two hours and another time broke down completely. They sat on a trunk beside the road from eleven o'clock at night until nine in the morning.

Forrest was delighted to be back in New Orleans, even if disappointed to discover that Jane Placide had departed for London. He and Bird explored the exotic wonders of the lively metropolis, dividing their time between the elegant drawing rooms and the rowdy waterfront taverns. Bird kept up a steady stream of reports to his mother and to his fiancée. He was fascinated by the pistol-shooting Creoles who took fire "at the appearance of insult, with all the quickness of suspicion," by "the negresses, and mulattoes chattering bad French," and by the sailors' taverns on the levee where there was always "a great din of laughing, swearing, and singing, and the stench of liquors." He liked the mint juleps, the French coffee, and the mosquito curtains which he was going to install over the beds in Philadelphia when he returned. He was convinced that this "Mecca of Mammon" was destined to be the greatest city the world has known.

They had intended to extend their peregrinations into Mexico and South America. Instead they turned north on May 19, going by steamer to Baton Rouge, Natchez, and Memphis. Perhaps the cholera epidemic in New Orleans had induced them not to risk exposure to the more fearful tropical diseases they might find farther south. Bird reported that they revised their plans because they could not endure the prospect of riding so far on "stupid mules."

At Memphis they separated. Forrest continued on to Cincinnati by boat, while Bird took the stagecoach to Nashville, "thirteen days over the hills and swamps of West Tennessee—oh the horrors and purgatoriosities thereof."

Both New Orleans and Cincinnati had given Forrest a cheering reception. He never tired of reading, as he did in New Orleans, that Othello had never been personated with "more energy and perfection," or in Cincinnati, that he had "his whole soul wrapt up in the business of the scene."

Some extra excitement was stirred up at the second performance of *The Gladiator* in Cincinnati on Monday, July 1, when Bird, who had rejoined him, was in the audience. During the arena scene, according to the *Advertiser*, Charles Hammond, editor of the *Gazette*, stood up and "in the manner of a rude bacchanalian which would have degraded the most ignorant boatman in the gallery, vociferously condemned the piece and the acting, and observed that 'the damned play should never be repeated.' With one accord the audience joined in the indignant cry of 'turn him out,' which was speedily done by one of the police officers on the spot." A lone voice did not stand a chance when most of the audience believed that the author "deserved to be ranked with the first American writers."

The returning-hero reception Forrest received in Cincinnati did not soften his financial demands. The managers continually reminded the public that the engagement had been arranged at a heavy expense. Whatever the expense, the eight hundred places in the pit and the three tiers of the Third Street Theatre were filled at every performance. When his departure was announced, the *Advertiser* "regretted much that this gentleman could not have made with us a longer stay."

On July 4, Forrest and Bird left Cincinnati, journeying north to Detroit and then to Buffalo to make their second obeisance to the mighty cataract before going home. They arrived in Philadelphia toward the end of July.

For most of the summer Forrest remained at home enjoying the attentions of his mother and sisters and buying new items for the house. His major purchases were a $70 set of French china, a $400 set of silver, and a case of champagne ($15!).

Before the summer ended he was restless to be back on the stage. He wrote to Francis Courtney Wemyss, who had temporarily abandoned his Philadelphia acting career for the manager's post at the new theatre in Pittsburgh. Wemyss urged Forrest to come immediately.

The trek from Philadelphia to Pittsburgh was a sentimental journey for Forrest. His first professional adventure, eleven years earlier, had begun over this same route. Traveling conditions, according to the brochures, had greatly improved; the three hundred miles were now said to be covered in four and a half days "without a single stoppage." Forrest was always intrigued with transportation and kept his library well-stocked with the most recent travel books. Well-worn copies of *The Traveller's Guide through the Middle and Northern States*, published at Saratoga Springs in 1833, and *The American Traveller: or Guide through the United States* by H. S. Tanner, printed at Philadelphia in 1837, are still in the Forrest Home Library. Then as now, comfort and speed never conformed to the advertising. When they took on additional passengers in Chambersburg, the stage was crowded to capacity with nine adults and five children.

The new theatre was a remarkable improvement over the barnlike structure in which he had first appeared. Every dressing room was carpeted and elaborately furnished. The greenroom was decorated in the style of a "modern drawing room," with piano, ottomans, easy chairs, looking glasses, and all the other accouterments of a first-class salon. Unhappily, a new theatre and a star actor were not enough to overcome the Pittsburgher's natural apathy. His $400 opening night was the only profitable night of the twelve; one performance of *Lear* sank below $100. Forrest considered this a personal affront. When he completed his commitment he departed immediately, determined to strike Pittsburgh from his list. He did not play there again until 1848.

For the winter season of 1833–4, Forrest confined his activities to the Bowery in New York, the Tremont in Boston, and the Pearl Street in Albany, where he knew his talents would be appreciated and rewarded.

Forrest had always felt indebted to the citizens of Albany for their early encouragement, and during his January visit made a partial repayment, a donation to the Young Men's Association. In his accompanying letter he praised their laudable motives in "forming an association for mutual improvement of young men of Albany," and hoped that a taste for American letters would be "carefully and sedulously disseminated among them; the false and parasitical opinion cannot too soon explode, which teaches 'nothing can be so good as that which emanates from abroad.' Our literature should be independent; and with a hearty wish that the iron fetters of prejudice which surround it may soon be broken. I herein enclose the sum of one hundred dollars, to be appropriated *solely* to the purchase of books PURELY AMERICAN."

Forrest grasped every opportunity to spread the nativist doctrine. He knew the letter would be widely quoted, and when his friends learned of the trip abroad he was now planning, it might reassure them that his Americanism was hardy enough to withstand foreign influences.

At the end of January Forrest was busy with another prize play by his friend Bird. The new play, *The Broker of Bogota,* was set in Bogotá, Colombia, in the eighteenth century and, unlike Forrest's other prize plays, was a domestic tragedy relating the pathetic story of Baptista Febro, a wealthy and honorable moneylender who lavishes all his love on his children and is rewarded by having them turn against him. The play got off to a good start. After the opening performance on February 12, Forrest wrote to Bird urging him to come to New York immediately so that he might have an "opportunity of seeing [his] last child in 'health and spirits.'" Bird was also preparing for a trip to England and could not come. Forrest, knowing that he would not be on hand for Bird's sailing, sent him a *bon voyage* note, enclosing a letter of introduction to James Wallack in London, urging Wallack to help Bird "in cultivating the acquaintance of some of the *elite* of our calling." Bird and Forrest did not meet again until August 1836.

Before Forrest himself went abroad, he felt compelled to cover his familiar haunts. After his February engagement he departed for New Orleans. As usual the Southern city turned out en masse to cheer him in his prize plays. This visit was marred by sad news from home.

As soon as he had docked in New Orleans he learned that his brother William had died on the very day his ship had sailed. That Monday evening, March 3, 1834, when the curtain was rung down after the opening piece at the Arch Street Theatre, the audience was told of the "melancholy occurrence." William had been at his regular duties in the morning and, according to one reporter, apparently "in the full enjoyment of health when the hand of the unsparing destroyer struck him down." The two brothers had been together in recent years only when Edwin occasionally lent his services to support William's managerial ventures; however they both had felt a strong fraternal bond, and when Edwin received the sad news, he wrote immediately to his mother:

My Dear Mother,—We have experienced a deep and irreparable loss. You are deprived of a dutiful and affectionate son, my dear sisters of a most loving and devoted brother, and I have now none on earth to call by that tender and endearing name. It seems but yesterday that I beheld him in the pride of his strength and manhood; and I can scarcely credit that his "sensible and warm motion had become a kneaded clod, doomed to lie in cold abstraction and to rot." . . . But for my sake, dear mother, for the sake of all your children, whose chief study in life is to make you happy, do not give way to grief, lest it impair your health and deprive you of the enjoyment of the many happy years through which it is our prayer that you may yet live to bless us. . . .

In spite of his grief he fulfilled his engagement (March 19 to April 26) before returning to Philadelphia to comfort his mother and to break the news that he was going abroad. As usual, she surprised him with her fortitude. Somehow the march of events, when she knew they were inevitable, never broke her spirits, and though saddened at his going, she made no effort to restrain him.

Back in New York, Forrest began a round of farewell performances: first at the Bowery, then in Albany and Philadelphia, concluding in New York on July 16. Everywhere he held almost exclusively to *The Broker of Bogota* and *Metamora*, reminding his audiences of his passion for native plays. This should assure them that here was one American who could withstand the corrupting foreign influences. His imminent departure received full attention in the press, and when he appeared in Albany on June 23, his old friend James Hunter, editor of the *Daily Advertiser* (and later of the *Albany Daily News*) gave him a grand send-off:

> This young man, who has given such lustre to the histrionic character of America, and who has shown that this side of the Atlantic can produce talent at least equal to the trans-atlantic shores, takes his farewell benefit to-night. He plays in a piece written by an American—John Augustus Stone.
>
> Edwin Forrest, independent of his universally admitted abilities as an actor, is a man of the most amiable and virtuous character. He is, to speak all of him briefly, A GOOD MAN. We know him well; we esteem him; we admire him; we love him; and we never knew of an acquaintance of his who did not.
>
> Pleasant breezes while going, and fast winds while returning, be your guerdon, and GOD be your guardian, OUR FRIEND.

The major farewell celebration was scheduled for New York. On July 10 a group of the first citizens requested the pleasure of his company "at a dinner at the City Hotel, on any day most agreeable to yourself." Forrest replied on the 12th, assuring them that no "additional memorial" was necessary to demonstrate their regard for him, yet "knowing the pleasure which generous natures feel in bestowing benefactions," he was happy to "name Friday, the 25th instant as the day when it will best comport with the arrangements I have already made, to meet you as proposed."

Everyone of any consequence in New York joined in the testimonial. In addition to his old friends W. C. Bryant, William Leggett, D. P. Ingraham, Fitz-Greene Halleck, James Lawson, Prosper M. Wetmore, and William Dunlap, a number of newcomers appeared on the list of the fifty-seven members of the arrangements committee: Philip Hone, businessman and socialite; Washington Irving, who had just returned from his post as Secretary of the United States Legation in London; James Fenimore Cooper, who was back from a tour of duty as United

States Consul at Lyons; William Gilmore Simms, the Southern novelist whose *Guy Rivers* had just been published. The roster read like a Who's Who of New York. Charles C. Ingham, one of the founders of the National Academy of Design, was commissioned to design a gold medal to commemorate the occasion. The medal (now in the New York Historical Society) shows a bust of Forrest, in profile, encircled with the inscription: *"Historiom Optimo, Eduino Forrest, Viro Praestanti"*; on the other side is a figure depicting the genius of tragedy with the line from Shakespeare: "Great in mouths of wisest censure."

At 6 p.m. on Friday, July 25, the company gathered at the City Hotel. Chancellor William T. McCoun of the Court of Chancery presided. The guest of honor was on his right, and on his left the Honorable Cornelius W. Lawrence, Mayor of the City. After the "removal of the cloth" the toasts and speeches began. The first toast was to "The Drama." The second to Shakespeare, and the third to Forrest. The climactic toast was preceded by an address by the chairman. McCoun recounted the actor's rise to his present eminence, praised his devotion to native drama, and commended his personal integrity. As he warmed up to his final tribute he pinned the medal on Forrest's chest: "You will mingle in throngs where jewelled insignia glitter on titled breast; but yours may justly be the reflection that few badges of distinction are the reward of qualities so deserving of honor as those attested by the humbler memorial which now rests upon your bosom."

He raised his glass. The entire group stood. "Gentlemen, I propose to you, Edwin Forrest—Estimable for his virtues, admirable for his talents. Good wishes attend his departure, and warm hearts will greet his return." The glasses were emptied, and a cheer went up for Forrest as he rose to reply. A simple brief acknowledgement would have seemed in order. Forrest gave them a full speech thanking them for their encouragement of his talents, their generosity at the box office, which enabled him to provide for his sisters and widowed mother, and, holding the medal in his hand, he concluded: "While I thus behold with feelings of deferential awe the last resting-places of those departed monarchs of drama [he had told them he intended to visit the tombs of Garrick and Talma], I shall then look upon this memorial; but, while my eye is riveted within its 'golden round,' my mind will travel back to this scene and this hour, and my heart be with you in my native land." He raised his glass and toasted the citizens of New York. Again there was a round of cheers.

After Forrest was seated, additional toasts were offered: to "talent and worth," to Hallam and Henry ("the Columbus and Vespucius of drama in the New World"), to Garrick and Kean, to Kemble and Talma, to George Frederick Cooke, and to the "dramatic genius of our country." Nor was this all; as a closing tribute the chairman read all the letters from the well-wishers who had been unable to attend. Nineteenth-century banqueters had phenomenal endurance.

A remarkable testimonial to a twenty-eight-year-old actor who had climbed to the top in twelve years, impelled by his own talent and industry.

CHAPTER ix

Romance and Red Tape in Russia

The next morning some sixty or seventy stalwarts, unwilling to let the celebration die out, hired a yacht to escort Forrest's ship down the harbor. Before committing him finally to the care of Captain Forbes, master of the *Sully,* Fitz-Greene Halleck spoke a few touching words wishing Forrest "hundreds of beautiful hours in beautiful places," and begging him to come back to them unchanged. According to Leggett's account of the departure which he sent to Mrs. Forrest, Forrest replied: "That is indeed the wish of a poet for his friend. You may be sure when I am at Marathon, at Athens, at Constantinople, I shall often recall your lines on Marco Bozzaris, and be delighted to link with them the memory of this your parting benediction." A salute of twenty-four cheers from the yacht concluded the festivities. The two vessels drew apart, and Forrest was on his way to France.

As long as the smallest speck of his native land was in sight Forrest stood at the rail, his eyes straining to fix the image in his memory. Whatever Old World enchantments he might encounter, the memory of home must be constantly on call.

The first night out Forrest kept to his cabin, reveling in his freedom from theatrical duties and dreaming of the adventures ahead. The second night and for the remaining nights of the two-week voyage he stretched a blanket on deck. Here he could savor whatever new sensations the churning water and the undulating panorama of stars might offer. He often remarked in later years that the loneliness and isolation that he felt on these nights, the awesome reminder of man's puniness in the vast world of ocean and sky, gave him new insights into the characters of Lear and Hamlet.

When the *Sully* docked at Le Havre, Forrest paid his respects to Captain Forbes and rushed on to Paris. Even without prior arrangements he found a comfortable room near the Tuileries and plunged immediately into his two tasks: bringing his New Orleans French up to Parisian standards and seeing the sights. His first letter to Leggett, just a week or two after his arrival, reported that he had already visited the Louvre, Place Vendôme, St. Cloud and almost half the twenty theatres that were then open. What a fascinating city it was: "One cannot go into the streets for a moment," he wrote, "but something new attracts his curiosity. . . . In your comfortable and handsome rooms, you may either breakfast, dine, and sup, or take only your coffee there, and dine at a restaurant. . . . Another agreeable thing in Paris is, that you may one moment be in the midst of fashion, pomp, and all the hollowness of the flattering crowd, and the next buried in the sincere quiet of your own chamber."

In the theatres he was particularly struck by the acting of Mademoiselle Georges at the Théâtre Porte St. Martin in the title role of Hugo's *Lucrèce Borgia*. "Her personation was truly beautiful. . . . How different is her and nature's style from the sickly abortions of the present English school of acting, lately introduced upon the American stage!—the snake-like writhing and contortion of body, the rolling and straining of the eyeballs till they squint, the shuffling gait, and the whining monotone."

Forrest was intrigued by another player, Mademoiselle Mars of the Théâtre Français, who had the "natural ease and grace which should characterize the most finished lady of the drawing room, and her quiet yet effective style of acting is the most enchanting and delicate triumph of the mimic art." In time he became well enough acquainted with Mademoiselle Mars to know that she possessed a splendid fortune, lived in a palace, and that her *salle du billiard* would "well serve for a corporation dinner." However, Leggett must not assume that his opinion of her acting was "influenced by personal attentions."

The only other actor who impressed him was an unknown minor player. Forrest had been asked by a theatre manager to observe a young player who, it was thought, showed great promise. Forrest, not sharing the manager's enthusiasm, advised him to watch "that Jewish-looking girl, that little bag of bones with the marble face and flaming eyes,—there is demoniacal power in her. If she lives and does not burn out too soon, she will become something wonderful." An acute prognostication. Some years later the "little bag of bones" was to be hailed as one of the great tragediennes of all time. We know her as Rachel.

In another report to Leggett, a five-page letter written early in January, Forrest described his first four months of Parisian delights. Lest Leggett think he had succumbed to French frivolity, he assured him that his first thoughts were always of America. He reported that President Jackson's recommendation of reprisals if American claims on France were not paid had dropped like a bomb in the Chamber of Deputies. They had had the effect, he wrote, "of once more *Americanizing* Americans, and revived within them that love of country which the pageantry and frivolity, the dreamy and debasing luxury of this metropolis serve materially to enervate."

Forrest deplored the French passion for pageantry, still he did not deprive himself of the pleasures it offered, and he wrote Leggett a long and detailed account of his presentation to Louis Phillipe.

One evening at about nine o'clock he had crossed over to the Palace of Tuileries, just opposite his hotel. After an hour or more of watching the "jewelled company constantly moving and intermingling: old ladies arranging their diamonds to the most dazzling effect of brilliancy, young demoiselles scrutinizing their relative pretensions in the way of decorations and personal beauty, and embroidered dandies twisting their long and grizzly mustachios," he and one hundred other gentlemen gathered outside the Hall of Council.

An usher took the name of each man and announced them to the court one at a time. "After hearing those of sundry marquises, counts, and others announced, it at last came to my turn. My name was audibly repeated, I entered, and made my debut before the King of France with not half the trepidation I experienced on presenting myself for the first time before a *sovereign* in New York—I mean the sovereign people—on an occasion you will recollect. The King addressed a question to me in French, and after exchanging a few sentences I bade him farewell, bowed to the Queen and others of the royal family, and withdrew."

It was a memorable experience even though Forrest took no stock in such ostentation. He urged Leggett to remind "our plain republicans" who often laugh at the mimic monarchs of the stage "for their want of grace and dignity," that the real monarchs are not remarkably endowed with those qualities.

The "*dulce*" had been the chief object of his search in Paris, yet he had not neglected the "*utile.*" He had visited the "perfumed chambers of the great and the poor abodes of the lowly, the institutions for science, literature and the arts, the resorts of fashion, of folly, and of vice." He had even gone to the Ste. Pélagie debtor's prison to study the barons, marquises, princes, and low-life denizens who shared a common incarceration. Wherever he went, he found something which not merely "served to fill up the passing hour, but that furnished either substantial additions of knowledge or agreeable subjects for future meditation and discourse." A holiday for Forrest was serious business.

After four months he had "tired of the glare and frivolities" and longed to tread again "the piled leaves of the West,—my own green forest land." France might be refined and polite; America was solid and sincere. Parisian pleasures were plentiful, still America was the land for true happiness.

Just before he left Paris, Forrest struck up an acquaintance with Henry Wikoff, a gay adventurer and would-be writer who had just been expelled from Yale and who, like Forrest, was on the grand tour. Forrest was intrigued by his knack for putting

117

a romantic bloom on the most ordinary day-to-day events and asked him to join him. Wikoff quickly agreed and on Tuesday morning, February 11, 1835, they departed for Italy.

As they traveled south, Forrest was amazed at the cheerless appearance of the open country, "somewhat like a wide uncultivated common or storm-beaten prairie," he wrote to Leggett. There were no neat farmhouses as in America, only untidy hovels; no signs of prosperity and thrift, only poverty and filth. After two days of this dreariness, they finally arived in Lyons where they stopped for a day to visit the Museum of Antiquities, the Cathedral, and the silk manufactories. Forrest was shocked to see the "attenuated sickly wretches" who wove the silk threads. Compared to their miserable existence, the slaves in America lived in luxury.

Forrest had been cautioned against crossing the Alps in mid-winter. Such talk of terror, though it might frighten "certain lap-nursed Europeans, who have never surmounted any but mole-hill difficulties," meant nothing to an American. At least not an American who has "seen something of his own magnificent country before hastening to examine the miniature feature of Europe."

They crossed to Turin by the Mont Cenis carriage road which Napoleon had built in 1811, and whose gentle ascent, according to Forrest, reminded him of the remark of a Kentuckian who thought the road from Albany to Troy "had the leetlest tilt from a level I ever did see!" The sun was just setting when they reached the summit, "and the slant rays lighted with dazzling lustre the snowy peaks around and bathed in a flood of light like molten gold the crags and flinty projections of the lightning-scathed and time-defying rocks. . . . A thousand features of rude magnificence filled me with admiration of the sublimity which marks this home of the tempest and avalanche." He apologized to Leggett for his inadequate description of the spectacle.

They arrived in Turin just as the sun was coming up. The streets were crowded with the sons of toil plodding to their morning labors and with revelers staggering to their beds. They had arrived in Turin at Carnival time. Even with the festive congestion, Forrest was immediately impressed by the cleanliness, spaciousness, and the general airiness of the streets, astonished too that, like Philadelphia, they were laid out at right angles.

However enlightened the Italians might be in this regard, he was shocked again at their attitudes toward the poor and lowly. Outside the church of St. Phillip he shivered at the heart-rending supplications of a blind man of eighty who "turned his orbless sockets to each passer, imploring charity in the name of Him whose crucified imaged he grasped in his attenuated fingers." Even more revolting was the brass plate which hung around his neck, "the inscription on which denoted that this mendicant had been regularly examined by the police, and had taken out his license to beg! What a source this from which to derive public revenue! What a commentary on the nature of government in this oppressed country! What a contrast it suggested, in turning my thoughts to my own land, where government is the people's choice, the rulers their servants, and laws nothing more than recorded public opinion!"

Forrest had a busy day in Turin, visiting the Museum and, in the evening, the Grand Opera House. The peculiar lighting fascinated him more than the performance. The six rows of boxes were dimly lighted with a single small chandelier suspended over the center of the pit. The rest of the lights were reserved for the stage, "by which the scenic effects are greatly heightened; but I doubt if what is gained in that respect would reconcile an American audience to sit in a sort of twilight so dim as scarcely to allow one to know the complexion of the person sitting at his side."

On Tuesday morning the two rovers departed for Genoa. Sleep was a problem. Forrest tried to nap as best he could between the jolts of the carriage and the sight-seeing interruptions. They took the old Corniche road to Genoa through the town of Asti, birthplace of the Italian dramatist Alfieri. Forrest paid his respects. Just across the Tanaro River they passed through the field of Marengo, where Napoleon had defeated the Austrian Army in 1800. They made their obeisance to history. At three o'clock on Wednesday morning, February 19, they arrived above Genoa, birthplace of Columbus! "The scene was like enchantment," Forrest wrote to his mother. "The moon was full and bright, before me was the Mediterranean Sea, calm and tranquil, the ships sleeping quietly in the harbour, and about, and above me rising in amphitheatral form was the city of Palaces."

When they descended into the city, the moonlight enchantment evaporated. Again he found the mass of the people "bowed down to the dust by unjust laws, and the fruits of their industry wrested from them, to support the idle pageant of a corrupt and despotic government," and again he repeated the old refrain, "I never felt so proudly the honor of being an American citizen." He was even prouder when he spied an American warship riding at anchor in the harbor, hired a boatman to row him out, and with the permission of the commander climbed up the side to stand for a moment under the American flag and be thus reunited with his native land.

The next stop was Florence where he dutifully inspected all the art treasures. He was more excited, however, over his meeting with Horatio Greenough, the American sculptor. In Rome Forrest found another compatriot, W. C. Bryant. The talk of distant scenes and distant friends was much more thrilling than the Colosseum and St. Peter's. From Rome they went to Naples, returned to Rome, then to Venice, Trieste, and Verona. Forrest gave Vesuvius a careful inspection. According to one story, of doubtful authenticity, he was unimpressed. His guide, an Italian Count, reminded him that America with all her wonders had nothing to compare with Vesuvius. To which Forrest was said to have replied: "Our great Niagara, if run into this thing, would extinguish it in two minutes."

The two travelers arrived in Milan at 11 p.m. on Friday, April 17, and early the next morning hired a *valet de place* to show them the sights. As Forrest has described it in his diary,[1] he walked through the galleries of the Palace of Fine Arts, and visited the library founded by Cardinal Borromeo where he inspected the manuscripts (a Vergil with marginal notes by Petrarch particularly fascinated him) and admired the Titians and the Raphaels. Like every visitor to Milan before and since, he worshipped before the faded "Last Supper" of Da Vinci in the refectory of the Convent of Santa Maria delle Grazie. He wandered among the four thousand marble statues in the gigantic cavern of the Cathedral, climbed to the highest cupola above the marble roof where he could look off at the Alps and the Apennines, and descended below the pavement of the church to the shrine of St. Charles Borromeo, the patron Saint of Milan. "There encased in gold and silver and crystal," he wrote in his diary, "we saw the ghastly and fleshless remnant of what 'once had a tongue and could sing.'" In Milan, as elsewhere, Forrest did not neglect the seamier side nor confine himself to purely cultural gratifications. He visited the Grand Hospital for the poor, and one evening, as he noted in his diary, he was " a fem[ale]."

On Sunday morning they were back at the Cathedral to hear the Grant Mass performed for the soul of the late Emperor. Forrest observed that the clerics were obliged to "call in the aid of the opposition." The chorus from the near-by La Scala Opera House supplied the music. After the Mass, Forrest in company with some 20,000 Milanese, promenaded upon the Corso. On Monday evening they went to the Opera and immediately after set out for Simplon Pass.

They breakfasted at the village of Arona on the shore of Lake Maggiore and then inspected the mammoth statue of St. Charles Borromeo. According to Forrest, it was the largest statue in Italy. He paid his respects by sitting on the Saint's nose. They stopped for the night at Duono D'Opola and at five in the morning began their ascent to the Pass, another of those invigorating gothic adventures in which Forrest delighted. "Morning clear," he wrote in his diary. "Set out to the

[1] Unless another source is indicated, Forrest's comments on his travels are taken from his diary.

Simplon and leaving the verdant plains and rich vineyards of Italy we were soon surrounded by mountains, perpendicular rocks, the wrecks of avalanches and listening to the wild roar of the foaming waters as they dash furiously through enormous fragments of displaced rocks." They breakfasted at ten at the village of Simplon and at three arrived at Brigg. Here the diary breaks off, not to be resumed until he returned to Paris in July. During the months of May and June Forrest traveled alone in Spain. Wikoff had apparently gone to England. No record of this part of the tour is extant.

On July 3 he wrote to his mother from Paris assuring her that though he had been out of touch he had been thinking of her. "All that I am I owe to you," he wrote. "Your necessities prompted my ambition; your affection led me on to triumph,— the harvest is your own."

He left Paris for Calais at 6 p.m. on July 8, arriving at Calais at 5 the next afternoon. His endurance was amazing. After riding a night and day in a crowded coach, he went to the Calais Opera House and then strolled on the ramparts before retiring. The next morning he crossed the channel on the *Firefly*; "boisterous, winds high, and all the folks sick." He stopped at Dover overnight; the next morning took a stage to Herne Bay, and from there the steamboat *City of Canterbury* to London where he registered at the Castle and Falcon Hotel in Aldersgate Street, supped and went to bed.

The next morning he breakfasted with Mr. Willcox, a gentleman from North Carolina whom he had met on the boat, and in the afternoon took a stroll in Kensington Gardens and St. James's Park where he and Willcox encountered the royal coach drawn by four gray horses and two outriders. According to Forrest, King William bowed to him.

During his three weeks in London, Forrest was besieged with invitations. An American was always a curiosity; a native American actor who had succeeded without benefit of British training was a rare phenomenon. Forrest reported to Leggett that he found "nothing but the warmest cordiality and kindness among men of letters, among the intelligent and worthy of the middling class of society, and among those of my own profession." Having arrived in London during the summer doldrums, he saw little of the theatre. He was, however, at Drury Lane the night James Sheridan Knowles, author of *Virginius* and *William Tell*, two plays already firmly established in Forrest's repertoire, made his first reappearance after his visit to America. According to Forrest's letter to Leggett, Knowles "took the occasion to advert, in very glowing terms, to the kindness he had experienced in America. He termed our country 'the bright land beyond the seas,' and our country-people his 'brothers and sisters.'" Forrest was cheered with this report from home, particularly hearing it from the lips of an Englishman.

On Tuesday, August 4, 1835, Forrest and Wikoff, who had now rejoined him, were preparing for the next lap of their journey. They paid their five pounds—meals and refreshments extra—for passage to Hamburg on the *William Jolliffe*. Just after midnight they went aboard, and at 2 a.m., sailed. They were bound for the dark and mysterious land of Russia. Happily, this part of the journey received detailed attention in the diary.

Some thirty passengers were aboard: Americans, Danes, Scotsmen, Poles, Germans, Spaniards, and others of undetermined origin. And, as Forrest noted, there was always someone among the passengers in a public conveyance who "will aim by some means or other to cut a figure or stand in *relievo*." In this case the character tempted by this "low ambition" was an "overgrown, fat, unwieldy, and as Shakespeare has it, almost spherical lady, dubbed on the way bill 'honorable,' and said to be the wife of a member of Parliament. This *dame passée* strove to ape the manners of a girl of sixteen and occasionally in a fit of would-be-young-again gave her huge frame a momentum on the promenade deck which, when in motion, looked for all the world like the wallowings of a great sea turtle in shallow water." A "British Count" also attracted attention "by blacking his new hedged mustachios with powdered lead upon a tooth brush."

The weather was fine, the wind favorable, and, in spite of the eccentric passengers, a general feeling of contentment permeated the decks. At 10:30 the next evening (Thursday, August 6) they anchored in the mouth of the Elbe. Because of the darkness, they were unable to proceed up the river until morning.

Forrest had expected Hamburg to be a dirty city, obsessed with commerce and alive with noise. He was agreeably surprised. His hotel, the De Rupie, was situated on the lake shore, and the ramparts fanning out on either side were "planted with handsome trees which afforded agreeable and shady retreats and the beds of flowers gave a delicious fragrance to the atmosphere." The general tone of the place was extraordinarily cosmopolitan, particularly on the fashionable promenade along the Aster where he encountered people of all nations and heard all languages spoken.

On Saturday he spent a considerable part of the day at the Russian Baths. Therapeutic water treatments always fascinated Forrest, and he gave a full account of the experience in a letter to Leggett:

Having reduced myself to nudity, a signal was given from an adjoining apartment, like the theatrical noises which attend the splitting of the charmed rock in the "Forty Thieves." A door now was opened upon the side, a blanket thrown over my shoulders, and I was told in German to go in. I obeyed. This was a small room, where the thermometer rose to about one hundred. Here the blanket was taken from my shoulders, a door beyond opened, and in stalked a naked man, who motioned me to follow him. I did so. I passed the portal, and was immediately enveloped in steam and heat up at least to a hundred and ten of Fahrenheit. This chamber was of oval shape and had on one side three or four shelves of wood, rising one above the other, on the first of which I was told to sit down. After striving to breathe here for five or six minutes, I was invited to sit upon the next, and after a certain time, to the next, and so on until I reached the last, near the ceiling, where the heat must have been at least a hundred and twenty. By this time the perspiration became profuse and poured off in torrents. The attendant now told me to descend to the third shelf; and then he commenced rubbing and whipping me with fragrant twigs. Then I was rubbed with soap, then told to stand in the center of the floor, when in a moment I was deluged with a shower of cold water. My probation was now nearly over,— three-quarters of an hour at least in the steaming purgatory. I returned to the first apartment, where I was laid, almost exhausted, upon a couch, and covered with at least a dozen blankets. Again the perspiration broke out upon me, and a boy stood by to wipe the huge drops from my face and brow. One by one the blankets were removed, and I was rubbed dry with white towels. Then I dressed myself, paid for the bath, about a dollar, and something to the boys. As I walked into the street, the atmosphere never before seemed so pure. Every breath was like a delicious draught. At every step I felt returning strength, and in about a half hour with a bottle of hock and a dozen oysters felt wholly myself again.

In the evening he and Wikoff went to the great Staat Theatre to see Schiller's *Don Carlos*. Forrest was impressed by the commodious appointments: the four rows of boxes arranged in horseshoe form and each furnished with four or five chairs instead of benches. Even in the pit the seats were arranged like armchairs, and many of these were engaged for the entire season. The citizens of Hamburg were obviously devoted to the theatre, a fact which became more apparent at 11 p.m. when after four and a half hours of sitting—"an English company could have acted *Brutus* twice over in that time"— they were still enrapt by what Forrest found a very tedious performance. "How a Yankee audience would have shuffled!"

Forrest needed rejuvenation before returning to the hotel. "From the theatre our *valet de place* took us to a *Salle de danse* called 'The Gas Light'—where a host of pretty girls were tripping away to the music of a half dozen fiddles, a cracked bass and a bleating clarinet. Here after taking supper in an adjoining room, I met a dark eyed Dutch girl who fascinated me home with her, and a storm coming on soon afterwards I was forced to remain with her until morning and in a damned cramped bed too!"

The next three days were taken up with tourist duties. They

inspected all the public buildings, joined in a harvest festival at Reinville, some three miles up the Elbe from Hamburg, and made return visits to the theatre and the *salon de danse.*

At the shank of the evening on Tuesday (August 11) he wrote in his diary: "Left my fair dame about twelve o'clock and went home by the light of the moon. I had been asleep about fifteen minutes when a ringing of a bell aroused me and supposing the alarmist to be my friend [Wikoff] who had not yet come home, I opened the window where I was confirmed in my supposition. I invited him in at the window but his fatigue cried 'no' to such exertion and I was forced 'sans culottes' to go and unbar the door for him. The devil himself could not waken a Dutch porter after the first snore."

The next morning they left for Lubeck, some forty miles to the northeast where they bought their passage for St. Petersburg (Leningrad): twenty-four ducats ($64) each for the 750 miles. They took a river boat to Travemunde, the Baltic port, and boarded the steamer *Alexandria.* Early on Monday morning, August 17, they arrived in Cronstaof (Kronstadt).

Forrest had heard of the backwardness of the Russians, yet he was amazed to discover that it was August 5, according to their barbarian calendar. "Time has rolled back for me," he wrote in his diary, "and I have the happiness to live twelve days over again, what a fool was he who said time once gone never returns." The reinstated days did not compensate for the tedium of the customs investigation. "A swarm of despot myrmidons came on board," sealing their baggage and inspecting their passports, plodding through the seventy passengers so slowly that they could not disembark at the St. Petersburg Customs House until four o'clock in the afternoon. Here the examination extended another two hours. It was 6:30 before he and Wikoff registered at Madame Wilson's hotel.

First thing in the morning, they hired a droshky and went to the Hotel de Paris in search of a better apartment. Finding that barnlike establishment no improvement, they decided to remain in "status quo." Madame Wilson learned of their expedition and when they returned agreed to improve their quarters. Thus assured, they "sallied out to see the sights," going first to the churches. In the four they visited, Forrest was impressed by the profusion of gold and silver and shocked to discover that the faces and hands of the Madonnas, saints, and figures of Christ were "represented in the color of the Negro." Everywhere the pitiful serfs crossed themselves and bowed their heads in the dust to these black Madonnas and Christs.

The next day (Thursday the 20th) they inspected the College of Miners where young men were being instructed in the art of mining before being shipped off to Siberia. After that, a session with Desirée, a French haircutter, who charged seventy-five cents for the tonsorial operation, and then to the Police Station to retrieve their passports only to discover that they had not yet been visaed by the secret police.

In the morning Forrest returned to the police and informed them that he was a Colonel of the 68th Pennsylvania Brigade — "whether there be such a regiment or not, I am completely innocent." He got his passport and saved himself ten rubles. "Nothing can be done in this stiff soldier government without a military title, so little is a private citizen respected that I have had to have recourse to a frock coat and a dash or two of braid a la militaire to secure even the commonest courtesies." When they went to the Palace of the Hermitage later that morning, the guards would not admit Wikoff because he did not have a dress coat. They were admitted to the church inside the adjoining fortress where they saw "an absurd representation of the grand Dieu holding the globe in one hand and his foot upon Europe with a bevy of little angels creeping from under his azure petticoats." As in all the churches, military standards taken from the Turks, Persians, and French were conspicuously displayed. "What a pride it is," Forrest wrote in his diary, "that amid all these we never see the Star Spangled Banner."

They visited the hut in which Peter the Great had lived while he planned his great city and then went on to the Alexander Nevski church, where Forrest was offended by the sight of "three old women going through the usual forms of xing [*sic*] themselves and bending down and kissing the earth while some priests stood laughing at them for their folly."

After dinner Forrest drove to "a house of momentary comfort" where he saw "a little girl who could not speak a word of any other language but Russian, but no matter, the action is the same in all lands and so I amused myself."

The next day (Friday, August 21), Wikoff having secured a suitable dress coat, they visited The Hermitage, the small museum on the opposite bank of the Neva that displayed Peter's mechanical contraptions and a collection of his old clocks, and the Academy of Fine Arts where the *chef-d'œuvre* was a monumental canvas showing the destruction of Pompeii. Recrossing the river by the wooden bridge, Forrest inquired about the covered boat that was gliding beneath them manned by a half-dozen soldiers. His guide informed him that it contained a "Polish nobleman who had been condemned to slavery and chain for the fault of loving liberty and his country too well." Assaults on freedom and human dignity appeared everywhere. Among the arcades of the Palais Royal he saw the miserable *castrati* money-changers. "Those whom they intend as money-changers they used to castrate (the practice had been abolished only a few years earlier) when infants so that they might be devoid of all passion and calmly calculate the value of kopecks. What a horrible crime against the dignity of nature and all for Mammon."

The next day they were out early for a jaunt into the countryside to see the royal palace. After pushing to arrive before noon, they discovered they would not be admitted until after two. One of the Princes was at home and did not intend to depart before that time. They were allowed to walk in the gardens which "are beautifully laid out, and the lakes (artificial) are filled with little fleets with their lilliputian sails fluttering in the wind. Little islands covered with umbrageous groves in which you see some miniature cottage." In another part of the gardens was the Emperor's Theatre, a handsome structure with an elaborately decorated royal box in the center of the horseshoe.

After lunch at the local hotel, they returned to the palace. According to Forrest's diary description, the palace was magnificent. "Its highly polished floors are formed with the most beautiful and various woods sometimes set in with pearls. The walls of one apartment are covered with amber, another with lapis lazuli, and another entirely with agate. The dining room is the largest in Europe." Evidently they were allowed to wander freely through the entire building.

The next day being Sunday, Forrest spent the morning observing the local worshippers. After church he followed the crowds into the Nevski, hoping, as he said, "to gratify his eyes with the sight of one handsome female." He hoped in vain.

After sleeping and studying French grammar for the afternoon he and Wikoff went to a Russian Restaurant to try a full-scale Russian dinner. We were "ushered into an apartment where a small table was arranged with a white cloth and about which were lounges stuffed and covered with green silk. On one side of the room hung a Saint before which burned the holy lamp. Thus was our meal sanctified." If the lamp cast a monastic atmosphere over the scene, there was certainly nothing monastic about the food. They went through some five courses: soup with two small meat pies, a fish covered with jelly (something like pickled salmon), two veal cutlets, a fowl (like a partridge), a salad of mushrooms, and for dessert some jellies and cake. All of this with a bottle of wine and cigars cost them the equivalent of four dollars. After this repast, it would seem an ample test of Forrest's hardihood to stagger back to the hotel, but he did not. The rest of the evening's adventure is best described in his own words: "Went to a special comfort house, but had no *capat*. Had to send my *valet de place* to the hotel to get the life preservers—then went ahead."

Although Forrest discovered friendly females, he was distressed that he saw no Russian beauties. As he wrote in his diary the next day: "I visited the churches, the public walks, the gardens. I tired myself in the vain search in the Nevski Prospect; I looked into the passing equipages, but they were freighted with nothing but ugliness. Even in the houses of a certain character where in most cities you can at least see the hectic flush of expiring beauty on the cheek of shame yet in these at Petersburg the wretched inmates could advance no such palliating witness to plead for their lost honor."

The next day, their last in Petersburg, he made a final round of the city and recorded his impressions. In the chapel at the Winter Palace he saw the *"veritable* hands of St. John the Baptist and the Virgin Mary, a piece of the *Vrai Cross,* a relic from the tomb of Lazarus, with many other holy cheats." A kind of fakiness characterized the entire city. The stuccoed and white-washed buildings were effective only under moonlight or "the uncertain light of a dusky evening." Most of the 450,000 inhabitants were homely, filthy, and superstitious. "A mower of beards would starve in the pursuit of his calling, for among the largest class of the community they never think of chin scraping." The mosque-like churches possessed a certain picturesqueness with their domes and bulbous towers painted a bright green or a deep blue and frequently studded with golden stars.

At 9:30 Tuesday morning, August 25, they packed their carpetbags, climbed aboard the coach, and drove into the dark, heathen country. In contrast to the primitive accommodations in St. Petersburg, the Moscow coach was luxurious: two compartments in the body of the "diligence" with two seats in each and additional coupés fore and aft; space for eight passengers. "There is a curtain of thick broadcloth which runs on a wire and if you wish privacy, or find your fellow passenger disagreeable you may draw the web 'and shut him from your sight.' Then you have pockets to hold your books, cologne water or any other small nicknack, a looking glass right opposite you where though heaven has given you one face you may make yourself another, and where the dandy may adjust his whiskers to a seeming propriety before he alights from his travel."

The road was a triumph of engineering; cut through the great larch and pine-tree forests with ample space provided on either side for cultivation, "neither ditches nor vallies occasion it to diverge from an almost direct line." The bridges, all of heavy masonry and with ornamental iron railings, were objects of beauty as well as utility, and what was most impressive, the entire stretch of 532 miles was macadamized. The accommodations and roadbed seemed less comfortable after the three days without a single overnight stop.

When they arrived in Moscow on Friday afternoon, they drove directly to the *Bureau des Diligence,* paid off the "conducteur," hired two droshkies, one for the baggage and one for themselves, and went to the Hotel du Nord. They had better luck than at St. Petersburg. They procured a comfortable room with two beds and furnished "a la Français with sofas, tables, and bureaus" for six rubles a day without meals.

Unable to hire a *valet de place*—most of the guides having gone off to the fair at Novgorod—they went to the Opera House where they saw a miserable performance of *Robert le Diable.* During the intermission they strolled into the salon "where the gentlemen retire to smoke pipes and take refreshments." The smoke was so thick, Forrest noted in his diary, "that you could scarcely recognize the features of those surrounding you. Everybody was partaking of a certain beverage from glass goblets and not to be out of fashion we ordered some of the same when lo upon tasting it proved to be Tea!! We hoped it something stronger."

On Saturday they made the rounds of the churches and visited the market place. In contrast to St. Petersburg, many more foreigners were on the streets: Greeks, Persians, Armenians, Georgians, Englishmen, and Americans. In the evening they attended the French vaudeville theatre and then went back to the hotel for their Saturday night bath which cost them five rubles each.

On Sunday and Monday, still having difficulty locating a satisfactory guide, Forrest spent most of the time in his room reading and writing. Tuesday morning a "dark Egyptian" offered himself as a valet. His appearance did not inspire confidence, still they hired him and set out for the Kremlin. They entered through the Holy Gate, where they were obliged to uncover their heads in deference to the image of St. Nicolas which hung above the gate. Forrest was fascinated by this gothic fortress with its embattled walls and towers and with its great bell, said to be the largest ever cast: twenty feet high, twenty-two feet in diameter, and weighing 440,000 pounds.

In the middle of the afternoon they returned to pack and move to Madame Howard's English House. They were annoyed with the landlord at the Hotel du Nord for neglecting to have their names published in the journal, "an indispensable form in Russia prior to your leaving the empire, in fact no one can leave Russia without advertising such intention three times in the public papers." After dinner at the Howards, Forrest commissioned the Egyptian to take him to a house where he might enjoy some Russian "fair ones." The Moscow style in nocturnal entertainment surpassed his expectations. The young lady had her true love stationed in the next room "playing the guitar while I —— *n'importe.*" Returning to the hotel he encountered another beauty and "as if the devil was in it—I 'talked' to her for a few minutes." He finally got home to bed at 2 a.m.

The next day, Tuesday, September 2, they returned to the Kremlin for a more thorough inspection. Forrest catalogued all the wonders. They saw the crown of Peter the Great with its 847 diamonds bordered with rich black fur; the crown of Catherine I "surmounted with a cross and ornamented with 2,536 diamonds with rubies and other precious stones"; the scepter of Valdimir "ornamented with 268 diamonds, 360 rubies and 15 emeralds"; the throne of Tsar Alexis Mikhailovitch "decorated in the oriental style with 876 diamonds and 1,224 precious stones and a multitude of pearls." They saw also a display of firearms of all ages and all nations, "the pride, pomp, and circumstance of glorious war."

Although the Kremlin buildings did not possess the regularity and beauty of classical architecture, Forrest observed that " if you consider them in a mass you are struck with admiration at the assemblage of their golden summits, the infinite variety of the designs and colors, the profusion of terraces, balconies and ramparts, and the peculiar roofs."

Before returning to the hotel for dinner, they stopped at a French café to sample "the small glutinous globules" of caviar.

It had "an ancient and fish-like taste," Forrest observed. In the evening their faithful Egyptian led them to the Hotel de Lupin where, as Forrest described it, "with a caput and some desire I lost an hour and a few rubles."

During the remainder of the week Forrest and Wikoff visited hospitals, the public gardens, the palace of the Empress, and numerous churches and convents. On Sunday evening they went to the Grand Theatre in Moscow for a performance of a "most stupid" Russian comedy, after which they supped with Mr. and Mrs. Priestly, an English couple, and "had a long chat about Negro Slavery."

To compensate for this misspent evening, the next night Forrest "sallied out again with the Egyptian to see some frail fair ones." By mistake he got into a respectable house where the ladies were all draped in black. Fortunately one of them spoke French, and with some embarrassed apologies he "got out of the scrape handsomely." Back on the boulevard, Forrest encountered Mr. Heilmann, a gentleman who had been a fellow passenger on the boat to St. Petersburg and who willingly joined him in his search for adventure. They met three girls: two Russians and one Pole, and went home with them. "I took two of them," Forrest noted in his diary. Returning to the hotel, Forrest was accosted by a policeman who lectured him about smoking a cigar in the street, "a thing prohibited; I took no notice of him and smoked on."

For some unaccountable reason Forrest spent the entire next day at the *Maison des Enfants Trouvés*. The *Maison* housed some five thousand children, sometimes admitted as many as fifty infants per day, and yet was in the "highest state of cleanliness and order." When a mother brought an infant to the home, no questions were asked except the name of the child and whether it had received baptism. A priest attended at five o'clock each day to give them a name and "sign them with the sign of the Cross." The girls remained in the institution until they were eighteen, and were taught Russian, French, German, the piano, drawing, and geography. The Livonian directress had difficulty in understanding that Forrest was American, being a white rather than red man. She knew America through the works of Cooper. The breadth of her education, astounded Forrest. Her Russian and German were perfect, her French fluent, and her English, which she had taught herself at the age of fifty, was passable.

During the next three days Forrest struggled with Russian red tape. The *Manual for the Use of English Travellers in Russia,* which he had bought in Moscow and which contained a vocabulary, guide to pronunciation, and simple facts about the country, evidently was of no help with Russian bureaucracy. His diary account of the entanglement sounds as if it might have been written today.

Wednesday. Went to Messr. A. Marc and to our bankers. Drew twenty-five pounds sterling or 559 rubles and six kopecks. M. Marc became security to the government that we should have no debts unpaid if permission should be granted for our departure before our names appeared regularly in the Gazette for the third time. We signed an instrument which was drawn up by M. Marc in which we pledged ourselves to make good to him any responsibility he might be liable for on our account. His security will be sent to the Vice-Governor today (the Governor being out of town) for acceptance and if it is we shall have permission to take our passports and leave the imperial domains of his most high Majesty the Autocrat of all the Russians.

The red tape stretched into the next two days:

Rose at 8 making preparations to leave Moscow—had got everything in the carriage when an officer from the government came in and told us that the sub-governor had gone out of town and therefore we must postpone our departure until tomorrow as he was not here to sign our passports. We have had more trouble than would clear fifty ships from the port of New York. And all this because Mr. Kopp chose to neglect the publication of our names in the Gazette when we first desired him.

Friday: We are disappointed again and cannot go today in all probability. Our passports and papers have gone through one hundred hands at least already and still there is no one who will take the responsibility that we shall leave town. Each one is afraid of losing his place and we are forced to lose our time. We have already given our banker as security for any debts that may be unpaid. We have sent in our petition to the Governor. We have fee'd officers to undertake for us and yet we can't go. All the delays and impositions practiced upon us during our voyaging in Europe put together could not make up this sum of perplexity.

Not until evening when he returned to the hotel was he able to write: "At last our passports are ready and we have permission to depart in peace. Took supper and went to bed."

Forrest's bitterness with Russian officialdom infected his other observations. He became annoyed with the spurious religious solemnity. "Today my very soul revolted at the sight of a well-dressed man who bowed his head to the very pavement, kissing the feet of the Holy Virgin who looked for all the world like a Virginia negress with a papoose in her arms."

On Saturday morning, September 12, they made their final preparations, and at one o'clock began the long journey to Odessa. At noon the following day they made their first stop, at Tula, a city of some 35,000, where they had breakfast and took their customary tour of the town. Monday's breakfast, cold tongue and bread, was at Orel and Tuesday's at Kursk, a town which had been built before the year 800, yet whose "white houses gave it the appearance of a town built yesterday." Wednesday they were among the Cossacks of Kharkov, and at 10 a.m. on Thursday arrived on the plain of Poltova, the historic spot where on June 27, 1709, Peter the Great had overcome Charles of Sweden. After inspecting the site, they breakfasted on sauterne, eggs, and bread and butter in the near-by town of Poltova. The party seems to have lived exclusively on breakfasts and often under unsavory circumstances. In Poltova Forrest discovered their waiter "spitting upon the teaspoons and wiping them with a dry cloth by way of cleaning them. Russian cleanliness!!"

When they reached the Dnieper at 3 a.m. on Sunday, after a day of rain and fearful roads, the "infamous scoundrels" who operated the ferry refused to transport the carriage for less than eight rubles. The regular price was two. They argued that they were not obliged to work at night. Forrest could match their stubbornness. He told the servant to put out the carriage light and advise the rascals that "we would wait until the morning and complain of them to the authorities. This done," Forrest wrote, "I got into the voiture and went to sleep. In the course of an hour one of the villains came and said he would take us over if we would pay but two rubles. To this we slowly acceded having kept the scoundrel in fear for some time. It was at the suggestion of Mr. W. that I gave up the point for I had resolved to expose the knaves. A greater race of vulgar cheats and low bred blackguards does not exist than these servants of his imperial majesty the Autocrat."

After eight days and nights on the road they finally reached Odessa on Sunday evening. They drove first to the Russian hotel which they found too expensive, then to the Richelieu, a French establishment.

In the morning they called on the American consul, John Ralli, were cordially received and invited to dine with him the next day. In contrast to the old Russian cities they had visited, Odessa was relatively modern, and, though founded only forty years earlier, already had a population of forty thousand. The streets were wide and airy, the houses spacious and well built, and a general air of bustle and business was evident on every hand.

At dinner that evening the landlord announced that General George Sonntag, another American, was anxious to meet them. Forrest was delighted to meet a fellow countryman, and, as it turned out, a fellow Philadelphian. When Sonntag came to the table, "a portly man of large frame and apparently about fifty," the conversation immediately "turned upon the land of free hearts." He was a man whom Forrest could admire. From a lowly birth he had by his "bravery, talents, and exemplary conduct raised himself to distinguished renown both in the Prussian and Russian service." He had come to Russia in 1815 and now held several orders for his achievements and was a member of the staff of Count Novrogow. He confessed, however, that he would gladly exchange all these foreign honors for the order of the American Society of Cincinnatus to which his father had belonged.

The next afternoon they had dinner at Ralli's country house where they met the French, Dutch, Greek, and "I don't remember how many more consuls," and on Thursday morning, September 24, rose at eight to prepare for their voyage to the Crimea.

Ralli brought their passports and a letter of introduction to Count Voronzow,[2] General Sonntag came to wish them *bon voyage,* and shortly after nine they climbed aboard the steamer *Peter the Great* bound for Yalta, the Black Sea port at the tip of the Crimean peninsula. In 1835 few Americans had ever heard of the place, probably no more than a half-dozen had ever been there.

On Friday morning they stopped in the harbor at Balaklava to discharge two young Russians. Up to that point the voyage had been peaceful. When they set out again the wind freshened, churning the waves so violently that most of the passengers became ill. Forrest stayed on deck testing his strength against the sea.

When they steamed past the village of Aloupka at six o'clock in the evening, they were greeted by a salute from Count Voronzow's cannons; *Peter the Great* replied. Just after dark they cast anchor in the bay of Yalta and took a boat ashore. Although they had intended to go immediately to the Count's castle, Wikoff was so exhausted from the voyage that he proposed they have supper, take lodging for the night, and set out early in the morning. Forrest insisted that they would never find suitable accommodations in Yalta and sent the guide to find a carriage.

In five minutes he returned, announcing that no horses could be procured until morning. "We soon perceived," Forrest noted, "that this was a devised plan between the fellow and the keeper of the house to detain us so that the house would reap

[2] Mikhail Semenovich Voronzow had been Commander of the Corps of Occupation in France from 1815–18, and, since 1823, Governor General of the Southern Provinces of Russia.

the profit. After I had spoken my mind to the fellow we told our servant Joseph to go and hail the boat, that we would sleep there for the night." Joseph soon returned, reporting that the sea ran high, that the lights were out on board, and he feared that the men could not hear his call. Forrest refused to be intimidated. He ordered Joseph to seek lodgings elsewhere. In a quarter of an hour he reported back. He had found a place.

"Away we went," Forrest wrote, "and soon entered a store in which was sold pipes, tobacco, coffee, fish, and axes, and the usual complement of a country store. To the left of which was our chamber, a filthy room with two benches covered with dirty blankets which were pointed out as our resting places. The glasses were broken from the sashes against which Wikoff commanded Joseph to hang a dirty rug to keep the wind away. Supper was now served which consisted of eggs, tea, and bread. I wrapped myself in my cloak and having the luxury of a tartar saddle for my pillow commanded me to sleep. The fleas and vermin struggled against me but at last overcome with exhaustion I dosed into forgetfulness."

Joseph routed them out at seven the next morning, announcing that the horses and voiture were ready for the ten-mile journey. The equipment was not impressive—two broken-down tartar horses and a dogcar mounted on four wheels and without springs—"but the morning was delicious and it offered haven by comparison to our lodging place."

The road from Yalta to Aloupka wound through wild and romantic country, past the palatial mansions of various princes and generals. Finding no one at Count Voronzow's castle, they took lodgings in the village. The next day the Count greeted them most cordially, conducted them through his gardens, showed them his new palace that was under construction and promised to be one of the architectural wonders of the Crimea, and invited them to dinner.

At five o'clock in the afternoon a gun was fired to indicate that it was time to dress for dinner. Half an hour later another gun announced that the guests were expected in the great hall. Forrest and Wikoff arrived at the castle before the second gun.

Forrest was unimpressed by the Russian nobility. Their table conversation—conducted in French—was senseless, and after dinner Forrest observed that some of the ladies smoked cigarettes and played cards. Beneath their showy elegance, he found them as mean and petty as any class he had ever met.

From Yalta they sailed across the Black Sea to Constantinople, that mysterious metropolis whose mosques and minarets, solemn cypresses, and spouting fountains, seemed at every hand to draw upon the wonders of the Orient. As viewed from the Bosporus, its romantic splendor surpassed anything Forrest had ever seen. From Constantinople they went to Smyrna and then across the Aegean to Athens. In Athens he tried with all the power of his imagination to convince himself "that this was the once proud city of Pericles, Plato, Aeschylus, Demosthenes, and the other men whose names have sounded so grand in the mouths of posterity." He wrote to his mother that he was obliged to ask, as Byron had:

> *Where are thy men of might? thy grand in soul?*
> *Gone,—glimmering through the dream of things that were.*

As so frequently happened Forrest was as impressed by a seemingly insignificant chance encounter as he was by the antique wonders. Tramping around the Parthenon, he tried to strike up an acquaintance with a picturesquely costumed Albanian, addressing him first in English, then French, and finally Spanish. He got no response, and the man walked away. Forrest later learned that he was the son of Marco Bozzaris, the Greek patriot, "one of the few, the immortal names, that was not born to die," as Halleck had described him. "This incident alone," Forrest wrote to his mother, "was enough to repay him for his whole journey."

From Athens they went to Corinth, then by way of the Ionian Isles up the Adriatic to Trieste. From Trieste they traveled across northern Italy back into Switzerland. They stopped at an inn in Chamonix to buy a copy of the hymn to nature that Coleridge had composed there, and again on the shores of Lake Lucerne to study the Tell country, and then went on to Dresden and Vienna. Forrest kept few notes on this part of his journey. On December 10 he wrote to his mother from Vienna: "I am weary with this wandering, and sigh for the sincere and tranquil joys of home. I hope, with the pleasure and instruction I have received from my journeyings, to entertain you during some long and friendly winter evenings, when we shall be cozily seated together in that snug little room of yours by a good coal-fire. How happy we shall be, dear mother!"

Back in Paris around the first of the year (1836), he summarized his travels in a letter to Leggett:

Since I saw you, I have indeed been in strange lands, and seen strange sights. I have traversed the Baltic and the wide dominions of the ambitious Autocrat,—crossed the Euxine and dipped into Asia and European Turkey,—"kept due onwards to the Propontic and Hellespont," wandered amid the faultless fragments of the bright clime of battle and of song,"—sailed by the Ionian Isles,—visited the chief town of the Germanic Confederation,—and here I am at last, safe and sound in the ever-gay capital of France. . . . I am free to confess Russia astonished me. I have sailed down the mighty Mississippi,—I have been in the dark and silent bosom of our own forest homes,—I have been under the eye of Mont Blanc and Olympus,—I grew familiar with Rome and London,—without experiencing the same degree of wonder which fastened upon me in Russia. I thought there to have encountered with hordes of semi-barbarians, yet I found a people raised, as it were, at once from a state of nature to our level of civilization. Nor have they apparently, in their rapid onward course, neglected the *means* to render their progress sure. And then, what an army,—millions of men! and the best forms of men,—the best disciplined, and able to endure the "labored battle sweat" by their constant activity, the rigor of their climate, and their ignorance of all pleasures which serve to effeminate. The navy, too, though in an imperfect state compared with the army (in sailors, not ships), will doubtless soon hold a distinguished rank. Only think of such a power, increasing every day,—stretching wider and wider, and all confessing one duty,—obedience to the will of the absolute sovereign!

Forrest's text would require few changes to make it appear to be the inside report of a mid-twentieth-century observer.

Romance and Red Tape in Russia

After a brief sojourn in Paris, Forrest returned to England to see the historic sites he had missed on his first visit, particularly Stratford-on-Avon. He visited Shakespeare's home and that of his father, Anne Hathaway's cottage, and the poet's grave with its "quaint and dread inscription":

> *Good friend, for Jesus' sake forbear*
> *To dig the dust enclosed here.*
> *Blessed be he who spares these stones,*
> *And cursed be he who moves my bones.*

For almost two years Forrest had wandered over the face of the old world. Now with a vast store of impressions resting in his memory, he boarded the *Poland* at Liverpool, happy to be turning toward home. Unable to cast an appropriate phrase of his own, Forrest chose some lines from Byron's *Don Juan* to conclude his diary:

> *What singular emotions fill*
> *Their bosoms who had been induced to roam,*
> *With fluttering doubts if all be well or ill,*
> *With love for many and with fears for some;*
> *All feelings which o'erleap the years long lost,*
> *And bring our hearts back to the starting post.*

In the fall reports were circulated that Forrest planned to make a book out of his travel diary. If he ever seriously entertained this notion, it progressed no further.

C H A P T E R   *x*

Wedding at St. Paul's, Covent Garden

On August 5, 1836, the *Poland* docked in New York. Forrest was thrilled to plant his feet on his home ground. The majestic towers of the Kremlin, the noble Parthenon, the sublime Mont Blanc, none of these could compare with the simple wonders of the sweet land of liberty. "An American needs to reside in Europe only a few months," he wrote to a friend, "to know and to feel that his own country is blessed beyond all others."

The welcoming party ushered him down the gangplank and proposed another banquet to celebrate his return. Recalling the protracted festivities of his farewell, Forrest urged them to postpone the affair. The first celebration was reserved for his family. Over and over his letters had teased: "Mother, do you sometimes wish to see your wandering boy and take him to your arms again?" In Naples he had raised a glass to her on his birthday. "My heart grew proud," he wrote, "while it acknowledged you the source of its creation."

The Philadelphia reunion continued for a joyous two weeks; Forrest luxuriated in the morning-to-night attentions and in the evening told the story of his travels. He took them to Paris, to Odessa, to Athens, and back to Paris. If some of the events became magnified and some more colorful, they all sounded true and exciting.

Forrest had not been on the stage for two years, yet when he returned to New York he apparently felt no need for rehearsal. On August 31, he plunged in immediately with a performance of *Damon and Pythias* at the Park Theatre, followed the next night by *Othello*. Then he rushed to Philadelphia for five performances, and back again to New York for a week, the kind of whirlwind schedule he enjoyed, particularly when supported by a crush at the box office and cheers in the house. He had forgotten how boisterous untamed Americans could be, and until the first sweet sound of applause floated over the footlights, he had not realized how starved he had been for their attention.

Every performance was sold out. The orchestra was dismissed to allow for more places; tickets were auctioned for as much as $25 each; people stood in line for hours to get standing room in the passageways.

In a way Forrest squandered the sure-fire appeal of his homecoming engagement by making it also a farewell. In a curtain speech after his first night in New York, he announced his plans for returning to England. A London engagement, he assured them, had not been of his seeking and he had consented only "in compliance with the wishes of a number of American friends, and partly to solve a doubt which is entertained by many of our citizens, whether Englishmen would receive an American actor with the same favor which is here extended to them." He had been hospitably received as a tourist, he might not be so kindly treated as an actor. He was resigned to that possibility: "If I fail—I fail."

He repeated the speech in Philadelphia, and in New York on his final night, choked up over the memory of his debut when, "a mere youth, emerging from severe hardships and still oppressed by poverty and a dark prospect," their generous applause had given him "a new zeal and a new strength to his motives." He would always remember them, and hoped that they would think of him during his absence, so that he might say, with the divine Shakespeare:

> *Our separation so abides and flies*
> *That you, remaining here, yet go with me*
> *And I, hence, fleeting, still remain with you.*

Throughout the happy month most of his time was occupied with his farewells; however, he squeezed in a few moments for personal affairs. He paid off William H. Moore "twenty-nine dollars in full for the funeral expenses of the late John A. Stone." His New York profits of $3,000, along with an additional $1,000, were sent to George Goodman at Niles, Michigan, to be invested in land [in that city] for his account and at Mr. Goodman's discretion. Goodman was an old Philadelphia friend who had moved to Niles the previous spring after the death of his infant son, Edwin Forrest Goodman. A man who had sought thus to perpetuate Forrest's name could be trusted to make a sound investment.

While he was still abroad, Forrest had written to Bird asking him to prepare a revision of Stone's *Metamora* that might be more suitable for English audiences. Bird had just completed the manuscript, and Forrest lent him $2,000. How much of this was intended as payment for his labors, and how much an outright loan, was not clear. A year later this misunderstanding precipitated an irrevocable break between the two men.

Forrest's final departing thoughts were reserved for his mother. He wrote a long letter from New York asking her forgiveness for running off and promising not to be "so neglectful as in the past in the 'letter-ary line.'"

Forrest approached his professional invasion of London in high spirits. His Philadelphia and New York engagements assured him that his absence had whetted the appetite of American audiences; a further absence would not endanger his local standing. His finances were in a healthy state. In spite of the heavy drain on his purse in two years of travel and no work and the impending theatrical gamble in London, he could still take a flyer in real estate to the tune of $4,000, and apparently he left his mother well supplied; in the middle of the winter she bought a new piano for $325.

Not all his New York friends approved his assault on London. Some urged him to delay and others to forget the whole project. James Kirke Paulding, who the year before had published his *John Bull and Brother Jonathan* in answer to the anti-

American slanders that had appeared in such books as Frances Trollope's *Domestic Manners of the Americans* (1832), argued that Forrest's reputation was secure without a British endorsement. "Washington never went to Europe to gain immortality," he wrote in a note to Forrest. "Jackson never went there to extend his fame. Why should you? Stay here, and build yourself an enduring place in the mind of your own country alone. That is enough for any man!" Forrest was unmoved. When the *Europe* sailed down the harbor on Sunday afternoon, September 18, he was happy to see his friends, again nudging alongside in their own chartered steamboat. Captain Marshall invited them to come aboard the *Europe*, and broke out champagne; they had a gay round of toasts as far as Sandy Hook.

Forrest was more luxuriously accommodated than on his previous voyage, having engaged a fancy stateroom and a valet. His old friend Andrew Jackson Allen had acquired this new assignment. Allen had begun his theatrical career in 1815 when he sang a Negro ballad at the Albany Theatre. Being inconvenienced by an "eccentric memory," he had never progressed as an actor. He had turned to costuming, and in the shadowy role of dresser, cook, and costumer for Forrest achieved an eminence that he could never have realized on his own.

It was a soothing crossing. Forrest was coddled by Allen and lionized by his fellow passengers. If he had felt any misgivings about his professional debut in the theatrical capital of the world, his fears were dissipated by the time he docked in Liverpool on October 9.

The arrangements for his London engagement had all been made by Thomas Willis Jones. Forrest had met Jones the previous spring and been impressed by his abilities. Up to that moment Jones had not invaded the London theatre, though he had had a successful career as manager of the Richmond Theatre, just outside London. Forrest's unfamiliarity with the English theatre had apparently led him to hire an intermediary between himself and the theatre manager and to give him *carte blanche*, even to the selection of his repertoire—certainly not an orthodox procedure for Forrest, and yet not the only peculiarity in the present arrangement. Forrest was scheduled to perform at Drury Lane, which at that moment catered to the more affluent theatregoers, maintaining a top price of seven shillings compared with Covent Garden's four. As if that handicap were not enough, Forrest discovered that the four shillings at Covent Garden would at present buy Macready as Othello, Vandenhoff as Iago, and Charles Kemble as Cassio all on the same evening. Macready and Kemble had not spoken to each other since 1823, yet they had now joined forces to combat the American invader.

Alfred Bunn, the Drury Lane manager, did all he could, except lower his prices, to assure Forrest a fighting chance. He announced that the theatre had been redecorated throughout "in the most costly manner" to give a proper welcome to the "principal tragedian of the United States." Jones planted a daily series of stories in the *Morning Post* for a week preceding the opening, describing Forrest's recent triumphs in Philadelphia and New York, and informing the public that the American tragedian had been receiving the phenomenal sum of £120 per night for his labors. On October 16, the day before the opening, an anonymous theatrical observer—perhaps Jones in disguise—commented on the sorry state of tragedy on the London stage. One is given only the choice between "the presumptuous and uninspired feelings of Mr. Bellwether Kemble, or the melodramatic jerks and pumpings of Mr. Macready." He also reminded his readers that every roguish actor who could borrow a shilling had infested the shores of the United States and brought back enormous sums, "more than they were worth and more than they could have made here." None of them had a tenth part of the talent or the genius of Forrest. And to forestall any disturbance at Drury Lane or at least to point the finger at the culprits, should a disturbance occur, he announced that "even the phrensied partisans of those bitter bad actors, Kemble and Macready, will not venture to show their teeth on this occasion."

Bunn had not been too optimistic about Forrest's chances when he signed the agreement with Jones. However, in his present war with manager Osbaldiston of Covent Garden he was willing to try anything. When Bunn heard Forrest speak

IX *Forrest married the vivacious Catherine Norton Sinclair at St. Paul's, Covent Garden, on June 23, 1837. Their marriage was terminated after a sensational divorce trial during which each accused the other of flagrant infidelities.*

Xa The living room of Forrest's town house at 436 West Twenty-second Street in New York. During the 1870's the house was occupied by Secretary of State Christian A. Herter's grandfather.

Xb Forrest as he appeared at the height of his career.

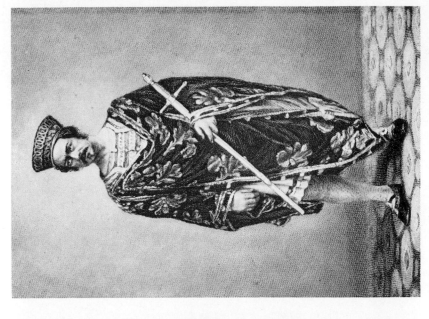

XIb Othello was one of Forrest's greatest roles. He was particularly proud of his make-up, a mixture of burnt sienna, unburnt sienna, and ivory black combined with almond oil.

XIa Forrest as Richelieu. Charles Kean called Forrest's impersonation of the canny French Cardinal the greatest acting he had ever seen.

XII Forrest's Fonthill Castle on the Hudson, with the George Washington Bridge in the background. Although the castle was built for his
wife, she never entered it after its completion. Fonthill is now the
Library of the College of Mount Saint Vincent.

SAINT CHARLES THEATRE . NEW ORLEANS

LUDLOW & SMITH PROPRIETORS & MANAGERS

XIII Although not so grand as the first St. Charles Theatre, the second St. Charles (1843) was equipped with gas lighting and with patent furnaces that "introduced hot air ad libitum."

XIV *Miss Lillie and Forrest in* THE BROKER OF
BOGOTA. *During his last years of touring, Miss
Lillie became his protégée and traveling com-
panion.*

XV Handsome "Prince John" Van Buren, son of President
Martin Van Buren, presenting his bill for legal services as
Forrest's counsel in the divorce trial.

XVI Thomas Ball's statue of Forrest as Coriolanus. Forrest
paid $10,000 for this white marble statue, which now
commands the main hallway of the Edwin Forrest Home
in Philadelphia.

his first lines at rehearsal, his skepticism disappeared. He had never heard such earnestness in an actor and never had seen such a noble athletic figure. After the rehearsal he commented to Jones that he was glad he was not obliged to fight with Forrest.

Jones had announced an all-American debut program with Forrest doing Spartacus in Bird's *The Gladiator*. It was a wise decision, and one to which Forrest willingly acceded. With expectation running high, any play would have served the purpose. "A money-loving country like England," the *Atlas* noted, "is always fascinated by a wealthy visitor from that 'money-getting country, America,' particularly an actor who, at the early age of twenty-eight, is said to have made a fortune of £20,000."

Forrest got off to a good start. *The Gladiator* allowed him to pull out all the stops and exhibit his most spectacular histrionics uninhibited by reverence for the text. Drury Lane was packed and when the final curtain closed, the audience bombarded him with a round of bravos that would have done credit to a Bowery crowd. One "honest fellow" in the gallery stood up and shouted: "Welcome to England!" and the rest of the audience took up the cry. When they quieted down, Forrest thanked them for the kind reception. Certainly it demonstrated that "England and America were joined by the closest good-will, that obviously the more enlightened portion of their population was superior to any feeling of national jealousy." This touched off another salvo. However, when he called for applause for his countryman Robert Montgomery Bird, only a few feeble hands responded—probably the scattering of Americans in the audience. The others shouted: "Give us Shakespeare!" Not precisely the all-out endorsement he had hoped for. Clearly they wanted more of Forrest and less of Bird.

The opening-night fever carried into the press, most of the official observers being overwhelmed by his herculean dimensions and the avalanche of physical energy that he poured into Spartacus. Never had an actor been so richly endowed with "thew and sinew," and such a "Jericho-trumpet" voice. His symmetrical torso, his elegant neck and head, according to the man from the *Atlas,* could have served as models for the *Farnese Hercules.* When he first came into view in the wings, the *Parthenon* observed, his five-foot-ten-inch figure seemed to rise to six feet. As he began to move and speak, it seemed to shoot up to seven. When he charged into combat, "he looked as if he could down the whole cohort" singlehanded. He may not have been "remarkable for the delivery of this or that pretty tinkling poetic passage," the *Sun* remarked, "but he gave free play to those rough natural passions which are intelligible all the world over." No actor had so electrified his audience since the memorable night in 1814 when Edmund Kean "burst on England as Shylock." All of this was music to Forrest's ear. What greater praise than to be compared with the master of the English stage!

The gentlemen from the *Morning Herald* and the *Morning Advertiser* detected "a provincial flavor of the backwoods" in his voice, "some degree of that *patois* which distinguished most Americans, even the best educated." His energy, his simplicity, sincerity, and above all his naturalness pushed such minor deficiencies into the background. In summing up his triumphant debut, *Figaro* insisted that "fame had blown her trumpet even more *piano* than the merits of the actor deserved and had she blown a blast of the most *fortissimo* description, it would not have been more than a just anticipatory tribute to his genius. He will go back to America a *forest* of *palms*, for the *palm* must at all *hands* be awarded to him."

Most of the reviewers shied away from the play and those who risked an opinion thought it deplorable. "This piece by Dr. Brien was heavily and feebly written." (The *Morning Post* had not even copied the author's name correctly.) *Figaro* said the "tragedy was bad, and the *bird* who wrote it must be a *bird* not much given to *soaring*." John Forster, in the *Examiner,* insisted that a gentleman would just as much think of "introducing a few real gladiators at an English supper-table as present such a succession of scenes in an English theatre." Only one unidentified reviewer, writing on the Sunday following the debut, showed any kindness toward Bird. According to him, no one in England, except Knowles, could have done half so well, "certainly neither of those brace of coxcombs, Talfourd and Bulwer who sat cheek by jowl in the stalls on Monday to witness the triumph of a man, whom, in the plentitude of their envy, hatred, malice, and all uncharitableness, they would have preferred to see hanging instead of acting."

One of Forrest's first callers during the week preceding his opening was William Macready, leader of the opposition at Covent Garden. Macready had to steel himself to this social chore. Though not yet obsessed with the bitter hatred that developed later, he did not approve Forrest's acting which he considered roughshod ranting. As London's chief actor, he felt obliged to welcome his American colleague, and surprisingly enough, at this first meeting, he found that he liked him. In fact, he was so impressed by his "noble appearance, his manly, mild, and interesting demeanor," as he noted in his diary, that he decided to invite him to dinner. After he had sent the invitation, the day following Forrest's debut, he regretted his hastiness. The dinner was set for Sunday, October 30, and Macready was forced to make the best of the intervening two weeks, keeping a sharp eye on Forrest's activities at Drury Lane and trying to put a damper on John Forster, the theatrical critic on the *Examiner*. Everyone knew that Forster was his close friend and literary adviser. Any sour comments on Forrest by Forster would automatically reflect on him. In his first observations on *The Gladiator*, Forster admitted "in cordial truth," as he put it, that Forrest was not an indifferent actor; still Macready feared that his good will would not endure. He sent Forster a note urging him to "deal liberally and kindly" with the American. At the same time he admitted to his diary that it "would be stupid and shallow hypocrisy" to say that derogatory comments on his competitor displeased him.

The two weeks were filled with annoyances. Some critics rashly hinted that Forrest was his superior. One morning Macready walked past Drury Lane and observed that Forrest was being proclaimed as "the Most Extraordinary Actor of the

Day." In the afternoon of the same day Charles Kemble and Stephen Price, the Park Theatre manager, who was in London hiring actors, called asking Macready to add his name to a complimentary dinner at the Garrick Club being got up for Mr. Forrest. It was "very indelicate," he noted in his diary; he had no alternative, he was obliged to sign the invitation.

On Saturday, October 29, the day before Forrest was to come to dinner, Macready read an advance copy of Forster's ill-natured and abusive review of *Othello*. Forster asserted that there was a vicious style in art which the public taste must be guarded against—Mr. Forrest was one of the professors of this style. Much as he regretted his duty, national politeness could not be permitted to interfere with his artistic judgment. Macready fumed at Forster for his harshness and for his bad timing. Certainly there must be some merit in Forrest's playing; if not, Forster might at least have held his full barrage for another week. It was too late now; the copy was already in the hands of the printer.

The next afternoon, however, when Robert Browning—the first guest to arrive—told Macready about Charles Dance's extravagant praise of Forrest's *Othello* in the *Athenaeum*, Macready was enraged that his "once friend" had gone over to the enemy. As much as he hated to admit to himself that he wished his rival "put down," and as hard as he labored to disassociate himself from any such scheme, he squirmed when Forrest was praised.

In spite of his inner turmoil, Macready affected a show of friendliness when he introduced Forrest to Browning, to T. N. Talfourd, author of *Ion,* and to Joseph Blanco White, the theologian and poet. Apparently everyone avoided the sore subject. Forrest was given the honor of escorting Mrs. Macready down. The dinner went smoothly, and they spent an agreeable and cheerful afternoon, though Macready was happy that his American friend was unable to return to the drawing-room after dinner.

None of Macready's distress was communicated to Forrest. He was flattered by the British actor's attention as he was by the courtesies he found everywhere. "I have received many grateful kindnesses," he wrote to Leggett, "in their hospitable homes, and in their intellectual fireside circles have drunk both instruction and delight." His friend Stephen Price presented him with a "rare copy" of Shakespeare and a "Richard" sword that Kean had used. Charles Kemble gave him two swords. One had belonged to his brother, John Philip Kemble, the other to the famous French tragedian Talma. At the Garrick Club dinner which Price had engineered as a spontaneous tribute, he was presented with a portrait of Garrick. These mementos are still preserved in the Forrest Home.

Forrest was not insensitive to Forster's hostility, yet the abuses of that "harbitrary cove," as one London cabman called him, were buried under the stream of favorable *Othello* notices. They described the elevation of thought and sentiment, the poetic grandeur, the picturesque in his conception of the character, which Kean had never achieved. His bursts of passion were terrifically grand. He embodied himself into strict identity with the character, discovered new ideas which his predecessors had missed, and where the others had ranted he spoke with dignified and quiet power. A twentieth-century press agent could have had a glorious morning lifting catch-phrases from the notices:

"The first tragedian of the age."—*Sun.*
"Heart-thrilling."—*Carlton Chronicle.*
"Truly great."—*John Bull.*
"A powerful and original actor."—*Morning Post.*

Even with most of the critics behind him, Forrest had to side-step occasional attacks. Forster found fault with everything, reminding Forrest that it took "more skill to finger and stop an instrument than to blow it," that he could have been a most useful actor had his ambition not been so great. Sometimes even his champions detected blunders. The *Morning Post* discovered too much of his national democratic manner in *Macbeth*. *The Parthenon* perceived a whining tone in some of the tender passages of *Othello*. There were freqeunt allusions to the harshness and provincialism in his speech and most of the reviewers, at one time or another, observed that he "syllabled his words rather too slowly," a habit of utterance to which English ears were unaccustomed. This was the only criticism that Forrest took seriously. These few sour notes did not distort the sweet melody that ran through the majority of the reviews.

Most of the newspapers confined their comments to their theatrical columns. Only *Figaro* became an out-and-out champion. They ran a serialized biography, sold their subscribers an engraved portrait of Forrest for a penny, and on November 12 announced that they would not tolerate Forster's nonsense: "When we make a man's reputation, no one else will be allowed to throw taint on it."

The enthusiastic press could not completely counteract the bad timing of his engagement. The triumvirate at Covent Garden with their bargain prices did have the good grace not to schedule their *Othello* and *Macbeth* on the same nights Forrest performed the plays, but they were not his only opposition. His own countryman, the minstrel-man T. D. ("Daddy") Rice was jumping "Jim Crow" [1] at the Royal Surrey Theatre and playing Gumbo Chuff in *Oh! Hush! or, Life in New York*. Even against the competition Forrest might have fared better with better scheduling. Jones had booked *The Gladiator* for three nights the first week, and in spite of its cool reception, insisted on sticking to his plan. The second week had three nights of *Othello*. Forrest decided to break with Jones—it appears to have been an amicable parting—and turn his affairs over to Bunn, the Drury Lane manager.

Bunn immediately tried to bolster the engagement by alternating Forrest's roles and adding extra attractions. On November 2 *The Yankee Pedlar* with the American comedian G. H.

---

[1] The famous "Jim Crow" song and dance routine was Rice's specialty. The dance was based on the eccentric jumping movements of a crippled stable boy and the song was Rice's own composition, the refrain of which went:

> "First on de heel tap, den on de toe
> Ebery time I wheelabout I jump Jim Crow.
> Wheelabout and turnabout and do jis so,
> And ebery time I wheelabout I jump Jim Crow."

Hill was run on as an afterpiece. The next week he replaced it with *The Siege of Corinth,* a spectacular operatic concoction that J. R. Planché had devised from Rossini's *L'Assedio di Corinto.* Anticipating a great rush to see Forrest and this magnificent bonus attraction, Bunn announced that the box office would remain open an extra hour daily and that additional agents had been "appointed both in the City, and at the West End of the Town." Bunn retained this combination for the remainder of Forrest's engagement. He also kept his eyes open for other possibilities. When Junius Brutus Booth arrived in the middle of November, Bunn hired him to act with Forrest; one night in *Richard III* and another playing Iago to Forrest's Othello. Bunn's efforts helped, but to fill the 3,500 seats of Drury Lane at his prices and against such strong competition was expecting too much. He settled for capacity in the three-shilling and six-penny sections and a respectable if sparse contingent in the seven-shilling boxes. Apparently Forrest was untroubled.

On November 19 he was honored with a gala dinner at the Garrick Club. The Club had been founded just three years earlier and was rapidly becoming one of London's exclusive establishments. To be ushered into its rooms on King Street was a distinct privilege, particularly for a foreigner. Among the some two dozen subscribers on hand for the Forrest celebration were Talfourd, who presided, Charles Kemble, Willis Jones, and Price.

Macready arrived late. Not out of disrespect for the occasion, he insisted, simply because Browning had detained him with a new play. Macready's health had already been drunk. Talfourd asked the company to raise their glasses again and Macready, succumbing to the sweetness and light that pervaded the atmosphere, responded. The attention was unexpected, he assured them; he had come to pay, not to receive, a compliment. His highly talented friend knew that "no one extended the hand of welcome to him more fervently or sincerely than myself, in doing which I only endeavored to repay a small part of the debt of gratitude which had been heaped on me by

the kindness of his countrymen." Macready's intimates may
have detected a certain emptiness in his little speech; Forrest
took it at face value. "His delicate courtesies and attentions,"
Forrest wrote to Leggett, "demonstrated his great refinement,
good breeding, and the native kindness of his heart." Macready could not endure the monotonous repetition of toasts to
the good fortune of his rival. He excused himself as quickly as
politeness allowed, insisting that he had to get back to Browning and *Strafford,* the new play. He did not escape before
Charles Kemble had trapped him into clinking glasses with the
guest of honor. Forrest missed the undercurrents. To him it was
just another testimony to his London success, additional assurance that the British frostiness his friends had warned him
against was just so much nonsense.

Three years later Forrest repaid the Garrick Club's hospitality, or, more accurately, shared with Thomas Sully, the Philadelphia painter, in repaying it. Sully had begun a portrait of
Forrest just before the actor had departed for England. When
Sully was in London in the fall of 1837, he was elected to honorary membership in the Club, so when the portrait was finished
in 1839, Sully and Forrest agreed that it should be presented to
the Garrick Club. It still hangs in their magnificent gallery of
theatrical portraits.

Forrest's Drury Lane engagement continued until December 19. In the two months he played thirty-two performances:
nine of *Othello,* seven of *Macbeth,* and eight of *Lear.* Only
Kean had matched his record of eight performances of *Lear*
within such a brief span. In addition to the Shakespearean
roles he had performed *The Gladiator, Damon and Pythias,*
and for his final and benefit night, *Virginius.* John Sheridan
Knowles, the author of the play, honored him by appearing in
the cast on this occasion, and after the final curtain Forrest
was feted by the *Corps Dramatique* and presented with a gold
snuffbox.

Jealously piqued at this attention, Macready noted in his
diary that a Drury Lane clown had been similarly honored for
"throwing thirty-one somersaults successively." To Forrest it

was a touching tribute, clinching proof, if any was needed, of his London success. He did not exaggerate his triumph when he wrote to his mother two weeks later: "I never have been more successful, even in my own dear land."

After two months of steady playing, Forrest willingly relinquished his share of the London theatregoers to Macready and his cohorts at Covent Garden. He advised Bunn that before he attempted another London engagement the prices must be lowered. In the meantime he would try the provinces. Just as at home, Forrest was not content to limit himself to the theatrical center: on Christmas Day he set out for a two-week engagement at the Theatre Royal in Liverpool.

Reports of his London triumph had preceded him, and the Liverpool patrons crowded the theatre nightly from December 26 to January 6. Again, his physical power attracted the most attention. The Liverpool *Mercury* reported that they had never seen an actor with a finer person and a stronger voice. One spectator was stupefied by his "extraordinary feat of lifting Lucullus [in *Damon and Pythias*] from the crowd by his throat and swinging him thus half round the stage." No British actor could have done it. Reporters and audience alike were overwhelmed by Othello's dying spasm. Forrest staggered toward Desdemona's bed after the blow had been struck, pulled away and finally fell backward and his head hitting the front edge of the stage. A fearful shudder passed through the audience. The Liverpool *Telegraph* thought that it was the most impressive piece of acting they had ever witnessed. As in London, some critics remarked that his speech was too "Yankeeish": "tears" became "teers"; "fears," "feers"; there was too much of a burr on the "r." However, these minor failings could easily be disregarded.

Forrest wrote to his mother from Liverpool: "Last night I finished one of the most successful engagements I ever performed during my professional career; not measured by the receipt of money, but in being crowned with the most hearty and distinguished applause. This intelligence I know will warm your kind old heart for I know you think with me that filthy lucre is not nor ought not to be the exclusive pursuit of our lives."

On Saturday afternoon, January 7, 1837, Forrest took the rail coach to Manchester, and on Monday moved into the Theatre Royal, replacing his compatriot T. D. Rice, who had been entertaining them the preceding week with his "Jim Crow" dance. Manchester, like Liverpool, gave him a rousing welcome. The Manchester *Guardian* wondered if "this was nature," but all agreed that he gave them a thrilling evening.

Forrest's provincial excursion had been an immense success. It had stirred up flattering offers from the theatre managers in Scotland and Ireland, which he had politely refused, and had given him a profit of £1,250.

Forrest was eager to return to London for another try at Drury Lane under more favorable circumstances, eager too to see the full-length portrait of himself as Macbeth that John G. Middleton had begun the previous fall, which was now on display at Somerset House. Back in London, he was besieged with invitations to tea, and to dinner, and willing as he was to spread his favors, he could not accept all of them. On January 28 he wrote to Mrs. Joshua Bates, wife of the American partner in the banking firm of Baring Brothers, regretting that a "previous engagement prevented his acceptance of her polite invitation to dinner on Sunday next." To placate Mrs. Bates he sent her a portrait and a letter of the late Edmund Kean to add to her "beautiful collection. If you prize these trifles worthy," he concluded in his politest rhetoric, "your acceptance of them will confer much pleasure upon yours with the highest respect, Edwin Forrest."

At Drury Lane everything was more happily arranged. Bunn had reduced his prices, though insisting that the scale of four shillings, two, and one was only an experiment. The Covent Garden combination had collapsed. Kemble had bowed out in December; Macready had just left for Manchester; only Vandenhoff remained. Even with the Covent Garden program supplemented with Henry Wallack in the farces, and the next week with Thomas Hamblin in Shakespeare, and with occasional appearances of T. D. Rice in *Virginia Mummy,* Forrest practically had the town to himself.

The change was happily reflected in the treasury; a full house at nearly every performance brought in a nightly average of two hundred pounds, fifty of which went to Forrest.

Forrest began with *Othello* on Monday night, February 6. Although he was fighting a cold that made his voice gravelly, the opening-night crowd and the next day's newspapers gave him an enthusiastic welcome. The major event of the engagement occurred on February 27 when he introduced a new spectacular production of *Richard III.* According to *The Times:* "His figure never appeared more erect and noble, nor his action more graceful and unconstrained" than in Allen's magnificent and tasteful costumes. One unidentified reporter wrote:

> *A tailor, 'tis said, makes a man,*
> *And often a strange man-ufacture;*
> *But this is the first time we can*
> *Say a tailor can make a great actor.*

Throughout the engagement the press lined up as it had in the fall: most of it unsparing in its praise and Forster equally unsparing with his abuse. In *Richard III* Forster insisted that the American "looked like a savage newly caught from out of the American backwoods," particularly in the fight between Richard and Richmond when the heavy strips of black hair that he had pasted on his head fell down over his face. Forster objected to Forrest's banging of his chest with his truncheon when he announced: "I am the Thane of Cawdor," and the way in which he manhandled the poor messenger who was obliged to report that Birnam Wood was moving. He lifted him bodily from the ground and "fairly flung him off the stage." A British actor, no matter how lowly, should not be subjected to such hazard and humiliation.

Forster's perverse views had no effect at Drury Lane. The engagement went along swimmingly until the end of February, when Bunn, anticipating a slackening-off in business, revised the program. Instead of giving Forrest his customary three nights a week, he limited him to Monday-night performances of *Richard III*. The other nights of the week he scheduled *Fair Rosamond*, a new operatic creation by John Barnett with scenery by the Grieves.

Forrest revolted. Macready was back at Covent Garden; he even announced his own production of *Richard III* for Monday night, April 3. Under these circumstances, Forrest told Bunn that he would not hobble along on his one night and one play a week. Bunn agreed to a slight modification. He gave Forrest a *Macbeth* performance on Wednesday, March 29, and again on April 5; however, when Forrest arrived at the theatre on Thursday, April 6, prepared for another night of *Macbeth*, he found that Bunn had changed the program. The same thing occurred the next Monday, his customary *Richard III* night. This was too much. In the backstage fight that ensued Forrest was reported to have cocked his fist but to have held the blow. Perhaps he recalled the stories of Macready's battle with Bunn and did not wish to be accused of yielding to an uncontrollable temper as Macready had. When the British actor's engagement at Drury Lane had been terminated the previous April, under similar circumstances, Macready had beaten the poor manager.

Forrest did not play again that season. Late in April Edward Fitzball, the prolific adapter of French melodramas, tried to work up a liaison between Macready and Forrest, proposing that Macready play Iago to Forrest's Othello. It is not clear that Forrest agreed to this proposition; Macready definitely did not. He insisted that he refused only because Iago was not his part. To assure Forrest of his continued friendship, he invited him to dinner again. He was not disappointed, however, when he received a note of regret from Forrest. He smugly noted in his diary: "If he have any justice he must admit my conduct most attractive to him."

Forrest would have grown impatient without a theatrical commitment, had he not, early in the spring, undertaken another project, the courtship of Catherine Sinclair. This enterprise required all his wits, for previously he had had only a passing acquaintance with the vagaries of the female heart. In Cincinnati he had agonized through a boyhood infatuation with Sallie Riddle. In New Orleans Jane Placide had introduced him to the pleasures and pains of the tender passion, and on his cultural journey abroad he had freely, if fleetingly, sampled female favors from Paris to Yalta. Until the spring of 1837 he had not seriously thought of marriage. Apparently Catherine was struck with the idea at their first meeting. "The impression he made was so instantaneous," she wrote to a friend several years later, "and so strong that I remember I whispered to myself, while a thrill ran through me, 'This is the handsomest man on whom my eyes have ever fallen.'"

This first impression had been made a year earlier when Wikoff had taken Forrest to call on the Sinclairs at 28 Alfred Place, just off Bedford Square. Forrest had then observed that she was strikingly handsome, intelligent as well as accomplished, and possessed of engaging manners; he had not, however, taken her seriously. She was eighteen. He was thirty. She was English. He was American. Now, a year later, these differences had lost their relevance. He felt no older, while she had been miraculously transformed from an engaging youngster into a desirable young woman. His notions about the British had been revised. Contrary to his expectation, he had found them very agreeable.

Perhaps Forrest's courtship would not have progressed so smoothly had he invaded a somewhat more typical and proper English domicile. The Sinclairs had been to America, and, more important, were themselves theatrical performers. John Sinclair, a handsome man with a sweet tenor voice, had a wide reputation as a singer of Scotch ballads. His wife, Catherine, though never more than a fill-in actress, had accompanied her husband on his theatrical safaris.

The Sinclairs came from Edinburgh, where they had been married in 1816. John had begun his musical career as a drummer in the Argyleshire militia, had made a feeble debut at Covent Garden in 1811 as Don Carlos in *The Duenna,* and since that time had been wandering on the Continent, taking occasional musical instruction from Pellegrini and Rossini. He never developed more than a simple prettiness in his singing and frequently critics complained that he was so addicted to ornamentation that the original melody got lost in the frippery. In spite of his faults he achieved a solid reputation as a reliable second-rater.

He made his American debut in 1831, and in April 1833, on his second tour, appeared on the same program with Forrest in New Orleans. Apparently neither he nor his future son-in-law took any account of this first meeting. Their paths had not crossed again until Forrest appeared at their home in Alfred Place. In the beginning the Sinclairs were flattered by Forrest's attentions; however, when his ardor appeared to be sweeping their young Catherine beyond a simple girlish infatuation, they became worried. They knew the fickleness of an actor's heart and the instability of his purse, and Mrs. Sinclair could not endure the thought of giving up her little girl. She had two others: Margaret, just two years younger than Catherine, and a year-old baby, Virginia Georgina. Her only son had died while she and John were in America in 1833, and she had not yet recovered from that loss.

Sinclair did not view the situation so gloomily; still he insisted on a clear understanding before the romance progressed further. He called on Forrest in his rooms at 5 Tavistock Row. If the actor's intentions were what they appeared to be, what settlement did Forrest intend to make on Catherine? This was the wrong approach. Forrest bristled at his "damned impertinence." He was not buying a female slave. His country had long ago abandoned these repulsive restraints on free love and free choice. He would not settle a single dollar on Miss Sinclair. If she could not trust him for her money, she had better not trust him for her happiness. This ended the interview. Sinclair returned to his wife and daughter and told them the marriage was off. He anticipated a tearful scene and a few days of mournful simpering. He did not anticipate the fiery protest that greeted him. Catherine's anger surpassed Forrest's. Her heart was not for sale. If Forrest had volunteered to bank a thousand pounds, or ten pounds, in her name, she would have refused it. Sinclair was grieved to find his sweet child infected with these mutinous American notions. When she calmly declared that Forrest was the handsomest, the kindest man in the world, the only man she could ever love or marry, and that if she was forced to accept him without paternal blessing, she intended to do so, Sinclair knew he had lost.

The first public notice of the impending change in Forrest's domestic status was attached to a short newspaper item in early June, reporting that the actor had visited the New Lion Brewery. Without suggesting any connection between the events, the reporter announced that Forrest had abandoned the theatre and was now going to appear "in a sprightly afterpiece entitled 'Matrimony'" after which he was going to honeymoon on the Rhine and in Paris before returning to the United States for a final farewell tour before accepting a seat in Congress. In 1837 newspapers gave little space to personal gossip. When they did, they squeezed in as much as they could, satisfied if half of it came close to the facts. In this instance, they struck somewhat above the average.

Early on Friday morning, June 23, Forrest hastily cleared up his private affairs. He called on his friend and theatrical adviser, Willis Jones, and presented him with a silver salver, politely inscribed: "As a small but sincere tribute, and as an acknowledgement of his friendly exertions, which overcame many objections, and prevailed on me to appear on the British stage."

In midmorning he joined the small company huddled together in the front pews at St. Paul's, Covent Garden. Described by Inigo Jones, its designer, as "the handsomest barn in England," St. Paul's was an appropriate spot for the ceremony. The church had always been associated with the theatre. The actor Charles Macklin and the dramatists William Wycherley and Mrs. Centlivre had been buried there. In more recent times it became the final resting place for Ellen Terry. The opening scene of the movie of Shaw's *Pygmalion* was filmed in front of its east portico.

The wedding was not a large affair. Besides the Sinclairs

and Forrest's friends Wikoff and Price, only a dozen other guests were invited: the United States Minister to Great Britain, Andrew Stevens, and his wife; Mr. and Mrs. Joshua Bates (the banker, later distinguished as one of the founders of the Boston Public Library); Mr. and Mrs. James Dunlop (he was a tobacco trader); Miss Gamble (Dunlop's niece and Wikoff's fiancée); Lady Mackenzie of Auck, Lady Knox, Lady Ferguson (friends of the Sinclairs); Captain Polhill (M.P. and theatre enthusiast); and a Mr. Vaux from the American Legation. Unfortunately, the season was not auspicious for a happy public demonstration: the city was in mourning for King William IV, who had died just three days before the wedding. The ceremony was conducted quietly and quickly. Forrest had chosen Reverend Croly, Rector of St. Stephen's, Walbrook, to officiate; probably because he had heard his famous sermon, "Divine Origin and Obligation of Marriage," and thought him peculiarly qualified. He was. He took less than ten minutes to speak the magic words.

After the ceremony "Forrest led his young and lovely bride to a new and splendid carriage expressly manufactured for the occasion, and with the aid of four beautiful gray horses, richly caparisoned, the happy couple started for Windsor where they were to pass the first portion of their honeymoon." This reporter obviously did not pursue the carriage. Before beginning the journey they paused in Alfred Place to share Mrs. Sinclair's "elegant dejeuner" with the guests, to accept the felicitations of their friends, and to give the ladies an opportunity to examine Catherine's gown of "chantilly blonde *en colonne*."

Anyone seeking portents for their future had many to choose from. In the evening a great balloon ascent took place at Vauxhall Garden; Macready appeared in *Othello* at the Theatre Royal, Haymarket; the announcements of the marriage in the next day's newspapers were inserted between the black mourning bands that outlined every column. Little space was given to the event, for the papers were filled with news of the King's household and plans for his funeral.

Forrest and his bride were happily oblivious of ill-omens. They spent a few days at Windsor, crossed the Channel for a quick tour of the Continent, and in early August came back to London. When they went up to Liverpool, the Sinclairs accompanied them, insisting on postponing the final parting to the last possible moment. Sending their daughter to live with the heathen on the other side seemed so heartless, and the assurances of Forrest and of Captain Holdridge that she would be well cared for did not relieve Mrs. Sinclair's apprehensions. But her tears could not restrain them. On Tuesday morning, August 8, the *United States* sailed.

Turning back to his native land was always the most exciting part of any journey for Forrest. With a new and permanent traveling companion to share his cabin, he began the most exciting voyage of his life. He had come to England to conquer the London stage, not to capture a wife. He had never pictured himself as a Benedict, and how he had slipped into this unfamiliar role, he did not know. The simplest explanation was probably nearest the truth. He had simply succumbed to his Catherine's extraordinary vivacity. No pictures of the nineteen-year-old bride have survived. In the later portraits she is pictured as a prim Victorian lady: tight lips, strong chin, and her black hair pulled tightly down across her forehead and woven in a bun at the back of her head. Although clearly outlining her face and figure, these portraits captured none of the sparkling exuberance with which she charmed Forrest, and later, it seems, other American males. She was so natural, so unlike the pasty drawing-room puppets he had encountered at London tea parties.

In the early morning Forrest would occasionally stand at the rail worrying about his new enslavement. These thoughts passed rapidly when he returned to Catherine; and as the *United States* rolled along over the north Atlantic, their days were filled with happy thoughts of the new life that lay ahead.

CHAPTER *xi*

A $33,000 Season

On Wednesday morning, September 6, 1837, Forrest was on deck before the sun. Standing alone at the prow of the ship, the spray splashing against his face, he strained his eyes for the first sight of land. When he caught the dim outline, he would go below and rouse his bride; he jealously reserved the first moment for himself alone.

As the *United States* sailed into her home port with that tantalizing snail's pace ships always reserve for the final stretch, Catherine stood beside him anxiously scanning the wonders of Manhattan. Forrest pointed to the crowd on the dock. He could see the hard core in the front line, his friends who found steady employment in these farewells and homecomings. The newcomers hung about on the fringes. Rumors had passed around that the American hero had succumbed to British snobbery; his friends wished to check for themselves. Most of all they wanted a first quick look at the lady who had captured his heart.

Forrest stepped to the top of the gangplank, threw back his head, and roared a welcome that could have been heard blocks away. Catherine tried to hide behind him. He pulled her forward, took her in his arms, and kissed her on the cheek with a loud smack. The crowd caught the cue and gave the honeymooners a lusty "Hip, Hip, Hooray!" However completely Forrest might have succumbed to his British beauty, he was still their brash and brawny hero.

He was proud of his bride, that was clear as he gallantly

passed her from one friend to another. If either had relinquished his birthright, Catherine had done so, not Edwin. She bowed graciously. She spoke softly. Every word, every gesture proclaimed her adoration for her husband.

For three fast and joyous days they rushed around New York, sight-seeing, calling on friends, and arranging his return engagement at the Park. Catherine was astonished at the attention she received as Mrs. Edwin Forrest; these Americans were fanatics in their hero worship. New York was, however, only the first test; the final examination must be passed in Philadelphia. Would his mother and sisters believe a frail youngster worthy or capable of taking care of their dear Edwin? That her rights were legally supported afforded little comfort. Mothers and sisters were apt to ignore such a feeble bloodless claim.

On Saturday morning, September 9, they started for Philadelphia. Catherine wept all the way and pleaded to turn back. Her intuition dredged up such a succession of worries that, by the time they reached his mother's house at 144 North Tenth Street, Forrest would gladly have back-tracked to his pre-England, pre-matrimonial bliss. He was certain that a devastating female battle was inevitable; he was not prepared for what happened.

He had barely ushered Catherine through the door when his mother, Henrietta, Caroline, and Eleanora caught her. Eight eager arms, flailing about like a giant octopus, enveloped her in a massive embrace. They giggled, squirmed, and wept. They passed her from one to the other. A separate hug, a separate kiss. Catherine fell in with the game as if this were exactly what she had expected. Edwin was pushed into a corner, perplexed at the chameleon-like agility of the female mind.

Finally, his mother pulled him into the circle to share the family blessings. She spoke a few solemn biblical phrases, a prayer, and then they all joined in a hymn. For thirty-one years his dear mother had centered her life on him. To break her solitary hold, admit the superior claim of a wife, Forrest knew, was not easy; yet she managed it graciously and tenderly.

For three happy days the household bubbled. The sisters

schemed against each other to invent new treats for the bride and groom. Forrest paraded Catherine around the city, proudly presenting her to all his old friends, guiding her among the romantic scenes of his childhood, and re-enacting the plain and fancy escapades of his first theatrical ventures.

On their last day his mother insisted that he go out alone; she must have a private heart-to-heart talk with her new daughter-in-law. Rebecca warned Catherine against Forrest's frailties; she must protect him from overexertion, watch for the first signs of chill or fever. He had never been robust enough to endure the exertions he inflicted on himself. One other matter. She knew that Edwin was a loving husband, a devoted son and brother; now he should be tested as a father. Catherine whispered shyly that she suspected a baby might already be on the way.

When the couple returned to the Astor House (on Broadway between Barclay and Vesey) on Wednesday, September 13, to prepare for Forrest's gala welcome-home engagement at the Park, Catherine's doubts and fears had completely evaporated. Their future now rested solely on their own love and devotion; in these her faith was firm.

The theatrical bills blazed with the announcements of Forrest's return. Before the Park Theatre doors were opened at 6:15 the following Monday night, the house was sold out. *Othello* had been chosen for the opening, more for personal than for professional reasons. With Shakespeare's eloquent lines he would proclaim to the world his passion for his new bride. He was still warm with honeymoon fever, and it did not occur to Forrest, nor apparently to Catherine, to listen to Shakespeare's prophetic warnings.

Catherine had expected strong applause when the curtains closed; she had not expected the wild cheering, stomping in the aisles, and hats sailing in the air. She had not realized a mere actor could command such adoration. When he stepped forward to speak, the audience hushed to catch every word. How eloquently he spoke even without Shakespeare's assistance! He praised his countrymen for their loyalty, their devotion to a fellow American whose constant wish was to please them. He touched on his desperate longing for home, his joy at being back. He bowed to Catherine's box and asked her to accept the hearty welcome of his friends. It was an incredible evening, like a gigantic family reunion.

Firmly settled into a four-week engagement at the Park, his popularity apparently running stronger than ever, the next order of business was to find a permanent New York home. As a roving bachelor, his mother's Philadelphia house provided an adequate home base. Now he was obliged to find a New York house that attested to his wealth and social station and did honor to his Catherine.

Unable to find a suitable place on the market, he temporarily sublet the home of the actor James H. Hackett, on Reade Street near Broadway. At least this would remove their private life from the public eye, an impossibility at the Astor House. To give Catherine and the establishment the attention they deserved, Forrest hired Mrs. Joseph Underwood, an Englishwoman who had just come to America, who had known the Sinclairs in London, and who would now be their housekeeper.

At the theatre, each successive night seemed a bit more crowded, the demonstrations more exuberant, and, on the whole, the press echoed the audience. Some quibblers noted that he was "still the actor physical rather than the actor intellectual," yet even their summations invariably turned soft. The *New York Morning Herald* reporter wrote on September 23: "No actor in England can at all compare with him except Macready. Forrest is all nature and Macready all art. The latter may give the more finishing touches but give me Yankee Doodle still."

In London, Forrest had opened with Bird and shifted to Shakespeare. In New York the order was reversed. He caught his stride in the second week when he turned to *Metamora* and *The Gladiator*. Some skeptical souls had argued that Forrest's year in England had softened him; a glance at Metamora or Spartacus was enough to convince them otherwise. "In these roles he has no rival," the *Courier and Enquirer* reported. "They require a physical energy, an almost awful power and vigor which we doubt if any actor on earth but himself can put forth."

Occasionally, when a reporter foolishly suggested that other American actors were in the running, he was quickly rebuked by one of Forrest's protectors. The following item appeared in the *New York Morning Herald* on October 4:

Elegant Theatrical Criticism. This Choice Epistle Comes to us Through the Post Office:

Mr. James Gordon Bennett. You say in your paper of yesterday that Forrest, Hamblin, Hill, Hackett, and Rice all went to England and that Rice succeeded best. You are a God damned liar! And if I ever catch you, you God Damned Scotch son of a bitch, I'll mash that God damned Scotch face of yours by Jesus Christ! You have once or twice intimated in your paper that Mr. Forrest's conduct while in England, manifested a lack of regard for the land of his birth. This is also a God damned lie, and you know it, God damned your Scotch soul! You have only got one eye now, and if I ever come across you in the vicinity of the Park Theatre, I'll knock out the other. By Christ! Beware.

Buskin.

Forrest's adherents were not shy. In fact, during this engagement they were frequently referred to simply as the "Loco Focos," identifying them with the radical wing of the Democratic Party and contrasting them with the more conservative souls who patronized the English actor George Vandenhoff at the National Theatre. Forrest may not have commanded the entire theatrical public, yet he certainly drew more than his share. When he closed with a benefit performance of *Hamlet* on Friday, October 3, he had grossed $18,434.50 for his twenty nights, $6,927.50 of which went into his pocket, "a larger sum than ever yet was realized by any individual [any actor] in the short space of four weeks," one reporter noted. Forrest divided the profits above the first $250, and took half the total receipts on his two benefit nights.

He was off to a strong start, and though his succeeding engagements in Boston and Philadelphia did not match New

York, in the three months before Christmas he had earned over
$16,000.

Forrest had not had time to see Bird during his first quick
visit to Philadelphia in the fall. When he returned in November,
he called on his old friend to report that he had not used the
revised version of *Metamora* in England and expected repayment of the $2,000. Bird refused. Apparently his new bride,
Mary Mayer, had insisted that Bird reappraise his professional
rights. Mrs. Bird recalled that she was in the parlor when the
gentleman arrived. She realized that it was a business matter,
and went upstairs. Not long after, "Dr. came up," she wrote in
her journal, "he looked irritated and, upon my asking who that
was, answered, 'That scoundrel Forrest; he is not fit to be in the
presence of a lady.' I imagine Dr. had requested an interview
to attempt to settle matters." Actually Bird had demanded
$6,000, which he thought Forrest rightfully owed him on the
plays.

Bird did not communicate directly with Forrest again, he
simply outlined his claim in a document entitled "Dramatic Authors and Their Profits." The essay was not printed, and Forrest
probably never saw it. Reading it now, one is struck with the
justice of Bird's demands and the appalling disregard for an
author's rights that then prevailed; one is also disheartened that
their "gentleman's agreement" had provoked such an irreparable rupture.

Bird claimed that Forrest had agreed to pay him $3,000 per
play and speculated that if he were to have received his just
share of the actor's profits he should have had $5,000 on each.
"The state of affairs between us is simply this," he wrote in summary. "I have received from him $1,000 on each of my plays,
The Gladiator, Oralloossa, and *The Broker of Bogota;* and
$2,000 in loan, for which he had my note. But he owes me still
(if there *was* a bargain between us, as I suppose there was),
$2,000 on each of these plays, in all $6,000, *minus* the $2,000
loan; that is, $4,000. He owes me also $2,000 for *Metamora*, re-
written; for so much I think it worth."

Bird's fulminations are interesting not only because they

disclose the arrangements between him and Forrest; they reveal the accepted practices of the day. Bird's prognostication of Forrest's eventual earnings from his plays was well below the mark. In 1853 Forrest performed *The Gladiator* for the one thousandth time, the first time, Forrest noted, that a play in English had achieved this record within the lifetime of the dramatist. After Bird's death in 1854 Mrs. Bird estimated that Forrest must have made at least $100,000 on this one play. It cannot be denied that Forrest made a fortune on Bird's prize plays, that he regarded them as his property, and that the playwright received a mere pittance for his labors.

His sad experience with Forrest persuaded Bird to give up playwriting. He did not, however, give up his quarrel with Forrest until 1851. In January of that year, his lawyer advised him that "if you have suffered Forrest to make copies of the plays and act them, you will have a great deal of trouble to get anything out of him, particularly since the length of time he has had them tends to strengthen his claim."

In 1869 Bird's son, Frederick, wrote to Forrest sounding him out on the possibility of publishing his father's plays. Forrest's reply was unequivocal: "The heirs of the late Dr. R. M. Bird have neither right, title, nor any legal interest whatever in the plays. They are my exclusive property, by the right of purchase, and for many years by the law of copyright."

In fairness to Forrest it should be noted that he did not always adopt this attitude. On February 25, 1856, Horace W. Smith, son of another prize author, Richard Penn Smith, received a much gentler reply: "The play of *Caius Marius* was purchased by me from your father, but I have not the least objection to your publication of it among his other works."

Now that authors enjoy such firm moral and legal protection, Forrest's treatment of Bird appears despicable—Bird's name does not even appear on the manuscript copies of *Oralloossa* and *The Broker of Bogota* that are now in the safe at the Forrest Home. Forrest did not, however, stray from the accepted practice of his time. A writer who submitted his compositions to an actor or manager knew he could expect only what largesse they felt inclined to bestow. Once his play was performed he also ran the risk of suffering from the piratical proclivities of other actors and managers.

The financial arrangements with the other principal contest playwright, John Augustus Stone, were more felicitous. Stone graciously accepted whatever Forrest offered. On November 2, 1829, he received $500 for the original version of *Metamora.* After that Forrest repeatedly bought clothes for him, paid hotel bills, and gave him cash. When Stone committed suicide by jumping into the Schuykill River, Forrest arranged for his burial and erected a monument over his grave in Macheplah Cemetery. Curiously, stonecutting paid as well as playwriting in 1834; Forrest paid $500 for the marker.

Distressed as he was that his homecoming was marred by the quarrel with Bird, Forrest had no time for brooding. Ever since his return from London, his Philadelphia friends had implored him to set a date for a homecoming banquet. He finally agreed to Friday, December 15, the week following his final performance.

On that evening some two hundred guests crowded into the Merchants' Hotel on North Fourth Street. Everyone with the slightest claim to local prominence had shared in the preparations. Nicholas Biddle, Director of the Bank of the United States, had presided over the arrangements committee. Mr. Sandeson, manager of the hotel, prepared a "gastronomical and bibulous tribute" guaranteed to surpass the New York farewell dinner. Forrest's name appeared everywhere: woven into a wreath at the head table, traced out with confectioner's sugar on the dessert, and embossed on each wine bottle.

Biddle was sick, undoubtedly overworked by his banquet rather than his bank duties, and was unable to attend. Joseph R. Ingersoll, Congressman, later Minister to England, and one of Biddle's six vice-presidents on the arrangements committee, presided. After the edible tributes had been consumed and the cloth removed, Ingersoll launched the verbal testaments. As usual on such occasions, the toasts extended until well past midnight.

Ingersoll praised Forrest's devotion to an honored profession, his patronage of all the arts, his generosity toward his colleagues, and his personal integrity. "We owe him thanks," Ingersoll concluded, "as members of a well-regulated community, that by the course and current of his domestic life, the reproaches that are sometimes cast upon his profession have been signally disarmed."

Successive testimonials were offered by Mayor Swift, two members of the State Supreme Court, Recorder and playwright Robert T. Conrad, and Richard Penn Smith. Some dozen letters from absentees were read and applauded.

Few lofty phrases remained untapped for Forrest's reply. He admitted that the words that rose to his lips were "too cold and vapid to denote truly the sentiments which prompt them." He told the story of a frightened youngster who had inhaled nitrous oxide in Tivoli Garden, and of the stranger who had taken this lad by the hand and announced to the crowd: "This boy has the germ of tragic greatness in him." Forrest paused, playing the scene for its full effect. He turned slowly to Mayor Swift. "Gentlemen, the present chief magistrate of our city was that benevolent stranger, and your guest tonight was that unfriended boy." According to the newspaper account, the cheers erupted as from a volcano.

As was customary on such occasions, once the toasts gained momentum they spread like wildfire. The atmosphere was so saturated with good feeling that once Forrest had been duly honored, the residual praise was freely distributed among the other illustrious citizens.

Forrest would have welcomed a few days to recuperate. Instead, he and Catherine hurried back to New York the next day to be ready for his opening at the Park the following Monday.

Since his return from England, Forrest had talked of adding a new play to his repertoire, and Leggett had urged him to become acquainted with the "insolent patrician" Coriolanus. Forrest was intrigued by the proud and passionate soldier. A character with such ambition, tenderness, daring, and haughty defiance of everything wrong or mean, even if he might lack

some democratic virtues, seemed tailored for his talents. However, when he introduced the play to the Park audience on
January 11, 1838, they did not share his enthusiasm. Less than
half the house was filled. The next night, his final and benefit
performance, he interspersed a few *Coriolanus* scenes with sure-
fire excerpts from *Metamora*. Even then his friends let it be
known that they did not approve his flirtation with Shakespeare's tyrant. Two weeks later he tried it in Philadelphia and
met the same rebuff. Forrest never allowed himself the luxury
of indulging his private enthusiasms if they conflicted with
public opinion. When the bills were posted for his spring engagement in New York, *Coriolanus* was not listed.

Except for the *Coriolanus* fiasco, the winter engagement
held up remarkably: a gross of $12,000 and a profit of $4,000 for
twenty performances.

His bulging purse was not the only source of delight that
winter. Catherine was definitely expecting. To be certain that
she received the proper care, Forrest took her to Philadelphia
to stay with his mother and sisters while he concentrated on
gathering funds to meet their new responsibility, first in Philadelphia, then in Baltimore, Washington, and Albany. In early
May he was back at the Park in New York.

He was still eager to get a new play into his repertoire and
decided to try Bulwer-Lytton's *Lady of Lyons* which had just
had its first performance in London in February. The story appeared promising: a low-born young man, Claude Melnotte,
disguised as a Prince, marries Pauline, an aristocratic lady.
When the ruse is discovered, Pauline is heartbroken. However,
as she discovers the devotion and homely goodness of the honest
young man, her shame evaporates and she also discovers the
humanity in her own love. Natural man and natural woman in
all their sentimental glory triumph over the wicked and super-
ficial infringements of society.

Forrest had not tried a contemporary British play before.
He guessed correctly that Bulwer-Lytton's sugary nonsense,
which currently passed for truthfulness to life, would please his
audience. He gave the first performance of *Lady of Lyons* on

Monday, May 14, with Pauline being played by Charlotte Cushman, the husky twenty-two-year-old Boston girl who had made her New York debut just two years earlier and who was now leading lady at the Park.

The audience indicated their approval at the box office—$789.50—and in their cheers at the final curtain. For the ensuing three nights, the termination of his spring engagement, Forrest clung to the *Lady of Lyons* with happy results: $530.25, $597.50, and $1,176.50 (his benefit). A remarkable turnout for four successive nights of the same play, and convincing evidence that Claude Melnotte should be retained in his repertoire.

No one at the Park was aware that Forrest had struggled through the engagement by sheer force of will. On the second day of the *Lady of Lyons* he received word that his first child had died at birth. He would have closed the play, if his mother had not assured him that Catherine had survived the ordeal, was rapidly recovering, and wished him to finish his scheduled performances in Boston, Baltimore, and Washington before coming home. Forrest's conscience troubled him, yet in a way, he was pleased to escape the melancholy scene. When he got to Philadelphia in mid-June, he was comforted to find that Catherine had regained her strength though remnants of sadness still hung over the household. He read the indelible reminder in the receipt book: "May 14th, 1838, of Mrs. Forrest, fifteen dollars and fifty cents in full for the interment of grandchild."

Back home in New York they could, at least partly, erase the memory in the company of old friends and in tabulating Forrest's spectacular homecoming year. For his 167 performances he had netted $33,399.07½. Recalling that in 1837 acting was not ordinarily a profitable profession, that Forrest had just passed his thirty-second birthday, that this was the year of financial panic, his profits were truly astonishing. If translated into present-day terms, Forrest would have been pushed into the ninety-per-cent tax bracket with an income of well over $125,000.

His well-packed purse, his wide popularity among the masses, and his passion for democratic causes inevitably brought him to the attention of the politicians. Forrest enjoyed talking politics, however, when someone suggested that his name be listed on the Democratic roster of eligible candidates, he refused. The proposition had come too rapidly. His friends backtracked and suggested that he merely participate in a political rally; to this Forrest agreed.

When the Democrats assembled at the Broadway Tabernacle in New York for their 1838 Fourth of July celebration, Forrest was on the stand as the principal speaker. Four thousand sweltering spectators jammed the hall to cheer the actor in his new role. Some reporters detected snatches of Leggett's rhetoric in the oration; none denied that Forrest rolled out the phrases as if they were his own, and though his periods might not rank with the best of Calhoun, Clay, or Webster, he came remarkably close to matching the professionals in his first (and last) major political utterance.

Fellow-Citizens,—We are met this day to celebrate the most august event which ever constituted an epoch in the political annals of mankind. . . . Where does the sun, in all his compass, shed his beams on a country freer, better, happier than this? Where does he behold more diffused prosperity, more active industry, more social harmony, more abiding faith, hope, and charity? Where are the foundations of private right more stable, or the limits of public order more inviolately observed? Where does labor go to his toil with an alerter step, or an erecter brow, effulgent with the heart-reflected light of conscious independence? Where does agriculture drive his team a-field with a more cheery spirit, in the certain assurance that the harvest is his own? Where does commerce launch more boldly her bark upon the deep, aware that she has to strive but with the tyranny of the elements, and not with the more appalling tyranny of man?

. . . The Old World is cankered with the disease of political senility and cramped by the longworn fetters of tyrannous habit. But the empire of the West is in the bloom and freshness of being. Its heart is unseared by the prejudices of "damned custom"; its intellect unclouded by the sophisms of ages. . . . What bounds can be set to the growth of American greatness? A hundred millions of happy people! A hundred millions of co-sovereigns, recognizing no law but the recorded will of a majority: no end of law but mutual and equal good; no superior but God alone!

Forrest feared that the audience would destroy the Tabernacle. The rowdies at the Bowery might raise a storm; they could not match four thousand frenzied Democrats who had just been offered such sure-fire stimulants as Jefferson, democracy, freedom, God, and country enlivened by Forrest's elocutionary pyrotechnics.

The Democrat Republican Committee printed the oration and circulated it throughout the country. In September they began pursuing him in earnest. Forrest had repeatedly insisted that he desired no further honor. "I can't afford to give my time for eight dollars a day," he wrote to the committee, "when I can make two hundred out of it. The day may come when I shall make the game of politics my study; and then it will be time enough to present myself to the suffrages of my fellow-countrymen." Fired with his Fourth of July success, the politicians still thought he could be persuaded.

The newspapers took up the cause. One reporter wrote: "Look at the play-writers in Parliament,—Sheridan, Bulwer, Shiel, Talfourd! Our friend Knowles is spoken of for a seat in the Commons. Why not Forrest?" Another speculated on what was to be done with Leggett. "They cannot be separated: they must go together, like two figs in a jar. If Forrest has a seat in Congress, Leggett must have a stool near him. . . . Suppose Forrest should break down in a speech on the North-eastern boundary, on the currency, on the Western land interests, or on any other great constitutional or legal question, he has only to turn around to his friend and say, in that remarkably silver voice of his, 'York, you are wanted!'" Although Leggett had disclaimed any part in composing the July oration, his denial had been cheerfully ignored.

In early October the New York nominating committee asked Forrest to become their candidate for the House of Representatives. On October 17 he informed them that though he was "impressed with a lively sense of gratitude to those who have deemed my name worthy to be placed among the number from which you are to select persons to discharge the important duty of representatives to the national legislature,—I am constrained to offer you a negative reply."

Thus Forrest terminated his brief political career. He never again came so close to the inner circle, nor delivered another oration, though he maintained his passion for political causes, contributed regularly to the Democratic Party, and supported all sorts of minor patriotic endeavors.

Forrest's political excursion, however brief and inconsequential, temporarily upset his fall engagement. When he began his New York season on Tuesday, September 4, he was forced to forsake the Park and go to the National Theatre. Stephen Price, the Park manager, observing Forrest's political dabbling, inferred that he intended to quit the profession and "so engaged the best of the season to foreigners and to the exclusion of all native histrions. I always take pleasure in welcoming to our shores any exotic talent," Forrest wrote to Wemyss in Philadelphia, "but certainly not to the entire exclusion of that which is 'native and to the manner born.'" His political activities also affected him in Philadelphia. Robert Maywood, the Chestnut Street manager, obeyed Price's dictates, and thus Forrest was forced into Wemyss's Walnut Street Theatre, at that moment a secondary house with second-class prices. Minor handicaps did not disturb Forrest nor his followers. For his three weeks at the National, a two-week stand at the Tremont in Boston, and thirteen performances at the Walnut Street, he netted over $9,000. Let the managers try to block him; the "real people" would rally behind him.

Forrest had additional troubles during the fall, more aggravating, and more difficult to cope with. Mr. and Mrs. Sinclair and their two children, Margaret and Virginia, arrived from London and moved in with them. Happily, Forrest was able to get out of town for a month. He could not bear to see his father-in-law lounging around the house. When Forrest returned from Philadelphia, Mrs. Underwood, the housekeeper, took him aside and reported that the place had been filled with "scenes of

revelry and disorder" during his absence. Forrest talked to
Catherine. He had been polite and decent and given her parents
the run of the house. A month and a half was long enough; they
would have to move on. Forrest was accustomed to have Catherine accept his proposals automatically. This time she rebelled.
If they went, she went. It was a frustrating fight for Forrest and
one he had no chance of winning on the present terms. He left
her weeping and went to bed.

The next morning he got out of the house before the Sinclairs were stirring and hurried to his friend and business adviser James Lawson. He made no attempt to explain the situation. He simply instructed Lawson to make a list of New York
houses presently on the market. He was going to Albany for
a week. When he got back he would make his choice. Before
Lawson had a chance to protest, Forrest departed.

When he returned from the Albany engagement on Saturday, November 10, Mrs. Underwood cornered him again. Affairs
in Reade Street had gotten worse. The house had been crowded
with company to all hours of the night. No one went to bed
before three or four o'clock in the morning. She herself was
afraid to retire for fear they would set the house on fire with
their smoking. Frequently, after the company had staggered
out, she had gone into the parlor and found Mr. Sinclair collapsed on the carpet and Mrs. Sinclair lying behind the door.

Forrest went immediately, if skeptically, to check on Lawson's progress. During the past year he had futilely looked at
one place after another. Lawson had been luckier. He had located a three-story mansion on West Twenty-second Street near
Tenth Avenue. Resigned to accept most anything, Forrest was
pleasantly surprised to discover that Lawson had found a magnificent establishment; in fact, some might regard it as too extravagant for two people. Forrest had no qualms about a bit
of ostentation. He asked Lawson to come to terms with the
owner, while he rushed home to Catherine with the good news.
She did not share his enthusiasm. Only after he had assured her
that they would take only enough furniture from Reade Street

to make the place habitable and that her parents could re-main in the old house, did she finally agree.

By the end of the week the deal was settled. The following week, while he took a break from the theatre, they moved in. Bivouacking in a bare house—only one bedroom and the dining room were partly furnished—did not please Forrest. At the mo-ment, however, he preferred anything to the obnoxious com-pany of his father-in-law, and he knew the arrangement was only temporary.

Now in the middle of his second season since his return from England, and with the demand at the box office slackening —he had performed a week each in Baltimore and Philadelphia after New York—Forrest decided to take Catherine on a tour of the country. She must see for herself that America was not limited to the tight triangle of New York, Boston, and Phila-delphia.

He had another motive for the journey which he did not reveal to Catherine. While they were gone, Lawson was to get the Sinclairs out of the Reade Street House, move the furniture to Twenty-second Street and have everything prepared for the Forrests' return. He gave Lawson $200 with which to bribe Sinclair, if that was necessary.

Shortly after the first of January they sailed down the coast, stopping at Charleston, looping around Florida into the Gulf and up to New Orleans, a peaceful and relaxing voyage. Forrest had not wanted to risk a rugged and jolting cross-country jour-ney. Catherine was three months pregnant and must be spared unnecessary hardships. The normal and unavoidable hazards along the Western circuit would make heavy enough demands on her strength. Ironically, Edwin, not the fragile Catherine, suffered the first illness. Some undiagnosed ailment struck him while they were still at sea.

Forrest had completely recovered when they arrived in New Orleans, a week before his scheduled opening. He immediately introduced Catherine to the fascinations of his favorite Southern city, imposing only such restraints on their perambulations as

179

were required by her delicate condition. A gay week climaxed on Monday, January 28, with his opening at the old Camp Street Theatre. He had been pushed into this run-down establishment—now in its last year as a theatre, because the new St. Charles was already occupied by J. B. Booth. Caldwell owned both playhouses; no matter whom the public favored, he won.

After a four-year absence and with the glowing accounts of his London triumph and his New York homecoming season filtering through, the citizens of New Orleans were eager for another look at their favorite. After all they had been among the first to recognize his talents. On opening night Catherine could not see a square foot of unoccupied space. When Forrest entered as Othello, the wild welcome reminded her of the first night in New York. The boatmen in the gallery seemed even louder and rowdier than the shouters at the Park and more partial to Edwin's extravagances. When she joined her husband backstage, she learned that the evening had been remarkable in other respects. The gross receipts of $1,370 and Forrest's share of $560 made it the most profitable night of his career. Two previous New York performances of *Metamora* had grossed $1,400. Unfortunately, on those occasions he had received a straight $200 per night; in New Orleans he shared equally with the management after the first $250.

After the *Othello* opening, Forrest had a touch of fever and was obliged to cancel the next night. He returned on Wednesday; on Thursday he was back in bed. He volunteered to give up his profits for the two missed performances; Caldwell and the public would not let him. Beginning on Friday, February 1, he played eleven consecutive nights, Sundays included.

Fortunately he got a few days' rest before his Mobile engagement, in fact, an extra day because the boat broke down. In Mobile the crowds were even more astonishing than in New Orleans, for the Government Street Theatre seated only five hundred and fewer than twelve thousand inhabitants lived in the town. One reporter noted that *The Gladiator,* on February 25, could well have taken in $500 more if there had been another inch of standing room in the building. Catherine continued to be amazed. For his fourteen nights he received $2,975. (New Orleans had given him $3,341 for thirteen.)

Catherine was also amazed and frightened by the rough frontiersmen who jammed the theatre and who worked up such a storm at every performance. She could not resist peering across into the upper boxes and thinking of the story everyone had been so eager to tell her. Just four years earlier, when Tyrone Power (great-grandfather of the late Tyrone Power, the movie actor) was performing there, a murder had been committed in one of the boxes during the play and the murderer had escaped undetected. Forrest laughed at her fears; still Catherine was relieved when the engagement was concluded.

From Mobile they went to Natchez. The ramshackle theatre there was worse than that in Mobile, and the stock company just a bit seedier. The actors attached to these frontier theatres did not warm the heart of a visiting star; the supers were impossible. Fortunately, the rugged characters in the audience did not object.

A writer for the *Natchez Free Trader and Gazette* who saw Forrest's *Metamora* on March 25 was less tolerant. He reported that the prompter spoke more lines than the actors, that the final climactic scene was utterly disastrous. After the intermission, during which the orchestra had provided a spirited rendering of "Coal Black Rose," the curtains parted to reveal an open country. Nothing obstructed the view but the head of the orchestra leader Mr. Mueller. A motley assortment of local rowdies charged on stage, pursuing Metamora. Someone shouted fire. In the wings three guns snapped; there was no report. The New England army was in despair. Metamora drew his bowie knife. "This will never do," exclaimed the prompter indignantly. "He deserted his post, rushed across to the opposite side of the stage and discharged a horse pistol. Metamora squeezed a small bag of red paint upon his dauntless countenance, turned to the audience, fell and expired." Thus, the local reporter described the tragic demise of Metamora in Natchez. In spite of the unfortunate collapse of his histrionic support, Forrest was wildly cheered. When he appeared in *Metamora*, it required more than trivial mishaps to prevent him from arousing his audience to a frenzy. The ten nights in Natchez increased his earnings by $1,403.75.

After Natchez they went back to New Orleans for a return engagement in the handsome St. Charles Theatre. This magnificent establishment, opened three years earlier, was unsurpassed in this country in size and beauty; only the opera houses in Naples, Milan, and St. Petersburg could match it. It was an astounding achievement for a city still under 100,000. The four tiers of boxes were decorated inside and out in a color scheme of pink, white, and gold, and each had its own private boudoir for the ladies. Suspended from the center dome was a gigantic chandelier twelve feet high and thirty-six feet in circumference, manufactured in London and valued at $10,750. The spectators in the pit must have worried about the hazard to life and limb; it contained 900 pounds of wrought iron, 2,300 pounds of brass, and 900 pounds of glass. Twenty-three thousand cut glass drops woven in concentric circles sparkled from the light of 250 gaslights. Each night the lamplighter took a half-hour, working with his long pole and wax taper, to illuminate the fixture. This gorgeous creation was Caldwell's pride and joy, a spectacular tribute to the splendor of gas lighting. Caldwell owned the gasworks. When he installed his system in 1834, New Orleans became the fourth city in the United States to be lighted by gas, and Caldwell had a thirty-year concession.

After a profitable fifteen nights at the St. Charles, Forrest and Catherine started up the Mississippi bound for St. Louis, stopping briefly for a week's engagement in Vicksburg (April 22–9). The Southern tour had been an incredible success. Adding the $960.50 he received in Vicksburg and the $4,083.41 for his final New Orleans engagement to his previous profits, his total for the four months came to $12,764.16. Some comparative figures for 1838–9 make his profits seem more astonishing as they also reveal that the theatre was healthier in New Orleans than in New York. For the entire season Caldwell showed a profit of $15,340 at the St. Charles, and $2,906 at the Camp

Street. In the same season in New York the Park lost money and the National had a paper profit of $26,400, of which $25,000 was earmarked for the previous season's deficit.

When they boarded the *Louisville* for the slow and easy journey up the Mississippi, they stowed the money in the safe and settled down to relax from the rugged routine of the past weeks. The spring rains had freshened the air and hurried the foliage. For days at a time the shore line resembled a primeval jungle with no sign of human habitation. But what excitement when the *Louisville* turned in to a landing! As soon as the inhabitants learned that Forrest was aboard, they streamed down to the waterfront to cheer the great actor and his wife.

On Sunday, May 5, 1839, the boat tied up at St. Louis and on Monday Forrest opened in *Virginius*. It was a disastrous evening. He had not been warned that three days before his arrival the vivacious singer Caradori Allan had begun a series of "musical soirees" at the Missouri Hotel. She had captured the St. Louis elite, and to hear her soulful renditions of "Angels Ever Bright and Fair" and "Jock o' Hazeldean," they ignored Forrest. Even on his second night with *Othello* and on the third with his new play *Lady of Lyons* he could not pry the audience away from Caradori.

Forrest was embarked on a ruinous engagement. After the third night Sol Smith, the theatre manager, advised his partner Noah Ludlow: "Last night the receipts were but $268!! What do you think of that?—At the Missouri Hotel, not only the room, but every nook and cranny leading to it, was jammed full! Fifty ladies more than could be seated—sweating, fanning, and admiring—while Caradori was warbling Italian music, the words of which were Greek to them! I went in—no, not in—I submitted to be squeezed in an ante-room—for a few minutes—and it is my honest belief there were not less than 450 people in and about there—and all theatrical going people." Smith and Forrest agreed that something had to be done immediately; they agreed too that *Metamora* offered the only hope.

The plan worked. On Friday night, May 10, the crowd abandoned Caradori and flocked to Forrest. Italian *bel canto* was no match for Indian war whoops. Friday morning Smith wrote to Ludlow: "*Metamora* resulted in a house of $951!— Come, not so bad, my master. 'Stocks is riz.'" Once the Indian play had broken the Caradori spell, Forrest did a thriving business for the remainder of the engagement: $3,159.06¾ profit for the twelve nights.

From St. Louis they began the homeward leg of their journey up the Ohio, stopping for a week in Louisville and another week in Cincinnati.

Immediately after they arrived in Cincinnati at the end of May, Forrest took Catherine across the river up into the Covington hills. Her enthusiasm for the view so nearly matched his own that when he discovered some thirty acres of hillside property for sale, he bought them. Forrest, like so many actors, yearned to subdue the itinerant and ephemeral nature of his profession with some sign of stability. He paid Israel L. Ludlow $8,500 for the Covington acreage, and before he left Cincinnati marked out a spot on the top of the hill for the carpenter who was to build a Swiss chalet for him. In later years Forrest referred to the place as his Kentucky cottage, though it could hardly be called a cottage. The chalet had eleven rooms plus a large wine cellar; its immense beams of neatly hewed native hemlock logs rested on a thick stone foundation. Irrefutable testimony to the craft of the builder, the house still stands and is presently occupied by a Cincinnati accordion teacher.

Five years later Forrest bought an adjoining plot from Ludlow, which he put into grapes, hoping therewith to stock his own cellars and perhaps initiate the whisky-drinking Kentuckians to the pleasures of wine.

Forrest relished the role of country squire and hired Thomas W. Whitley, an English landscape painter, to superintend the grape arbors. For a time the arrangement worked well. In 1847, however, Whitley insisted that he had been abused, deceived, and insulted by Forrest. He even wrote a melodrama which he proposed to send to Forrest's contest, in which the actor was portrayed as an insane villain who is finally committed to a madhouse. Whitley remained on the property until he moved to New York in 1850 and shifted from cultivating grapes to selling wines and spirits over the counter.

However troublesome the role of absentee landlord became, Forrest retained his sentimental attachment to the Kentucky hillside throughout his lifetime. When he died, he still held title to the forty-four acres, which later became incorporated into the present Devou Park.

After the completion of the week's engagement in Cincinnati, they continued up the river, stopping for a week at the Pittsburgh theatre before beginning the rigorous overland journey home.

Forrest had now completed his second full season since his return from England, with a profit of $33,956.82½ for the 158 performances. This was $500 more than the previous year, with nine less performances, and with more than half the season spent on the Western circuit. No actor, American or British, had ever had such a spectacular season.

Edwin and Catherine had covered some 4,000 miles with only the anticipated aggravations. When they got within a hundred miles of Philadelphia, their luck ran out and they had to stop in Harrisburg. The ceaseless jogging of the carriage from Pittsburgh had apparently precipitated the event Forrest had hoped to celebrate in Philadelphia. On June 27, 1839, he wrote to his mother from Harrisburg: "We expected to be with you in Philadelphia today but have been prevented by the entrance into this breathing world of a little girl. Catherine is doing very well and begs to be remembered to the family."

Two weeks later the trio reached Philadelphia. After Forrest was certain that Catherine and the baby were thriving, he returned to New York.

He had been back in the city only a week, happily preparing for his new engagement and working with a new play, when he received a sad note from Catherine. The little girl had died. It hardly seemed possible; a few days before her tender cheeks had been so fresh and blooming. It appeared now that Catherine could not bring a child beyond those first sweet days. Perhaps this was the season for bereavements. Just before he got back, his dear old friend William Leggett had died, and at the happiest moment of his sad life. President Van Buren had just appointed him Minister to Guatemala.

CHAPTER *xii*

Town House in "Old Chelsea"

Forrest plunged into preparations for a new production, to burn out his sorrow for the death of the little girl in his work.

He had chosen *Richelieu,* a drama of conspiracy and intrigue based on the life of the canny French Cardinal, because of its success at Covent Garden the previous March and because of his fortunate experience with the other Bulwer-Lytton play, *Lady of Lyons.* Both of these plays had been initially performed in England by Forrest's would-be friend and arch-rival-to-be, William Macready.

Andrew Jackson Allen had been engaged to make the Richelieu wardrobe for Forrest and for the other principal characters as well. Allen produced a magnificent set of costumes, said to be exact copies of robes and gowns worn at the Court of Louis XIII and to surpass anything previously seen on the American stage. Allen was one of the few serious practitioners in this field. He frequently boasted that Forrest had reached his present eminence largely with the help of the splendid costumes Allen had designed for him. He supplied the actor's entire stage wardrobe from 1826 to 1843.

"Dummy" Allen, as he was called, was born in New York in 1788 and began his theatrical career in Albany. Although he acted occasionally even after he joined Forrest, he was on call to Forrest as valet, jester, and costumer. Not only was Allen dexterous with the needle, he had a sharp eye for comic possibilities in any situation and a penchant for concocting escapades to dupe the public. He once advertised a balloon ascension. Two daring aeronauts, Monsieur Gageremo and Mademoiselle Pussieremo, were to fly into space. When the gaping spectators arrived on the scene, they discovered two cats harnessed into tiny baskets ready to explore the upper air.

In 1850 when Allen became too feeble to follow Forrest's arduous schedule, he settled in New York and opened a saloon. During the three years he operated this establishment, until his death on October 29, 1853, he lost none of his comic spirit, judging from his frequent announcements in the press:

> Dum Vivimus, Vivamus
> While we live, let us live!
> Respectfully I inform the whole union that the
> Rialto Saloon, No. 37 Bowery (upstairs),
> is one of the most respectable resting places in the city, where gentlemen, without fear of intrusion, may rest from their labors, and call for refreshment as good as that of any similar establishment in the union. The Rialto Saloon has no union with the amphitheatre or circus saloon next door, as some people suppose.
> Andrew Jackson Allen is "himself alone."
> Walk up and see the old man! You shall have a cordial welcome; he himself will do the honors.

When Kossuth, the Hungarian patriot, arrived in this country in 1851, Allen changed the name of his establishment:

> Now Open—The Kossuth Divan!!!
> No. 37 Bowery (upstairs)
> Andrew Jackson Allen
> Internal and External Costumer

Allen's costumes for *Richelieu* were not ready for the initial week at the National, so from August 19 until the end of the month, Forrest played his Shakespearean repertoire with occasional nights of *Virginius* and *The Gladiator*. On Wednesday, September 4, 1839, *Richelieu* opened and for four successive nights drew capacity audiences. The costliness and elegance of the costumes were duly noted by press and public; the principal attention was, however, focused on Forrest and his new role. The critics pronounced it a masterly creation with genuine "flashes of genius." They detected an enlarged intellectuality in his playing, an incisive grasp of the mercurial range of the Cardinal's temperament, a greater finesse and subtlety. Forrest's adherents in the audience were more impressed with the grandeur and passion, with the democratic ideals of the aristocratic Cardinal who recognized only natural and heavenly endowed superiority, who loved his native land, and who dared to challenge the King's royal prerogatives. Charles Kean, after seeing a performance, was reported to have said to his wife: "Ellen, this is the greatest acting we have ever seen or ever shall see."

Forrest was delighted with the range of possibilities in the role. In the subdued passages he portrayed Richelieu as a feeble, tottering old man, thus giving himself emotional elbowroom for the passionate explosions. Clearly the French Cardinal would take his place in his repertoire with Metamora and Spartacus.

After the Saturday night performance on September 7, Forrest packed the Allen costumes in his trunk and went to Philadelphia. As in New York *Richelieu* was not introduced at the Walnut Street Theatre until the second week of the engagement. When manager Wemyss heard about "Dummy" Allen's magnificent costumes, he determined to go a step further and provide settings of equal richness and authenticity.

When Forrest got his first glimpse of the lavish decor Wemyss had contrived, he was utterly amazed. In addition to new drops, the manager had procured chairs and tables of the period; an uncommon concession to authenticity. After the initial performance on September 24, Forrest called Wemyss to his dressing room, and, according to the manager's account, "after many compliments, concluded by saying, 'For what you have done for the honor of the profession I will play one night gratuitously for you at the end of the engagement; select any play you think proper.'" Wemyss was overwhelmed by Forrest's magnanimity. Even after the benefit—he chose *Metamora* —had netted him a meager $289 compared with Forrest's $400 from his own benefit the night before, and knowing that the actor was departing with $2,904.22 in profits for the thirteen nights, Wemyss wrote: "Such a proffer, on such an occasion, from such a man, was a feather in the cap of a manager, which no one has been able to pluck away from me."

Forrest was delighted with the success of *Richelieu*, with the flattering attention to scenic elegance of the Walnut Street Theatre. The real pleasure on the first night came, however, from seeing Catherine in the stage box. Her old vivacity, which had been so brutally stamped out in the summer, was returning. As he watched her through the performance, he could see that she was caught up with the Cardinal and had for the evening forgotten her sorrow.

She was not ready, however, to follow his mad whirl, or he would have taken her with him. He closed in Philadelphia on Tuesday night, October 1, opened at the Front Street Theatre in Baltimore on Wednesday, and for thirteen nights from then until October 16, struggled against bad business and an "execrable" company. The poor attendance he could understand. Baltimore was too fired up with the local elections to take time for the theatre. One night a "grand democratic procession," some five to six thousand strong, carrying illuminated banners, stopped in front of the theatre "with cheers for your humble servant. You will I am sure be gratified to hear this," he wrote to Catherine, "in spite of your *pretended* aristocracy."

Catherine wanted to be home in New York, and he longed to be with her. The most he could arrange was a few days off to take her back to Twenty-second Street before rushing on to Boston. Happily, this was time enough to quiet her fears, to promise her that he would not accept an engagement in the South this season, that as soon as his fifteen weeks were finished he would be home.

On Tuesday, October 22, when he opened a ten-night stand at the Tremont in Boston, his thoughts were still with Catherine in New York. Every night when he returned to the Tremont House, exhausted from Metamora or Spartacus, he "could not resist the pleasure of communing" with his beloved Catherine and "tracing a few lines to repeat how much, how very much, I love her." "As I wandered through the park today," he wrote on another evening, "a thousand pleasant reminiscences crowded upon me of our many pleasant walks there together. In fancy you were by my side again, and the bracing air, had called upon your much loved cheek its rosiest hue." In a few days they would be together again to enjoy the "luxury of reality, and then our joys shall be intenser by our distance now." In the meantime he sent her some quinces for preserves, some squash which Allen insisted were the finest quality in the Union, and promised in a few days to send her some game which at the moment was available in great abundance in Boston.

He closed in Boston on Saturday, November 1, spent the next week in Providence and then hurried to New York. His profits ($5,000) for the past twenty-eight performances had not equaled his lush proceeds on the Western circuits, yet he felt sufficiently prosperous, when he was back in New York, to indulge his charitable impulses. Beginning on November 11, he did a series of seven benefit performances at the new National (the former Niblo's) for the "company and manager of the late National Theatre." On September 23, the old National had burned to the ground, taking along with it the African Methodist Church, the French Church, and the Dutch Church. No one could claim that God's wrath was striking at the house of the devil.

Forrest now had only four weeks until he completed his fifteen-week commitment: two in Philadelphia and two in New York. Although he was eager to finish at the Bowery by Christmas, he agreed to postpone his benefit night of *Metamora* until New Year's Day. For some unaccountable reason the Indian play was thought appropriate for January 1, and evidently it was. It drew $1,785, the largest sum Forrest had ever drawn into a theatre's treasury. Unhappily, he did not share in the good fortune at the box office. He received a mere $200.

With the strenuous fall season concluded, Forrest was happy to forget the theatre and devote himself to Catherine and the new house. He had not yet had time to become familiar with his new residence at 436 West Twenty-second Street, which Catherine had been busily shaping into a home.

Already the place was being pointed out as one of the fashionable residences in the "Old Chelsea" area. Situated on the south side of Twenty-second Street, a block north of the General Theological Seminary and a block south of London Terrace, an area now largely surrounded by Puerto Rican tenements, the solid brick structure still retains some of its former dignity. The house that sheltered the Forrest newlyweds in solitary splendor is now partitioned into nine separate apartments.

Built in 1827 by an English cotton factor named Cargill, who had purchased the land from Dr. Clement C. Moore (the author of "Twas the Night Before Christmas"), the house was designed by Cargill to duplicate his wife's girlhood home in London. When she died in 1837, Cargill tried to remain there alone for a brief period. He finally gave up and sold the house to Forrest. For the next twelve years it became the domestic center for Catherine and Edwin and the scene of many gay parties.

Forrest sold the mansion in 1850 to Don Alonzo Cushman. During the 1860's Cushman's daughter, Mrs. Pristor, lived there, and during the following decade it was leased by Christian Herter, the interior designer who decorated J. Pierpont Morgan's New York house and who was the grandfather of Christian A. Herter, the Secretary of State. In 1877 the property was sold to Dr. Isaac Wyman Drummond, the Boston paint merchant. (His father was founder of the DeVoe and Reynolds Company, and he later became chairman of its board.) Fortunately, Drummond kept the house, until his death in 1933, much as it had been during Forrest's time and the detailed pictures of the interior, taken during Drummond's occupancy, give a glimpse of the elegant surroundings in which the Forrests lived.

The three-story brick and brownstone façade, rising almost fifty feet above the street level, was topped with an iron-rail snow guard. Four window balconies along the third floor, tucked under the mansard roof, were also protected with iron railings. The main entry, slightly off center and nine steps above the street, was tunneled into the façade and flanked with two pairs of Greek columns topped with pediments. The raised first floor brought half the basement above ground and thus gave the house essentially four full floors of living space.

Inside the main door the large entry hall was spread with a marble floor leading to the wide circular staircase with its intricately carved balustrade that wound to the top of the building. At the right of the entry hall was the dining room, pantry, and lift. Straight ahead and stretched across the entire back half of the main floor was the drawing room. Each of these principal rooms was laid with a highly polished parquet floor. The white wall-panels, door frames, and fireplaces, here as well as throughout the house, were designed in the best Adam tradition. Every room had its own fireplace, and every door was framed with fluted pilasters. Even for a fashionable New York house of the period, the rooms were extraordinarily large. The drawing room measured thirty-four feet by twenty-five feet, the full width of the house and half the depth. Beyond the drawing room was an outside porch, duplicated on the second and third floors, that stretched across the back of the house, overlooking the garden.

Forrest's library was on the second floor directly above, and of the same dimensions as the drawing room. Three bedrooms occupied the remainder of the second floor. Two bedrooms for the servants, a small study, a workshop, and a den were located on the third level. Even a person endowed with Forrest's expansive disposition need not feel crowded.

When Forrest concluded his New Year's Day *Metamora*, he settled in as Lord of the Manor. In his absence Catherine had valiantly attempted to establish a domestic order that would please Forrest, though her natural inclination toward alfresco living was not conducive to the strict arrangements Forrest demanded. His library was to be his sacred domain. The books were not to be disturbed and only Mrs. Underwood was to do the cleaning. Dinner would be served at two o'clock. If occasionally guests arrived in the evening, the waiter and cook must stay up. Ordinarily the house should be quiet at ten. Most of their entertaining would be done on Sunday.

Forrest's seclusion on Twenty-second Street during January

and February 1840 did not erase his name from the public's mind. Now and for the remainder of his life the Forrest name maintained a remarkable ubiquity. Race horses were named after him, yachts, club boats, pilot boats, steamers, merchant-men, locomotives, military companies, fire engines, and fire companies. At least seven thespian groups called themselves the Forrest Dramatic Association.

His noble features were recreated in marble in six busts and one full length statue. Samuel Lawrence, the English painter whom Thackeray had urged to come to America, William Page, the specialist in somber portraits, and innumerable anonymous artists painted his portrait. The principal, as well as the minor, daguerreotypists circulated idealized likenesses, whether pic-turing him in mufti or in the abbreviated costume of one of his roles.

Many actors who could not succeed on their own specialized in Forrest imitations: Charles Eaton, McKean Buchanan, J. M. Scott, and Augustus A. Addams. Eaton was probably the least successful because he mixed in imitations of Booth and Vanden-hoff. Buchanan's copies were apparently too exaggerated. J. M. Scott was acclaimed by one reporter for the "faithfulness with which he reproduced the mannerisms of Forrest"; and Addams, who resembled Forrest in appearance, was said to have fallen "into this mode of imitation so readily that anyone hearing him, in ordinary conversation, without seeing him, could not possibly have told whether Mr. Forrest or Mr. Addams was the speaker."

Forrest took no account of these imitators. As long as they did not infringe on the plays that he regarded as his exclusive property, he willingly let them trade on his mannerisms.

Forrest stayed away from the theatre until he reappeared at the Bowery for five nights in mid-March. He could not, how-ever, divorce himself completely from theatrical affairs. He had been pestering Judge Robert T. Conrad—the same Conrad who spoke at Forrest's testimonial banquet in Philadelphia—for a manuscript of *Jack Cade* (sometimes billed as *Aylmere*), a new play which Wemyss brought to Forrest's attention the previous fall. On March 6, 1840, Forrest wrote to Wemyss complaining that Conrad had not yet sent the play and promising him that as soon as it arrived he would advise him of the scene requirements.

Wemyss was not deceived by Forrest's apparent friendliness. Clearly the actor had conveniently forgotten Wemyss's vested interest in the play. *Jack Cade* had a curious history. Judge Conrad had originally written *Cade* for Addams, the Forrest imitator. When the play was scheduled for a first performance at Wemyss's Walnut Street Theatre on December 7, 1835, Addams had been too drunk to perform and David Ingersoll had appeared in his place. Conrad was dissatisfied with the results and retrieved the manuscript.

During the next winter season, 1840–1, Forrest continued his negotiations with Conrad, supplying him with a constant stream of suggestions. He also intimated that the play would be considered with the "prize plays" and had more than a reasonable chance of winning. The culmination of the Cade project was still a year away.

After Forrest broke his vacation with the reappearance at the Bowery and felt the pleasant rub of the harness, he was trapped for the rest of the season. In April he performed ten days at the Tremont in Boston. Then he returned to New York for a one-night stand at the Bowery on April 20 with Thomas Hamblin doing Iago to his Othello, went to Philadelphia for eleven nights at the Walnut Street, and then to Baltimore for seven performances at the Front Street Theatre. Wherever he went his thoughts turned to home. He wrote to Catherine from Baltimore that he was counting the days until he would "be restored to my dearest one." Allen also missed her and sent her some succulent green peas, which he claimed were better than any she could buy in New York. Forrest was sorry to report that Baltimore had been disappointing. The weather had been bad, and business was poor. He had to listen to the intolerable optimism of the Whigs prancing about the city, so positive that Harrison would be elected and that the Democratic Party would be overthrown. He hoped that they would "be sadly disappointed" in their folly.

The spring season seemed depressed everywhere. Even Forrest's final session at the Bowery (May 25 to June 5) fell far below the fall engagement in New York. His final tabulation for the year was less impressive than that for the two previous seasons: a total profit of $21,808.36¾ for 113 nights, making an average of $195 per night. In 1837–8 the average had been $200, and in 1838–9 had reached $213. Forrest was not alarmed.

Edwin and Catherine remained in New York for the summer waiting for the arrival of another baby. Again their happiness was quickly turned to sorrow. The baby died at birth.

Where was the third-time charm? Forrest desperately wanted a child, preferably a boy to carry his name. What profit in the wish if the child would not be born? The sadness and doubts that might have pushed Catherine and Forrest apart seemed to draw them closer together. When Forrest left for his engagement in Boston in October suffering from a slight cold, Catherine wrote immediately for a full report. He assured her that he was quite recovered, even happy in the beautiful Boston sunshine, "that is, as happy as I can be in the absence of *one* who forms so big a share of all the good which is allotted me." Most every day throughout the year he reminded her of how weary he was of being alone, how much he loved her, how he longed for the day when they would be together.

Forrest had planned a heavy road season. After his opening engagement at the Bowery (September 7 to 18) and except for a benefit night of *Richelieu* for the Bowery manager on October 2, he did not return to New York until the following May. For the first time he devoted his season almost exclusively to the Eastern circuit: Philadelphia, Boston, Baltimore; then, Philadelphia again, Washington, Baltimore, and Washington; then to the Marshall Theatre in Richmond, Virginia, his first appearance there since his return from England. After Richmond, he played two nights in Petersburg before taking the boat to Charleston, South Carolina. The Charleston engagement, announced for twelve nights, was reduced to eleven when a severe storm forced the closing of the theatre on January 20.

From Charleston he returned to Washington for five nights

and then went back to Richmond for seven. In Richmond, on Saturday, February 20, President Harrison was in the audience. His inauguration was only two weeks away, yet when he came backstage, he and Forrest avoided any reference to politics; instead they reminisced about Cincinnati. Forrest had, of course, voted for Van Buren. After Richmond, nine nights in Norfolk, two in Portsmouth, and then by steamboat to Baltimore for a week. On April 12 he concluded his hectic tour. "How he runs from one theatre to the other," one reporter wrote, "like the fox, doubling until he reaches his starting ground again, more attractive by his temporary absence. It is a dangerous experiment, which his popularity alone enables him to pursue with success. Managers rail at it as an ungenerous course, but they are all eager to make engagements with him."

On Monday, April 5, he settled down at the Arch Street Theatre in Philadelphia for what now seemed an interminable nineteen nights. Finally, on the first of May he rejoined Catherine in New York.

He was overjoyed to be home and excited at the prospect of a new play for his Park engagement. In Philadelphia Conrad had given him the completed manuscript of *Jack Cade,* doctored to Forrest's specifications. As soon as Forrest got the engagement underway, he put the play into rehearsal so that it might be ready by the last week of his schedule.

The role of Cade was tailored for Forrest. Conrad had chosen as his central character the same fourteenth-century English rebel whom Shakespeare (in *Henry VI, Part II*) portrayed as a vulgar demagogue and transformed him into a vengeful patriot revolting against the feudal system and its wicked abuses. One critic called the drama "a battle song of liberty, written in blood and set to music."

Before the play begins, Jack Cade has fled to Italy. He had struck Lord Say after Say had killed his father. When the play opens, Cade, now called Aylmere, has returned to England with his wife and child to avenge the killing of his father and to lead a rebellion of the bondsmen. Like Metamora, Cade had been called to his duty in a vision. One night in Rome he had dreamed that he had been summoned from his couch. He walked about the eerie ruins of the Colosseum and "there in the darkness, leaning against a mossy wall, thought upon my country," and swore "to make the bondsmen free."

Cade rallies the insurrectionists, charging them to demand:

> *All that just nature gave and they have taken:*
> *Freedom for the bond! and justice in the sharing*
> *Of the soil given by Heaven to all; the right*
> *To worship without bribing a base priest*
> *For entrance into heaven; and* ALL *that makes*
> *The poor man rich in Liberty and Hope!*

The rebellion is filled with horrors: Cade's mother is burned to death in her cottage; his child is killed; his wife is captured, abused by one of the nobles, and driven mad. Still Cade clings to his noble cause. When Lord Say commands him to abandon his foolish notion that commoners can live on equal terms with men whose fathers had been "made noble by a king," Aylmere replies that Jack Cade was made noble "by a God! . . . The people are God's own Nobility; and wear their stars not on their breasts, but in them!"

The revolt finally succeeds. Cade kills Lord Say and in turn is mortally wounded by him. As Cade is dying, the charter declaring the bondsmen free is brought in. Cade seizes it, clasps it to his bosom, sinks to the floor, and dies.

In Conrad's play Jack Cade became the symbol of rebellion against arbitrary and wicked power. A few timid critics suggested that the play encouraged class hatred; Forrest's democratic disciples, never known for their caution, cheered the bondsmen's revolt. They welcomed another drama glorifying the common man, and Forrest was delighted to add another democratic tract to his repertoire.

The May engagement generated no new enthusiasm except that which greeted *Jack Cade* on May 24. Attendance was steady, though not up to its previous level. Even after adding post-season dates in Philadelphia, Pittsburgh, and Albany, the season's record was disappointing: $18,500 for 153 performances, down roughly $3,000 from the previous year and with forty more performances. The peripheral towns on the Eastern circuit might boast more culture per capita than the Western outposts; they could not match them in their passion for the theatre.

Forrest came down the river from Albany anticipating a happy summer at home. Catherine was nearing the end of another confinement, and the house was bubbling with activity. Mrs. Underwood was transforming the spare bedroom into a nursery. Catherine Levins, the cook, pestered the greengrocers for fresh fruits. Anna Flowers, the chambermaid, kept a steady, if sometimes embarrassingly intimate, vigil over her mistress. Ordinarily Forrest would have avoided such confusion; instead he joined the circle, sitting with Catherine almost constantly and guarding her against unnecessary exertion. He even bought a pamphlet on "Infant Treatment, with Directions to Mothers for self-management before, during, and after Pregnancy." They never talked of the previous misfortunes; each knew the dreadful question that floated just under the surface. By common consent, if they skimmed near the subject, one or the other would grasp at some ridiculous irrelevancy.

Caution and care could not break nature's design. The child lived only a few minutes. For a week following the sad event Catherine wept constantly. Forrest sat beside her bed fumbling for comforting words that he could never find. The pitiful weariness and disappointment in her face became almost unbearable to him. Between his visits to her room he shut himself in the library or walked the streets.

Catherine had desperately wanted children to salve the loneliness she felt when Forrest was away. He had wanted a son. His brothers were dead, none of his sisters had married, perpetuating the Forrest name was his responsibility. In a way, the blow struck deeper at him. Four times he had happily prepared himself to assume his parental role, a role that he was eager to play. Each time the defeat had become more humiliating. Now it appeared that the Forrest name would pass into oblivion.

If Catherine's incapacity for giving him a child weighed

more heavily on him than on her, he had an easier escape. He could pour his fury into Spartacus or Metamora and heap the engagements one on the other, leaving little time for brooding.

Beginning in the middle of August, he shuttled between Philadelphia, Boston, and New York. His new play, *Jack Cade*, was in demand everywhere, and to satisfy the clamor he abandoned his usual system of alternating plays. In each city he gave a solid week to Conrad's play.

As might have been expected, his success with *Cade* brought a series of pitiful solicitations from Wemyss. The one-time Philadelphia manager was down on his luck, had taken the second-rate post as manager of the Front Street Theatre in Baltimore, and was now grasping at every past association that might revive him. He wrote to Forrest, reminding him of the extraordinary production he had given *Richelieu*, hinting at his claim on *Jack Cade*, and begging him to play Baltimore. Forrest had no sympathy with such sniveling. He replied on November 22, 1841; he had no objection to playing in Baltimore if Wemyss could produce an adequate company to sustain him. On the matter of terms, he could see the manager flinch as he wrote: "I shall expect the undivided half of the night's receipts." As to the other subject, please, "specify in your next, what that 'little claim' is that you think you have upon the play of *Jack Cade*."

Wemyss answered immediately, carefully avoiding any reference to his feeble acting group, and respectfully reminding Forrest that he first gave him the Conrad manuscript. In regard to the terms for Baltimore, Wemyss begged for a ten-per-cent deduction from the gross for the house rental before Forrest took his half.

Managerial supplications did not disturb Forrest. He shot back his answer: "I cannot consent to the deduction of ten per cent from the receipts." As to the Conrad play: "I am not in the least convinced that you show the slightest cause for your alleged claim upon the tragedy of *Jack Cade* which Judge Conrad wrote for me."

That settled the matter for him, if not for Wemyss. The

manager immediately advised Forrest that if the actor appropriated *Jack Cade* in this fashion, he, Wemyss, might now adapt *Metamora* to his own use. This was too much. Forrest went to Baltimore at the end of January 1842, played at the rival Holliday Street Theatre, and further taunted Wemyss with repeated performances of *Jack Cade.*

During the spring, Forrest continued racing between New York, Philadelphia, and Boston, with side excursions to Richmond and Norfolk, finally concluding the season at the Chatham Theatre in New York on May 30, 1842, with a performance of *Lady of Lyons.* Josephine Clifton had been his leading lady throughout.

Forrest had never before carried a leading lady with him. Why he chose this amazon, Miss Clifton, is hard to understand. Perhaps her brawny physique, almost equal to his, fascinated him. She was an athletic giant, weighing over two hundred pounds, and, according to one reporter, "with a bust finely developed, a physiognomy indicative of great firmness of character and a mind rather of a masculine turn." When she appeared in England in 1834—she was one of the first Americans to take this risk—one critic commented that "the six foot specimen of transatlantic genius did not make the impression which was anticipated. Her lungs are inimitable and her arms beautifully brawny, but here praise must cease."

Perhaps Forrest was weary of femininity. Certainly Miss Clifton's muscles and masculinity were her crowning glories. She was just seven years younger than Forrest and of questionable parentage. Less charitable reports suggested that her mother was a prostitute. She made her New York debut in 1831, played with Forrest in Philadelphia in 1836, and in 1837 achieved her only histrionic distinction until that time in *Bianca Visconti,* a blank verse tragedy by N. P. Willis.

Her support of Forrest this season was apparently not confined to the theatre. However, the image of her forbidding size and "manly mind" makes it hard to think of their relationship in romantic terms. Perhaps it was the love of one athlete for another. They appear to have had very chummy travel arrangements, and according to "Dummy" Allen, usually occupied the same suite of rooms; at least they did in French's Hotel in Norfolk. Allen said he saw them kiss and embrace, and one morning observed that Forrest's bed had not been slept in. Allen's snooping cannot be accepted at face value. This statement was made some nine years later and after he and Forrest had parted company.

During the summer Miss Clifton and Forrest played together in Albany and Buffalo. On the night boat to Albany they were reported to have occupied the same stateroom, and on the train from Utica to Rochester Miss Clifton was said to have been stretched out on a sofa in the saloon at the end of the car in such agony that John Hawkes, a physician of questionable reputation, was certain an abortion had taken place. Hawkes was not attending her, and his report, like Allen's, was given some years later.

For the month of August and the first half of September Forrest was back in New York with Catherine. In the fall he again returned to the road with Miss Clifton. His reunion with the Amazon did not push Catherine out of his mind. He wrote from Boston, thanking her for sending the Richard costume, the winter vest, and the hoarhound candy. All were most welcome. How he wished he could cut off his engagement and come home to her. If Catherine was suspicious of his traveling companion, his protestations should have comforted her.

Forrest was in good spirits during his three weeks in Boston. The little Fox girl, whose father was property man at the Tremont, recalled that the actor took great notice of her and taught her to recite Lady Macbeth's speech about "Out damned spot!" This tot later married G. C. Howard and became famous as the Topsy in *Uncle Tom's Cabin*. Her daughter, Cordelia, starting at age four, made a lifetime career out of playing Little Eva.

After Boston he had a two-week engagement in Philadelphia and a happy reunion with his mother and sisters, then returned to New York in a fearful snow storm and immediately left for Albany, in spite of Catherine's protestations. He reminded her that the weather had never kept him from fulfilling an engagement.

The trip to Albany was rugged. The ice in the river was so heavy that he and Miss Clifton were forced ashore twelve miles below the city. In spite of the storm a large and cheerful crowd appeared for the opening night. Forrest wrote to Catherine that in New York "under the same circumstances, there would probably not have been more than twenty people in the house." The fearful weather continued throughout the engagement, still the theatre was filled; people came in on "sleighs from all the neighboring towns."

When Forrest returned to New York in December, he found the theatre in the doldrums. Even his patronage, which ordinarily kept up in spite of any contrary trend, deteriorated so badly during Christmas week that on January 2, 1843, he decided to quit and take a three months' recess.

Invigorated by his layoff, Forrest expected a rejuvenation in public interest when he returned in April. It was not forthcoming. In some respects the situation was worse, for he was obliged to compete against his old friend Junius Brutus Booth, who had returned from retirement to stagger through his Shakespearean repertoire. Both men deplored the rivalry. They were old friends, not bitter antagonists. Frequently the two actors had supper together after their performances. One evening when he arrived at Booth's dressing room at the Park, Forrest found his namesake, young Edwin Booth, picking out "Old Zip Coon" on his banjo. Forrest began jigging, Junius joined in with a fancy heel-and-toe. In a few minutes the room was shaking with their wild steps, while the stage manager pled with Booth to return to the stage for his curtain call.

In June Forrest again decided to bolster his sagging profits with a summer season. When he boarded the Albany boat this time, Catherine, not Miss Clifton, was with him. After a week in Albany, they took the canal boat to Buffalo, then a lake steamer to Detroit. Forrest had never played Detroit, and though he was accustomed to primitive frontier theatres, Detroit possessed the shabbiest establishment that he had ever encountered. Inadequate scenery never bothered him; still, this place was impossible. According to Forrest, the red brick house on the drop used for Brabantio's Venetian abode (in *Othello*) needed only a poll parrot in one of the windows and a Jerusalem cherry tree in the other to be a Mercer Street dance house. (Mercer was then known as one of New York's "shadier" streets and not because of the trees.) The Detroit patrons were not troubled by the brick façade. In fact, they welcomed Forrest with such a clamor that the six nights he had bargained for had to be extended to eleven, and he was honored by another testimonial banquet, given by Lewis Cass, the former Governor General of the Territory of Michigan who later became a Senator and Secretary of State under President Buchanan. Forrest was always delighted to accept the hospitality of a fellow democrat.

On the return trip the couple stopped in Buffalo for a two-week engagement, where Catherine wrote a long letter to Forrest's sister Eleanora, detailing their adventure in the "Far West." After finishing in Detroit, they had gone by railroad to Jackson, the capital of Michigan, and then by stage to Battle Creek. "After this we abandoned the public conveyances so long as we travelled in Michigan—the routes taken by the stages being generally through the most uninteresting portions of the country, and the additional expense of a private conveyance being small, and the additional comfort great."

Catherine, like her husband, leaned toward romantic extravagance in reporting the wonders of the American countryside, though she occasionally sprinkled in practical observations. "Leaving Battle Creek, our road lay through one of the most beautiful portions of the State. For nearly twenty miles we rode through magnificent forests of huge old oaks, unencumbered by any undergrowth, and surrounded on all sides by wild flowers of every form and hue, roses, lillies, and the vivid scarlet lobelia everywhere growing up in the richest luxuriance."

In Kalamazoo they inspected the property his friend Goodman had purchased for him. Catherine noted that with the expected completion of the railroad the following year, these lots should increase in value. After a night in Kalamazoo they went to Niles, where "Goodman, who was standing at the door of his store, immediately recognized Edwin and stopped the carriage." They stayed with the Goodman family for two days, and Catherine was happy to report that "Edwin has settled all his business with him, and is satisfied that he [Goodman] has acted honestly." From Niles they went to St. Joseph on the shore of Lake Michigan, where they took a boat to Chicago, "a very pretty town." They stayed in Chicago only a day, then boarded the steamer to Mackinac, "a most beautiful little island, where there is an annual meeting of most of the Indian tribes, who gather there to receive their pay from the government. We walked on shore, saw a sufficient number of Indians to satisfy all reasonable curiosity, and in a condition which tends to destroy the romantic ideas we are apt to form of them." Forrest ignored the Indians; they were not acceptable company for Metamora.

According to Catherine, the journey had done wonders for Forrest's health. When they arrived in New York in mid-September, he was eager to get back on the stage. First he had a social obligation to perform: welcoming the British actor, William Macready, who had just arrived in the city. Forrest called on him at his hotel, took him for a walk to see the reservoir and the aqueduct, and brought him home to tea with Catherine. On October 3 Forrest gave a dinner party in his honor. Macready reported to his diary that the affair was "too large for comfort, but most kindly intended." He enjoyed his conversations with Bryant, Halleck, and Inman, the painter, and thought his host, "a clear headed, honest, kind man."

Macready relished the attention that was showered on him by Forrest and by others—Longfellow was one of his regular callers. He was not so happy in the theatre. He feared that American audiences had become too accustomed to exaggeration and extravagance to appreciate him. He was convinced when he saw Forrest play *Lear* in Philadelphia on October 21. His reactions have a special pertinence because at this moment no hatred or vindictiveness was apparent in his appraisal.

Macready reluctantly concluded that his prophecy of seventeen years earlier had been correct, that the young man would not properly cultivate his talents. "He has great physical power," Macready admitted, "but I could discern no imagination, no original thought, no poetry at all in his acting." One could not trust the liberal applause of the audience, for "the state of society here and the condition of the fine arts are in themselves evidences of the improbability of an artist being formed by them." Forrest had become the darling of this unintelligent crowd; a grave misfortune because he is essentially "an upright and well-intentioned man."

The English actor took a less charitable view a few days later. On Monday night he acted *Macbeth* at the Chestnut Street Theatre; on Tuesday Forrest did the same play at the National. On Saturday, October 28, Macready wrote in his diary: "Saw some papers affecting to make a comparative criticism on Mr. Forrest and myself in *Macbeth*! It was too bad, as the ignorant creature [the critic] showed in what he was obliged to state that Mr. Forrest did not understand the character; nor does Mr. Forrest understand Shakespeare. *He is not an artist.* Let him be an American actor—and a great American actor— but keep on this side of the Atlantic, and no one will gainsay his comparative excellence. Much disgusted. Rested and thought on *Richelieu;* determined to act it well, if I could, as Mr. Forrest, not handsomely, I think, was put up for the same night."

Macready was beginning to reveal his touchiness. Forrest was overstepping his bounds when he invited direct comparison. Such behavior reaffirmed Macready's opinion that he lacked taste. However, he was careful not to broadcast his views. When Wallack called and "declaimed against Forrest," Macready reported that he was "cautiously silent." He was becoming less cautious in his diary. On November 9 he noted: "Mr. Forrest's engagement at New York has failed; as it was got up *in opposition* to me and so *carried through*, I cannot affect regret at it." And later in Boston he wrote: "The more I reflect upon Mr. Forrest's acting and the impression made by myself, the more I am disgusted with the knavery and impertinence of Messrs. Willis and Co." N. P. Willis had been castigating him and praising Forrest in the *New York Mirror*.

Apparently no hint of Macready's growing resentment was communicated to Forrest. On December 8 Forrest called on Macready at the Astor House in New York to tell him of the friendly letter he had just received from Catherine Macready, the actor's wife.

The theatrical managers saw potential profits in the rivalry. E. A. Marshall, manager of the Chestnut Street Theatre in Philadelphia, proposed a spring engagement in which Macready and Forrest would appear on alternate nights. Macready declined the invitation; he knew the rabble would declare Forrest the victor. The Park Theatre contemplated a similar venture. "It is understood," one reporter noted, "that they propose a Napoleon-like movement, Macready, Forrest, and Josephine Clifton three nights per week and opera the other. Try it Simpson. Go ahead, old fellow!" This project, like Marshall's, went no further.

Macready's distress with the American audiences was shared by Forrest, for another reason. Macready deplored their uncouth behavior; Forrest, their lack of attendance. He reported in a letter that the Park had "lost its charm as a temple of the muses." The managers had talked of converting it to a circus arena, "a proposal which has my support. The sooner the change takes place the better."

With the depressed state of the theatre, to say nothing of the horrible weather, Forrest decided to go to New Orleans. He had another good reason for the trip, if one was needed: Macready had embarked on a Southern tour at the end of December. Forrest thought that his Southern friends should be given an opportunity to make a comparison.

Several changes had occurred in New Orleans since his last visit. The St. Charles Theatre had burned down in a spectacular conflagration on March 13, 1842. The fire had started in a small workshop near the rear windows of the theatre, invaded the paint room, and then "darted like a mad fiend among the paint and oil," the *Picayune* reported, "gathering such strength in three minutes that the flames seized the scenery and away it went raging with the rapidity of a powder explosion around the whole interior." Construction of a new St. Charles had begun the following fall and on January 14, 1843, the new theatre opened. Not so grand nor commodious as its predecessor, it seated only 1,500 compared with the first theatre's 4,000. There was no chandelier. Instead the dome was decorated with sixteen panels with white emblematic devices set against a salmon background. Above the proscenium a painting of Shakespeare floated "in a halo of light upon the pinions of America's eagle." The seating was arranged in a semicircle, (rather than an ellipse) so that the center box was only fifty-one feet away from the stage. The pit, divided into single numbered seats, became the most desirable part of the house for "those who attended with a sincere desire to see and hear the play." It was also equipped with patent furnaces "which introduced hot air *ad libitum.*"

This new establishment was under the management of Noah Ludlow and Forrest's old Cincinnati friend, Sol Smith; his former rival, Caldwell, had retired. The Ludlow and Smith partnership, begun in 1835, was to continue until 1853; "an extended quarrel for eighteen years," someone called it. Ludlow shifted back and forth between Mobile and Natchez. He had had five theatres in Mobile, two of them in partnership with Smith, and all five had burned down. The partners had moved into New Orleans in 1840 in protest against Caldwell's invasion of Mobile. With Caldwell now out of the running, Ludlow and Smith held almost complete control of the Western circuit.

Heretofore, Forrest had merely announced his bill, roared through his repertoire, acknowledged the ovation, and picked up his bundle at the box office. Now he had to combat Macready. Rivalry with a second-rater like George Vandenhoff, or a friendly match with the fading Junius Brutus Booth had never bothered him; Macready offered stiffer opposition. At the present moment Macready clearly held the advantage. He had been playing at the St. Charles since February 7, and had just closed his engagement on Friday, March 1. When Forrest began his two-week assignment on March 4, 1844, he faced not only an inevitable comparison with his predecessor, but also the problem of sustaining interest at the box office. Happily, he succeeded in both. The audiences still preferred the American actor's vigor to the Englishman's elegance. The *Picayune* observed that Forrest's *Richelieu* was "much freer and bolder in outline and had much more startling effects" than Macready's.

During Forrest's run at the St. Charles, Macready moved to the Royal Street Theatre in Mobile. After two weeks they shifted: Macready back to New Orleans and Forrest to Mobile, and when Forrest returned to New Orleans, Macready went up the river to St. Louis. Forrest did not relish the follow-the-leader role. He had no choice; Macready had started first.

Their engagements balanced out fairly evenly; Forrest was slightly ahead in New Orleans, Macready in Mobile. Forrest held an edge in public attention outside the theatre. On April 2 a group of the first citizens proposed a dinner in his honor so that "your many friends in New Orleans and the state may take you warmly by the hand for 'Auld Lang Syne' on the evening of your departure from the city." Forrest declined the invitation. His commitment in Cincinnati compelled him to leave immediately after his final night. He hoped to be back the next season for a farewell engagement. "My wishes and inclination," he wrote, "have for some time tended towards other pursuits than those which pertain to the stage." He did not elaborate on the "other pursuits"; probably they were not clear in his own mind, for this was the first time he had hinted that he might desert the theatre.

On his homeward journey Forrest bypassed St. Louis in order to catch up with Macready in Cincinnati. He made it just in time to move into the theatre when Macready moved out. Forrest was certain that the Cincinnati competition would put him clearly in front. He missed his guess, at least during his first week.

The *Cincinnati Enquirer and Message* insisted that the poor attendance resulted from his choice of plays. Their old favorite had forgotten his pledge to support the native drama. "We have waited in vain," they wrote, "for the personation of any of the sterling pieces which American writers have given the stage. The half-filled boxes of the National show, we think, that the public have heard enough of *Richard, Hamlet* and *Othello*. These plays have long since become a drug on the market. Give us *Jack Cade* and *The Gladiator*. . . . A word to the wise is, or ought to be, sufficient." It was. When Forrest shifted to the American plays during the second week, he re-established his pre-eminence and built his profits to $1,340, thus beating his rival.

The game of tracking Macready ended in Cincinnati. The English actor went up the Ohio to Pittsburgh and on to Philadelphia. Forrest swung back to St. Louis.

During his stay in Cincinnati, Forrest had been busy inspecting his Covington acreage and negotiating for the purchase of an additional plot of land. He and Catherine roamed over the Kentucky hills and slept in the new cottage for the first time. "The farm is looking in most excellent condition," he wrote to his mother. "Next year I think you might make a visit to the great West to see what improvements have been made."

When the Cincinnati engagement closed on May 20, they took a circuitous route to St. Louis, stopping first at Mammoth Cave, where Forrest insisted that Catherine crawl with him through the subterranean wonderland. From there they went to Nashville to visit "the brave old man at the Hermitage [Andrew Jackson], whose health I am rejoiced to hear has much improved in the last month or two," he wrote to his mother. "May he be spared yet to witness the downfall of the reckless party whose chief desire seems to be to benefit the few at the expense of the many."

From Nashville they struck out cross-country for the Mississippi, where they boarded the river boat *Frolic*. They arrived in St. Louis on Sunday, June 9.

Ludlow had expected them on Saturday. When they did not arrive, he announced a special benefit Monday night for "The Sufferers by the Late Great Fire in New Orleans." When the Forrests turned up on Sunday, he quickly pasted Forrest's name on the billboards. Again, as in Cincinnati, the audiences preferred the American plays. *The Gladiator,* on June 13, brought the largest gross ($519.50) of his St. Louis engagement and his most enthusiastic press notice. The *Republican* (June 14) insisted that "Those who see a superiority in Macready over our own great actor, must be blinded by prejudice; for not only have foreign critics pronounced him great, but the applause forced from the coldest spectators of his efforts, manifests that skill in the actor, which Macready fails in."

From St. Louis the Forrests went to Chicago and Detroit, then via lake steamer to Niagara Falls. They stopped in Buffalo for a brief engagement (July 4–13), then went across to Albany on the Erie Canal and back down to New York. It was a happy journey, retracing with Catherine the tour he had taken with Bird ten years earlier. In their five months of traveling together they had recaptured the faith in each other that a year ago seemed to be slipping away. Forrest's letters to his mother spoke regularly of Catherine's wifely devotion and invariably closed with some variant of "Kate joins me in sincerest love to all and I remain your devoted son."

When they arrived in New York toward the end of July, they went immediately to Philadelphia for a family reunion. After the cool refreshing breezes on the Lakes, the Philadelphia summer was unbearable, and Forrest bought a "summer blower" [1] for his mother's house to give them some semblance of comfort while he waited for his fall engagement.

---

[1] Forrest's receipt book gives no details about the "summer blower." It may have been an American version of Dr. J. T. Desaguilier's manually operated centrifugal blowing wheel (1734), or Dr. Stephen Hale's blower box (1741), a contraption employing valves and a diaphragm, also manipulated by hand, or the "air or ventilator pump" (1832) invented by two Philadelphians, George Harley and John Segwick. Unfortunately, the description of their device was destroyed in the patent-office fire in 1835.

CHAPTER xiii

Hisses in London and Edinburgh

Forrest had just begun his engagement at the Walnut Street Theatre on August 26, 1844, when he discovered that Macready planned to challenge him on his home ground. To enliven the competition Forrest took a layoff after his opening week, thus delaying his second week to run concurrently with Macready's. To tease his rival further, he put on a single night of *Damon and Pythias* on the Saturday before the Monday Macready was to open. He invited the English actor to attend, and, as if that were an inadequate taunt, announced that he, like Macready, would perform *Hamlet* on Monday.

Macready was not happy about the arrangement. He wrote in his diary on Saturday night: "Saw Forrest act Damon—a very dull, heavy-mannered, unpleasant performance. He is not a good actor—not at all an artist. He acts Hamlet on Monday in opposition to me, and I hear, made this *engagement to oppose me!* This is not the English generosity of rivalry."

It may not have been "English generosity"; neither was it good sense. Forrest was pitting one of his weakest roles against Macready's strongest. And if Macready's diary can be trusted, clearly the challenger won the opening round: "Forrest had not more (if he had that sum) than $200 to his *Hamlet*," he wrote. "If it be so, he is justly punished for his ungentlemanly conduct."

For the remainder of the week Forrest retreated to firmer ground with *The Gladiator* and *Metamora*. Except for one performance of *Richelieu* by Forrest and one of *Lady of Lyons* by Macready—plays common to both their repertoires—their respective adherents were given no further opportunity to make a comparison.

However miffed Macready may have been at Forrest's "ungentlemanly conduct," he maintained an outward show of friendliness. On Sunday, September 15, the day after their engagements closed, he "talked with him and went to sit with Mrs. Forrest, whom I like as pretty and amiable." They chatted for the entire afternoon without touching the tender subject.

Neither audiences nor press had yet split sharply into opposing camps, though signs of a split became increasingly apparent. On September 10, the Philadelphia *American Advocate* observed that the theatres offered "Native Americanism vs. Foreignism. Which of the two to choose? Why Forrest, of course." One reporter described Forrest as "a rough jewel of the first water; Macready a paste gem, polished and set off with every counterfeit gleam art could lend. The fire of the American commands honest throbs and tears; the icy glitter of the Englishman, dainty clappings of kid gloves."

Macready returned to New York on Sunday evening, and after a two-week engagement and an additional two weeks in Boston, went home to London. Happy as he was to escape from the land of the barbarians, he had been annoyed to learn that Forrest contemplated a trip abroad and even spoke of trying an engagement in Paris. Was this uncouth American intent on shadowing him wherever he went? Macready had himself scheduled a Paris engagement for December and January that looked unpromising enough without further complications. Helen Faucit had been engaged as his leading lady. She was a capable actress. Macready was aware, however, that she now had her own following and would probably be unwilling to subjugate herself to his will. A *Punch* reporter had once chided him for his arrogant disregard for her talent, remarking that Macready must have been fascinated with the beauty of Miss Faucit's backside. When they played together, that was the only part of her that he allowed the audience to see. If he were to contend with both Faucit and Forrest, Paris would be miserable.

All the brooding was done by Macready. Forrest was too busy crowding in as many nights as he could in New York, Boston, and Philadelphia before his departure. Even had he been less occupied, he was not inclined to fret over his problems, professional or domestic. He took his stand, announced it publicly, and drove toward a showdown on whatever course seemed clearest, quickest, and surest. He was incapable of burying his anxieties in the pages of a diary as Macready did.

Departing on a foreign junket was not so easy as it had been eight years earlier when he had neither wife nor house, nor so easy as packing his trunk for a month in Boston or a tour of the Western circuit. He anticipated at least a year away from home, perhaps more, and his wardrobe must be ready for the sharp eyes of Paris and of London. Allen was no longer tending his costumes; that task had been taken over by Catherine. She was industrious and willing, but she had neither "Dummy's" knack nor experience.

Catherine's sister Margaret, Mrs. Voorhies, volunteered to move into the house while they were away. James Lawson was to supervise all Forrest's financial affairs, giving Margaret as much money as required. Mrs. Underwood agreed to continue as housekeeper, and Catherine Levins as cook. Anna Flowers, the pathetic chambermaid who had been with them since June, volunteered to continue her service even though she was pregnant. The father, she confided to Mrs. Forrest, was Mrs. Forrest's friend, Captain Howard. Catherine gave her thirty dollars to buy clothes for the baby and advised her to forget about Captain Howard. Only one post in the household complement was unfilled. Barney McCabe, the waiter, had been dismissed the month before when the cook caught him in bed with Anna. Even without his services, Mrs. Voorhies had an ample staff, particularly since they had little to do except keep an eye on each other.

Forrest and Catherine finally cleared their way through the domestic and theatrical confusion, assigned their trunks to Captain Eldridge's care, and sailed on Christmas Eve. The pursuit of Macready was not Forrest's sole mission; he was eager to test his theatrical powers in Paris and again in London, and Catherine wanted to see her old friends. In the seven years they had now been married she had never been home.

The *Liverpool* docked in Liverpool on Sunday, January 12. The next day they went to London where Forrest left Catherine with her family. On Tuesday he hurried on to Paris. He had not bothered to make preliminary arrangements; he was certain that an engagement could be worked out when he arrived. He was too optimistic. Macready had advised Mitchell that Forrest was coming and urged the manager not to see him. Colonel John Mitchell controlled British theatricals in the French capital, as he also controlled the French companies that visited London. Forrest tried repeatedly to talk to Mitchell without success. At the hotel he was told that Mitchell was at the theatre. At the theatre they said that he was at the hotel. Disgusted with this evasion, Forrest gave up and returned to London, though not without sufficient snooping to convince himself that someone, and most probably Macready, had hatched the plot to keep him out of Paris.

Forrest did not brood over the rebuff. He quickly arranged a London engagement with J. M. Maddox, lessee of the Princess's Theatre in Oxford Street, and enlisted the American actress Charlotte Cushman as his leading lady. She had not yet made her London debut. To profit from the enthusiasm built up for that event without taking the edge off his own reappearance, it was agreed that she would open solo on Thursday, February 13. Forrest would join her the following Monday. This schedule had another advantage: if any anti-American sentiment was present in the house, it could be dissipated on her before he appeared.

Forrest's success in engaging Miss Cushman did not endear him to Macready. When she had arrived in London the preceding December, Macready had urged her to join him and had proposed that she replace Helen Faucit as his leading lady in Paris. Miss Cushman had gone to Paris to investigate the possibility. When she discovered that Macready wanted an actress who would play a soft second to him, she quickly rejected his proposal.

Maddox announced the February 17 opening night as an "immense attraction." Forrest felt on solid ground. He had excellent support, a powerful role, Othello, and his competition was far less formidable than that which he had encountered on his first visit. Drury Lane offered a Parisian dance troupe plus a Balfe grand opera, *The Daughter of St. Mark;* Covent Garden, Vandenhoff [1] and his daughter in Sophocles' *Antigone,* with music by Dr. Felix Mendelssohn Bartholdy executed by sixty male voices; and the Haymarket, a Douglas Jerrold comedy, *Time Works Wonders,* with Charles Mathews and Madame Vestris. Forrest had Shakespeare to himself.

He began the evening in high spirits, confident that he would overwhelm the audience with his matured interpretation; when he reached the final stabbing he was so unnerved that he was tempted to strike the blow in earnest. On his first entrance he had been welcomed with some honest applause and cheers, yet threaded through the applause he detected an ominous snaky hiss mixed with unflattering titters. He had never before been greeted in this fashion. That he was the object of disaffection was all too clear. Had Charlotte Cushman received the same treatment, it could have been attributed to anti-Americanism, but the hissers were conspicuously quiet when she appeared.

Forrest was thankful for a day's rest from the ordeal—he was scheduled only for alternate nights. When he returned on Wednesday, the villains were back to torment him. Obviously someone had engineered the affair. Forrest had his suspicions, but he was not to be tempted into a hasty accusation. For the moment he would ignore the rascals and give them and their manipulators a chance to reveal themselves.

Even though he carried on against the ungentlemanly oppo-

[1] John Vandenhoff must not be confused with George Vandenhoff, who had frequently been in competition with Forrest in New York and who later became Mrs. Forrest's tutor.

sition, it was a distressing engagement. On his previous visit, seven years earlier, he had expected to be challenged by the critics. Instead, most of them had showered him with praise. Now when he had reached his prime, they were lukewarm. *The Times*, previously one of his staunchest advocates, thought he had tried too hard to counteract the impression that he was "a physical actor" and had become too calm and deliberate, weighing every word instead of trusting his own impulse. The *London News* reporter found himself yawning while Forrest ruminated. According to the *Era*, Othello's address to the senators was read: "Most potent (pause) grave (another pause) and reverend sineyours," and so on through the entire speech; and included such horrendous pronunciations as "verches" for virtue, "meddercinal" for medicinal.

On Friday, February 21, Forrest shifted to *Macbeth* for five performances. This brought the critics up a notch, though they still chided him for his plodding declamation. Not until he turned to *Lear* on March 6, did he get off the ground; here he soared. The *Sun* called it a "decisive triumph"; *The Times*, "a masterly, intelligent, and powerful performance"; even the *Era*, which had been most harsh in its condemnation, found it hard to believe that this was the same man: "He was Lear from first to last." Only John Forster in his "Theatrical Observer" column in the *Examiner* continued to attack him. He labeled Lear "a roaring pantaloon, with a vigorous totter, a head waving as indefatigably as a china image, and lungs of prodigious power."

If Forster had tempered his tongue, his remarks might have been passed off as simple prejudice against the actor's American manner. He went too far. He thought Forrest's smile in *Othello* was "like the grin of a wolf showing his fangs"; his *Macbeth* excited more mirth than the best of our comic actors. Forster's barbs were so poisoned that their purpose was unmistakable. Forrest knew, as everyone did, that Forster was Macready's friend, his literary adviser, and his parasite, as one writer called him. From what Forrest learned of his character, he was convinced that Forster was capable of the vilest behavior. He was, according to one of his enemies, ashamed of his birth—his father had been a butcher—and was willing to become a "toady and lick spittle of the meanest sort" if it would elevate him in society. Undoubtedly Forster had hired the hecklers and may even have prejudiced his fellow critics against Forrest.

When Macready read of Forrest's "disastrous and total failure in *Macbeth*," he remarked to his diary that he was "truly sorry for him (without wishing him *great* success) and deeply sorry for his wife." He never revealed, even in his diary, any active participation in the plot to push Forrest out of the Princess's. His circumstantial connections with the affair were, however, impossible to escape.

At the end of February Forrest wrote to Bulwer-Lytton, requesting permission to add *Richelieu* and *Lady of Lyons* to his repertoire at the Princess's. Macready had introduced these plays in London, and Bulwer-Lytton, like Forster, was an intimate of Macready's. On March 4 the playwright replied. Forrest could do the plays—on exhorbitant terms: fifty pounds in advance, each play was to be given ten performances, and all twenty performances had to occur within a period of five weeks. No actor at that moment could have met Bulwer's conditions.

Other annoyances appeared to stem from Macready. Forrest was again unsuccessful in attempting to arrange with Mitchell for a Paris engagement. Certainly Macready's diary entry of March 2 hints that he had some secret knowledge of the attempt: "Called on Mr. and Mrs. Forrest," he wrote, "with whom were several people; to me he observed that he was going to Paris, where he would be better appreciated than he is here. I fancy *not*." In May, and again in June, Forrest was still futilely trying to take a company to France. He never succeeded.

Having his Paris plans thwarted angered Forrest. Before his departure he had announced to a Philadelphia audience that one of the great joys he anticipated was the opportunity to perform for the French, "those brave people who had been our allies during the War for Independence." The speech had been reprinted in the French papers, accompanied by flattering remembrances of Forrest's first visit and assurances that they longed to see this "Talma *de l'Amerique*," thus comparing him to their greatest tragedian.

There were other sources of irritation. An unidentified friend of Macready reported that when Macready called on Forrest on March 2 to invite him to his birthday party the next day, Forrest declined. Another said that in February Macready had asked the American actor to dinner and that Forrest had ignored the invitation. Another version suggested that Forrest was irritated because Macready had not asked him to dine. In later years, when the dispute became public property, such secret knowledge of the initial cause was bound to appear; even then each side denied responsibility for precipitating the final fight between the two actors.

Forster, Bulwer-Lytton, and Mitchell all disclaimed any share in machinations to suppress Forrest; however, their lengthy testimonials, which Macready solicited in 1848 when the quarrel approached a showdown, protested their innocence somewhat too extravagantly. Bulwer-Lytton wrote on December 16, insisting that Macready had "never directly or indirectly expressed even the remotest wish that Mr. Forrest should not act in any play of mine." In a later letter Bulwer claimed that impugning Macready was as "ludicrously glaring, as if we had heard a report that the Duke of Wellington had been broken for cowardice, or the Archbishop of Canterbury went to the Treadmill for picking pockets."

In this same series of letters, which Macready had printed in 1849 under the title *The Replies from England to Certain Statements Circulated in This Country Respecting Mr. Macready*, Colonel John Mitchell protested as fully and faithfully as Bulwer. Macready had not "in any manner direct or indirect, with me personally, or to my knowledge with any other person, attempted to interfere with, or prevent, any arrangement that Mr. Forrest might have desired to make with me for his appearance at Paris."

For some unexplained reason, John Forster, who undoubtedly knew more about the Forrest affair than the others, was represented in Macready's collection by proxy. Albany Fonblanque, proprietor of the *Examiner,* replied for Forster, asserting that he could not go so far as to say that Macready "never attempted to influence the *Examiner* as to Mr. Forrest; for I am aware that you did attempt to influence it to forbearance towards him."

Macready may have exercised forbearance during Forrest's visit to England in 1836; pitifully little evidence of it appeared now in 1845. At this moment Macready was disinclined to invoke charitable feelings for any fellow actor. Helen Faucit was outdistancing him in audience favor. Charlotte Cushman continued to rebuff his solicitations. "This woman is full of the idea of her own importance," he moaned to his diary. And Forrest held on at the Princess's in spite of the opposition. To add to his unhappiness Macready had to admit to himself that he condemned his competitors "as much from a feeling of envy as an impatience of injustice. . . . In this profession we seem to suppose that distinction, except to oneself, is an obscuration of oneself. This is very narrow and poor and bad." Macready's private repentance did not help Forrest.

The reception of *King Lear* had restored Forrest's confidence momentarily. After the Easter holiday, when he tried *Metamora,* he lost the ground he had gained. The few feeble cheers for his portrayal of the Indian were overshadowed by the complete condemnation of the play. *The Times* said that they had never seen "such utter rubbish." The *Era* called it a senseless production: "To untangle the plot of *Metamora* was as difficult as to discover perpetual motion."

Forrest's chances of getting a solid hold at the Princess's appeared painfully remote. When he received an offer of an engagement from Sarah Macready, manageress of the Bristol Theatre, he quickly accepted. Charlotte Cushman had been included in the invitation. She refused, and for good reason. London had not seen a full-bodied, Mrs. Siddons-like actress in some time, and they meant to hold her. Pleased as Forrest was to have a fellow countryman so well received, his spirits were not raised by seeing the preference cast so unmistakably for her and observing her continue triumphantly until the 15th of July while he was driven to the provinces.

Forrest concluded at the Princess's with a final *Lear* on April 7. On the following Monday he began a week of four performances with Mrs. Macready: three at the Theatre Royal, Bristol, and the fourth, Saturday night, at the Theatre Royal in Bath. He was happy enough to escape the battle at the Princess's, though not overjoyed to seek refuge with his rival's stepmother. The audiences gave him a warm enough reception; the press was less kind. The *Bristol Mirror* observed that he was an actor of "considerable merit," that if he nursed his talents they might "do much to form and reform the uncultivated minds of his fellow countrymen." This patronizing pronouncement did not endear Bristol to him.

At the end of the week he returned to London. Soliciting engagements in the provinces was not easy; too many actors were available. James H. Hackett, the American comedian who had come over on the same ship, was on the road, as were Macready, Helen Faucit, Mr. and Mrs. Charles Kean, the Vandenhoffs (father and daughter), Master Betty, the child prodigy, and Ira Aldridge, "the African Roscius." Forrest had arrived in a crowded season.

He decided to try Dublin. Macready was playing in Belfast, and if he went immediately he could head him off from Dublin. Forrest suspected that if the English were down on him, the Irish would cheer him. He was right. Even before he opened, on Saturday, May 3, the *Freeman's Journal* announced that they had read his notices both from his native land and from England and that they were "more disposed to place confidence in their American friends than that of the more pretentious tribunal in London." Forrest possessed the revolutionary fervor and flamboyant manners to stir up the Irish. They had never seen an actor like him. For a solid month the crowds at the Theatre Royal shouted and stamped like the boys at the Bowery. The critics, too, perceived his superiority. His Othello was "glowing with the divine fire of genius, that wonderful electricity by which the inmost nature of man is moved." Not since

Kean had there been such a Lear. Forrest was particularly thrilled that *The Gladiator* aroused the Irish. They loved to see his brawny muscles generously exposed—only his waist and upper thighs were covered—and to hear Spartacus' noisy invectives against tyranny.

One performance of *The Gladiator* (May 15) might have ended calamitously had not the audience secretly applauded Forrest's impolitic behavior. The royal box was occupied by the Lord-Lieutenant of Ireland, Sir Edward Blakeney, Major General Wyndham, and a full complement of officers from the garrison. During the play Forrest ignored them and at the final curtain studiously avoided bowing toward their box. He was a democrat; he loved the Irish and despised their English masters and refused to strike a hypocritical pose just to ease the tension. Neither the English nobles nor the Irish commoners acknowledged the affront, yet both caught its significance. The incident passed without comment.

When Forrest concluded in Dublin on May 29, he returned immediately to London. Coming back to Catherine would have been more pleasant if he could have escaped the reunion with the Sinclairs. He spent as little time in the house as possible. On several evenings he went to the theatre with N. P. Willis. Willis was one of the American journalists who had spoken out for Forrest and against Macready during the British actor's recent visit to the United States. Now he appeared to be so inflated with British culture that Forrest suspected that he would change his tune when he returned home. Forrest was always depressed when he saw an American succumb to British snobbery. Let it happen to Willis; it would never happen to him.

Forrest could not endure hanging on in London, camping with his in-laws, with the uncomfortable reminder of his spring fiasco so close at hand. Charlotte Cushman was still going strong at the Princess's. He took Catherine up to Scotland for the summer where he could escape his professional worries and at the same time indulge his passion for ancestor worship, tramping around Edinburgh County among the scenes of his father's boyhood.

When they returned to London, Forrest settled Catherine with her family and departed. He had no intention of humiliating himself with another engagement in the city. Let Forster gloat if he wished; Macready could have a free field in London. He would seek his fortune in the provinces. Unhappily, even there he did not command the red carpet. When he arrived in Manchester on September 29, he discovered that the edge had been taken off his appearance by Charlotte Cushman's visit the week before. What was even more annoying, he was obliged to appear at the "second" house, the Queen's Theatre, in opposition to Jerrold's *Time Works Wonders* at the Theatre Royal. On opening night all the local officials chose Jerrold instead of *King Lear*. The next day the newspapers clearly indicated that the "second" theatre had the top attraction. The *Manchester Guardian* reported that his "energetic muscular action, his fierce shouting and hoarse ravings" surpassed anything ever heard in the city.

This was higher praise than Forrest at first realized; the Manchester audience was well acquainted with "shouters." Gustavus Vaughan Brooke, the principal supporting player at the Queen's, was Forrest's British counterpart, a man of powerful physique and strong lungs. When Brooke played Iago to Forrest's Othello during the Manchester engagement, his fellow actors goaded him to try to outshout the American. It was a noisy evening; neither won, but each developed a friendly respect for the other's laryngeal prowess. When they discovered their common distaste for Macready, they became fast friends.

On Monday, October 6, Forrest opened at the Theatre Royal in Liverpool. Although scheduled for a single week, the theatre was so crowded every night and he was hailed with such "vehement applause," that a second week was added, and finally an extra benefit performance on Monday the 20th, at which he played *Lear* and the first two acts of *The Gladiator*.

Forrest had a difficult time in the provinces, not because of Forster's campaign to undermine him—it had not carried outside of London—nor from any chill in the audiences, but simply because there was too much competition. After Liverpool, he scheduled five performances in Belfast during the last week in October and seven in Glasgow in mid-November. These were the only dates he could secure. In December he went back to London to spend the holidays with Catherine and to map his campaign for the spring.

He kept up a steady correspondence with the provincial managers and by early January had arranged a solid schedule for the remainder of the season, beginning in Sheffield on January 19, 1846.

Sheffield gave him a strong welcome. Audience, critics, and actors combined to make it his best engagement to date. The critics properly noted his tremendous power, yet praised him more highly for his delicate handling of the quiet passages. On Othello's line, "And you, ye chaste stars," for example, instead of staring up into the stage house, he looked out the window. The *Iris* reporter thought that this demonstration of "natural" acting was a stroke of absolute genius.

The supporting actors, including Brooke in the secondary roles, were heads above any he had found previously, and apparently Forrest rewarded their competence by treating them more politely than was his custom. At any rate, after his benefit night, the actors ushered him to the greenroom and presented him with a silver snuff box, inscribed "To Edwin Forrest, Esq., by the members of the Sheffield Theatrical Company, as a mark of their esteem for him as an ACTOR and a MAN. January 30, 1846." These ceremonial boxes—the one he had received at Drury Lane on his previous visit was made of tortoise shell and gold—were the conventional tokens for such occasions. No implication that the recipient was a snuff addict was intended, or that he was being encouraged to take up the habit. Forrest was touched by the honor and told them so. According to a press account of the occasion, he said that these little courtesies shown to one another could be "productive of a vast amount of good. I cannot but remember that I, too, have gone through the 'rough brake,' that I, too, began the profession in its humblest walks; and I have not forgotten the pleasing and inspiring emotions that were awakened in my youthful breast when I have received a kind word, or an approving smile, from those who were 'older and better soldiers' than myself." Sheffield was all sweetness and light. What a heartening contrast to London!

His next stops were in Edinburgh (February 9 to 15) and Aberdeen (February 24 to 27). At the Theatre Royal in Aberdeen the gallery was full on opening night. However, only three ladies and less than a score of gentlemen occupied the boxes, and four rows of empty benches were evident in the pit. The *North of Scotland Gazette* reporter, who made this calculation, insisted that Aberdeen was unwilling to pay advanced prices for this "accidental star." Ordinarily, Forrest would have rebelled at both complaints. Instead he donated his services for one night of *Othello*, permitting the prices to be lowered. Perhaps his charitable impulse arose from some feeling of loyalty to his father's native land; whatever prompted him, his generosity was wildly applauded.

In Edinburgh he was not obliged to make any concessions. Press and public alike gave him a strong reception. One perverse critic complained that his Othello was painted to look more like a Shawnee or Mohican than a Moor,[2] but the *Weekly Chronicle* asserted that he was one of the great actors of the age. His intellectual grasp, his vigorous and striking execution, and above all, "his rare faculty of expressing by face what neither pen can write nor tongue can tell," entitled him to be compared with the best. The public was urged to return to the theatre in two weeks when they could see for themselves how he compared with Macready.

Throughout the fall and winter Macready and Forrest had

---

[2] Max Factor cosmetologists would probably shudder at Forrest's make-up formula. In 1827 he recorded in his notebook: "Composition for the face of Othello. Burnt terra de sienna, unburnt terra de sienna, ivory black number one quality; the above colors must be ground with almond oil on a glass stone—to be ground to the utmost then placed in a bladder and tied up."

followed separate paths. During October and most of November Macready had remained at the Princess's in London. In December he had gone to Belfast; in January and February he was back at the Princess's. Even with Forrest and his other rivals out of sight, he was perpetually oppressed with hostile thoughts. "Reflected much on the tendency to selfish and envious feelings in my nature," he wrote in his diary on October 6. "I *have no right* to be dissatisfied with any performer, male or female, whether I have helped them to obtain distinction or not, for choosing the course that seems most eligible to them, even though that course be in direct hostility to my interests."

On October 28, 1845, Macready had arranged with manager William Murray for a March engagement in Edinburgh. On Friday, February 27, 1846, he concluded his run at the Princess's, and on Sunday arrived in Edinburgh. Forrest closed in Aberdeen on the 27th, and with a week's break before his next engagement, he decided to go to Edinburgh and have a look at his rival.

On Monday night Macready paced through his *Hamlet* at the Theatre Royal, encouraged that the Edinburgh audience seemed more attentive than usual. He was unaware that he had a distinguished visitor in the upper box. When he reached the crucial court scene where Claudius' guilt is exposed, Macready was confident that he was giving one of the best Hamlets of his career. The King and Gertrude were on the throne, the "players" ready in the wings, awaiting Hamlet's summons to enter and re-enact the "foul murder." Hamlet surveyed the scene, and on the line, "I must be idle," began dancing back and forth at the front of the stage pretending unconcern. Before he completed one full circuit a loud and stinging "Hissssss" sprayed from the upper-right box. "The audience took it up," according to Macready, "and I waved the more, and bowed derisively and contemptuously. . . . It discomposed me, and alas! might have ruined many; but I bore it down."

Forrest never denied the hiss and made no effort to conceal

his identity. However, not until two days later was Macready convinced of Forrest's villainy. On Tuesday, his fifty-third birthday, he began to suspect that Forrest was the offender. He was not fully persuaded until Wednesday when he got the report of eye-witnesses and of the police officer who had been on duty. "I feel glad," he noted in his diary that day, "that it is not an Englishman—but no Englishman would have done a thing so base; indeed he dared not have done it, and that is one argument in my mind for my belief in Mr. Forrest's guilt. I do not think that such an action has its parallel in all theatrical history! The low-minded ruffian! That man would commit a murder, *if he dared*." Once Macready's suspicions were confirmed, he envisioned all sorts of diabolical possibilities.

Forrest did not shy away from the consequences. He intended the rebuke and had no wish to apologize. He was surprised at the storm. The hiss apparently kept ringing in Macready's ears for the next three years.

The first public accusation appeared in the *Scotsman* two days after the event. It insisted that the audience had been loud and enthusiastic in their admiration, only a single culprit had "made himself unenviably conspicuous by loud and repeated *solitary* hissing." What was more deplorable, the offender had been a brother actor, though not a member of the English dramatic fraternity. Forrest did not dispute the fact. He did object to the aura of villainy that was cast around him. When he learned that Macready had sent the *Scotsman*'s report to London where it was reprinted in *The Times* and *Examiner* on March 12, Forrest wrote to the *Scotsman*. When they ignored his letter, he sent a copy to *The Times* of London, where it was printed on April 4.

Forrest insisted that he did not wish to prolong the argument. He felt obliged to speak only because the affair had assumed such a "questionable shape." As every one knew, there were two "legitimate modes of evincing approbation and disapprobation in the theatre, one expressive of approval by clapping hands, and the other by hisses to mark dissent." Hissing, he maintained, was "a salutary and wholesome corrective of the abuses of the stage." He had not approved of Macready's fancy dance; it desecrated the scene. A fellow actor, when he was on the grounds as a spectator, had as much right as anyone, and certainly he was better qualified than the layman, to determine when a hiss was appropriate. Since the general public received their only knowledge of the affair from the newspapers, he must point out that he had "warmly applauded several points of Mr. Macready's performance," and several times when the audience had been unwilling to "second me in so doing." As to the pitiful charge of "professional jealousy," that was sheer nonsense. Any of his associates in England or in America could testify to that point.

Forrest's statement did not terminate the argument, though the wildest exchange of charges and countercharges did not occur until two years later. On November 20, 1848, Macready renewed the quarrel when he told the audience at the Arch Street Theatre in Philadelphia that he had never shown any hostility to any American actor in England. He declared, on his "sacred honor," that all such reports were completely false. On the other hand, he had been hissed in a public theatre by an American actor, "an act which I believe no other American would have committed."

The next day Forrest countered with a "Card" in the *Public Ledger*. Why, he asked, did this pussy-footed Englishman allude to "an American actor? Why not openly charge me with the act, for I did it, and publicly avowed it." Other observations in Macready's curtain speech must be corrected. "I assert, and solemnly believe," Forrest wrote, "that Mr. Macready connived with his friends to hiss me, with the purpose of driving me from the stage, and all this happened many months before the affair at Edinburgh, to which Macready refers, and in relation to which he jesuitically remarks that, 'until that act, he never entertained toward me a feeling of unkindness.' Pah! Mr. Macready has no feeling of kindness for any actor who is likely by his talent to stand in his way."

The matter did not rest there. In December 1848, Macready solicited letters from his friends in England that would, he thought, provide an unshakeable defense. Some of these have already been noted; others dealt with the simple question of the "hiss." In spite of Forrest's willing admission that he was the man in the upper box, Macready insisted on amassing testimony to prove his guilt. William Murray, the manager, and John Ryder, an actor in Macready's company, both identified Forrest as the culprit. J. Gordon, High Sheriff of Edinburgh wrote: "Believe me, there was but one hiss and one hisser. Forrest was the hisser—Forrest's was the hiss." These letters were only concerned with pointing the villain. Further details of what occurred at the Theatre Royal on the evening of March 2, 1846 must be found elsewhere.

Probably the most vivid account of the incident was supplied by John Coleman, the actor who played Marcellus. In his *Fifty Years of an Actor's Life* he wrote:

> Macready wore a dress, the waist of which nearly reached his arms; a hat with a sable plume big enough to cover a hearse; a pair of black silk gloves, much too large for him; a ballet shirt of straw-coloured satin, which looked simply dirty; and, what with his gaunt, awkward, angular figure, his grizzled hair, his dark beard close shaven to his square jaws, yet unsoftened by a trace of pigment, his irregular features, his queer, extraordinary nose—unlike anything else in the shape of a nose I have ever seen —and his long skinny neck, he appeared positively hideous. . . . Macready had acquired various tricks, one of which was to strut from side to side just before the play scene, extravagantly flirting his handkerchief above his head and behaving less like Hamlet than Osric. On this Edinburgh night, when he knew himself to be acting with particular power and discrimination and the audience was cordially with him, he came to the line "I must be idle." As he spoke, he waved the handkerchief, and from the upper boxes on the right-hand side of the stage, there issued a long, sustained hiss like the sound of a steam engine.

Coleman peered from the wings and spotted the man, "his square brow, noble head, dark eyes, blue-black beard, bulldog jaw above a turned-down white collar, and arms folded on his broad chest. It was Edwin Forrest, looking as he had in *The Gladiator* when he said, 'Let them come; we are prepared.'"

If Coleman's description of Macready's Hamlet is correct, the audiences must have been remarkably tolerant not to have expressed their disapproval long before Forrest gave them the cue. No doubt they had become accustomed to Macready's prancing, for according to Forster he had been using this "business" in *Hamlet* since 1835.

What happened on the succeeding nights of Macready's engagement? Here the evidence is less reliable. Some insisted that when Macready performed *Hamlet* again on March 9 and 16, "the whole house hissed." Macready noted, on the 9th, that he "felt rather nervous and uneasy from the uncertainty whether this American ruffian may not have left some colleague or hireling here instructed to renew the insulting outrage on me." And on the 16th, "Perhaps the editor of the *Weekly Chronicle*—Mr. Forrest's friend—might say there was hissing at the handkerchief tonight!!!" Macready referred to an article in the *Edinburgh Weekly Chronicle* of March 14. The reporter had asserted that on Monday, the 9th, when Macready again introduced the *pas de mouchoir,* a few injudicious admirers attempted to applaud the harlequinade, while most of the house hissed. The High Sheriff insisted that no hissing occurred on either the 9th or the 16th.

Forrest was not in the theatre on either of these occasions. Apparently he was on hand for *Lear* on March 4. Macready reported to his diary the next day that the "poor creature" had been "conspicuous by laughing and talking in my principal scenes." One reporter noted that Forrest accosted a Mr. Gibson in the theatre that evening and asked him if he was not the editor of the *Scotsman.* The man shrunk away, muttering that he was not. "That is fortunate for you," Forrest was reported to have said, "for had you been, by the living God I would have flung you over the balcony into the pit!"

Macready struggled along with his Edinburgh engagement until March 17. He was liberated from Forrest's annoying presence, if not from the critics and the audiences. The *Weekly Chronicle* was particularly vicious in comparing him with Forrest: his Hamlet was "too tortured," his Lear had none of the American's electrifying quality. Most of all Macready was oppressed with the "slaughterous work" of acting to audiences who preferred such uncouth ruffians as Charles Kean, Helen Faucit, and the vile American. "I am not one of the Edinburgh wonders," he moaned. When he tallied his proceeds, he sadly discovered that he had earned less than he had twenty-one years earlier for a similar engagement. If he could have fixed all the blame on Forrest's villainy, he might have been less unnerved. Unfortunately, he could not.

Forrest did not stay in Edinburgh to observe his rival's disintegration. He went to Carlisle for three nights, beginning on Monday, March 9, and on the 16th rejoined Brooke for a two-week engagement in Manchester. News of the Edinburgh incident had spread rapidly in the profession, and most members of the brotherhood cheered Forrest's protest. They shared the view of the *Weekly Chronicle* reporter who had said that Macready's mechanical system of acting utterly destroyed the vitality of the other performers. They "go like clockwork to particular spots," turn their backs to the audience, and stand like wooden Indians, not daring to "lift a hand or move a muscle." Macready's face was the only one on view. Apparently at least one other actor, emboldened by Forrest's success, had registered an additional protest. When Forrest went to Dublin in mid-April, he wrote to Brooke: "If it be true that Mrs. Leigh Murray *has* chastised that brute Macready for his insolence, she should be rewarded by the profession with a handsome and valuable piece of plate, the actors here say they will subscribe with pleasure." After the Edinburgh affair, Forrest did not conceal his distaste for Macready. He once remarked of an actress whom he disliked that her face looked as if Macready had sat down on it. He was the first to applaud any actor who invented new devilment for his arrogant adversary.

After his humiliation of Macready, Forrest would probably have found London more antagonistic than it had been a year earlier. In the provinces the public became more enthusiastic. The *Carlisle Journal* said that not since Kean had they seen an actor with more "energy and truthfulness." The *Manchester*

Guardian insisted that he was even better now than he had been in the fall. The Irish were ecstatic.

Forrest had a wild two weeks in Dublin. He had feared that the audience might be reduced because he was succeeding Charlotte Cushman and her sister Susan. Their curious production of *Romeo and Juliet*, Charlotte doing Romeo to Susan's Juliet, had been drawing tremendous crowds. Forrest's opening night, April 13, cleared away his doubts. The Theatre Royal in Hawkins Street had never been so packed. In fact, the gallery had been oversold and the spectators in that region kept up such a tumult throughout the evening, chiding their more comfortably accommodated neighbors in the pit and boxes, that Forrest had difficulty in making his *Richard III* carry over the noise.

It was a thrilling, if somewhat odd, engagement. Forrest was accustomed to the inconsequential farces that were presented after the tragedy. In Dublin, for the first time in his career, he shared the stage with a dog. The celebrated French dog Emile, acclaimed for his "extraordinary sagacity," appeared each evening in *The Dog of the Pyrenees* following Forrest's play. Dublin had a passion for eccentric bills. On Forrest's benefit night, April 22, he played Act Two of *King Lear*, Act Three of *Macbeth*, Act Two of *Hamlet*, Act Two of *Richard III*, and Act Three of *Othello*; all this in one evening, plus Emile.

The Dublin engagement concluded on Saturday, April 25; the following Monday he opened in Cork. Although scheduled for a single week, so many would-be spectators were stranded in Cook Street outside the theatre that the engagement was extended for a second week. Cork provided an inspiring finale to his English adventure, which had begun so badly. Never had he received such extravagant attention. The reporters declared that he was "glowing with the divine fire of genius"; he was unquestionably the "foremost living actor." *Jack Cade* sent the audiences into a frenzy. The invectives against class tyranny, "unveiling at a glance the narrow foundation upon which it bases its power and usurpation," struck at the fiery soul of every Irishman. This was not *acting*, the *Examiner* insisted. "Forrest seemed so thoroughly and entirely to identify himself with the struggles of an enslaved people; every spirit-stirring sentence was dashed off with the energy of a man in earnest as if it had its birthplace in the heart rather than in the conceiving brain."

After his final night on May 11, billed as "positively his last appearance in Europe," the audience refused to leave the theatre until Forrest spoke to them. He was exhausted after *Macbeth*. If they would forgive his weakness and his feeble language, he would attempt a few words. He assured them that he would never forget their courtesy and hospitality. In bidding them adieu he hoped, as they did, "that the dark cloud that overhangs this fair country will soon pass away; that a happier and brighter day will beam on her, and that Ireland and her people will long enjoy the prosperity and happiness they are so eminently entitled to." When he stepped back with a final bow, such a roar burst forth that the manager feared that his theatre would be shattered before their fever cooled.

Cork was a minor, out-of-the-way spot on the theatrical circuit, yet the Corkers gave Forrest the wildest reception he had had since leaving home. On his final day they summoned the local poet laureate, who was also named Edwin Forrest, to compose a tribute. His sonnet, printed in the *Cork Examiner*, might not place high in a poetry competition, but the Cork and Philadelphia Forrests alike were enchanted:

> *O'er the rough mass the Grecian sculptor bent,*
> *And, as his chisel shaped the yielding stone,*
> *Rising, the world-enchanting Venus shone,*
> *And stood in youth and grace and beauty blent.*
> *Thus o'er each noble speaking lineament*
> *Of thy fine face, thy genius, FORREST, shines,*
> *And paints the picture in perfection's lines. . . .*

Recalling his sour initiation at the Princess's a year earlier, Forrest was happy to conclude on such a strong note. It had been a satisfying spring. Audiences and critics had cheered him, and in Edinburgh he had partly avenged the malicious treatment he had received in London.

From Cork Forrest went to Killarney to rest from his labors, to tramp around the lakes, and to explore the ruined castles and monasteries before returning to London. Back with Catherine and the Sinclairs, he was impatient to be on the move again. He stayed only long enough to deliver the principal speech at the American colony's Fourth of July celebration at the Lyceum Tavern. The next day he and Catherine sailed for a vacation in the south of Spain and for a side excursion to Mauritania (Algeria). Catherine apparently contracted a fever somewhere along the way that was to plague her for the next few years. Forrest bought two Spanish paintings that were later installed in his New York house. Nothing more is known of the journey; he kept no record.

On August 8 they were back in London, and a week later sailed for home. A farewell performance was announced for Liverpool just prior to his departure. For some reason it never materialized.

The *Rochester* was a slow vessel, taking twenty-eight days for the crossing. Forrest did not complain; he was happy to be away from London, alone with Catherine, and on his way home. At the first sight of the sun in the early mornings he was out of his cabin for a rapid hike around the deck and a chat with Captain Britton on the bridge before going down to join Catherine for breakfast. He and the Captain became great friends, and during the next few years John Britton never sailed into New York harbor without stopping for a visit at Twenty-second Street, usually arriving with a barrel of flour or a case of London porter.

CHAPTER *x i v*

Scandal in Cincinnati

When the *Rochester* docked in New York in early September 1846, the pier was crowded with the usual noisy reception committee. Forrest begged them to hold off their full welcome until after his *King Lear* on the following Monday night. He had inhaled too deeply of the Atlantic's windy blasts and was being punished with a cold. Given four quiet days to gargle it away, he would be ready to acknowledge their greeting.

Monday was a hot day. In spite of the temperature, the spectators squeezed into the suffocating atmosphere of the Park, and when the final curtain closed, "the pit rose in mass, and long and loud was the applause, clapping of hands, thumping of canes, waving of hats, and handkerchiefs, ending with nine cheers." The same reporter noted that though Forrest was still struggling against a cold he responded with a short curtain speech in which he assured the audience that "while a pulse beats here or memory continues, I shall ever remember the emotions of my soul at this reception."

As he ranged through his repertoire during the next two weeks, the critics carefully scanned his performances to see if his British sojourn had affected his acting. They were delighted to report that without losing his old fire, he had become "more subdued and quiet," his "actions and attitudes appeared more classic," and in general his performances depended less on "unrepressed energy and overwhelming physical power." Lest anyone think in reading these reports that he had gone over to the British, on his final benefit night Forrest explained that he was still the champion of "American dramatic letters" and "of our own meritorious and deserving actors." To set them straight on the Macready business, he declared that he would "blush to imitate that narrow, exclusive, prejudiced, and I may add, anti-American feeling which prescribes geographical limits to the growth of genius and talent." When he took his final bow, " a garland, enclosing a copy of verses addressed to him, fell at his feet." He raised it and retired while the orchestra and the audience struck up "Home, Sweet Home."

One critic maintained that Forrest had returned to this country "a soured and disappointed man." The evidence does not support this view either in the theatre or at home on Twenty-second Street, where the house was filled with callers and the mailbox with letters welcoming him home. On October 11 he received the inevitable proposal for a jubilee celebration:

> Dear Sir,—The undersigned, your friends and fellow-citizens, desirous of expressing to you personally the high estimation they entertain for your public and private character, avail themselves of the occasion of your return from Europe to invite you to a public dinner and request that you will set apart one of the few days you are to remain with us, that may be most convenient to you, to accept this slight tribute to your professional excellence and private worth.
>
> We are, with great respect,
> Your obedient servants

The list of forty-four "obedient servants" read like a New York *Who's Who*. Among them were William Cullen Bryant; Parke Godwin, Byrant's son-in-law, author of the recently published *Popular View of the Doctrines of Fourier*; Fitz-Greene Halleck, author of "Marco Bozzaris," the stirring poem on the Greek struggle for freedom; Evert Duyckinck, prominent bibliophile, whose magnificent library has now become one of the invaluable possessions of the New York Public Library; Judge Charles P. Daly, brother of Augustin Daly, the future theatrical impresario. It would have been difficult to prepare a more distinguished roster.

Scandal in Cincinnati

On Friday, October 16, Broadway between Washington Place and Waverly Place was crowded with carriages jockeying up to the entrance of the New York Hotel. The banquet hall was decked with flowers and ribbons. It was a gala affair, the first big event of the fall season. William C. Bryant sat in the president's chair, flanked by Forrest and four honorary vice-presidents. After everyone was satiated with food and the covers removed, the speeches and toasts began. The first was to "Our Country"; the second, to "The American Stage: its brilliant morning gives promise of a glorious day." The third, to the guest of honor, was proposed by Byrant after an appropriately flamboyant introduction. Bryant praised Forrest's skill in infusing the shadowy outlines of the dramatist with "the blood and breath of life." Yet he commanded greater honor for his personal virtues. "In the intense competitions of the stage," —here Bryant alluded to the Macready trouble—"Mr. Forrest has obeyed a native instinct in treating his rivals with generosity. He has preserved the magnanimous silence of conscious greatness." Bryant concluded in the manner of a twentieth-century master of ceremonies introducing a guest star: "Gentlemen, I will no longer withhold from you the toast,—I give a name, without a sentiment,—a name which suggests a volume of them,—I give you our guest, Edwin Forrest." "The toast was drunk," according to one newspaper account, "amidst a tempest of demonstrations."

When the cheers subsided and the glasses were back on the table, Forrest responded. As in his previous testimonial replies, he alluded to the old familiar voices that were raised in kind approval of his early efforts. Taking advantage of Bryant's opening, he spoke for the first time since his return of his troubles abroad: "Even before I had appeared I was threatened with critical castigation, and some of the very journals which, upon my former appearance in London, applauded me to the echo, now assailed me with bitterest denunciations." He was pleased to report that the "sober second thought of the people rebuked the malice of the hireling scribblers, and defeated the machinations of theatrical *cliques*." In Edinburgh his reception had been extremely gratifying and as for Ireland, "I need scarcely tell you that in the land of the warmhearted Irishman an American is always at home."

When a description of the banquet reached Macready, he was depressed to hear that such seemingly intelligent men as Bryant and Halleck had spoken of Forrest's "professional excellence and private worth!! . . . America!! Give me a crust in England," he wrote in his diary.

After the celebration, Forrest threw himself into a furious homecoming schedule: two weeks in Philadelphia, two in Boston, back to Philadelphia for another two, and in early December back to the Park in New York. A strain on him, yet nothing to what it was for the local actors. Before going to Boston, he advised the manager of the Federal Street Theatre to call a rehearsal of *King Lear* at ten o'clock and of *Metamora* at eleven thirty on the morning of his arrival. What miraculous rehearsal maneuvers must have been used to put *Lear* in shape for the evening with an hour-and-a-half sprint through a three hour play!

In spite of his absence of almost two years, the ranks of his followers had expanded. Only infrequently did a spectator or a reporter dare to suggest that Forrest was not the best of all possible actors. One off-beat writer in the Boston *Pilot* maintained that Forrest indulged in too much sound and fury; " 'He puts in his licks whenever he gets a chance,' as Yankee Doodle would say, and as often as he can raise a plaudit by so doing." In *Othello*, "he snorts and howls through five acts, looking and talking up to Heaven every two or three minutes, with a countenance like Satan, and deporting himself generally like a man in hydrophobia, and at the end metamorphoses into a suicidal fop, makes a magnificent speech, and sends himself to perdition like a sentimental gentleman who has committed forgery."

Another perverse complaint came from an inconspicuous reporter on the *Brooklyn Eagle* named Walt Whitman. (This was nine years before the publication of *Leaves of Grass*.) Whitman recognized Forrest's genius in making "the hearts of the masses swell responsively to all those nobler manlier aspirations in behalf of mortal freedom." He deplored the evil influence that he exerted on his vapid imitators, who lacked his control. "If they have to enact passion, they do so by all kinds of unnatural and violent jerks, swings, screwing of the nerves of the face, rolling of the eyes, and so on. . . . It is a common fallacy to think that an exaggerated, noisy, and inflated style of acting—and no other—will produce the desired effect upon a promiscuous audience."

As long as the audiences stormed the box office, Forrest could brush aside these minority reports. Happily, they did. He had a strong New Year's Day *Metamora* at the Park, a profitable two weeks in Philadelphia, and on January 16 went south for three weeks of work and sunshine in Charleston, Augusta, and Savannah.

Forrest had been acquiring real estate at such a rate that he could not afford a vacation if it did not at the same time produce profit. Since his return from England, he had bought a house on Twenty-first Street directly back of his own, two rental properties on Twenty-second, a cottage in New Rochelle, and while in Savannah had had word from James Lawson that his $10,000 offer for acreage on the east bank of the Hudson, just below Yonkers, had been accepted.

The balmy Southern weather and his pride in his new affluence could not take his mind off a new worry. Before he left Philadelphia, his mother had not been well. When he had offered to cancel his trip, she had insisted that nothing other than her eighty-four years was responsible for her frailty. When he returned in March, she seemed weaker, yet she was strong enough to insist that he fulfill his April engagement in New York. When he came back to Philadelphia in May, she was relieved to have him by her side. In the evenings he must go to the theatre, with her assurance that she would not die while he was away. She kept her word. She passed away quietly in her sleep on June 24, 1847. The next day Forrest wrote to his friend James Lawson:

My mother is dead. That little sentence speaks all I can say, and more—much more.

> Yours truly,
> Edwin Forrest

The sorrow sounded from the depths of Forrest's heart. He had lost the one person to whom he had anchored his whole being. Somehow every step he had taken as long as he could remember had been guided by her. As he once wrote to a friend: "When I was tempted to do wrong, thought of my mother, of her love for me, of her faith and character, of what she would wish me to do and to be, came and drove the offending temptation away." His mother's passing was a shattering blow from which he never completely recovered.

Long after her death he visited her grave regularly. Some twenty years later he copied a poem into his notebook entitled "My Mother's Grave," the last lines of which ran:

> *I have but one sad wish, when life is o'er,—*
> *Whatever fate is mine, on sea or shore,*
> *Who'er may claim my ashes for a trust,*
> *They still may come to mingle with thy dust.*
> *'Tis fit this troubled heart, when spent with care,*
> *Again should turn to that unfailing breast,*
> *And find at last the home my childhood shared,—*
> *The quiet chamber of my mother's rest.*

Shortly before his death, Forrest wrote to a Boston friend: "When I saw her great eyes fixed on me, beaming with satisfied affection, and listened to words of approval from her lips, O it was more to me than all the public plaudits in the world! My God, what a joy it would be to me now to kneel at her feet and worship her! And they say there are no such meetings hereafter. I know not, I know not. I hope it *is* so."

No one, not Catherine nor his sisters, knew how much of himself was buried in the St. Paul's churchyard. He struggled to piece together the remnants, to fashion a conscience of his own that might guide him as his mother had. He never completely succeeded. He did not shy away from choice, from decision, from judgment, nor hesitate to defend his rights, yet somehow he never captured the assurance he had always felt with his mother to sustain him. Before her death his personal and professional life had ascended smoothly and rapidly. After she was gone he was hounded with one shattering experience after another. The louder he protested, the more his troubles increased. His professional powers were unaffected; he still packed the theatres. But between performances he was bedeviled with problems and doubts.

During the month of July he stayed in Philadelphia, comforting his sisters and trying to find peace for himself. In August he broke away, returned to New York, and on the 30th plunged into his fall season at the Park. It got off to a bad start. After his opening night of *King Lear*, he had another attack of the hoarseness that had plagued him the year before. He was forced to withdraw for a few nights. This was not the only annoyance. The Park Theatre had almost collapsed. There were holes in the floors, the benches were covered with rags, a foul odor polluted the atmosphere; and, according to one reporter, the spectators in the pit were obliged to keep their feet off the floor to give the rats running room as they raced back and forth during the performance.

During the twenty-seven years of the Park's second incarnation, Forrest had often been the principal attraction; his first *Metamora* had been done there. Now the old glory had faded. October 29, the final night of his re-engagement (he had taken a two week interval in Boston), marked his farewell to the Park. In December the house was turned over to a circus, and a year later it burned down.

Its dilapidated condition was not the only factor that hastened its final demise. The Park could not withstand the competition of two new theatres: the Broadway and the Astor Place Opera House. The Broadway, a large and sumptuous house seating 4,500, located on the east side of Broadway between Pearl and Worth streets, had opened in September. During the next ten years it replaced the Park as the "theatre of stars," and the scene of Forrest's new triumphs. Some thought it began badly by catering too much to imported stars. Bryant, in an editorial in the *Evening Post,* asked if "it was to be an American establishment of the highest class, or did it propose to go on the old beaten track, merely a house of call for such foreign artists as may find it agreeable or profitable to visit."

The Astor Place Opera House, on Astor Place just off Broadway, opened in November. It seated 1,800 and was designed for the aristocracy. The first-night playbill, for Verdi's *Ernani,* announced that no lady was to be admitted unaccompanied by a gentleman. This "kid-glove" approach never proved profitable. After five years of struggling to entice the upper-crust, the Opera House abandoned theatricals, shifted to books, and became the Clinton Hall Library. Its one period of exciting notoriety came in May 1849, when the disastrous Astor Place Riot occurred during a Macready engagement.

After his last night at the Park, Forrest made the melancholy journey to Philadelphia for a three-week stand at the Walnut Street Theatre, three weeks among the gloomy reminders of his mother's death. By the end of the month he was so thoroughly depressed that he had to escape. He wrote to the Western managers telling them that he was available, returned to New York, and plunged into the project he and Catherine had been mulling over: a castle on the Hudson. Now they would settle the matter, get the building under way, and sail for New Orleans.

Day after day during December and January Forrest braved the winds that blasted down the Hudson and whistled around the hills at Riverdale (just south of Yonkers). He climbed up and down the slopes above the river searching for the site that would give a commanding view of the river. He paced off tentative perimeters, drove stakes, and then circled around to view the castle as it would look from various angles. In the evenings he and Catherine sat before the fire on Twenty-second Street with sketches and books fanned out around them, trying to piece together their dream castle. One of the books they must have pored over—it is still in the Forrest Library—was John Rutter's *Delineations of Fonthill and Its Abbey.* This

XVII Forrest *first played* KING LEAR *when he was twenty-*
one. Throughout his life he made a study of insanity and
in his mature years insisted that he knew more about the
subject than most doctors.

XVIII In 1866 Crosby's Opera House in Chicago was the scene of one of Forrest's greatest professional triumphs, with gross receipts of $11,385 for five nights.

XIX Forrest and James "Acorn" Oakes were devoted friends for forty-five years. They were said to have become so much alike that one was frequently mistaken for the other.

XX Forrest's final appearance in New York City in 1872, reading Shakespeare from the platform in Steinway Hall, where Charles Dickens had appeared some four years earlier.

XXI Forrest had a private art gallery and a little theatre in the south (left) wing of his Philadelphia town house at Broad and Master.

XXII After Forrest's death his Philadelphia town house was purchased by the Philadelphia School of Design for Women (now the Moore Institute of Art). The above picture of the garden was taken at graduation time some years ago.

XXIII The present Edwin Forrest Home at 4849 Parkside Avenue in Philadelphia was opened in 1928. Here twelve old American actors are invited to spend their declining years, all of their needs provided for by the Forrest estate.

XXIV The entrance hall of the Edwin Forrest Home, as it now looks, filled with Forrest memorabilia.

"make-believe [English] Cathedral, looking like a church turned into a drawing-room by a crazy bishop," as Forrest described it in a note on the flyleaf, was located at what is now called Fonthill-Gifford, two miles north of Tisbury, about six miles northwest of Salisbury. It had been built in 1796 by the eccentric traveler and country gentleman William Beckford, whose father had been Lord Mayor of London. Since the time of King John, the site had been variously labeled Fountell, Fontel, Funtell, and finally Fonthill, presumably "from the local circumstance of the abundant springs that gush from the sides of its hills." What remains of the Abbey at Fonthill-Gifford is now inhabited by a Major James who jealously guards its antiquity with a forbidding chain and "no trespassing" sign at the main gate.

By the middle of January, with repeated inspections of the grounds and with long architectural evenings in the library, Forrest and Catherine finally settled on plans for their American Fonthill Castle, turned them over to the Hudson Valley builder, Thomas L. Smith, and boarded a boat for New Orleans.

As many times as he had visited New Orleans, he invariably found something new; this time, a new American Theatre, a plain and neatly decorated establishment seating 1,500, which had been built in 1842 on the site of its old namesake. The American boasted a removable stage that could be struck in a few minutes, leaving a "fine arena" for equestrian performances. Forrest would have gone to Ludlow and Smith's St. Charles had it not been pre-empted by the "Viennese Children," an Austrian ballet group. Ludlow and Smith were not disturbed; they controlled both theatres. Forrest, however, was not happy to compete with the forty-eight prodigies from Vienna. While they were averaging a gross of $800 per night, the best he could do for his opening (February 7) was $500.

It was probably not his annoyance with these terpsichorean moppets, nor the attack of gout that forced him to miss two performances, nor the sprained ankle from a fall on the wet pavement that kept him out for two weeks in the middle of the run, that prompted him to announce his retirement from the stage.

According to a newspaper account of his final night (March 24), Forrest told the audience that "the little bell which a short time since sounded for the fall of the curtain, rang also the knell of my professional experience in your city." He planned to withdraw from "the laborious toils of the stage while yet in possession of an unimpaired constitution," in order to pursue other tasks, "entirely unconnected with public life." For the first time Forrest intimated that his castle building was to become a full-time enterprise.

Forrest had intended to stop in St. Louis on the homeward circuit, until Smith rebelled at paying the $200 per night guarantee. He bypassed St. Louis and went directly to Louisville. Louisville also had a new theatre, completed just two years earlier: a handsome four-story building with three tiers, and with all the seats stuffed with hair and covered with the finest Brussels carpeting. The new upholstery did not help his engagement. The houses were pitifully small. Several nights running the receipts dropped $50 below Forrest's $200 guarantee.

Bates hoped to recoup his loss when Forrest moved on to his Cincinnati theatre. Even without that prospect he would have hesitated to trifle with Forrest as Smith had. Managers learned to their sorrow that it was futile to haggle over terms. When Forrest received a plea from Smith to come back to St. Louis under any arrangement, he ignored the letter. When Smith wrote again, Forrest finally replied from Detroit, three months later: "Sir, I regret I cannot appear in St. Louis under your management; no amount of money could induce me to do so." According to Sol Smith, this was the last letter he ever received "from one whom I had cherished as a sincere friend for twenty-six years." Friendship and charity were forgotten when Forrest was dealing with managers.

The engagement at the National Theatre in Cincinnati turned out as Bates and Forest expected. The manager had profited by his Louisville experience; he raised the prices, advising the public that no one who desired to see Forrest should "carp at the manager's endeavors to save himself." No one objected; Forrest was greeted with "deafening applause" at each performance. He was in good spirits. On Tuesday, the 18th, he even allowed Bates to schedule John Brougham's burlesque, *Metamora; or the Last of the Pollywogs,* as an afterpiece following his own *Metamora.* Normally Forrest would not have permitted this spoof of his ranting stage Indian. The bill was a managerial coup; according to one reporter, it drew the "largest house ever crowded into the National Theatre."

For his final two weeks the theatre was filled every night even though he was competing with Barnum's midget, General Tom Thumb, and Hudson's *Panorama of the Ohio and Mississippi.* Before his last night, word had evidently leaked out of his proposed retirement. One reporter remarked that it was "as if the sun were to set at midday." On his final benefit night, May 13, Forrest announced his plans.

The audience wept at the thought of losing their old favorite. No one who heard the farewell speech guessed that the month in Cincinnati signaled a turning point in Forrest's career more radical than his proposed retirement. The public was unaware of what one reporter later called, "the first intimation of a kink in his domestic relations."

One afternoon Forrest and Catherine had invited George Jamieson to accompany them to a lecture on phrenology. Jamieson had played Iago to Forrest's Othello at the Park the previous spring and was now in the Cincinnati company. The lecture was at three o'clock; at one Forrest went for a sitting to a local portrait artist, leaving Catherine alone at the hotel. Not finding the artist at his studio, Forrest returned sooner than expected. The account of the episode is best given in Forrest's own words as recorded in an affidavit three years later:

> When I entered my private parlor in the City Hotel, I preceded S. S. Smith [not Sol], who was with me, some yards, and found Mrs. Forrest standing between the knees of Mr. Jamieson, who was sitting on the sofa, with his hands upon her person. I was amazed and confounded, and asked what it meant. Mrs. Forrest replied, with considerable perturbation, that Mr. Jamieson had been pointing out her phrenological developments. Being of an unsuspicious nature, and anxious to believe that it was nothing

more than an act of imprudence on her part, I was for a time quieted by this explanation.

The affair precipitated no immediate outburst. Forrest maintained a show of affection toward Catherine, though the seeds of suspicion had been planted. When they left Cincinnati, he noticed that Catherine "carefully preserved about her person a bundle of letters." He did not at the time question her about the parcel, but he was unable to gloss over the episode completely; he began to piece together past incidents. He wondered if Catherine's passion for partying—giving dinners and soirees even when he was away—was as innocent as he had believed. N. P. Willis and his wife had been regular visitors. Frequently they had been accompanied by Willis's brother, Richard, who came ostensibly to help Catherine's sister, Mrs. Voorhies, with her singing. Forrest knew Catherine depended on socializing much more than he, and certainly she deserved compensation for the loneliness his absences inflicted. Much as he brooded, he did not confront Catherine with his suspicions.

From Cincinnati they went up the river to Pittsburgh. If Forrest was preoccupied with his domestic crisis, it was not apparent in the theatre. He was delighted and astonished with his Pittsburgh engagement. According to the *Post,* Forrest captivated even "the persons who stoutly aver that 'the theatre is a sink of vice.' There is something in his acting that brings out the best instincts of the soul." Forrest must have wondered how he had missed bringing out the best instincts in Catherine's soul. If he had known more of her activities, he would have been even more concerned.

When they backtracked through Cincinnati on their way to Chicago, he did not know that she had another visit with Jamieson, nor did Forrest see the letter she wrote from Chicago to James Lawson in New York. This was the famous Fourier letter, so called because she adapted her text from Charles Fourier's freewheeling doctrines, which had been widely circulated by Parke Godwin, Horace Greeley, and the Brook Farm crowd. Catherine explained to Lawson that it was a "fearful thing to think of the numbers who, after a brief acquaintance, swear solemnly to love each other while they 'on this earth do dwell.' Men and women boldly make this vow, as though they could by the magic of these few words enchain forever every feeling and passion of their natures. There would be fewer family jars if each were pecuniarily independent of each other. The relative position of husband and wife must be that of companions; not mastery on one side, and dependence on the other." Clearly Catherine thought that their marriage had been too hasty, that she was now enslaved by her dependence on him.

Whatever inner doubts may have tormented him, Forrest continued his professional schedule. He performed in Chicago for the first time. Although he had visited the city on previous occasions, not until the Chicago Theatre, located on Randolph Street near Dearborn, had been completed during the preceding year did the city offer an inviting opportunity for the actor. Now under John B. Rice's management—he was later to become Mayor—the new theatre had placed the city on the map of the Western theatrical circuit. During a busy and profitable two weeks Forrest suppressed his suspicions. However, when he closed on June 21 and announced to Catherine that their next engagement was to be in Detroit, she rebelled. She insisted on returning to New York.

Ordinarily he would not have submitted to her whim. Under the present circumstances, he thought it the wiser course. He advised the Detroit manager that the engagement must be delayed, took Catherine home, stayed with her for a week, and then set out to fulfill his commitments in Detroit, Cleveland, and Buffalo, leaving her alone in New York. When he returned, Mrs. Underwood, the housekeeper, told him that Catherine had entertained Jamieson on two occasions during his absence.

Two days later, he received a letter from his sister Eleanora hinting that she had read in the newspapers some oblique references to trouble on Twenty-second Street. Forrest replied immediately: "They are lying chronicles and the amount of truth they utter upon any subject might be put in a nutshell." Their only trouble was that "Kate has been suffering from severe headaches caused by exposure to the sun when we were in the south of Spain, but I hope by great care and restricted diet she will soon be restored to her usual good health." He did not intend to let a clique of wagging tongues jeopardize his domestic bliss.

In fact, when he began his month's engagement at the Broadway Theatre on August 28, 1848, and Catherine, while he was at the theatre began to hold open house for her friends with what he thought was too much wine-sipping and cigar-smoking, he did not complain. If he had known that when he took to the road later in the fall, the parties were to become more raucous and stretch into the early hours of the morning he would have prohibited them immediately.

His success at the theatre may have partly blinded him to what was happening at home. On his opening night all of the 4,500 seats at the Broadway were filled and some 3,000 people were turned away. The *New York Herald* predicted that it would be "the most brilliant season ever known to a New York theatre." Similar reports appeared day after day throughout the month: "The theatre could have been filled three times." "There was such an immense assemblage that one could scarcely get a peek at the stage." "Forrest draws a class of people who seldom attend the theatres—numerous Germans and foreigners who scarcely understand the language, yet they appreciate his genius." He was riding high on Broadway if not on Twenty-second Street.

Forrest had apparently forgotten his retirement announcement in New Orleans and Cincinnati. He did, however, desert the theatre during the first two weeks in October to take over as "straw boss" at Fonthill. The heavy gray granite stones of the outer shell were nearly in position. In a month or less the roof would go on. He and Catherine could begin the delightful task of transforming the castle into a home. If it now looked like a monolithic monument perched above the Hudson, Forrest visualized it as it would appear in the spring when the foliage softened its grim outlines and he and Catherine took up their posts as lord and lady of the manor.

He interrupted his construction duties only long enough to fill a two-week engagement in Boston. In early November he was back in New York, and on Saturday, November 11, Smith and his men were ready for the "roofing ceremony." Forrest loved these commemorative occasions and, with a chance to stage it himself, he gave the workmen the biggest celebration that the Hudson Valley masons and carpenters had ever seen. An improvised banquet table was set up in the central hall. After they had all gorged themselves, the cloth was removed. Forrest insisted that everything should be arranged as if they were gathered in a fancy New York hotel. More wine was brought on for the toasts, and Forrest began the speechmaking. He praised the men for their industrious and temperate habits. From the laying of the cornerstone to the roofing, no accident had occurred and no harsh words had interrupted their harmonious consecration to their task. For those among them who might question his motives in raising such a monumental structure, he read a copy of the document that had been placed in the cornerstone:

> In erecting this edifice I am impelled by no vain desire to occupy a grand mansion for the gratification of self love; but my aim is to build a durable spacious and comfortable abode for myself and my wife to serve us during our natural lives, and at our death to endow the building with a sufficient yearly income, so that a certain number of decayed or superannuated actors and actresses of American birth (all foreigners to be strictly excluded) may inhabit the mansion and enjoy the ground thereunto belonging, so long as they lived, and at the death of any one of the actors or actresses inhabiting the premises, his or her place to be supplied by another from the theatrical profession who from age or infirmities is unable to obtain a livelihood upon the stage. The rules and regulations by which this Institution is to be governed will be framed by me at some future date.

Forrest concluded with a pat on the back for Thomas L. Smith, their kind and liberal architect. Now that the task was nearly completed, he prayed that "the Great Architect of the Universe would smile upon and bless them all." The newspaperman who wrote up the event reported that they gave him a rousing "nine cheers" that reverberated through the empty castle. After the cheers had subsided one of the workmen, who had been spotted as the orator, replied:

> That great artist, who honors you today by his company was once a poor boy—a very poor and unknown boy—with scarcely a friend to say "God speed you." But he knew that industry and perseverance would help him onward to wealth and fame. . . . You have raised a monument that will stand as a beacon-light to the present and future generations; for, so long as that noble river, the Hudson, shall lead its thousands and tens of thousands of human beings onward, so long the uplifted eye will look upon the rays of the rising or the setting sun that will linger on the summit of those towers, and the lesson on which every person may learn will be, that as industry, perseverance, frugality, temperance and genius have raised stone upon stone, so there is hope for you all.

Forrest would have liked to continue his daily excursions to Fonthill, to speed up the day when they could move in. He was obliged to turn to more pressing matters. He had heard that Macready was planning to play in Philadelphia; he thought it only proper that he should be on hand to welcome him.

"*Sweet Consuelo*"

Ever since Forrest had left England in the summer of 1846, Macready had been smarting under the Edinburgh hiss and had become increasingly depressed over his failing theatrical fortunes in England. He finally decided his only hope was to try America again. When he arrived in Boston, he immediately questioned his decision. "I fear it is not *possible* to live here," he wrote in his diary, "how *triste* and gloomy! What a hopeless dilemma: No peace in England! No peace in America!" His spirits were badly in need of repair even before he braved a theatre audience. Longfellow noted in his journal that when he came to dine on September 25, he looked "pale and ill."

When Macready opened at the Astor Place Opera House in New York on October 4, his confidence was temporarily restored. A polite and appreciative audience reminded him that Americans were not all blackguards. Still he was on the defensive. When he acted *Hamlet* on October 12, he feared "some friends of Forrest might be in the theatre on purpose to give colour by their disapprobation to the 'justice' of his outrageous conduct in hissing me." Ironically, Laertes and not Forrest's friends ruined this performance. Macready was badly cut up in the final sword play.

The sympathetic audience at the Opera House could not counteract the persistent annoyances. The newspapers were filled with scurrilous attacks. When he assured W. C. Bryant that he "had been passive throughout all that had occurred" in England, the poet appeared to distrust his protestation. The other theatrical managers attempted to disrupt his engagement by concurrently offering two disgusting burlesques: *Who's Got Macready? or; a Race to Boston* and *Mr. Macgreedy; or, a Star at the Opera House.*

When he returned to Boston on October 30, he was chastised by the Boston *Mail*: "Mr. McReady [they refused to spell his name correctly] has at length arrived, and next to the grand water celebration will create such excitement, as will emphatically mark the present epoch in time's calendar. He plays this evening at the Howard Athenaeum, and refuses to show himself for less than one dollar a ticket." This extravagant demand at the box office was not his greatest offense: "It is his conduct in his own country in relation to Mr. Forrest, that we are about investigating; his inhospitality, his crushing influence, his vindictive opposition, and his steadfast determination to ruin the prospects of that gentleman in England, that we bring to his door. Let him deny them if he can." After his performance of *Lear* on November 8 he was utterly depressed. "The curtain fell," he wrote in his diary, "and the audience, who would have cheered on a thick-headed, thick-legged brute like Mr. Forrest, took no notice of this, my best performance. This is the civilization—the growing *taste* of the United States!!!"

If prospects for the future had been less gloomy, Macready might have withstood the butchering attack on his ego in these two initial engagements, but he saw no hope. He had not yet directly encountered his adversary. While he was in New York, Forrest had been occupied with his castle. When he returned to Boston, Forrest had just departed. However, when he arrived in Philadelphia on Saturday, November 18, one of the first persons he met on the street was the rude American: "I did not look towards him, nor speak, as that would be to acquit him of the unworthy and ungentlemanlike conduct he has displayed to me."

On Monday night they both opened in *Macbeth*. Macready was not consoled when he read the *Public Ledger's* announcement of the event. "This evening commences a week of theatrical rivalry. . . . Macready has to contend with age. Forrest is in the prime of a vigorous and robust manhood." Macready needed no reminder of this melancholy thought.

To prepare himself for the ordeal, Macready ate a light dinner and took "no stimulant." Before the play his friend and fellow actor, John Ryder, warned him that there would likely be a disturbance. There was. When Macready entered, the applause was mixed with the "hissing, coarse noises, etc., of the ruffians." "I received it unmoved," Macready reported to his diary, "and went on braving it." He braved a copper cent thrown at him during the third act, a rotten egg in the fifth, and a continuing clatter of "noise and outrage" throughout. At the final curtain the applause of the "bulk of the audience" prevailed, and he was able to deliver his curtain speech unmolested. As already noted, he protested his innocence in the London affair and assured them that if they wished him to relinquish his engagement as of that night, he would gladly depart. Macready reported that this proposal was greeted with a "No! No! No!" and that when he concluded his remarks "the applause was most fervent."

According to the next day's newspaper accounts both actors had immense audiences. Forrest had the upper hand in the battle. Not only was he on home ground; he wisely held his fire until Macready made the first move. His "Card" (already quoted) published in the *Public Ledger* on November 22 pointed out the nonsense in Macready's speech and concluded with a stinging insult. Forrest insisted that many friends had urged him to rally his followers and drive the villain from the Astor Place Opera House at his first appearance one month earlier. Forrest advised them to "let the superannuated driveller alone"; he would destroy himself. Some of Forrest's adherents thought that his "Card" was too harsh. In a letter to one of them he explained that "the axe and not the pruning hook was necessary." Englishmen must be cuffed into a proper conduct toward us; a milder treatment would have no effect.

Macready could not ignore Forrest's "Card." He ordered his own "Card" "to be put into the hands of all who entered" the

Arch Street Theatre on the night of November 22. Forrest's charges were completely without foundation, yet he did not propose "to bandy words upon the subject." He requested the public "to suspend their judgement upon the questions until the decision of a legal tribunal." The next day he turned his case over to two Philadelphia lawyers, W. B. Reed and George Meredith, "with authority to commence such legal proceedings as they might deem advisable." Two days later (November 25) he dispatched a bundle of letters soliciting evidence from his friends in London and Edinburgh. Before the replies reached him in the middle of December—the pertinent passages from them have already been cited—his lawyers persuaded him to abandon his plans for a libel suit. Macready could not, however, bear to conceal the damaging indictments contained in the letters from England. He had them published in May 1849.

While Macready was busy building his case, he could not escape the nightly humiliation of playing in opposition to the American villain. Forrest continued to badger his rival. As soon as Macready's evening program was posted, the bills at the Walnut Street Theatre announced Forrest in the same attraction. Only if Macready chose one of his inferior roles in *The Stranger* or *Werner,* which were not in the American actor's repertoire, could he escape the disrespectful taunts of his adversary.

The public thrived on the excitement. "This theatrical *emeute*" the *Public Ledger* observed, was "the most laughable affair that has recently happened. The two great thespian rivals making speeches and shooting paper pellets at each other's scenes in the form of cards, remarkable only for exceeding bad temper and coarse language. Somebody should dramatize this great feud immediately."

Forrest's attack shattered Macready's composure. When he read Forrest's "Card," he felt that his "personal safety" was not to be relied on, and ordered the Treasurer to post "at least ten police behind the scenes," and before going to the theatre emptied his "purse of some of its gold, in case I should be assaulted." The more he wrote of his worries, the more he exaggerated the danger. "If Mr. Forrest could have induced my assassination, he would have rejoiced in doing it, and if he dare take my life, I am confident he would gladly do it. Let me once get from this country and give me a dungeon or a hovel in any other, so I be free from this."

Macready could not afford the luxury of leaving the country immediately. He had to be satisfied with the temporary relief of getting out of Philadelphia. He closed his engagement with *Hamlet* on Saturday night, December 2. On Sunday he went to New York, leaving Forrest to gloat over his success in driving him away.

When Catherine heard that Macready had acknowledged defeat by cutting short his engagement, she sent Edwin her congratulations. During the fall she had followed the affair, cheering her husband on. When Macready had first appeared in New York in October, she had written to Forrest in Boston reporting that the "superannuated" actor had gotten little attention but "there's a good time coming for him in Philadelphia." When she read of the exchange of "Cards," she urged Forrest "to give it to him."

If some might question the propriety of her partying in his absence, certainly her letters revealed a constant wifely solicitude. When Forrest caught a cold in Boston, she advised him, "for mercy's sake to wear his flannel when he was acting, and to keep taking his *nux vomica* [an old East Indian remedy]— two drops on a small lump of sugar, once a day." She was busy at home copying *Metamora* parts for him and sewing a new Spartacus costume. When Forrest was in his last week in Philadelphia, she asked, when is "my own precious childie" coming home? And she appeared genuinely disappointed when he went to Baltimore from Philadelphia instead of coming to New York.

Forrest's side of the correspondence was equally sweet and ardent. He hated to be away from her, was delighted that she approved his "Card," and overjoyed with her reports on Fonthill. From Baltimore, he wrote: "This is a warm, bright, beautiful day, and I am sitting at an open window in the Eutaw

House; and while I write, there is above me a clear, blue, cloudless sky—just such a day as I yearn to have with you at Fonthill."

During Macready's week respite in New York, the English actor gave two Shakespearean readings at the Stuyvesant Institute. On Saturday, December 9, he went to Baltimore to begin his Southern and Western tour. Braving the American wilds and contending with stupid actors and uncouth audiences was not a happy prospect; as if this were not enough, on Sunday he discovered that Forrest was also in Baltimore. Just as in Philadelphia, when Macready announced his evening bill at the Front Street Theatre, Forrest challenged him with the same play at the Holliday Street Theatre. Both actors drew large audiences, and apparently no disturbance occurred. Forrest insisted that his Philadelphia "Card" had actually been of great service to Macready in a pecuniary way; it had stirred up public interest in seeing his "*pas de mouchoir,*" which, according to Forrest, he was now rendering with "*tours des forces*" (*sic*). Forrest was not the only one who held this view. Dickens wrote a joshing letter to Macready, asking if it were true that he had paid Forrest five thousand pounds to "perpetrate his published card"; it would have been cheap publicity at twice the price. Good business was not enough to placate Macready. Although scheduled for two weeks in Baltimore, he could not endure the torment. He quit after the first week, leaving Forrest again in command.

He went to Washington and Richmond, and then down the coast to Charleston. Released from Forrest's needling, he still found little peace of mind. He worried over his meager profits, his advancing years—"I saw in the glass today [January 4] that I really am an old man," and everywhere he found some stupid reporter praising Forrest for his courage and honesty. Macready was scheduled to open in New Orleans on January 29. He refused, however, to leave Charleston until he was assured that the cholera epidemic in the Crescent City had subsided. When he finally arrived on February 12, Sol Smith insisted that he include Sunday performances to make up for his late arrival.

For four weeks he played nightly at the St. Charles. The rigorous schedule was not the only annoyance. Macready insisted that he had never encountered a stupider group of actors. The only pleasant memory he took from New Orleans was that of the farewell dinner given for him at the Verandah Hotel on March 29, at which his place was set with a model of Shakespeare's home at Stratford made out of confectioner's sugar.

In Cincinnati, acording to the *Enquirer* "not only the B'hoys with the machine [fire engine] but the 'bully butcher boys' of our 'Brighton' area" made life miserable for the English actor. At a performance of *Hamlet* on April 2, he reported to his diary, "an occurrence took place that, for disgusting brutality, indecent outrage, and malevolent barbarism, must be without parallel in the theatre of any civilized community. A ruffian from the left side of the gallery threw into the middle of the stage the half carcass of a sheep!"

Ever since he landed in Boston, Macready had become increasingly depressed, and the future looked even gloomier. He read in the New York papers that "friends of mine and this blackguard Forrest" intend to make the occasion of my reappearance "a signal for a conflict." He received a telegram in Cincinnati, saying that Forrest had been engaged to open at the Broadway Theatre on April 23, just long enough in advance of his own engagement to stir up trouble. When he arrived in New York on April 28, his spirits were sagging, yet he doggedly refused to side-step the inevitable showdown.

During Macready's absence, Forrest had refused all offers of an engagement. Only once did he break his pledge. On February 8 he appeared in *Macbeth* at the Astor Place Opera House in a benefit for the Dramatic Fund Association, just three months before Macready was to begin his ill-starred engagement in the same play, at the same establishment.

Forrest had not retired to conserve his energies, or because he schemed to spring at Macready when he returned to New York. He was too absorbed with his domestic problems—finishing his castle and fighting to sustain his faith in Catherine—to worry about Macready. At moments it looked as if he might end up with a well-feathered love nest on the Hudson and with no lovebird to share it.

On Thursday evening, January 18, 1849, Catherine had gone to a party at her sister's, Mrs. Voorhies, at 40 Great Jones Street: a farewell get-together for her husband, who was going to California. Forrest had stayed at home, not only because he detested Catherine's sister Margaret, but because he avoided such soirees whenever possible. Some thirty guests, including the Bryants, Godwins, Lawsons, Willises, George Hall, the former Mayor of Brooklyn, and two clergymen, Rev. Samuel Parker and Rev. Joel T. Teadley and their wives, participated in the gaiety. Late in the evening, after the clergymen departed, Catherine, Lawson, and some others retired to an upstairs parlor where, according to Lawson, Mrs. Forrest gave him a cigar and lit one herself. They also had a few rounds of brandy to toast the departing Mr. Voorhies before the party broke up sometime after midnight.

Normally Forrest would have retired early. This evening, according to the later testimony of the housekeeper, Mrs. Underwood, he "seemed to be very wretched and was walking about and sighing." When Catherine returned, she saw a light in the library and stopped to put it out before going to her bedroom. She was shocked to see Forrest still at his desk. He stared at her a moment and then asked her to sit down. He inquired about the party, about the guests. Why hadn't her gracious sister included their friend Andrew Stevens? Catherine assured him the guest list was Margaret's business and not his. This innocent defense of her sister set him off. Forrest leaped out of his chair, charged back and forth across the room, flailing the air with his arms and accusing Margaret of the grossest indecencies. A degraded sister-in-law might be endured; she could be shut out of the house. When her lures drew his wife into the iniquitous whirlpool, that could not be tolerated. Spartacus and Metamora had conditioned him for long tirades; now the thoughts were torn out of his own seething brain. For four hours he roared, shifting his abuse back and forth from Margaret to Catherine, finally centering on Catherine, and in a wild climactic fury he declared that she was no longer his wife. She had lost her right to share his house. He stormed out of the room, leaving Catherine sobbing on the sofa. Through the tempest she had been screaming "It's a lie! It's a lie!" Forrest never gave her a chance to say more.

The next morning when Mrs. Underwood came in to Mrs. Forrest, she could see that she had been crying and asked her what was the matter. This drove Catherine into another spasm as she explained that she had not gotten to bed until six and that "Mr. Forrest has something terrible in his head; I don't know what is the matter with him."

After Forrest left the house for Fonthill without so much as a "good morning," Catherine soon discovered the reason for his rage. Mrs. Underwood described the events of the morning. "I was making the bed when Mrs. Forrest came from the library into the bedroom. She went to her bureau and opened the bottom drawer with a key, stepped back and exclaimed, 'Oh, Good God! Oh, sister Katten, what a fool you are! (Katten was her nickname.) Forrest has opened my drawer and got all my letters.' I asked, 'What letters?' And she said, 'All my correspondence with my sister the time we were in the South and a foolish letter from Jamieson amongst them that I didn't want Forrest to see.' She then went upstairs and brought down a bundle of other letters, and was burning them till near two o'clock." Mrs. Underwood tried to distract her from her frenzied activity, insisting that Forrest was only trying to frighten her. Catherine knew better. She had never seen him so angry nor "so serious."

The letter that had shattered Forrest's faith was the famous "Consuelo" letter that Jamieson had written to Catherine in Cincinnati some three weeks before they had been discovered together in the parlor of the City Hotel, and which later became the center of endless argument during the divorce trial. Whether or not Catherine shared the ecstasy so vividly described was irrelevant to Forrest; the letter clearly implied that she had expressed sufficient ardor to float Jamieson on a sea of poetic fantasy. "And now, sweetest Consuelo," the letter read:

our brief dream is over, and such a dream! Have we not known real bliss? . . . Can slander's tongue or rumor's trumpet summon us to a parley with ourselves? No! No! A doubt of thee can no more find harbor in my brain, than the opened rose could cease to be the hum-bird's harbor. And as my heart and soul are in your possession, examine them and you will find no text from which to discourse doubt of me. . . . Be happy, dearest; write to me and tell me you are happy. Think of the time when we shall meet again. Believe that I shall do the utmost to be worthy of your love; and now, God bless you, a thousand times my own, my heart's altar.

I would say more, but must stow away my shreds and tinsel patches. Oh! how hideous they look after thinking of you.

> *Adieu! adieu! and when thou art gone,*
> *My joy shall be made up alone*
> *Of calling back with fancy's charm,*
> *Those halcyon hours when in my arm*
> *Clasped Consuelo!*

> *Adieu! adieu! be thine each joy*
> *That earth can yield without alloy,*
> *Shall be the earnest, constant prayer*
> *Of him who in his heart shall wear*
> *Sweet Consuelo.*

> *Adieu! adieu! when next we meet,*
> *Will not all sadness then retreat,*
> *And yield the conquered time to bliss,*
> *And seal the triumph with a kiss:*
> *Say Consuelo?*

To have his marriage bed desecrated and to have the adventure so vividly described was unbearable. Nor did it console him to know that Jamieson had lifted his sticky sentiments and borrowed his endearing name for Catherine from George Sand's *Consuelo*; the sentimental novel that had been the rage of New York for the past five years. When Forrest borrowed the three volumes from Parke Godwin two days after the tormenting night, and discovered that Sand's bohemian heroine was remarkably amiable and chaste, he was not relieved. He still had the letter; he could not resist the torture of reading it again and again.

After the initial outburst, Forrest said nothing more to Catherine about his suspicions; he simply ignored her. She pretended that nothing had changed. She copied parts for him, repaired his wardrobe, and during the spring embroidered a new costume. When Forrest deserted the dining room and took his breakfast alone in the library, she brought up the tray. She even carried up the coal to keep his fire going.

According to Rev. Elias Magoon, who professed a secret knowledge of their habits, Edwin and Catherine still occupied the same bed, though as "brother and sister." Mrs. Underwood corroborated his statement. She testified that Mrs. Forrest had told her "to leave the bed a little from the wall so that she might get in as her and Mr. Forrest had no communication with one another." Mrs. Underwood helpfully suggested that she "could coax Mr. Forrest if she wished." Catherine rejected this shabby female tactic.

Catherine was little more than an "upper servant" in the house. Except when she was serving him, Forrest forbade her to enter the library. He sat there alone most of the day and night brooding on his misfortune.

The imagined scenes of his wife's infidelity tracked through his brain so repeatedly that he was unable to think of anything else. The beautiful, innocent young girl of nineteen who had captured his heart was now a tarnished woman. Forrest recognized only two classes of women: those who had fallen, those who had not. Once a respectable lady crossed over, there was no return. Some pitiful flaw in Catherine's character had sent her tumbling into the ranks of the "dysgenic females." The shame, the grievous cut at his pride, gnawed at him day after day.

They could no longer live as man and wife, that much was settled. He did not yet know how to punish Catherine for her folly and at the same time relieve himself from the haunting humiliation. For the moment he settled on a course of self-deception; he would hide the skeleton.

When one of his friends wrote that there "were circumstances under which even guilt might be palliated," he quickly replied that "there was no guilt—would to God there was!" When Catherine asked if he held anything against her as a wife, he protested that if there were he would not be suffering such agony. To complete the self-hypnosis, he persuaded Catherine to sign a vow, which he had prepared, protesting her innocence:

> With the sincere and awful conviction that I now stand in the presence of Almighty God, I call him to witness and record the truth of what I now utter, and also that I utter it without mental reservation. I have never been unfaithful to the marriage bed; I have never at any time permitted any man whatever to take a liberty with me that might not be warrantable in the conduct of the purest wife; I have never permitted the caress or caresses, the embrace or embraces, of any other man than my lawful husband.
>
> All this, in the presence of Almighty God, I swear, and if it be not true, may peace, comfort, and happiness forsake me in this life, and forsake my soul forever in the life to come.
>
> Catherine N. Forrest
>
> January, 1849.

After Catherine signed, she pled with Forrest to abandon his plans for a separation; no document could ever convince the public that any cause but her "departure from virtue" had torn them apart. Forrest argued that he could hold off the gossipers. If anyone insulted her or questioned her purity, he would defend her. Forrest was not convinced by his own arguments.

A few days later they talked of Catherine's future. Forrest thought that her vanity might tempt her to go on the stage. He warned her that if she did she was most certainly lost. She would descend step by step from bad to worse, and at length become a criminal. The weakness in her character could not withstand the corrupting influence of the stage.

Throughout the spring Forrest tortured himself and tortured her. He repeatedly postponed the fatal day of their separation, hoping for some scheme to reduce the shock. Time and again Lawson volunteered to attempt a reconciliation. Forrest insisted that it was useless; no third party ever interfered between man and wife with advantage.

He tried to find peace in turning his attention to Fonthill, occasionally staying overnight in the gardener's cottage, where a room was reserved for him. Smith's workmen had come back on the job in early March after the winter's layoff. It looked now as if the place would be ready by May. That might be a good time to break up their housekeeping on Twenty-second Street. He would sell the town house, and if the river castle was not ready, he could move to Philadelphia temporarily.

With this prospect in mind, Forrest shook off his brooding and turned to his professional affairs. He knew that Macready was on his way back to the city, and in preparation for his return Forrest scheduled a spring engagement to begin at the Broadway on April 23. He also sent the *New York Herald* a copy of a letter he had received from his friend Wikoff which asserted that Macready had instigated "the foul stream of unmanly abuse" in England. This should set the New Yorkers in the right frame of mind for his opening and for Macready's arrival.

On Sunday, April 22, the Godwins and Lawsons were invited to Twenty-second Street for dinner. Forrest did not reveal that he regarded the event as a final farewell dinner. Lawson and Catherine, the only ones who knew a separation was imminent, wondered if his jovial spirits indicated a change of heart, or if he was merely excited by the thought of his return to the theatre the next day.

Catherine had not been told when the final break would occur. Before he went to rehearsal the next morning, he casually announced to her that he planned to close the house the next weekend. With the exception of some special treasures that he wanted, she could take anything she wished. The rest would be moved to Fonthill. Catherine had expected that before the final moment, he would make some provision for her. Now it was clear that she had to make her own arrangements.

That evening after Forrest had gone to the theatre, she decided to swallow her pride and tell someone the whole story, or so much of it as might be necessary, to assure herself a temporary home. She chose her closest friend outside the family, Fanny Godwin, Bryant's daughter. The Godwins listened patiently and insisted that she must come to them.

The final fearful week was almost unendurable. How rapidly their twelve years of married life seemed to slide away. Each day the house was stripped of a few more items. Catherine sent her bedstead to her sister's and a chair and mirror to the Godwins. She took nothing else. She worried over the final departure. How would it be managed? She thought of hiring a carriage. Mrs. Underwood said that would be improper. Someone must come for her, Mr. Godwin or Mr. Lawson.

On Thursday morning, when Catherine heard that Forrest planned to go to Wall Street, she asked him to send Lawson around to see her. When she explained that she intended to ask Lawson to take her to the Godwins, Forrest assured her that he himself would arrange her final departure.

The last days were sadder for her than for him. He was busily occupied at the theatre with little time to brood over his changing domestic life. However, on Friday evening before he left the house, he presented Catherine with a copy of Shakespeare, one of his most treasured volumes. The flyleaf bore the simple inscription: "Mrs. Edwin Forrest from Edwin Forrest, 27th April, 1849."

On Saturday morning Catherine's personal belongings were loaded into the carriage. Forrest helped her into the seat and climbed in beside her. Propped against his knees was a heavy four-by-four-foot frame, his portrait that had hung in the dining room. The companion portrait of Mrs. Forrest had already been sent to Fonthill. The sad silent journey from Twenty-second Street over to Lexington Avenue took only a few moments. When they arrived at the Godwins, a servant ushered them into the parlor. They shook hands. Forrest leaned the picture against a chair beside Catherine and returned to the outer hall. Mrs. Godwin was just coming down the stairs. He touched her hand in a quick greeting, motioned to the parlor, and went out.

For the remainder of the morning he rehearsed *Jack Cade*. After the evening's performance he spent the night at the Lawsons, and early Sunday morning went out to Fonthill.

Catherine began the sad duties of a rejected wife by trying to compose a letter to her parents in England. She finally gave up and sent a note to Lawson, asking if he would be so kind "as to write by the steamer which leaves tomorrow, a few lines to my father at 5 Clipstone Street, Fitzroy Square, informing him of all that has taken place lately concerning myself? . . . I am sorry to give you this trouble, but you are the only person, except myself, who could with propriety write to my father on the subject."

Lawson obliged immediately, shielding the Sinclairs from all the nasty implications that he knew would be widely circulated in the next few days. He explained to her father that painful as it was he must reveal the "unpleasant circumstances that have happened in Twenty-second Street":

On Saturday last (28th April), Mr. Forrest took your daughter to the house of Mrs. Godwin (Mr. Bryant's daughter), and there left her, with the intention of a formal separation. The cause of this separation I do not know, and neither party may ever disclose. It is now about three months since the first intimation of a difference came to my knowledge; it seemed impossible, but it has happened. . . .

From the time this unhappy affair was concluded on between them, Mrs. Forrest has conducted herself as she always does, with admirable discretion; not a murmur has escaped her lips. Mr. Forrest has always been kind and considerate, and nothing in his conduct gives warrant for angry feeling or unkind treatment. He thinks he has made a self-sacrifice for some high principle; what I know not.

I am persuaded that both parties are still warmly attached to one another; he, judging by his looks, has suffered deeply, and has grown ten years older during the last few months; she is not less afflicted. These things all considered, make this separation appear a mystery, which I cannot fathom.

Of one thing I can assure you, your daughter's honor is unsullied. No breath of suspicion can touch it, and all who know her will bear testimony in her favor. The mutual friends of both parties remain the friends of each, and no effort shall be left untried to bring about a reconciliation; but I dare not hold out the hope of a successful issue. . . .

Before delivering the letter to the post office on Wednesday morning—obeying Catherine's request to get it aboard the *Europa*—he showed it to Forrest. Edwin only commented that it would do.

Later in the week Lawson talked with Catherine about the letter. She approved of it and thanked him for his kindness. She simply questioned the part about her honor being unsullied. Why should he speak of that which nobody had ever doubted? Lawson explained that if he were in her father's place that would be the first thing he would want to know. Lawson had begun a task that was to occupy him for the next year: attempting to dampen suspicion and subdue the antagonism of both parties in hopes of a final reconciliation.

At the beginning there were hopeful signs. During the first week of May Forrest visited with Catherine at the Godwins on two occasions. The first time he stayed only a half hour; the second time he was distressed because Fanny Godwin had to run out and bring Catherine back from her sister Margaret's.

Immediately after the separation, however, Forrest was much too occupied with Macready to worry about Catherine.

CHAPTER *xvi*

A Bad Night in Astor Place

Macready had arrived in New York on Friday, April 27, the day before the separation, and on Saturday Colonel William Niblo and James H. Hackett, the proprietors of the Astor Place Opera House, "respectfully informed the public that this splendid establishment" would house the eminent English tragedian during his farewell performances, commencing with *Macbeth* on Monday, May 7. Macready had ten days of worrisome waiting at the New York Hotel just a half-block down Broadway from the Opera House. On May 2 he tried an evening of readings at Hope Chapel, across the street from his hotel, for the edification of the New York school teachers. Most of the time he stayed in his room rereading the letters that he had solicited from England and preparing them for publication. He could not escape the daily reminders that his adversary held the advantage.

Forrest had opened at the Broadway on April 23 and was going strong. The newspapers were filled with articles on the two actors. The *New York Herald*, particularly, found them good copy. They had run a series of letters from Forrest, reprinted from the *Pittsburgh Morning Post*, covering all the details of his London experience. On April 5 they had suggested that Forrest play the Bowery and Macready the Broadway, each for six nights and each at an admission price of one dollar, then on the true American principle of the "almighty dollar," give the thespian crown to whoever brought in the most dollars. They were certain that the "unsophisticated energy of the daring child of nature" would win out over the "glossy polish" of the Britisher. Any good American preferred "the tomahawk to the toga."

Some of the papers pleaded for a truce; if not truce, at least, temperance. On May 1 the *Morning Express* insisted that both sides should forgive and be forgiven. If these two "ornaments to a liberal profession" could be reconciled, "it would not only redound greatly to their own credit, but it would gladden the hearts of 'troops of friends,' on both sides." The feeble attempts to placate the adversaries and minimize the danger with playful allusions to the fuss fooled no one, least of all Macready.

On Monday morning, May 7, Macready rehearsed *Macbeth* with "much care." In the afternoon he retired to his hotel to rest and to read the papers. What he read did not reassure him; for example, the *Herald's* observation: "During the last thirty-six hours the excitement among the theatre-going people has been rising to fever heat." Prospects for a triumphant opening of his farewell engagement were not bright. Forrest, true to his malicious nature, had also announced *Macbeth* for the same evening; and Thomas Hamblin, at the Bowery, not wishing to let the stars have "all the fun and dollars to themselves, put his oar in," offering a *Macbeth* for the neutrals.

Even though no one seriously anticipated more than the usual shouting and hissing at the Opera House that evening, Chief of Police Matsell stationed a half-dozen deputies in the auditorium as a precautionary measure. Before the play began, the house was jammed; the entrance doors on Astor Place were shut; a dense crowd continued to mill about outside. According to one reporter, "the gallery presented a sinister and ominous appearance." A rhythmic "tramp, tramp, tramp" reverberated in the upper tier, a sure sign that the Bowery B'hoys were out en masse.

The first two scenes went smoothly. C. W. Clarke, an American actor who played Macduff, was given a resounding welcome. (In Macready's version, Ross's lines in Act I, Scene 2, were spoken by Macduff.) In his dressing room below the stage, Macready thought the audience had mistaken Clarke for himself; he soon learned otherwise. When he made his entrance in the next scene, he was deluged with groans and hisses. The cheers from the boxes and the waving handkerchiefs of the ladies were no match for the rebels. For fifteen minutes the play stopped; the actors in the gallery took over. Macready was pelted with eggs "of doubtful purity," potatoes, asafeotida, and "a copper coin." Two banners were unfurled: "No apologies, it is too late!" "You have proved yourself a liar!"

Macready braved the attack. He stooped down, picked up the coin and bowed "with mock humiliation to the quarter of the gallery from which the visitation had descended." After the rascals had been allowed a proper interval for their devilment, he stepped forward to speak. He misjudged the endurance of his adversaries. They responded with a renewed onslaught; they waved the banners more furiously. He gave up, drew back among the actors, and told them to proceed with the play. The remainder of Act One went on in "dumb show" with the actors dancing about to dodge the debris.

During the intermission the company urged Macready to give up. He refused. Much as he deplored the disgrace such rowdies "inflicted on the character of the country," he must fulfill his obligation.

Throughout the second act, the actors' speeches were completely inaudible against the tumult, but they kept going. In the third act, the rowdies finally accomplished their mission. Having exhausted their vegetable ammunition, they began throwing chairs. The first fell short of the mark, causing "a prestissimo movement among the musicians." The next three were more effective: one splintered in front of Lady Macbeth (Mrs. Pope), and the other two winged within a hairbreadth of Macready's head. Their aim was improving. A fifth would probably have floored the actor had not the curtain been rung down. Macready climbed over the shattered furniture and went to his dressing room.

One of the actors marched out in front of the curtain with a banner stating that "Macready has left the theatre." The rebels greeted this with a shout of "Down with the codfish aristocracy!" Finally, a half-hour later, the B'hoys had exhausted themselves with their repeated, "Three groans for the English bulldog!"

Throughout the evening Chief of Police Matsell and his cohorts stood by and watched the fracas. He later reported that though some five hundred had been involved, he did not perceive any action that warranted an arrest.

The mob made no attempt to pursue Macready. He got safely back to the New York Hotel and sat down to record the events of the evening. "Pray God," he wrote, "I may do what is right. I will try to do so. I thank His goodness that I am safe and unharmed."

The prepared banners and the unison rumblings of the rowdies suggested an organized opposition, yet no one charged Forrest with complicity in the affair. One account hinted that late in the evening the rascals had been treated to champagne, "manifestly at the expense of persons concealed." Even this reporter did not intimate that Forrest had paid for the refreshments.

Forrest was more than a mile away from the Astor Place area and more happily occupied than his rival. His *Macbeth*, like Macready's, was repeatedly interrupted, but only to permit him to acknowledge the "bursts of applause" from an "enraptured audience."

Macready spent a long and dreary night. He could not sleep. Whenever he began to doze, he would hear an egg sailing past his ear and splashing against the backdrop. In the morning he decided that it was futile to battle such odds, to risk further humiliation and possible injury. He wrote to Hackett, informing him that the engagement was terminated. He sent a hotel porter to cancel his scheduled sailing for June 7 and to book him on the *America*, which was to depart the next day.

His firm morning resolve became less firm as the day progressed. A steady stream of visitors came to apologize for the shameful conduct of their fellow citizens and to assure him that those of "highest respectability, in and out of official station," would prevent a repetition of the disgraceful episode. He must not endanger his worthy reputation nor satisfy these blackguards by running away. Their argument was convincing, particularly when submitted in writing and signed by forty-seven leading New Yorkers, among them David Colden, M. M. Noah, Washington Irving, Herman Melville, Evert A. Duyckinck, and Cornelius Mathews, editor (with Duyckinck) of the literary journal *Arcturus*. These last two had evidently shifted their sympathies. Their names had appeared on the testimonial banquet invitation to Forrest in October 1846.

Macready was unable to resist such a flattering petition from the respectable element; he agreed to stay. When he went to the Opera House on Wednesday morning to arrange the resumption of his engagement, Hackett and Niblo urged him to take up again that evening. Macready thought that it would be better to wait until Friday. The managers argued that the delay gave the opposition too much time to regroup their forces and to build up tension that might then explode more violently. They finally compromised on Thursday, and to assure them that he did not fear a repetition of the Monday night disturbance, nor the ill-luck so commonly associated with the play, he would repeat *Macbeth*.

Once he had settled his course, Macready pitched into the quarrel with new vigor. On Tuesday afternoon he hastily wrote a foreword to his *Replies from England*, charging that although he had intended to defer to the advice of his counsel and "reply in silence" to Forrest's Philadelphia "Card," "the outrages of Monday evening [made] it necessary" to abandon this resolution. Early Wednesday morning he delivered the packet of letters to the printers, Stringer and Townsend, and received their promise that the pamphlet would be ready for distribution on Friday morning, May 10. Having committed himself to a showdown, Macready was more intent on proving Forrest a scoundrel than he was in assuring himself a quiet evening at the Opera House.

Throughout the week Forrest remained silent, proceeding with his scheduled performances as if nothing had happened.

His aloof, hands-off policy was not shared by the press and public. On Tuesday the newspapers limited themselves largely to detailed accounts of the Monday night performance, each with slightly different versions of what happened. Only one, the *Courier and Enquirer,* blamed Forrest for the outrage, and insisted that "the cost of the victory" would probably not bother him "now that he has reduced his household expenses." This scurrilous attack brought an immediate reply from Theodore Sedgwick, Forrest's legal adviser. Sedgwick demanded a retraction: "Every charge against Mr. Forrest," he wrote, "is absolutely and grossly false, and as the attack is coupled with reflections of a most improper and offensive character, I hope that you will see the propriety of retracting and withdrawing the accusation." The next day they apologized, claiming that the item had been inserted without the approval of a responsible editor.

Sedgwick's quick action may have frightened the other editors. On Wednesday, when they began to editorialize, they avoided direct condemnation of either Forrest or Macready. They dwelt on the inherent rights of spectators and of actors, and the duty of the police to protect those rights. The *Tribune* (May 9) labeled the affair, "a wanton, tyrannous and scoundrelly outrage . . . a cowardly theft of the money which the quiet portion of the audience had paid for the expected pleasure of seeing the play." The police bore the brunt of the newspaper attacks. According to the *Morning Express*: "There was no fact more prominent, upon that occasion, than the utter inefficiency of the Police, which was present in considerable force, but without doing anything whatever towards preventing or stopping the riot."

On Thursday, May 10, the city was alive with anticipation. There were probably few citizens unaware of the trouble at the Opera House, few who had not committed their sympathies. Macready's *Replies* were in the bookstalls. The full text was also printed in the *Herald* and a complete summary in the *Daily Tribune*.

Forrest's case was stated more succinctly. The city was flooded with handbills that bore the simple charge:

WORKINGMEN

SHALL

AMERICANS OR ENGLISH RULE

IN THIS CITY?

The crew of the English steamer has threatened all Americans who shall dare to express their opinion this night at the English Aristocratic Opera House!!

We advocate no violence, but a free expression of opinion to all public men!

WORKINGMEN! FREEMEN!!

STAND BY YOUR

LAWFUL RIGHTS.

American Committee

No one was misled by the "committee" label. The group was not limited to a small hard core of Forrest champions. It was a coalition of the Bowery B'hoys and the various nativist societies: Native Sons of America; Patriotic Order of Sons of America; Order of United Americans (forerunner of the "Know-Nothing" party). Macready was a natural target. All of them advocated "America for Americans." Leading the "committee" was the infamous adventurer and rabble rouser E. Z. C. Judson, better known as "Ned Buntline" (the same man who is remembered for his "Buffalo Bill" novels). The forty-six signators to the petition urging Macready to return to the Opera House had neither the organization nor the adventurous disposition of the "American Committee." Throughout the day the "committee" members charged about the city, rallying their forces; Ned, according to his wife, "decked out in his blue frock coat with gilt buttons and tall hat."

Macready's sedate champions were not actively engaged. They hung their faith on the moral force of decency and respectability and fixed the responsibility for maintaining order on the Opera House management and the city officials.

273

Mayor Caleb S. Woodhull, who had just assumed office the day before, called a meeting in his office at 11a.m. Present were Recorder Tallmadge, Sheriff J. J. V. Westervelt, Chief of Police G. W. Matsell, General Sandford, and the theatre managers, Niblo and Hackett. When the Chief of Police informed Woodhull that a serious disturbance might occur, too serious for the civil forces to control, the Mayor urged the managers to cancel the performance. Niblo and Hackett refused. This was Macready's farewell engagement. The public could not be deprived of their right to see him, and they must be protected. Woodhull reluctantly agreed, ordering Matsell to post a full police detail and General Sandford to hold a "sufficient military force in readiness."

Niblo and Hackett returned to the theatre and barricaded the windows with inch-and-a-half boards. The Mayor ordered his street cleaners to remove all the stones "which had been raised for the purpose of constructing a sewer in the vicinity." The only precautionary measure that would have helped had been ignored: closing the theatre.

When Macready arrived at the Opera House a few minutes before six and saw the mob milling around the main entrance, he wished he had stuck to his original resolve. Even after he was safely inside, undetected, and assured that three hundred and twenty-five policemen were prepared to protect him, his fears were not dispelled. A little before seven he could hear the mad stamping as the doors were opened and some 1,800 spectators rushed in.

At curtain time, seven thirty, the actors were ready, the audience was ready, the police were ready. Some two hundred "stars" were distributed in strategic spots throughout the theatre. Fifty police were on the Eighth Street side of the building, the remaining seventy-five at the main entrance in Astor Place. The military had been mustered at their downtown drill rooms: two hundred members of the Seventh Regiment, two "troops of horse," plus a stand-by unit of hussars.

Neither Macready, the other actors, nor the audience were fully aware of this mass of military might. And except for the glittering badges, and the somewhat larger assemblage, Thursday night seemed like Monday. The performance followed the same pattern. Clarke was cheered. When Macready entered the dam burst. His speeches were obliterated by an unceasing racket of boos, hisses, and groans. He did not attempt a speech. A board was pushed in from the wings reading: "The friends of Order will remain Quiet." The "friends of order" may have obeyed, the friends of disorder did not. Some of the police were itching to take a hand; Chief Matsell refused to give the signal. He watched the pressure build through the fourth scene and then sent an emissary for Recorder Tallmadge. The Recorder and the Chief conferred in back of the parquet and finally decided to arrest the more conspicuous offenders. Just before the curtain was rung down on the first act, six stalwart "stars" marched down the aisles and tapped three selected rowdies. They struggled with the officers, were overpowered, dragged out, and locked in a basement room.

The tactic of setting an example with these minor arrests backfired. When the actors began their second-act dumb-show and the B'hoys their noisy accompaniment, someone broke one of the upper windows, stuck his head out, and informed his comrades in the street that the police had incarcerated three of their friends. The outside mob stormed into action. Bricks and paving stones pounded against the barricades and soon came crashing through the windows. A plank sailed across the balcony and knifed into the balustrade. A large stone "took effect upon the magnificent chandelier hanging in the center of the theatre and ruined it."

The Recorder and Sheriff rushed out of the building, the Recorder into Eighth Street, the Sheriff into Astor Place, yelling to the police to arrest anyone seen throwing a stone. It was a futile order, for the police were backed up against the building. Some daring officers dashed out and collared a half-dozen rioters and dragged them into the building. More police were injured than rioters. The Recorder and Sheriff dodged around among the police, ducking stones and trying to rally their dwindling forces. They finally gave up and ordered the "stars"

inside the building, charging them to protect the building until
the military arrived. A runner was dispatched to General Sandford. It appeared that a long and fearful evening lay ahead;
the actors were mumbling through the last scenes of Act Two.
Considerable concern was expressed over the ability of the
police to withstand the siege until reinforcements arrived.

Just after the third act began, about nine o'clock, the military appeared at the corner of Astor Place and Broadway. Leaving the infantry stationed on Broadway, General Sandford led
his fifty horsemen, ten abreast, into Astor Place. They slowly
cleared the street up to the entrance of the theatre; when they
pressed beyond the Bowery, the stones came sailing so rapidly
that they were forced to dismount and turn the operation over
to the infantry. The foot soldiers forced their way with fixed
bayonets, finally circling the building around to Eighth Street.
When they cleared this side of the Opera House, and were replaced by policemen to maintain the positions they had secured,
they marched down Broadway and back into Astor Place.

Forcing the mob away from the front of the theatre was
not easy. After the cavalry and infantry units had passed
through the first time, the crowd had again taken command of
Astor Place. Finally the soldiers got through, prodding the
rioters with bayonets. Then they backed up four deep against
the length of the building. Sandford commanded them to separate in the middle of the formation, and force their way across
Astor Place, one section fanning out toward the Bowery and
the other half toward Broadway. They advanced only a few
paces before a massive barrage of stones felled half the men in
the front rank. The rioters, gaining confidence and convinced
that the military would not fire, became more daring. The soldiers were forced to retreat to the wall of the theatre, and the
officers went inside the building to plan their next move.

The Mayor was now in the lobby. He had stationed himself
at the New York Hotel with Governor Hamilton Fish (grandfather of the recent congressman from New York). When he
had observed the military pass the hotel, he walked up to the
Opera House, certain that the appearance of the soldiers would

clear the area. He had misjudged the fury and determination of the rioters. When he saw that guns might have to be used, he ducked the responsibility for giving the order, hurried out of the building and back to the hotel.

It was now clear that if the men were not given the order to fire, they would be forced to abandon the street and leave the theatre and the audience to the mercy of the mob. The Sheriff and Recorder agreed that before the order was given the rioters should be warned of the impending slaughter. Unfortunately, with all the clatter, few heard their admonitions. When Sheriff Westervelt finally gave the fearful command, the men were ordered to aim over the heads of the rioters, between the first- and second-story windows of Mrs. Langdon's house (opposite the entrance of the theatre). The first volley of musket balls splashed against the house with a loud crackle. The shouting suddenly stopped. The mob retreated into Lafayette Place and back toward the Bowery. Word quickly spread that no one had been injured by the blast. Someone began shouting: "They've got leather flints and blank cartridges."

The mob could not be frightened by the mere sound of gunfire; they attacked with renewed vigor, now aiming their stones directly at the military instead of lobbing them at the building. Again the Recorder made a futile attempt to remonstrate with them. He was shouted down with cries of "Burn the damned den of the aristocracy!" "Fire into this breast. Take the life out of a free-born American for a bloody British actor! Do it, Ay, You darsn't!"

General Hall gave a second order to fire, screaming to his men to keep their muskets low. "Don't hit above the legs!" Battling the shouts of the rioters and the general confusion among the military, his command did not reach everyone. Some who heard refused to obey, revolted at the thought of drawing blood, even from the legs, of an American. The disorganized blast dropped a dozen or more rioters and drove the others back. There was only a brief respite while the rioters dashed out to retrieve the dead and wounded. When they charged again, Hall made not attempt to control the aim of the muskets. He

stormed back and forth among his disorganized ranks screaming: "Fire! Fire! Fire!" Fortunately, the slaughtering third blast
broke the spirit of the rioters; the military probably could not
have repelled another charge. Three hundred men had marched
up Broadway an hour earlier; now only fifty were still available for duty. Reinforcements had been sent for, but they did
not arrive until after the final retreat of the mob.

The performance inside the theatre had concluded before
the spectacle outside. The audience had been led out through
a cordon of military and police through Astor Place and over
to Broadway. Macready, disregarding the pitiful pleas of his
fellow actors, had stubbornly insisted on carrying through to
the end of the play. The spectators were willing to give up before Macready. During the fourth and fifth acts most of them
had abandoned their seats and huddled together in the lobby.

When reinforcements marched into Astor Place shortly after
the last firing, both sides began mopping up. Wounded police
and soldiers were carried into the Opera House. Civilian casu-
alties were distributed among the drugstores in the area, the
Fifteenth Ward Police Station, and the City Hospital. Some
seventy of the protectors of law and order were treated for cuts
and bruises; none died of these injuries. The rioters and "innocent bystanders" suffered most. Five days later when the tabulation seemed as complete as it ever would be, thirty-one were
reported dead and forty-eight had sustained injuries demanding
treatment. Many more had rushed off to nurse their wounds in
private, not wishing to be listed with the rioters.

Macready had escaped the theatre disguised as "Malcolm,"
and had spent the night at the home of Robert Emmet
(nephew of the Irish patriot). The next morning he took the
train to Boston, and on Tuesday, May 22, sailed for home on
the Cunard steamer *Hibernia*.

The day following the massacre everyone was talking of
the riot. The *Herald* bragged that it sold over 33,000 copies.
The gruesome task of identifying bodies continued throughout
the day. The Astor Place area was crowded with curious spectators. Philip Hone, the socialite and diarist, who lived just two

blocks down Broadway, reported his visit "to the field of battle in Astor Place. The Opera House presents a shocking spectacle and the adjacent buildings were smashed with bullet holes. Mrs. Langdon's house [She was John Jacob Astor's youngest daughter.] looked as if it had withstood a siege. Groups of people were standing around, some justifying the interference of the military, but a large proportion were savage as tigers with the smell of blood."

Late in the morning a new set of handbills was distributed about the city:

AMERICANS
Arouse! The Great Crisis
Has come!!
Decide now whether English
ARISTOCRATS!!
and
FOREIGN RULE!!
Shall Triumph in this
AMERICA'S METROPOLIS
or whether her own
SONS
whose fathers once compelled the base-born miscreants to
succumb, shall meanly lick the hand that strikes, and
allow themselves to be deprived of the liberty of
opinion—so dear to every true American heart.
AMERICANS!!
Come out! and dare to own yourselves sons of the true hearts
of '76!

America

The meeting was called for City Hall Park at six o'clock that evening (May 11).

The Mayor countered with a proclamation, issued from City Hall at two o'clock in the afternoon, urging "all citizens, for some days, to remain as much as possible within their own dwellings, and abstain from swelling public assemblages, and from all acts that tend to encourage the riotously disposed. . . . THE PEACE OF THE CITY MUST AND SHALL BE MAINTAINED, by the whole civil and military power of the County."

279

In spite of the Mayor's admonitions, some ten thousand citizens gathered at City Hall Park in the evening to hear the rousing orations of Mr. Strahan, Mike Walsh, and Captain Rynders. They chastised Macready and his "kid-glove" crowd and castigated the military for their murderous attack on innocent citizens. After the meeting more than half the angry crowd marched up to the Opera House. They were completely frustrated in not being able to get near the place. More than a thousand soldiers, nine hundred police, and a thousand special deputies held a defensive circle, blocking Broadway at Ninth Street on the north, Waverly Place on the south, and shutting off the Bowery and Lafayette Place approaches; and, as if this were not enough, a cavalry unit kept up a constant gallop around the building. Niblo and Hackett had closed the theatre.

The military remained on duty through Sunday night. On Monday and Tuesday the defense was taken over by the police, and on Wednesday, the theatre was turned back to the proprietors. The Opera House was a shambles, and could not be reopened until the following December. Judging from the ill-luck that was to plague it for the next (and final) three years of its life as a theatre, the managers should have adopted the suggestion of the *Herald* reporter who wrote on May 29: "We advise the proprietors of Massacre Place Opera House to convert it into a church—into a place for hearing sermons, and singing of psalms, and making prayers, and repenting of sin, for assuredly there has been enough of sin committed in that region to be repented of in sackcloth and ashes."

On Monday afternoon, May 14, the Coroner's Inquest decided that "the circumstances existing at the time JUSTIFIED the authorities in giving the order to fire." They maintained, however, that if a larger number of police had been on duty, the use of the military might have been avoided. The termination of the official post-mortem on the riot did not end the public discussion. The press continued to speculate on who was to blame; none reached a settled opinion; all regretted the mob violence and the recurrent suggestions that this was a class war and not merely a feud between two actors. The final chapter was written the following September when ten of the rioters were tried and sent to jail for terms ranging from a month to a year. Ned Buntline got a full year.

Forrest had stayed completely clear of the Astor Place activities. On the day following the fateful night he had written a long account of the affair to his friend Oakes in Boston. "This blood," he wrote, "will rest on the heads of the Committee who insisted that Macready should perform in despite of the known wishes of the people to the contrary, and on the heads of the public authorities who were requested by many of the citizens to close the house, and thereby prevent any further demonstration." Some officials had urged Forrest to cancel his engagement. He refused, maintaining that he contributed more to the interests of law and order by continuing.

There was no question about who had won the final battle, and Forrest, although protesting his innocence in the affair, was delighted with the flood of congratulatory messages. He must have been surprised to hear that George Jamieson, the author of the "Consuelo" letter, had told a Cleveland theatre audience that Forrest should be decorated by the profession for having driven out Macready; the time was now at hand, Jamieson was reported to have said, when "American actors would do the American acting."

On Saturday night, May 19, Forrest concluded his New York engagement. He had intended to go immediately to Philadelphia, but apparently the pressure under which he had been living since January finally broke through his resistance. His doctor ordered him to bed and insisted that he leave his quarters at Florence's Hotel and move in with the Lawsons.

While he was at the Lawsons', Forrest got the first taste of the complications attending his separation that were to hound him for the next few years. On Saturday, June 2, Lawson received a letter from Catherine, outlining her financial needs. Evidently Forrest had balked at allowing her the $2,000 a year she demanded, insisting that she would squander it in support of her unworthy sister. Now she explained to Lawson that she had no intention of living with Margaret, and in response to

Forrest's claim that a single woman could live on much less, she pointed out that comparing her to his sisters in Philadelphia was unfair. They were established in a regular house and have "been accustomed to practise habits of more strict economy than I ever knew anything about." She assured Lawson that she did not despise economy; instead she hoped that with a little practice she might emulate Forrest's sisters. She meticulously added up all her anticipated household expenses; they came to $1,900. Certainly Forrest would not begrudge her the $100 cushion she requested. If he insisted, she could move into a boarding house, though that "would be a very wretched life for me and one which Mr. Forrest would not willingly doom me to. No one knows better than he does the horror of being surrounded constantly with strangers."

Forrest must have been moved when he read Catherine's plaintive description of her loneliness: "You may conceive how sad and painful it is to be forced to make plans for my future, disconnected with all that has brightened some years of the past. It is the first time in my life that I have felt homeless and poor. Truly, for whatever wrongs we may commit in this world, our punishment is here."

Lawson replied on Sunday morning, reporting that when Forrest had returned from Fonthill the night before, he would have called on her had he not been exhausted. He took a bath and went immediately to bed. He had read her letter and was very touched by her concern over his welfare. "He does not wish, however," Lawson wrote, "to trouble you, as he is in want of nothing to make him comfortable." Catherine must have been reassured by the closing paragraph: "Pray rest in patience while he is sick. I shall do all in my power to bring up the amount as high as possible. He has much kind feeling for you, but none for your sister. If he goes to Philadelphia, you shall hear from me, and I shall try to get the check, if he cannot call himself." Catherine's younger sister, Virginia, had stopped in to see Forrest that morning, and when she was leaving, Lawson gave her the letter to take back to Catherine.

Just after she had gone, Forrest called Lawson to his room

and pointed out that Catherine's letter required a more considered reply. In spite of her pledge to frugality, Forrest detected a certain female wiliness in the letter. She bewailed the meagerness of the $2,000 allowance as if Lawson had proposed the amount and as if she now found it inadequate. Actually no figure had been settled on. Forrest had intended to give her $500 a year and a rent-free house on Twenty-second Street (not the one they had occupied). If she did not accept that, she could move into a boarding house. Lawson had urged him to greater lenience, suggesting $1,500 per year and no house, arguing that if Forrest did not give her a respectable allowance, he might be sued for alimony and be forced to pay considerably more.

Forrest also pointed out that Lawson had not replied to her postscript in which she accused him of breaking his vows to secrecy regarding their separation. Lawson wrote again: "My Dear Mrs. Forrest—When I wrote you a brief note, about an hour ago, by Virginia, I mentioned that yours of last night was at that moment in the hands of Forrest." On rereading it, Forrest now wished to remind her that the $2,000 was her proposal, not his. Such a large sum was out of the question. On the cause of separation, he assured her that Forrest had "not even hinted to me the 'unhappy cause.'" He had only said that "he was not the cause." Lawson was struggling to keep the door open for a reconciliation: "All that I say from one to another," he concluded, "must not be misconceived."

Nothing was really settled. Forrest still deluded himself with the notion that when he had delivered Catherine to the Godwins he had terminated his troubles.

Late in the morning Dr. Gray called, surveyed Forrest's throat, gave him some medicine, and advised him to stay in bed. As soon as the doctor left, Forrest got up, dressed, and took the train to Philadelphia. He had given himself two weeks of sick leave; that was enough. His Philadelphia engagement had been postponed once; he did not intend to postpone it again.

CHAPTER *x v i i*

Revelry on Sixteenth Street

Forrest struggled through his week at the Walnut Street Theatre, trying to confirm the management's announcement that he had "recovered from his recent severe indisposition." When he reached Saturday night, he was glad to quit. He had not realized how the turmoil of the past month had shaken him.

When he returned to New York on June 20, he found the city still fired up about the riot. Stringer and Townsend, the printers, had done so well with Macready's pamphlet that they had brought out *A Rejoinder* compiled by an "American Citizen," purporting to give an impartial review of the "lamentable occurrences at the Opera House." Forrest still refused to be drawn into the affair; he went to Fonthill, settled in the gardener's cottage, and on the Fourth of July staged a patriotic celebration for his neighbors. What a happy relief to be away from the city, out of range of the riot talk, and free from the haggling over the settlement.

Forrest loved his castle. He loved to roam over the gentle slopes and climb through the empty rooms. From the staircase tower, rising seventy feet above the ground, he could trace the ribbon of the mighty Hudson from as far north as Sing Sing until it broke past Staten Island and spilled into the sea. He wandered down the path from the caretaker's cottage at the crack of every dawn to catch the morning light splashing against the battlements. The castle was an impressive Norman and Gothic mound of gray granite with a cluster of six octagonal towers, the central tower capped with a corniced coping and the five flanking towers laced with notched embrasures, each cutting the sky at a different level.

In contrast to the forbidding exterior, the interior was warm and inviting. Two massive pairs of oak doors, one on the river side, the main entrance in Forrest's time, and the other directly opposite, opened into the main rotunda. For the convenience of the students at the College of Mount Saint Vincent—the castle is now their library—the landward portal has become the principal entrance. The floor of the central-hall octagon was inlaid with encaustic tiling around a small central octagon of translucent green glass. One of the sisters discovered the weird power of this glass hub a few years ago when she entered the darkened building after hours. The furnace man was in the basement and the rays from his lantern rose through the glass pane, bathing the rotunda in an eerie green glow.

The principal rooms were clustered around the central octagon: library, dining room, drawing room, and boudoir on the first floor; four chambers on the second floor. All the rooms were octagonal, and all were paneled with richly polished woods. The castle was solidly built. For over one hundred years it has withstood the sharp wintry winds that sweep down the Hudson, and it now appears that Fonthill will hold its sentinel post indefinitely.

In July 1849 Forrest distrusted any signs of permanence. He had believed that his marriage was permanent. He had built Fonthill for Catherine. Now as he walked through the lonely castle, he could not suppress the bitter thought that the place must be transformed into a bachelor's retreat. After a week of battling his melancholy, he went home to his sisters.

He remained in Philadelphia for a month, returned to New York for a week, talked with Lawson about the allowance, finally agreeing to $1,500, and then came back to Fonthill. Forrest had begun the restless search for peace of mind that was to occupy him for the next two years, and, in a way, for the rest of his life.

Catherine was also shifting from place to place. When the Godwins closed their house, she moved in with the Willises, then with the Bryants at Roslyn on Hempstead Bay, Long Island. Finally, in August, after stopping in New York to collect the first installment of $375 on the $1,500 yearly allowance that she had reluctantly accepted, she took a room in a farmhouse near New Bedford, Massachusetts. When she returned to the city in the fall, she and her two sisters, Margaret and Virginia, rented a house on Sixteenth Street, just off Sixth Avenue.

According to some reports, the Sinclair sisters maintained a gay household on Sixteenth Street. One observer said that the house "was visited by gentlemen without their wives; that there was drinking and disorder." John Brougham, the paunchy actor and author of the burlesque on *Metamora*, was said to have been a frequent visitor, as was Dr. John B. Rich, an unlicensed physician who operated a physical training institute. The doctor later explained that his work at the institute kept him until nine o'clock, so that when he came to apply leeches to relieve Mrs. Forrest's neuralgia, he necessarily arrived late in the evening. One reporter suggested that either Catherine had perpetual neuralgia or the Doctor's leeches worked slowly.

In October James Lawson began a serious campaign to effect a reconciliation. He received little encouragement at Fonthill and even less on Sixteenth Street. Forrest would only say that he blamed Margaret for his wife's downfall. Catherine argued that if couples were not allowed to separate when their love had evaporated, marriage was no more than legalized prostitution.

After three weeks of shuttling back and forth between them, Lawson finally broke through one of the barriers. Catherine wrote that she had reluctantly asked her sister to move out and at "extreme pecuniary embarrassment." Lawson confidently hurried to Fonthill with the letter. His hopes were quickly shattered. Pleased as Forrest was to learn that his wife had shown the good sense to get rid of her sister, he was still unwilling to talk of a reunion.

When Lawson returned to Catherine, he evaded her questions about Forrest's response. Instead he pressed for further information about their separation. He had no wish to know the cause. Could she simply tell him who was wrong? Mrs. Forrest bowed her head and answered that she was. Lawson assured her that confession was the first step to repentance and since the cause was known to them alone, a reconciliation should not be difficult. Catherine did not share his optimism, for the cause was known to a third party and Forrest could never forget that fact. While Lawson waited for her to say more, she shook his hand and walked back into the house. It was their last interview, and very unsatisfactory as he recalled it. They had talked in the hallway, because Henry Placide, the actor, was in the parlor. Lawson's future efforts were carried on by mail. However, with each successive letter his hopes for a reconciliation grew dimmer.

When Forrest came to town on Friday evening, November 30, Lawson pleaded with him for some small morsel of encouragement to pass on to Catherine. He had tried to sustain her faith; now she was backing away and only a firm proposal could restrain her from an irrevocable retreat. Pushed to an answer, Forrest declared that there was no hope. Catherine had broken their pact of silence; worse than that, she had charged him with the blame. To whom she made this revelation he did not say. He almost wept as he spoke. He had begun life as a poor boy, had struggled hard to reach the pinnacle; when he reached it, he had been stricken down. She had been the only woman, besides his mother, whom he had ever loved or ever could love. Now she looked ugly. Her face, which had once been fresh and beautiful, was now black and hideous.

One substantiated report said that Forrest raved and ranted and that at one point in the evening "dropped upon the floor, with such suddenness and violence that he hurt himself considerably." Lawson did not remember any groveling on the floor, though he did recall that Forrest had been deeply moved.

The next morning Lawson wrote a sad final letter to Catherine:

My Dear Mrs. Forrest:—Not unmindful of your interests, I laid the whole matter before Mr. Forrest, in the best phrase I could command, and asked him to think calmly, and let me know his feelings. It was only last night that I received a decided answer. You were right. You said it was impossible, that a cause insuperable existed and I was only working in the dark. I see no chance of reconciliation. . . .

I am satisfied that Mr. Forrest has suffered—suffered acutely—he is unhappy—no bright future before him, and the cloud that darkens his pathway is cast over it by the only woman on earth he ever loved or ever can love. He did not, of course, tell me the cause. . . .

Lawson was unprepared for Catherine's reply. She blamed him for deceiving her as to the state of Mr. Forrest's feelings. "Mr. Forrest and I parted friends," she wrote. "I learn with sadness that his feelings have changed, and to you alone can I ascribe the blame. That this should be a matter of little importance to you I can understand, but your Christmas will gain nothing in mirth or content by the reflection that you have wounded one already suffering deeply."

After his efforts to heal the breach, this was Lawson's reward, not an uncommon reward for the helpful friend in a domestic crisis. He now aligned himself completely with Forrest, and Forrest took up the correspondence himself.

On December 24, 1849, he wrote to Catherine explaining that he was compelled to address her in strong terms because he had learned from various sources that she had disregarded their pledge not to reveal the cause of their separation and had been "making statements in regard to it, intended and calculated to exonerate" herself and to "throw the whole blame on me." She knew as well as he that "the cause of my leaving you was the conviction of your infidelity," the proof of which (the Consuelo letter) he still had in his possession. "Let me know at once," he commanded, "whether you have by your own assertions, or by sanctioning those of others, endeavored to throw the blame of our miserable position on me. My future conduct will depend on your reply. Once yours, Edwin Forrest."

Catherine replied immediately. The rumors and reports

were "utterly *untrue.*" When asked "the cause of our sad differences, I have invariably replied, that was a matter known only to ourselves and which would *never* be explained." She did not really blame Forrest for his suspicion. His mind had been poisoned against her by those "with evil motives of their own." He could not know how she had suffered. "Some day, perhaps one so distant that it may no longer be possible for us to meet on this earth, your own naturally noble and just mind will do me justice, and you will believe in the affection which for twelve years has never swerved from you. I cannot, nor would I endeavor, to subscribe myself other than, Yours, now and ever, Catherine Forrest."

Her noble sentiments might have appeased Forrest if she had let the matter rest. Five days later, and before Forrest had replied, she wrote again.

On rereading his letter and "weighing it carefully" she now feared that her silence regarding the proof of her guilt that he said he possessed might be construed as "assent to that accusation." Certainly he could not be so foolish as to consider an anonymous letter a proof of guilt, unless perhaps he had ulterior views and sought "to found some grounds for a divorce." Divorce had not been mentioned in previous correspondence, though they had apparently talked of it before. "I repeatedly told you," Catherine wrote, "that if a divorce would make you more happy, I was willing to go out of this State with you to obtain it," but she implored him, "for God's sake, to trust [his] own better judgment." If he did, certainly his future would not seem brighter for having cast "disgrace upon one who has known no higher pride than the right of calling herself your wife."

If the sequence of letters had been reversed, there might still have been some hope. Her afterthoughts could not be ignored. "It is utterly untrue," Forrest wrote on January 2, 1850, "that since the discovery of that infamous letter, which you callously called 'foolish,' I have ever in any way expressed my belief of your freedom from guilt. I could not have done so, and you know that I have not done it. I have no desire to injure or crush you; the fatal wrong has been done to me, and I only wish to put a final termination to a state of things which has destroyed my peace of mind, and which is wearing out my life." He knew that her second letter had been written "under instruction." Parke Godwin had told him that he had advised her to write it.

This ended the correspondence. Forrest hired Theodore Sedgwick to represent him in New York and Josiah Randall in Philadelphia and started divorce proceedings. Both were prominent lawyers and close friends of Forrest. Sedgwick had been an attaché in the United States Embassy in Paris and had edited William Leggett's *Political Writings*. Randall was a leading Whig and civic reformer.

When Godwin read Forrest's final letter, he advised Catherine to employ Charles O'Conor to represent her. O'Conor was one of the top-ranking lawyers in New York. He was prominent in the Democratic Party, later became Jefferson Davis's chief counsel, and had a strong hand in breaking up the Tweed Ring. O'Conor agreed to take the case, and on Tuesday morning, January 29, the three lawyers met in Sedgwick's library at 37 Irving Place.

Randall explained to O'Conor that they intended to petition the Pennsylvania legislature for the divorce. Only minimal charges would be filed against Mrs. Forrest. No information would be given to the press, and the case would not be placed in the files of the legislature. O'Conor doubted their ability to restrain the press and to withhold charges that would be damaging to Catherine's character. Too much public interest had been aroused by the Forrest affair. He was obliged, however, to transmit his client's willingness, as she stated it, "to consent to a divorce if the application does not contain a reproach upon my honor, so that when I go forth to the world without a husband, I may not be reproached as a vile woman." Sedgwick assured him that his client respected her wish. To be certain that no "impeachment of Mrs. Forrest's chastity" occurred, O'Conor insisted that he be allowed to have an agent in Harrisburg, to be paid by Forrest, who would see that the stipulation was respected. After the meeting Forrest's lawyers were convinced that O'Conor was going to be troublesome. They decided to bypass him and communicate with Mrs. Forrest through William Cullen Bryant.

They could not have selected a more suitable mutual friend of both parties: the poet's professional and personal reputation was above reproach. Bryant held two interviews with Mrs. Forrest. At the first they talked in general terms about the divorce; at the second about Sedgwick's specific plans for presenting the case to the Pennsylvania legislature. She agreed to the proposal with the understanding that all parties, including O'Conor, hold a preliminary meeting to be certain that everything was clearly understood. Bryant communicated her answer to Sedgwick on February 9, and on Friday morning, February 15, he advised Sedgwick that Mrs. Forrest would like to hold their conference at three o'clock that afternoon. Sedgwick agreed and sent an invitation to O'Conor.

At the appointed time Bryant was in Sedgwick's office. Mrs. Forrest and O'Conor did not appear. O'Conor had exploded when he discovered that they had circled around him and forbidden Mrs. Forrest to attend. The next morning he wrote to Sedgwick, explaining that although his client was "willing to suffer any personal deprivation which might conduce to her husband's happiness," she was unwilling to acquiesce to any charge that she had failed in purity as a wife, and if she gave them blanket permission to proceed in Pennsylvania, she would be admitting as much.

Sedgwick had reached an impasse. O'Conor had apparently convinced her that any charges no matter how delicately "couched" were apt to become "uncouched." Sedgwick advised O'Conor that nothing was to be "attained by the continuance of our correspondence." He was compelled to proceed without the benefit of a preliminary conference.

Forrest had not participated in the initial explorations. He was in Philadelphia and had apparently broken his silence about the affair. On January 25, Colonel John W. Forney, editor of the *Pennsylvanian* and later Secretary of the United States

Senate, wrote to George Roberts, editor of the *Boston Times,* who was at that moment visiting in New Orleans. Forney explained that Forrest was about to apply for a divorce, that eighteen months earlier Forrest had caught "Mrs. Forrest in a very *equivocal* position with a young man in his own parlor— not in actual connection, but near it." This young man, George Jamieson, was now performing in New Orleans. Forney wished Roberts "to obtain in some way an admission from Jamieson. He is fond of a glass, and possibly, in a convivial mood, might admit, as a thing to be proud of, his connection with Mrs. Forrest." Jamieson's drunken confession was never obtained.

On February 19 a copy of the petition to the Pennsylvania legislature was transmitted to Mrs. Forrest. O'Conor was furious when he read it. Sedgwick had assured him that the word "criminal" was not to be employed, yet there it was. "Your memorialist makes this appeal," the petition read, "averring an entire incompatibility of temper and feeling, and the utter impossibility of happiness to either party in the continuance of the matrimonial connection. That his wife has committed criminal acts inconsistent with the dignity and purity of the marriage state."

On February 28 a commission from the legislature came to New York for a three-day session at the Astor House to take depositions. Mrs. Underwood, the housekeeper, and Robert Garvin, another servant in the house, did most of the talking. They implicated nine different persons in "indelicacies amounting to adultery" with Mrs. Forrest. In addition to Jamieson, the list included N. P. Willis; Richard Willis, his brother; Samuel Raymond, an actor; Captain Calcraft; Captain William H. Howard; Dr. John B. Rich; Forrest's friend Henry Wikoff; and Professor Hackley of Columbia. Although O'Conor and his client had been invited to this initial exposé, they did not attend.

O'Conor filed a simple protest with the legislature, stating that Mrs. Forrest had "never in deed, word, or thought deviated in the slightest degree from entire purity and chastity."

Forrest was in Harrisburg throughout the spring. At first he was disgusted that the matter was not settled immediately.

In April he seemed pleased with the progress. He wrote to
Boyd Hamilton, Forney's associate on the *Pennsylvanian:*
"Things are now in such a train as to warrant the belief that
the bill can be carried triumphantly whenever it comes up in
the House." Two weeks later he was less hopeful: "The recon-
sideration of my bill has not yet been moved and it is quite
uncertain if Senators can be found to take charge of the matter
on Monday next. The time allotted will expire and if not then
accomplished, I shall abandon the project and return to the
city." His fears were not ill-founded. When the legislature adjourned in the middle of May, no action had been taken. Forrest was furious that a native son should be treated so shabbily.
He found little comfort in the fact that his home-town press
supported him.

The promise to suppress newspaper comment had been
abandoned when O'Conor refused the original proposition. On
May 26 the *Philadelphia Sunday Mercury* wrote: "Mr. Jamieson says his note was merely a 'farewell,' written after having
'indulged rather freely in wine!' Can Mr. Jamieson induce his
wife to credit such a preposterous assumption? Would Mrs. Forrest keep it, if she felt the writer had no reason to assume such
familiarities? This is sillier than the scribblings of Mr. Willis
though we did think it was impossible to surpass, in folly, the
rigamarole of this person. How can Mrs. Forrest relish two
such ninnies?"

N. P. Willis had become involved in April when he wrote
a series of articles in his *Home Journal,* reprinted in the *New
York Herald.* He charged that the Lord of Fonthill in England
could never have behaved in this despicable fashion; "undoubtedly the standard of delicacy to a lady is lower among
the owners of castles in America." Willis maintained that Forrest had married from pride. He wanted a "woman of lofty
mien who would show well as the mate of 'nature's nobleman.'"

Forrest had never liked Willis, even when he attended the
theatre with him in London. He had tolerated his company out
of deference to Catherine and because Willis had written down

Macready in 1844. The chubby, name-dropping dandy who lectured on women's fashions had always revolted him. Even some of Catherine's devotees would gladly have dispensed with Willis's support. One unidentified reporter commented on April 13: "Cannot some friend of Mrs. Forrest's repudiate the idea of his being her champion? Will not some one occupy him with the subject of hair ointment, or a new slope to a skirt, till the case is brought to some safe point?"

Willis had good reason for attacking Forrest, or thought he had. In January Forrest had stopped him in front of the Astor House and given him a "coarse and indecent" tongue lashing. The next day, Willis reported, his wife had received an anonymous letter charging him with improper relations with Mrs. Forrest. He was certain that the letter had been sent by Forrest.

On the evening of June 16 Forrest and his jeweler friend Andrew Stevens encountered Willis in the Washington Parade Ground (Washington Square). When Willis was six feet away, Forrest jumped in front of him, "looking at him steadily in the eye and shaking his fist in his face." Willis made a movement, "as if to draw a weapon," according to Stevens, whereupon Forrest knocked him down, "took away his cane, placed his foot on his neck, and laid upon his person with the cane." While they struggled, Forrest shouted, "gentlemen, this is the seducer of my wife; do not interfere," and Willis screamed for the police. A few days later Forrest told Parke Godwin that if the police had not arrived he would have "cut his damned heart out."

Willis's account of the fight, given in a "Card" in the *Herald* the next day, differed from Stevens's in one essential detail. Willis charged that Forrest had attacked him from behind.

Forrest could not ignore this sneaky implication. On the 25th he published his own "Card": "I most solemnly aver, that when I first struck N. P. Willis, I stood before him, face to face, and with my hand alone felled him to the earth." With that, the Willis affair rested temporarily; it was not concluded.

Forrest had more important duties than whipping Willis. He and Sedgwick were ferreting out new evidence preparatory to making a new appeal. Forrest had asked Sedgwick to track down Anna Flowers, who had been Catherine's personal maid. Sedgwick found her through an advertisement in the *New Orleans Picayune* and had paid her passage to New York. Anna proved a gold mine of backstairs gossip. Her stories were far more graphic and lurid than Mrs. Underwood's. She had seen one man buttoning up Mrs. Forrest's dress; she had caught N. P. Willis with his arms around her; and one night she had discovered Mrs. Forrest in bed with Captain Howard.

During their summer conferences, Randall, Sedgwick, and Forrest decided to abandon the plea to the legislature. On August 9, 1850, they filed a suit in the Court of Common Pleas in Philadelphia. Only a single charge was altered from the original petition: Hackley, the Columbia College professor, was dropped from the list of seducers.

With the complaint now shifted to the law courts, O'Conor went into action. Early in September he filed a restraining suit against Forrest in the Superior Court, charging him with attempting to dispose of his property and of forcing Catherine to appear in Philadelphia. Mrs. Forrest signed an affidavit stating that "between 11:00 and 12:00 at night, on June 15, and divers other times, he had prowled about her house in a stealthy and secret manner, having in his hand a loaded stick, and threatened forcibly to carry her out of the said State of New York." O'Conor asked for a writ of *ne exeat*, preventing Forrest from leaving New York, an order prohibiting him from visiting Catherine, and an injunction restraining the Philadelphia proceedings. Only the final request was granted, yet O'Conor had accomplished his immediate objective, stopping Forrest's case in Philadelphia.

During the fall Forrest spent most of his time at Fonthill, to escape the humilating reminders he invariably encountered when he came to town. On September 25, for example, walking from Lawson's to Florence's Hotel, where he took his meals, he met Captain Granby Calcraft, who was listed as one of Catherine's intimates. Forrest glared at him for a moment and then shouted: "When are you going to England? I advise you to go to England!" Calcraft testified that he replied warmly but not discourteously: "I have no idea at present of going to England; that is my own affair." Forrest restrained himself from giving him a physical chastisement to avoid further complications.

On November 19 O'Conor filed a suit in the New York Superior Court for an absolute divorce on the grounds of infidelity. Sedgwick countered with the first of a series of requests for postponement, demanding more time to assemble the evidence. With the initiative now shifted to Catherine and with her apparent intent to carry through to the end, Forrest advised Lawson to cut off her allowance. The $375 paid on November 1 would be the last.

In January Forrest had another brush with Willis, and on Wednesday morning, January 8, Willis published another "Card," advising the public that he had again been abused by Forrest and "in the presence of a lady." Forrest answered with his own "Card" on Thursday: "It is true," he announced, "that on Monday last I met N. P. Willis on Fifth Avenue and addressed him in these words: 'You infernal scoundrel, liar, and coward, this is the first time I have seen you since the horsewhipping. Don't turn pale; I will not lay violent hands on you.' On the evening of the same day I again met him in the lobby of the Opera House and repeated the same epithets. Mr. Willis walked into the dress circle and then, for the first time, I knew he was accompanied by ladies. I did not speak to him after." Forrest felt obliged to inform the public that however great his distaste for Willis, he would not humiliate him in the presence of a lady. Willis was not satisfied with the apology; he immediately filed a suit for damages based on Forrest's assault of the previous June.

Forrest was too busy with his main action to worry about Willis. Sedgwick had been forced out of the contest by illhealth. In his place Forrest had engaged John Van Buren and H. W. Robinson. "Handsome Prince John" Van Buren, so called because he had once danced with Queen Victoria, was the son of the former President. He had been Secretary of the Ameri-

can Legation in England and in 1845 was the Attorney General
of New York State. Robinson was his law partner and had been
his Deputy Attorney General.

It would have been impossible to pick two stronger champions for the final battle. Both Van Buren and O'Conor were
among the top ten lawyers in New York.

With his case now in expert hands, Forrest turned his attention back to the theatre for the first time in over two years.
On Monday evening, September 15, 1851, he made his triumphant reappearance at the Broadway Theatre in *Damon and
Pythias*. It was a gala occasion. "Long before the hour appointed," the *Herald* reported, "the crowds of anxious auditors
filled the street to the opposite side of Broadway. On entering,
we found the theatre filled to its utmost capacity, the orchestra
playing with admirable effect 'Hail Columbia,' followed by the
enlivening air of 'Yankee Doodle.' When Forrest entered he was
received with the most vehement cheering—hats and handkerchiefs were waved—men stood up from their seats, and the
ladies vied in their enthusiasm till the whole house seemed one
moving mass of human beings."

Forrest made the most of his first opportunity to address
the public since the divorce gossip had started. The play was
only a minor part of the evening's program; his curtain speech
was the main attraction.

He assured the audience that he was deeply touched by
their enthusiastic greeting. As they all knew, he had been "the
best abused man in the United States" during the past two
years. He had been "abused, villified and misrepresented by a
mendacious dungeon lawyer who, under the color of his trade,
without the slightest shadow of justice, has prosecuted and per-
secuted me; one who has admitted to me, in the presence of
others, that his client was a *****." (The *Herald* reporter
could find no euphemistic substitute.) Why had he been so
mistreated? Simply because he "would not tamely submit to the
most infamous of all wrongs—the dishonor of my house." The
applause and cheers continued for ten minutes after he left

the stage. Forrest must have wondered why he had not sought this emotional therapy sooner instead of torturing himself in private with his shame and humiliation.

After his two-week engagement in New York, he played three weeks in Philadelphia, two weeks in Boston, returned to the Broadway for a week, and on Saturday, November 29, concluded his whirlwind tour with a performance of *Metamora*.

Happily, he was exhilarated and not exhausted from the adventure. After repeated postponements, most of them instigated by Sedgwick or Van Buren, the case of Forrest *vs.* Forrest was scheduled to come to trial in mid-December.

CHAPTER *xviii*

Forrest vs. Forrest

On Tuesday morning, December 16, 1851, the first act of the Forrest courtroom drama began. At the crack of dawn spectators gathered in City Hall Park, and by the time the doors opened at 10:00 a.m. "every avenue promising access to the Supreme Court Room" was thronged. It took only a moment to fill the hundred places. Most of the crowd was forced to hang about in the corridors or wait in the park for news of the proceedings.

When the spectators were settled, Chief Justice Oakley entered, followed by Charles O'Conor and the plaintiff, and John Van Buren and the defendant. Mrs. Forrest was attended by her sister, Virginia, and Mrs. Parke Godwin. The principals made a striking impression. "Mrs. Catherine N. Forrest has a good figure, and very erect carriage," the *Herald* wrote. "She was habited in black, wore a black silk bonnet lined with a white cap, with a black lace veil covering her face." Forrest looked "extremely well and was marked with all the outward characteristics of a gentleman." He wore his customary dress, a black frock coat with velvet facings, and "collar a la Byron, with an ample exhibition of snowy linen covering his broad chest."

After the respective counsels had agreed on twelve jurors, O'Conor began his opening statement, charging the jury "to bring public opinion to the test, on a fair, impartial and just inquiry; whatever may have been said out of doors, or published in the newspapers, you are called upon to stamp the seal of your repudiation on what is false." He outlined the Forrests' marital history, alluded to the underhanded attempt to push a quick divorce in Pennsylvania and to Forrest's dastardly misrepresentation of the Jamieson letter. In fact, he credited Forrest with only one charitable act: the list of nine adulterous accomplices in the original charges had now been reduced to six. He alerted the jury to the shady characters that the defense would parade before them, particularly the disreputable Anna Flowers. He previewed Forrest's plot to get Jamieson drunk and thus persuade him that admitting adultery with Mrs. Forrest "would be a feather in his cap."

Seven issues must be decided by the jury: (1) Whether the defendant since his marriage with the plaintiff has committed adultery. (2) Whether both parties were inhabitants of this state at the time of the commission of such adultery. (3) Whether the defendant's adultery was committed within this state. (4) Whether at the time of such adultery and at the time of the commencement of this action, the defendant was an inhabitant of this state. (5) Whether the plaintiff has committed adultery. (6) Whether at the time of the commencement of this action, the plaintiff was an actual inhabitant of this state. (7) Whether at the time of the commencement of this action the defendant was a resident of this state.

With the case clearly outlined, O'Conor called three witnesses to testify that Forrest had voted in Yonkers in the general election of November 6, 1849, thus establishing his legal residence in New York State. When it looked as if O'Conor were going to dally along with the supernumeraries, he quickly snapped everyone to attention. He called Forrest.

As the actor strode calmly to the stand, Catherine hastily asked Mrs. Godwin to hustle Virginia out of the room. It was not clear whether this move to protect her innocent ears (she was then fifteen) was engineered by O'Conor for its effect on the jury, or whether Catherine genuinely feared the revelations that might follow. If she did, she need not have worried. Forrest's first appearance—it was also his last—merely provoked a spate of legalistic wrangling. Forrest admitted his association with Miss Clifton. He had performed with her and traveled with her, although infrequently and never on long journeys. O'Conor's climactic question: "Have you ever, since you were married to Mrs. Forrest, had sexual intercourse with Josephine Clifton?" was never answered. It touched off a hassle between the two lawyers that carried over into the next day's session. Oakley finally ruled the question inadmissible: "The witness could not be called to testify in favor of his wife."

Obliged to abandon the direct attack, O'Conor called two of Forrest's former employees: Thomas W. Whitley and Andrew Jackson Allen. Both of them relished the opportunity. Allen had been discharged as Forrest's costumer, and Whitley still insisted that Forrest had cheated him when he was tending the grapes in Covington. Whitley knew nothing of Miss Clifton. He had, however, frequently met Forrest in New York when the actor was on his way to a house of ill-fame.

Allen was more explicit. He had first observed Forrest's fondness for the brawny actress at French's Hotel in Norfolk. "I am hard of hearing," he testified, "and could not hear everything that was said; but I can see as far as most folks; I saw them kiss and embrace, but I did not see anything criminal; I did not hold a candle for them." He had never peeked into "Miss Clifton's room; I am an old man now, and I never interfere with the ladies." On another occasion he was just leaving Miss Clifton's lodgings in White Street in New York when Forrest entered. The actress was in bed. He could not be certain whether or not she was dressed. He saw one leg with a stocking on it, but that was "*as far* as I saw her legs."

When Allen finished, O'Conor announced that he would rest his case for the present, whereupon Van Buren proposed that if this was the plaintiff's evidence supporting the adultery charge, that issue could be decided by the jury immediately. Justice Oakley thought this a bit premature and advised Van Buren to proceed with his opening argument.

After a few prefatory allusions to Forrest's exemplary reputation, Van Buren tackled the prejudice that he knew was to be his big stumbling block: "It is inherent in manhood to have sympathy with a woman; it is creditable to the human mind and human heart," yet the jury must consider how far Mrs. Forrest's vile charges were "consistent with female delicacy." Was it consistent with female delicacy to besmirch Josephine Clifton's name seven years after death?

As much as he shared the jury's desire to protect the helpless female, he was obliged to reveal some painful evidence. A husband, however charitable his disposition, could not overlook the Cincinnati episode with George Jamieson and the impassioned "Consuelo" letter. He asked the jury to listen closely while he read the letter.

He got no further. O'Conor was on his feet. The letter could not be introduced until it had been "proved in evidence." Van Buren delighted in his protest, knowing that the jury would assume that O'Conor was afraid to have the letter read.

Van Buren willingly settled for whetting the jury's appetite with a teasing description of the forbidden document: "It will be found that in that letter he addressed her in language of deep affection. . . . It will be found that that letter speaks of the realization of a voluptuous enjoyment. . . . It will conclude with a poetic picture, descriptive of when they lay enfolded in each other's arms in the enjoyment of a kiss." What would a virtuous wife do with such a letter? Treasure it? No! She would bravely lay it before her husband and say: "Here is a man who has dared to address me in terms implicating my honor!"

The discovery of this document had led to Forrest's renunciation of his beloved wife in January 1849. This was only the beginning. He later learned of Catherine's disreputable friends and the shocking parties held in his home during his absence. Van Buren knew he could stir up a few prejudices in the minds of his twelve honest-men-and-true. They were clearly not from the upper-crust and undoubtedly would be scandalized by such loose living.

Van Buren regretted to report that one of Mrs. Forrest's most constant companions, her sister Mrs. Voorhies, had had the misfortune of having a child out of wedlock. And yet, in-

stead of doing penance for her folly, she had brazenly participated in the "scenes of wassail" in Twenty-second Street. Who
were the other debauchers? Gentlemen, "it was a literary
coterie, by the fiat of whom every man must fall, led by the
notorious Mr. N. P. Willis." He taught Mrs. Forrest "to look
down upon the simplicity of her husband's character." There
were others. Richard Willis, who was closeted in an upper
room for three days. Captain Granby Calcraft, who was "seen
coming up the stairs with decanters and glasses." Captain
Howard, who was caught in "criminal connection with Mrs.
Forrest," and who later debauched the servant girl, Anna
Flowers.

If the opposing counsel attempts to discredit the testimony
of the servants, these simple souls from the underprivileged
ranks who observed the revelry, he has two courses open: bring
forth a sworn contradictory statement or indict the witness
for perjury. "No one who knows Mr. Forrest," Van Buren concluded, "would believe that he is capable of hiring testimony
to injure his wife—such an idea is contrary to humanity—it is
contrary to his nature." Thus the second day ended.

The Thursday and Friday sessions were taken over by Van
Buren's first witness, Mrs. Underwood. She had intimate knowledge of everything that transpired in the house and was delighted to share her observations.

She recalled one of N. P. Willis's visits in December 1844,
shortly before the Forrests went to England. Mrs. Forrest was
"packing up her clothes and she said she expected a gentleman
to call at two o'clock. She went down to the drawing room for
half an hour. When she returned she looked rather flushed and
flurried; she said she was afraid Mr. Forrest would be home
soon, and she regulated her hair."

Two other meetings stuck in Mrs. Underwood's memory.
One stormy afternoon about two o'clock Willis and Catherine
were together in the drawing room with the blinds shut. One
evening, when she returned from prayer meeting, Mrs. Forrest
stopped her in the hall and said that Willis was in the house
and that she wanted to sneak him out. Mrs. Underwood oblig-

ingly guarded the kitchen area while Willis came down the stairs. On both of these occasions Mr. Forrest was away from the city.

She remembered an all-night party in the fall of 1848. At six o'clock in the morning, she had heard loud talking and had come down to investigate. She met Catherine in the hall and asked what was happening. Mrs. Forrest replied: "We have been sitting up all night amusing ourselves."

Samuel Raymond, the actor, had been a frequent visitor during the summer and fall of 1848. One evening after dinner Mrs. Forrest said she had tripped on the stairs and sprained her ankle. "She sent me to the druggist for some liniment. When I returned Mrs. Forrest was lying on the sofa in the parlor about to have her foot rubbed by Mr. Raymond." In the morning "Mrs. Forrest said to me, 'that wretch,' or 'that devil,' I don't recollect which, 'stayed all night' and she wanted him to stop for breakfast. I asked her where did he sleep? and she said, 'in the spare bed.' She also told me that Raymond had caught hold of her petticoat that was lying on the bed and asked her if that was a tin petticoat." This remark brought a roar from the spectators, and Justice Oakley, missing the point, inquired, "A what?" "A tin petticoat: you know they put such a deal of starch in them," Mrs. Underwood explained.

Captain Granby Calcraft was another regular. When he could not come, he sent bouquets and boxes of "little white segars, tied with blue silk." On at least one occasion the Captain, and his English nobleman friend Fortescue staged an all-night party with Mrs. Voorhies and Mrs. Forrest. Mrs. Underwood was awakened at three in the morning, got up and looked down the back stairs and saw Calcraft and Mrs. Voorhies noisily stumbling up with a tray of glasses and bottles.

Under cross-examination Mrs. Underwood admitted that some of her testimony was based on hearsay. She had not seen Mrs. Forrest raise a wine glass to her lips; she had merely seen the bottle and the glass. She had seen her smoke only twice. Unwittingly, O'Conor's probing brought out some additional

details. She reported that Mrs. Longstreet, Mrs. Forrest's landlady on Sixteenth Street, had once asked if one of "all those
gentlemen with the hairy faces that were coming to call" was
Mr. Forrest. O'Conor was not happy with Mrs. Underwood. Although he forced her to admit that she had never actually seen
any man take criminal liberties with Mrs. Forrest, he knew
that the circumstantial framework of her story had registered.

On Saturday morning Van Buren continued with the Forrests' servants. Robert Garvin, their waiter, elaborated on
some of the incidents and personalities introduced by Mrs.
Underwood. He recalled a day when Captain Calcraft had
dined with Mrs. Forrest, and she was so tipsy that she could
"scarcely carve the chicken." Later that same evening, he discovered "Mrs. Forrest sitting on Captain Calcraft's knee with
one arm leaning on his shoulder and the other across his
breast." Once when he was working on the back piazza, he
had seen N. P. Willis sitting on the sofa with Mrs. Forrest. "In
what condition?" Van Buren asked. "Called lying on each
other," Garvin replied. After they left the room, he had found
hairpins and an elastic garter on the sofa. Garvin had a sharp
memory for incriminating incidents: the night Captain Calcraft
broke Mr. Forrest's library chair; the evening he found Mr.
Raymond and Mrs. Voorhies lying on the carpet.

O'Conor's cross-examination was brief. He quickly discovered that his questions merely loosened Garvin's gossipy
tongue. He was happy to get him off the stand before he gave
the jurors more juicy morsels to chew on over the weekend.

Immediately after court convened on Monday morning,
Van Buren called Anna Dempsey Flowers, his star witness.
She reported that Parke Godwin had once stayed all night in
the library; one morning N. P. Willis had been ushered up to
the second floor when Mrs. Forrest was still in bed. On another
occasion she had seen Mr. Willis "with his arm round Mrs.
Forrest's neck and he kissing her." Anna's big story involved
Captain Howard. She explained that when Mr. Forrest was
away she frequently slept with Mrs. Forrest. One night, early

in September 1844, she recalled: "I awoke in the middle of the night, and Mrs. Forrest came in and undressed herself for bed; she did not say anything until she got into bed; she then called me, but I did not answer. She then left the room in her night clothes. I was afraid I had misunderstood her and got into the wrong bed, as I heard whispering and a noise of the bedstead in the next room. I got up and took the lamp that was lit on the hearth and went into the next bedroom. I went to the foot of the bed and looked over it, and I saw Mrs. Forrest and Captain Howard; they were in the bed; both in the same bed." The next morning Mrs. Forrest advised her to forget what she had seen and to take a comb and brush and one of Mr. Forrest's shirts upstairs to Captain Howard.

Three days later Anna herself was in bed with Captain Howard and with more serious consequences. She had a child by him.

Van Buren had to gamble on the momentary damage of this evidence in order to demonstrate that Mrs. Forrest had contributed to the support of the child to keep Anna quiet. Even when the Forrests had gone to England, Mrs. Forrest had instructed her sister Margaret to look after Anna's baby.

Van Buren held his monoply on Anna as long as he could. In the late afternoon, he was obliged to release her to the opposition. O'Conor began gently with a few miscellaneous items, revealing, among other things, that Anna's expenses to New York had been paid by Lawson, as they had been on her previous visit in June 1850; that during this first visit she and Sedgwick had connived to blackmail Mrs. Forrest. The exact nature of the scheme was not explained. He flashed a letter under her nose, asking if she had addressed it to Mrs. Forrest. Anna agreed she had. O'Conor read the letter and passed it to the jurors. Although not an orthographical masterpiece, its message was clear:

Dare Mrs. Florrist I have just arrived from New Orleans, and I want to see you very much before I see anybody else. I am going to Brookling this morning, but I will be hear at half past 5 this afternoon. Do pleas com and see me for I have so much to tell you. I don't want to be seen hear until I see you. Call at 142 Mercer Street, Willson's hotel. Please send answers by the barer.

Anna Dempsey

O'Conor pointed out that her request to see Mrs. Forrest *first* was sheer nonsense. Anna had already been quizzed for two days by Forrest and Sedgwick.

For the remainder of the afternoon and most of the next morning, O'Conor dredged up unsavory incidents from Anna's past. She admitted that she had been caught stealing and had spent several years in the House of Refuge, though she preferred to call it a "Boarding-school." When O'Conor asked if she had had intercourse with the Forrest's waiter, Barney McCabe, Anna was shocked. "No sir," she protested, "he was nothing but a small, dirty boy." Anna was particular about her bedmates. When the laughter subsided, she was dismissed, and O'Conor turned the proceedings back to Van Buren.

To assure the jury that his case did not rest entirely on loose-tongued females, Van Buren spent the final hour and the entire next day with C. Edward Lester, former United States consul at Genoa, and John Kent, a servant of the Willises.

Lester and Kent testified to Mrs. Forrest's unwifely conduct. According to Lester she was much too solicitous in urging strangers, including himself, to come into the house during her husband's absence. Kent reported that Mrs. Forrest had a bedroom at the Willises, ostensibly to give her a place to rest when she was there nursing Mrs. Willis. One night Kent had seen Mr. Willis coming out of Mrs. Forrest's room in his stocking feet and heard him call, "Goodnight, dear." In cross-examination, O'Conor forced Kent to admit that Willis might have been calling to his daughter Imogene who occupied a room on the same floor.

The trial dwindled down to a relatively peaceful level before court was adjourned for the Christmas holiday.

During the one-day recess, O'Conor and Van Buren took stock of their progress. Each was confident that the case was moving in his favor. On Christmas Eve Justice Oakley visited

307

the Gramercy Park home of his old friend George Templeton Strong, the lawyer and tireless diarist. Strong thought that the proceedings were "dragging through the Court like a wounded skunk," and though he despised "the king of blackguards, Edwin Forrest," he feared the "evidence was beginning to pinch Mrs. Forrest pretty closely." He chided Oakley for ruling out the "Consuelo" letter, informing him that George Sand's heroine was not a naughty woman but a "super-human and boldly-refined extract of all kinds of sublime virtue." The old Judge—he was then sixty-eight—admitted that he was not up on the latest literature and that perhaps the letter should be admitted.

Friday's session was relatively dull and repetitious: further details from Anna on Mrs. Forrest's support of Anna's child and an expanded report of Lester's visits with Mrs. Forrest.

Throughout the third week of the trial Van Buren continued his attack on Mrs. Forrest, shocking the jury with the most scandalous passages from the "Fourier" letter and from the affidavit which she had signed in December 1850. Van Buren savored her confession to one all-night party and two all-night visitors: Samuel Raymond and Richard Willis. Her claim that they were accommodated with the greatest propriety did not worry Van Buren. If her protestations of innocence did not appear too vehement, he could make them seem so. Let her say that she had "never committed adultery or been guilty of any unchaste, impure or immodest conduct whatever"; who among the jurors would believe her when they considered the testimony of Mrs. Underwood, Anna Flowers, and Egbert Demming, his new witness? Demming lived on Twenty-first Street, directly back of the Forrests. One evening, in the fall of 1848, he had seen Mrs. Forrest and N. P. Willis standing by the window "side by side, with one of his arms around her waist."

For anyone unconvinced by these eye-witnesses, Van Buren still held a trump card, the "Consuelo" letter. Finally, on Friday, January 2, after a long argument in the Judge's chambers, Oakley admitted the letter. Knowing that the spectators had been waiting almost three weeks for this moment, Van Buren gave an impassioned reading, relishing each sweet phrase.

O'Conor recognized the futility of a point-blank denial of Jamieson's love song. The best he could do was raise a few questions. If Forrest had actually discovered the "Consuelo" letter and believed his wife an "abandoned woman," would he have taken her to a "virtuous home" like the Godwins'? Would he have continued "to lay with his wife for long winter nights, with plenty of spare beds in the house?" Could anyone honestly believe that during these long winter nights in the same bed he had "no marital intercourse with her?"

With these doubts planted in the minds of the jurors, O'Conor turned to his direct attack: discrediting Van Buren's star witness, calling his defenders of Mrs. Forrest, and building his case against Forrest.

Dr. Charles Lee, one of Anna's former employers, and David Terry, Superintendent of the House of Refuge, agreed that they would not "place a straw on her word." Harriet White, from Norwalk, remembered a night when Anna had locked herself in a room with two men. James Curzon, a daguerreotypist from New Canaan, recalled an evening in Mr. Dickinson's kitchen; he was cleaning his gun when Anna appeared in her night clothes and said: "James, if you will make me a corsetboard, I will grant you any favor you ask." Catherine Levins, another Forrest servant, insisted that Anna carried on with Barney all the time: "I saw him catch hold of Anna and kiss her before I caught them in bed; he'd kiss her whenever he came into the kitchen and in the area, and the garden, and in the yard."

O'Conor summoned Barney McCabe to complete the demolition of Anna's character. When Barney's name was called, "a general buzz and bustle of anxiety was manifested throughout the court." His appearance bore out Anna's description. He was a "miserable-looking, ill-clad, shirtless individual with a downcast look." O'Conor brought him right to the point: "Had you at any time sexual intercourse with Anna?" McCabe was just as direct in his reply: "I believe I had once or twice;

I believe it was in the bedroom next to the bathroom; I believe it was the day before the night I was caught in her bed."

With most of these witnesses, Van Buren limited his cross-examination to one point: how much they expected to be paid for their information. All agreed that they anticipated something but were not sure how much.

To counteract the case against Mrs. Forrest, O'Conor called a number of the principals who had been implicated. Samuel Raymond admitted one overnight visit when there was a severe rainstorm; the sleeping arrangements had been very proper. Captain Calcraft recalled the time he and Mrs. Voorhies had carried trays and glasses to the library; they were not "disguised with liquor." They were shouting and laughing about their awkwardness. He had never observed embraces or sitting on laps.

Mrs. Willis clearly remembered the circumstances of one all-night party. After the main gathering had broken up shortly after eleven, she, Mrs. Voorhies, Richard Willis, and Mr. Ibbotson had remained. Mrs. Voorhies was eager to try some of the songs Richard had brought back with him from Germany, many of them his own compositions. Shortly after the song fest began, it started raining. They continued singing while waiting for the rain to stop and became so engrossed in their music that it was morning before they realized it. There had been no indelicacies.

Nathaniel Parker Willis concentrated on the specific accusations made against him. As expected, he had the proper answers. He had not kissed "any part of Mrs. Forrest's person, nor lay upon or against her person, or any part of it." Both Willises told the same story about Mrs. Forrest's visits to their home. After the birth of their child in the spring of 1848, Mrs. Forrest had frequently stayed overnight. The "goodnight, dear," which Kent heard, had been addressed to Imogene, Willis's daughter by his first marriage.

Richard Willis, Nathaniel's brother, echoed Mrs. Willis's account of the all-night music session. He could recall only

one other time when he had been in the Forrests' house overnight. He had stayed too late for the last omnibus and "since
he was a stranger in the city and unacquainted with the lo-
calities of New York, he had accepted the hospitalities of the
house." He had never been concealed; he had never taken
liberties with "the person of any lady" there.

O'Conor's witnesses withstood most of Van Buren's cross-
examination attack although some of the edge was worn off
their testimony. Raymond was hazy about the breakfast that
had followed his overnight visit. Calcraft became confused
about his frequent visits to the homes of other New York ladies.
N. P. Willis was obliged to admit a close friendship with Josephine Clifton. He had written two plays for her, and she had
frequently visited his home at Glenmary, Tioga County, New
York. Richard Willis became completely tangled up. He did
not know how many nights he had stayed in the Twenty-second
Street house. Finally, he agreed to more than three and less
than ten. He was certain that he had never been there for three
consecutive nights.

If this part of the case seemed to end in a draw, O'Conor
was not distressed. His heavy ammunition was reserved for
the adultery charge: Forrest's affair with Josephine Clifton and
his frequent visits to Mrs. Ingersoll's, a house of assignation at
355 Greenwich Street.

O'Conor began with Caroline Ingersoll. On two or three
occasions Forrest had engaged rooms at her establishment.
She had not observed anyone with him, nor would she admit
anything peculiar about the fact that her house had an over-
abundance of "chambers." This was true of any rooming house.
O'Conor did not quesion Mrs. Ingersoll's testimony; he merely
paraded his other witnesses. William Mackeller, Clerk of the
Chief of Police, testified that 355 Greenwich Street had been
listed as a "suspicious place." John D. Hilbert, who kept a
butcher shop across the street, was certain it was a "bad house."
He had once seen a female at one of the windows "put her
finger to her nose to a man who was passing by." Six policemen
and a doctor reported professional visits to her establishment.

O'Conor presented such a line-up that one reporter commented: "Mr. Forrest may think himself very fortunate that he was not indicted for keeping a disorderly house."

If this circumstantial evidence might not weigh heavily, at least it provided a prelude to the more explicit reports on Forrest's relations with Miss Clifton. William Foster had seen the actor coming out of Miss Clifton's room at the Eagle Tavern in Albany with "nothing on but his linen and a cloak." Robert Freeman, a New York tailor, had observed them going into the same stateroom on an Albany steamboat. Dr. John Hawkes and his wife Laura had traveled with the couple in the railroad cars from Utica to Rochester.

Hawkes explained that because his wife had been ill, he had secured a place for her on one of the sofas in the saloon at the end of the car. Josephine Clifton was stretched out on the other sofa, "groaning and twisting" in great pain. Just after the train left Syracuse, Forrest went into the saloon and requested Mrs. Hawkes to depart for a moment. Laura went back to her husband. One half-hour later Forrest came out of the saloon and told Mrs. Hawkes that she could return. When Dr. Hawkes led his wife back to the sofa, he observed that Miss Clifton's "contortions" had ceased. Repeatedly O'Conor led Hawkes to the crucial question: "What, in your opinion, caused the change?" Each time Van Buren stopped him with an objection. Finally, Oakley allowed the question. Hawkes gave his answer: "From all I saw and heard, I formed the opinion that an abortion had taken place."

Van Buren had given most of the recent witnesses only a token cross-examination. The doctor required more attention. After a few moments of sparring, Hawkes admitted that he was really a druggist. He practiced medicine as an avocation. If this was not enough to convince the jury of his incompetence, Van Buren had other witnesses in reserve, ready to be called if necessary.

O'Conor's final witness to Forrest's relations with Miss Clifton needed no cross-examination. In fact, after she began speaking, O'Conor wondered how she had got into his camp.

Nancy McLoughlin, the housekeeper at the American Hotel in Buffalo, swore that she had never seen Forrest enter the actress's room at the hotel. When she left the stand, she shook hands with Forrest, commenting to O'Conor in a loud voice: "He's a nice gentleman, more gentlemanly than you. I haven't seen him for years, and I'm glad to see him." After this break, O'Conor knew he could not recover the jurors' attention for the remaining hour. He was relieved when Oakley announced an early adjournment.

On Wednesday morning, January 14, O'Conor began with William H. Doty, his principal witness to Forrest's infidelities. Doty's story, like Anna's, was richly detailed. He had known Miss Clifton in Saratoga, where he had worked and where she had been a frequent guest. When she and the actor came aboard the Albany night boat at the foot of Cortlandt Street, Miss Clifton had told Doty that she and Ned were going off "to take a little turn in the country." Late at night Doty had heard Forrest's voice in her room and had heard them kiss. In the morning he heard her say: "Come Ned, it's time to get up." After they left the boat at Albany—Doty was going on to Troy—he looked into their room and "saw a bed made up on the floor and no mattresses in the berth."

Under Van Buren's questioning, Doty floundered on many details. Of one thing he was certain: the incident had occurred early in July 1843. Van Buren was pleased to have him reinforce the date.

O'Conor had three more witnesses: Forrest's old friend Henry Placide whom he had once called "the best comedy actor on the English-speaking stage"; Ellen Lawless, a hotel maid; and George Boyd, a carpenter.

Placide knew of one all-night party on Twenty-second Street when Forrest was present. Some twenty guests had been served a midnight supper and a select few an additional supper of wild duck at 2:00 a.m. The Forrests and he were still at the table when sunlight began seeping through the shutters. They had topped-off the party with a morning mint julep. In reply to Van Buren's questions, he admitted that this was an unusual evening; ordinarily he "felt uneasy at keeping Forrest up after twelve o'clock."

Neither the spectators nor Van Buren—judging from his meager cross-examination—detected O'Conor's motive in the testimony of Ellen Lawless. The characters in her story were all anonymous. A woman had rented a back room on the third floor of Mr. Wilson's hotel on Mercer Street. "I went into the room toward evening with a pitcher of ice water for her," Ellen explained. "I think a gentleman was there. There was a new piece of muslin in one of the back windows and also in the door to the bedroom, fastened with pins or tacks." That was her story. The point of it was to come later.

George Boyd contributed a single item: he had put up an extraordinary number of bedsteads for Mrs. Ingersoll. Aside from this fact, he had observed no "action which illustrated Mrs. Ingersoll's mode of life." Skipping from one story to another and closing with such an inconsequential witness might have weakened O'Conor's case had not Van Buren adopted the same tactic in his rebuttal.

During the next two days, Van Buren introduced six friends of Anna who swore to her good character. He called Thomas L. Smith, the Fonthill builder, to testify to Mrs. Forrest's bad character. Smith had seen her drink whisky punch, smoke both small and regular-size cigars, and had once observed her "lying on the ground at Fonthill in an indelicate position."

Van Buren's principal attack was leveled at the testimony of Dr. Hawkes and William Doty. Four reputable physicians— even O'Conor recognized their high standing—attributed Miss Clifton's distress to her normal menstrual pains and her relaxation to nature's own curative powers. She had been "relieved by flooding"; there was no evidence of abortion.

Doty's story was demolished just as completely. The auditor of the Hudson River Railroad Company, an agent for the New York Steamboat Company, and a steamboat joiner, all testified that in 1843 the *Albany* had no staterooms; she was a day boat and had not been converted to a night boat until the following year.

O'Conor was unwilling to give up. He called twelve witnesses to attest to Doty's honesty, and Doty himself to correct his story about the Albany night boat. He now claimed that the incident had occurred in 1844 instead of 1843. Van Buren immediately challenged the new date. From June 10 to July 13, 1844, Forrest had been performing in St. Louis, Detroit, and Buffalo. After checking Mrs. Forrest's records, O'Conor granted the point, reluctantly abandoned Doty, and shifted to another consideration.

O'Conor proposed that the jury should fix the amount of alimony as well as pass on the guilt or innocence of the defendant. To prepare them for the task, he called Thomas Whitley to survey Forrest's financial status. Whitley valued Forrest's six houses and lots on Twenty-first and Twenty-second at six to seven thousand dollars each; his own home at some eighteen to twenty thousand; Fonthill between fifty and sixty; the Covington property about twenty-five; the six or seven lots in downtown Cincinnati from fifteen to twenty. He could not report on Forrest's Michigan property nor on his personal possessions. Where Whitley got his information was not indicated. Oakley remarked that it coincided closely with the estimate prepared by Mr. Forrest himself.

Whitley was the last witness. When he finished, there was considerable shuffling about in the courtroom. Mrs. Forrest and her companions, Virginia and Mrs. N. P. Willis, departed. Van Buren gathered his notes and just after eleven o'clock on the twenty-eighth day of the trial began his summing up.

The jurors must appreciate what a sad blow the separation had been to the defendant. Forrest had admired and loved his wife. After they parted, he had protected her from abuse and refused to speak to anyone of the degradation that had forced them apart. Tempted as he was, by friends and enemies alike, to reveal the cause of their separation, he refused to break his silence until he was forced to defend his character against Mrs. Forrest's evil insinuations.

Van Buren sketched the negotiations between Sedgwick and Bryant, emphasizing Mrs. Forrest's willingness to permit the action to go before the Pennsylvania legislature. He returned to the theme touched on in his opening remarks: "the prejudice of courts and juries in behalf of the gentler and more dependent sex." She possessed an additional advantage: the funds to procure counsel "whose acuteness and energy are exceeded by none who practise at the bar," and the means to enlist "witnesses from every part of this State and from several of the other States of the Union to testify in respect to the most trivial, the most insignificant circumstances."

With all these advantages, what had the plaintiff actually offered to support the charge of "carnal connection with and carnal knowledge of Josephine Clifton," and similar relations with a long list of unidentified females? Their ridiculous case for adultery had been built around the fabrications of William Doty, who was sneaking around Miss Clifton's cabin on a non-existent Hudson River night boat. His testimony had been proved to be rank perjury. Why had they struggled so desperately with their parade of low-life characters and prostitutes? "Reflect upon the fact that there is not a living man in the city of New York better known than the defendant in this suit. Testimony regarding his whereabouts, during the whole course of his life, is readily available." They had resorted to perjury because their charge of adultery could be supported in no other way.

Reluctantly, Van Buren was obliged to dwell on certain unsavory aspects of Mrs. Forrest's conduct. No one could deny that she associated with persons of whom her husband disapproved. Few would accept the free-thinking principles outlined in her "Fourier" letter. Certainly he doubted if any of the jurors had had such "frolics in their households" as those held on Twenty-second Street.

The jury must discriminate between the witnesses. Garvin's wild story about washing the windows and peeking into the library was unworthy of serious attention. However, Mrs. Underwood's reports could be taken at face value. What about Anna? Several circumstantial facts must be noted. If her illegitimate offspring had been the child of Barney McCabe, would

Mrs. Forrest and Mrs. Voorhies have treated her so charitably and provided for the child's care? And what about the other persons involved with Anna? At the moment of this trial, "tell me why it is, that a simple woman, as if by magic, drives them all away. Howard to the Sandwich Islands; Godwin to Europe; the Voorhies to Europe?" Simply "because she holds within her a truth which can destroy them, and they don't dare to confront her." "I trust," he continued, "that when the counsel comes to sum up the other side, he will not forget that she is the 'Flowers' of his 'Forrest,' and not of mine."

Van Buren read again from the notorious "Consuelo" letter, interspersing his recitation with an explication of the text. He was dismayed, as undoubtedly the jurors had been, to discover that "however refined and intellectual literary people may be, apparently the mode in which they make love resembles that of ordinary mortals." Jamieson's confession was incontrovertible. "When you come to declarations of love, when you come to avowals of confidence, when you come to clasping people in your arms, and sealing meetings by a kiss, you come to what, with ordinary mortals, is regarded as the evidence of adultery."

The history of the letter was now well known. One gloomy January night, when Catherine had abandoned her husband for the empty gaiety of another party, Forrest discovered the letter. Alone in his library, how those sickening phrases must have torn at his heart. What of the author of these rapturous lines; has he stepped forward to deny them? No! George Jamieson, like the others, has not dared to appear. Is it not strange that this lady's loyal protectors: Jamieson, Howard, Godwin, Voorhies, and even Bryant, have all fled from her? Except for her legal adviser, the only men to whom she could turn for counsel and comfort were Mr. Forrest's friends: James Lawson and Andrew Stevens.

Van Buren thanked the jury for their patient acceptance of his "rude and unpolished manner." For a moment would they allow him a brief personal observation? He had found Forrest so uniformly kind, so simple in all his tastes and feeling, so perfectly frank, and so religiously regardful of truth that it had produced on him the strongest conviction that the actor had been wronged, deeply wronged. Since the separation, this honest man, one of our country's first citizens, had been forced "to occupy a room in a hotel, a bedroom in his sisters' house or an outhouse at Fonthill," instead of the comforts that he had so ably earned and so well deserved.

Finally, he must caution the jury against sickly sentimentality toward the unprotected female, against the delusions of the literary clique with their "sportive tricks" and "looking glass amblings." If the jurors heeded the promptings of their own honest natures, he would be content.

On Thursday morning, January 22, O'Conor began his summation, touching first on the unwarranted abuses of parties not on trial and parties not present to defend themselves. He swept along in grand style. How could anyone believe the vile charges against "a woman, who, at the bright and blooming age of nineteen was captivated by the fame and personal attractions of the distinguished young American. She gave him her hand, and trusted her virtue to him; and since then—at all events until the year 1849—eleven long years, nay, about twelve long years—she devoted herself to him; finally in such an abject manner, that that spiteful woman [Mrs. Underwood] said she was little better than an upper servant in the house of her lord."

O'Conor addressed the jury man-to-man: "I know not how you felt, gentlemen, when that woman uttered that remark, but I may say, for myself, it was the stage of this case—the stage in which I thought of the tendency of the human heart to fiery indignation, which, on fitting occasions turns as it were the milk of human kindness into gall and makes man feel as if a rattlesnake had prepared to strike."

O'Conor shifted to specific matters. He did not ask them to accept Doty's story; they could not, however, ignore the eye-witness accounts of Forrest's chummy hotel arrangements with Miss Clifton. They could not ignore his repeated visits to Mrs. Ingersoll's bawdy house. Certainly the actor did not go there "to say his 'pater noster.'"

They must weigh this evidence against the feeble fabrications on the other side: the Jamieson episode and the ridiculous "Consuelo" letter. To disprove the defendant's evil construction put upon them, one need only examine the record from May 1848 to May 1849. If Forrest were filled with "galling doubt," could he have written such affectionate letters to Catherine, letters utterly devoid of reproach? Recall the events after the argument over Mrs. Voorhies's farewell party in January 1849. "Why what a patient, mild, innocent, self-denying creature this must be, who when he found his wife unchaste, would lay his pure and uncontaminated person on the same bed with her for four long months? Do you believe it?"

Much had been made of the all-night parties, yet only one of them had been clearly substantiated and that by Mrs. N. P. Willis, the noble lady who has been by Mrs. Forrest's side throughout the trial. You recall her refined description of that song fest. "Mr. Forrest must have felt debased in his own estimation when he heard that innocent story, and said to himself, 'My God, how I must appear before this community! Am I not like some obscene animal which has escaped from its slough and looks out from its place of concealment at the refined and delicate society from which he shrinks, lest his presence should contaminate it?' "

The jury must consider all the despicable machinations of the defendant: Colonel Forney's scheme to trap Jamieson into a drunken confession; the attempt to hoodwink Mr. Bryant and Mrs. Forrest, a calamity that was narrowly averted when she "fell into the hands of an individual [himself] who would not allow her to slide down the slough of destruction." Undoubtedly the jury had already discredited Anna's testimony, but had they perceived how shamefully this creature had been used? When Anna was housed in Mercer Street in a dark room with muslin hangings over the windows and over the door leading to an inner room, she had invited Mrs. Forrest to visit her. The scheme was simple. If Mrs. Forrest had been thus discovered in this backroom of a disreputable house, what fearful accusations would have been heard at this trial. Finally, the jury must observe that all the diabolical stories of the witnesses bear the mark of a single diseased brain. These poor souls have been unwitting tools. Pity them, but do not pity the man who manipulated them.

O'Conor was confident he had carried the jury. "A single minute's reflection," he concluded, "can scarcely be required to enable you to arrive at the conclusion which will relieve from the name of this lady, the only thing which, under present circumstances, she regrets being obliged to say she feels to be a stigma—that name, which she will be at liberty to abandon when you render the verdict which law and justice requires."

Before Oakley gave his instructions to the jury, O'Conor was allowed a statement on the alimony and Van Buren, a brief rebuttal to O'Conor's summary.

Forrest's estate had been estimated at $150,000; his income from these holdings, $4,000 a year; and everyone knew that he could derive a princely revenue from even a moderate practice of his profession. O'Conor requested one third of his fortune for the support of Mrs. Forrest.

Van Buren ignored the alimony question. He concentrated on Jamieson, rereading Smith's account of the Cincinnati episode, and on Mrs. Ingersoll, charging that O'Conor's attempt to put an evil caste on Forrest's visits to her home was so much verbiage. No proof had been offered.

Although they had reached adjournment time, Oakley insisted on getting the case to the jury. He explained his duty to isolate the salient points, as he saw them, cautioning the jury not to be unduly influenced by his opinions. They must make the final judgment. As he saw the case, the only evidence of adultery on Mr. Forrest's part related to Miss Clifton and to Mrs. Ingersoll's establishment. On the charges of infidelity against Mrs. Forrest, he was inclined to rule out Richard Willis, Captain Calcraft, and Samuel Raymond; the decision rested on the charges involving N. P. Willis, Captain Howard, and George Jamieson. One legal point, peculiar to this action, must be observed. If both parties are judged guilty of adultery, "the law will leave them where it finds them: the law never grants divorces to guilty people." His final observation related to the "Consuelo" letter. He thought it peculiar that Mrs. Forrest would have preserved such a letter.

Just before five o'clock the jury retired. Two hours later they asked for further instructions: were visits to a house of ill-fame to be construed as proof of adultery? Oakley refused to give a ruling, and they returned to their deliberations. At eight o'clock they sent out another message, advising Oakley not to hold the court. After consulting with O'Conor and Van Buren, Oakley called for adjournment until ten o'clock Monday morning, instructing the jury to seal their verdict if they came to a decision before that time. An hour-and-a-half later the jurymen reached an agreement and went home. Apparently, they all kept their pledge to secrecy. No word of the verdict leaked out over the weekend.

The trial was winding up after a full six weeks. Everyone was exhausted but tenaciously hanging on for the final crucial moment. On Monday morning, January 26, 1852, "the excitement was intense," the *Herald* reported. "Thousands and thousands of the anxious public thronged the park. At ten o'clock, the Chief Justice took his seat upon the Bench, and the anxiety depicted on every countenance for the breaking of the sealed verdict was intense.

"Mrs. Forrest was in court, as was also Mr. Forrest, at an early hour. The fortitude which never left Mrs. Forrest during the protracted investigation seemed now to have almost deserted her, and she was faint with anxiety, restless, watchful, and uneasy. Mr. Forrest looked anxious, but he looked like a man resolved to meet the worst that could befall him.

"The Clerk of the Court called over the names of the jury and all answered. He then said, 'Gentlemen, have you agreed?'"

The Foreman replied that they had and handed the sealed verdict to the Court. "A breathless silence reigned throughout

the room while the Chief Justice was perusing the verdict."
Oakley handed the verdict to the Clerk and ordered him to
read it aloud. The Clerk began.

Gentlemen, hearken to your verdict as it stands.

First—Has or has not the defendant, Edwin Forrest, since his
marriage with the plaintiff, Catherine N. Forrest, committed adultery as in the complaint in this action charged? *He has.*

Second—Were or were not the said plaintiff and said defendant
inhabitants of this State at the time of the commission of said
adultery by the said defendant? *They were.*

Third—Was or was not such adultery by the said defendant
committed within this State? *It was.*

Fourth—Was or was not the said defendant a resident of the
State of New York at the time of the commencement of this action? *He was.*

Fifth—Has or has not the plaintiff committed adultery as alleged against her in the answer to this action? *She has not.*

Sixth—Was or was not the plaintiff a resident and inhabitant
of this State at the time of the commencement of this action?
She was.

Seventh—Was or was not the plaintiff an actual inhabitant of
this State at the time of the commission of such adultery by the
defendant within this State, and also at the time of the commencement of this action? *She was.*

Eighth—What annual amount of alimony ought to be allowed
the plaintiff? *Three thousand dollars.*

The jury say that they find for the plaintiff on the whole issue
in the pleadings and that in answer, they find in the affirmative on
the first, second, third, fourth, sixth and seventh questions of fact
specified in the order of December 24th, 1850, and in the negative
on the fifth question of fact specified in the said order.

And they find that alimony be allowed the plaintiff to the
amount of three thousand dollars per year.

Mrs. Forrest had won a complete victory.

Forrest was the first to leave the court, and "as he descended
to the Park he was saluted with vociferous cheers from the
assembled multitude who continued to shout and cheer him

on halfway up Broadway." This friendly demonstration re-affirmed what he had suspected from the beginning: the final verdict rested with the people. He was unaware of the equally enthusiastic reception for Mrs. Forrest on the other side of the building. She had departed by the back door into Chambers Street.

The feelings that had been aroused by the trial were not subdued by the jury verdict. "In every public house," the *Herald* reported the next day, "in every barroom, on the ferry boats, in the cars, in the omnibuses, and in every hole and corner of the city, amongst all kinds of society, from the literary coteries and codfish aristocracy down to the merest jabberers on the Five Points, the facts, the incidents, and above all, the verdict, were freely discussed." Many thought the verdict would be regarded as a "premium paid for licentiousness." One reporter deplored its effect "in the regions of uppertendom. Walking into the property of her husband to the extent of $3,000 per year would have not only a pecuniary but a moral bearing." Divorce actions "against the lords of creation" would increase at a merry clip.

O'Conor was widely praised for championing the helpless lady. The members of the New York Bar gave a dinner in his honor, and on February 24, 1853, thirty ladies presented him with a silver vase as a token of their appreciation for his noble work. (No gentleman was permitted to subscribe!) O'Conor accepted all tributes, for he received no reward beyond the personal and professional glory. Someone estimated that the trial had cost him $6,000 out of pocket, to say nothing of his services, for which he had not been paid.

Public interest in the Forrest case might have been dissipated in a month or two had there not been so many conspicuous reminders.

First, Willis's assault action came to trial; then, Forrest's counterclaim for damages; at the end of the year, the perjury trial of William Doty; and, finally, Forrest's protracted appeals for a reversal of the alimony judgment. He would not let the wound heal. "A great wrong has been done," he wrote in his notebook shortly after the trial, "and to prevent a repetition of it—the offenders should be scourged and what scourging is so effective as to keep the names of these ermined tyrants, a mockery and a scorn forever in the mouths of men." This task occupied Forrest for the rest of his life.

CHAPTER *xix*

The People's Verdict

Publicly proclaimed an adulterer and sensitive as he was to damaged pride, Forrest might reasonably have retired to his castle. Instead, he went to Philadelphia for two weeks, allowing time for the public to read the court proceedings in one of the half-dozen editions that had been rushed into print. On Monday, February 9, he appeared at the Broadway Theatre to hear their verdict. From his first entrance until the final curtain, when someone produced a banner announcing, "THIS IS THE PEOPLE'S VERDICT," their decision was clear.

According to a newspaper account of the occasion, Forrest happily let them roar for a half-hour after the play before he tried to quiet them. Finally, he stepped forward. The audience settled back in their seats, and he spoke: "Instinctively I ask myself the question, why is this vast assemblage here tonight." Had they come to see a favorite actor in a favorite play (*Damon and Pythias*)? No! They had come to express their "irrepressible sympathy for a deeply-injured man." He would not comment on the late unhappy trial; the courts would be given a chance to rectify their error. "In the meanwhile, I submit my cause to you,—my cause, did I say?—no, not my cause alone, but yours, the cause of every man in the community, the cause of every human being, the cause of every honest wife, the cause of everyone who cherishes a home and the pure spirit which should abide there. I submit my cause to a tribunal uncorrupt and incorruptible."

For the next twelve weeks the crowds gathered nightly at the Broadway to cheer their hero, a total of 80,000 according to one estimate. At the fiftieth performance, April 9, manager Marshall staged a gigantic jubilee: a transparency illuminated the front of the theatre and "many persons in the neighborhood, sympathizing with the general feeling, illuminated their dwellings." When "this great and prosperous engagement unparalleled in the history of the stage" concluded on April 30, Forrest assured the audience that their demonstrations had vindicated him more than a thousand verdicts, for they had the power to "make and unmake judges." Even after Forrest had departed for Washington, New York kept up the clamor. Each night Christy's Minstrels added an extra verse to their "Jordan Am a Hard Road to Trable":

> *For sixty-nine nights the immortal Forrest played,*
> *And sixty-nine crowds he had accordin';*
> *In Macbeth, Damon, and Jack Cade*
> *He's the greatest actor on this side of Jordan.*

During his spectacular run at the Broadway, Forrest's daytime hours had been occupied with the pesky Willis trial. Although Willis had asked for $10,000 damages, the jury awarded him $2,500. Some of his newspaper colleagues thought even this was too much. One reporter figured Willis's actual damages at $56.28, including such items as: "Loss of time for editing the *Home Journal,* twelve cents; outraged honor through receiving a public castigation, three cents."

The Willis trial was not the only daily nuisance; Forrest was contending with a new theatrical rival. On February 2, one week before he opened at the Broadway, Mrs. Catherine Norton Sinclair Forrest had begun an engagement at Brougham's Lyceum, appearing as Lady Teazle in *The School for Scandal.* Many believed that this shocking declaration of independence was a tacit admission of her debased character. In the mid-nineteenth century a lady did not skip from parlor to stage without arousing suspicion.

When her allowance had been cut off in November,

The People's Verdict

Catherine had hired George Vandenhoff to coach her for the stage. Vandenhoff was a young English actor, who, like his father, had made a minor reputation in America. He thought Catherine devoid of talent and too old (thirty-three). He could not, however, ignore the box-office power of her name. In exchange for his coaching and for appearing as her leading man, he was to receive half the profits from all engagements. During the court proceedings little time was available for extralegal activities; most of their rehearsing had to be concentrated in the one week between the end of the trial and her debut.

With the excitement over the divorce still running high, and aware that the "Cossacks of the Bowery" had not approved the verdict, Mayor Kingsland feared another riot. He packed Brougham's Lyceum with "stars" and ordered a detachment of militia, veterans of the Astor Place Riot, to stand by. His precautions were unnecessary. Except for a drunk in the gallery who toppled over when he tried to lead "three groans for Mrs. Forrest," there was no disturbance.

Most of Catherine's friends thought that she performed remarkably for a beginner. Her voice was weak, and some thought that she was "too highly rouged." One reporter was shocked to hear her recite the indecent passages with such "imperturbable nonchalance." This might "tell much in her favor as an actress, but it involuntarily suggests many an unpleasantness against her as a woman."

No one claimed that she was a great actress, yet everyone was amazed that she had learned so much; and after she had performed the five plays Vandenhoff had taught her, the critics began to praise her skill in "cool and cutting irony," and her remarkable "ease and gracefulness." In the four weeks at Brougham's she played the leading roles in *Lady of Lyons*, *Love's Sacrifice*, *Much Ado about Nothing*, and *The Patrician's Daughter*, in addition to *The School for Scandal*. Probably no aspiring actress ever began her career on such short notice and with such a repertoire.

After the month in New York, she performed two weeks in Philadelphia and two weeks in Boston. Both managements

327

took full advantage of her notoriety, billing her as Mrs. C. N. Sinclair, "the late Mrs. Forrest." During the next year she toured the country, terminating the season with an engagement at Maguire's San Francisco Hall. In November she became actress-manager at the Metropolitan Theatre in San Francisco, and two years later assumed the same duties at the Forrest Theatre in Sacramento with Edwin Booth as her leading man. In light of his later prominence it is startling to see "Edwin Booth" in small type on the playbills and "MRS. C. N. SINCLAIR" in boldface.

During the 1856-7 season she played in Australia, and in September 1857, opened a month's engagement at the Haymarket Theatre in London. The critics were kind. Although perceiving little talent, they praised her "handsome and expressive countenance"; the *London Morning Post* noted that she possessed "a figure perfectly *en bon point*." After touring the provinces, she returned to the Haymarket the following September for a final four weeks, introducing two new plays: Arthur Murphy's *The Way to Keep Him* and Mrs. Inchbald's *Wives as They Were and Maids as They Are*. She could speak with authority on both subjects.

Two years later she returned to America, and after a final performance at the Academy of Music in New York on December 18, retired from the stage. For ten years she lived in an old mansion on Staten Island with her sister Virginia and Virginia's husband, Henry Sedley, the actor and critic. When her sister died in 1869, Catherine and Henry moved to a brownstone house at 62 West 84th Street, where she remained until her death on June 9, 1891.

Except for occasional chance encounters and the required communication via their lawyers, Catherine's and Edwin's paths never crossed. The irreparable loss of the deep affection that they had once felt for each other was only perversely apparent: in Catherine's patient waiting for the alimony and Forrest's extravagant efforts to set aside the judgment of the court.

During the spring of 1852, while they were competing in

the theatre, the real torture had not yet begun. Catherine was successfully trading on the name that she had hoped to abandon; Forrest was thriving on the nightly affirmation of the people's verdict, in New York, Washington, Baltimore, and finally, in Philadelphia.

On the Fourth of July, James Lawson and Andrew Stevens joined Forrest at Fonthill to commemorate the sacred day and to celebrate his recent triumph in the theatre, a combined tribute to the ultimate power of the people. Fonthill was an ideal spot for the observance. Hitched to the highest turret, the flag caught the warm winds that swept up from the valley and proclaimed that the master was at his patriotic devotions.

Forrest remained at Fonthill for the summer. In the fall he returned to the theatre for his first full season since the Riot. During the previous spring, the theatre public had turned out en masse to countermand the verdict of the court. Now they were welcoming him back to his theatrical duties. The packed houses, the wild cheers, and the treasurer's reports in New York, Philadelphia, and Boston assured him that his professional life had not been damaged. His seventy-night engagement in New York even surpassed his record of the year before by one performance.

Except for an occasional week in Baltimore, Forrest held to the three theatrical centers throughout the next two seasons. The public maintained their solid support; he faced only the normal occupational hazards. As usual, he complained regularly about the incompetent supporting actors. He wrote to a friend that one manager "had enough 'sticks' to start a crutch factory." Why was it, he asked, that "whenever a young man is incapable of learning a trade, is incompetent to be a store porter, is too lazy to beg, and afraid to steal, he takes to the stage as a proper field for the profitable exercise of his idiocy?"

Anyone who knew Forrest could tell that he had cast aside his gloomy preoccupation with his domestic crisis. In Philadelphia he demanded that one of the actors be dismissed because he had been drunk "upon the stage." In Boston he refused to perform with John Gilbert, the stock company's leading man. When Forrest heard that E. L. Davenport, the handsome comedian, had appropriated *Jack Cade,* he sent him the inevitable ultimatum: "If you act this play again, I will test your moral right to do so by an action in a court of law."

One aggravation was more difficult to combat. During his 1855 spring engagement at the Broadway Theatre, his acting was viciously criticized in the *New York Tribune* by Edmund O'Flaherty, alias William Stuart, alias "Fry." O'Flaherty had left Ireland under a cloud, adopted the name of Stuart when he arrived in America, and to shield his true identity further, adopted "Fry" for his by-line.

Stuart condemned Forrest's performance in every role. In the players' scene in *Hamlet* he insisted that the actor "had far more the air of some huge gypsy watching with roguish glance an opportunity to rob the hen-roost." The grand emotional outbursts, which, in Shakespeare, "gushed from the deepest depths of Othello's heart, seemed to come from the deepest depths of Mr. Forrest's stomach." Stuart grudgingly conceded that Forrest's audiences held a contrary view. He suggested that if these ill-bred "butcher's apprentices" had become so accustomed to the bellowing of bulls that they delighted in sub-human throat rattles they might better listen to the "firing of cannon and the filing of saws." Such noises produced just "as agreeable sensations."

Forrest would probably have horse-whipped him if the Willis affairs had been less vivid in his memory. Once again Forrest placed his faith in the judgment of the people. They did not disappoint him. Each night their cheers seemed louder, and on his final night of the season, the "Forrest Light Guard," appearing in full uniform in the front seats of the parquet, gave him a resounding "hip-hip-hurrah."

After the costumes were packed away for the summer, Forrest broke his customary end-of-the-season routine. Instead of seeking his rejuvenation at Fonthill, he went to Philadelphia. Not only did he crave the companionship and loving attention of his sisters, he had a new project in the back of his head.

One day in the middle of July he interrupted his morning stroll to examine the construction of a brownstone mansion at the southwest corner of Broad and Master. Inquiring of the workmen, he learned that it was being built for Frederick Gaul, a well-known Philadelphia brewer. Later the same day, he went to the brewery and offered Gaul $23,000 cash for the unfinished house. Apparently he had chosen a persuasive figure; Gaul accepted. Forrest took one minor precaution in completing the transaction: the deed was recorded in his sisters' names. If the courts ever attached his property, they could not touch his home.

He had been driven to his purchase not only by his irrespressible passion for real estate; he wanted a Philadelphia town house as a permanent residence. In spite of his continuing efforts, Fonthill had failed him. The river castle had been built for Catherine, and whenever he was on the grounds, he was inescapably reminded of that sad fact.

Staying away from Fonthill did not, however, free him from the nagging thoughts of his marital calamity. Just after he began his 1855 fall engagement in New York, a new novel appeared in Philadelphia, exposing the Forrests' entire domestic history through a tissue-thin disguise. Everyone understood why the author of *The Match-Girl: or, Life Scenes as They Are* chose anonymity. Forrest was called Oakwood; Catherine, Caroline; the Parke Godwins, Mr. and Mrs. Field Close; and Nathaniel Parker Willis acquired the fanciest moniker, Bazallel Wagstaff Bayes. Even the characters as depicted in the illustrations bore an unmistakable resemblance to the originals.

The description of the couple's separation was one of the high spots in the novel. Just before they departed from the Twenty-second Street house, Edgar strode to the doorway: "His face, haughty in its habitual expression, was colder and haughtier now than ever, and his step, measured and equal, as though he trod the stage, on which he knew no rival; for he was the greatest artist of his country, who now was acting out in all the agonies of reality, the deepest, saddest of life's dramas." They walked out to the carriage. " 'Caroline,' said he, as he placed the portrait beside her, 'Will you like this?' 'Thank you!' faintly murmured the weeping wife." The final moment came when they stood together in the entrance hall in her new home. Mr. and Mrs. Close were descending the stairs. Oakwood stepped toward his wife. " 'Edgar,' she said, in a low voice, 'they are looking at us!' Edgar bent his head, and touched her forehead with his lips, then letting go her hand, he turned away. . . . He was gone, and so they whom God, and man, and love, had joined together, were separated forever."

The author did not stick as close to the facts in other episodes. In some he was more scandalous than Anna Flowers. Caroline regularly visited Bazallel Wagstaff Bayes's filthy hall bedroom where he scribbled out his pieces for the "Fireside Gazette." Night after night they drank themselves into an alcoholic frenzy—how dog-eared these pages became—and plotted their life together after the divorce. She would get "a splendid allowance, and that, added to her reputation as the most injured and virtuous woman, would give them fame and freedom over the whole world."

The novel was an unsavory prelude to the next act in the Forrests' real-life drama. When Forrest concluded his December engagement in Philadalphia, he returned to New York to explain to the Superior Court why he had not paid the alimony. The case began on January 10, 1856, with O'Conor and Van Buren again representing the two parties.

"Handsome John" opened the argument. His client had ignored Justice Oakley's directions for good reason. Public opinion, the final arbiter, had outstripped the tardy court and reversed the opinion of Oakley and his jury. Mr. Forrest has never been more universally respected and admired than at this moment, while Mrs. Forrest, "whose innocence had been declared by the verdict has been an exile from the city either upon the coast of the Pacific, or in some Islands beyond, and pursuing courses, if my information can be relied on, which would make any respectable friends she may formerly have had now the least anxious of all other persons to see her here again."

Van Buren did not rest his case on the present status of the two principals. He asked the two Justices to consider the twenty-seven errors in the divorce trial, ranging from the numerous instances of irrelevant and immaterial testimony to Oakley's error in allowing the jury to fix the alimony.

Although the hearings occupied only five court days, they extended until the end of the month. Even then, the judges quashed Forrest's hopes for a speedy decision. They would take the matter under advisement and report their findings in due time. Unhappily, their notion of "due time" did not coincide with Forrest's.

When he concluded his spring season of brief engagements in Baltimore, Washington, and Philadelphia, the judges were still silent. Finally, the first week in July, they handed down their decision. The jury had been correct in granting the divorce; they had erred in specifying the alimony; and Oakley had been wrong in ruling that if Catherine accepted the alimony, she relinquished her dower rights in Forrest's estate. Both of these matters must be decided by a competent referee. They assigned Alvin C. Bradley to the task. Forrest had hoped this would be the final chapter in his domestic travail; now the villains proposed to prolong his agony. Fortunately, he could not know that Bradley would take three years and five months to arrive at a more damaging decision.

Stung twice by the legal minions, Forrest determined to brace himself against them as best he could. The first step was to dispose of Fonthill. If the wily O'Conor led Catherine to attack his estate, undoubtedly they would first lay siege to the castle. He found a buyer immediately. Archbishop Hughes was looking for a home for the Sisters of Charity of St. Vincent de Paul. Under other circumstances Forrest would have sought a more solvent buyer; now he was quite willing to accept $25,000 down and a 6 per cent mortgage for the $75,000 balance. In fact, Forrest was so pleased with the bargain that he donated $5,000 to the Sisters of Charity. After Forrest had begun the negotiations, apparently, he could not bear to relinquish his entire claim to the lovely hill. He retained thirty acres.

As further precaution against plunder, he copyrighted his

plays. Congress had just passed the first strong copyright law, giving the author of a play "along with the sole right to print and publish the said composition, the sole right also to act, perform and represent the same." Forrest interpreted the law to suit himself. The authors had relinquished their rights when they sold their plays to him.

With his defenses prepared and a fortune of $158,000 to draw on, not counting his real estate, Forrest resolved to give up the theatre. To spend three hours every night roaring through *Metamora, Jack Cade,* or *Lear* to pile up cash that might be raided by the courts seemed a futile enterprise.

Forrest did not announce his retirement immediately. Instead, he tapered off with a reduced schedule during the fall and on February 5, 1857, began his farewell engagement in New York. He never reached the final night on which he had intended to inform the public of his plans. Four days after the opening he was stricken with the gout and was forced to suspend his performances. On Saturday night, February 13, he sufficiently subdued the infirmity to struggle through *Jack Cade.* When the curtain closed, he knew he had to give up, angered as he was by such an inglorious swan song. He went home to Philadelphia and for the next two months remained in bed.

Some of his friends ascribed his collapse to his heavy program of exercises and his too frequent Turkish baths. Unfortunately, the jargon used by his contemporaries to describe his ailments does not translate readily into the jargon of present-day medical science. His eulogistic biographer, W. R. Alger, reported that his "rheumatic inflammability—a contracted and congested state of some part of the capillary circulation and the associated sensory nerves accumulating force to be discharged in hot explosions of twinging agony—might have been cured by an aesthetic gymnastic adapted to free and harmonize all the circulations—the breath, the blood, the nerve-force."

In June Forrest had recovered sufficient strength to walk in the garden, and in early July Tom Maguire, the San Francisco impresario, reported that he found the actor in good health. Maguire had brought a letter from Governor James N. Johnson urging Forrest to come to California. Though flattered by the invitation, Forrest reluctantly declined. He had not changed his mind about retiring.

By the middle of July Forrest was well enough to take a jaunt to the country. No notebook entries or letters indicate where he went; the *Philadelphia Sunday Mercury* simply reported, on September 6, that he had been visiting "celebrated springs, mountains, lakes, and valleys."

In the early fall Forrest concentrated on his new home. He arranged to have the Fonthill furniture moved by boat to Philadelphia and hired Thomas Heyl to start work on a stable on the back of the lot, facing Carlisle Street. With affairs on Broad Street progressing smoothly and with his health firmly re-established, he packed his trunk and headed west. For the first time in his life, he intended to travel as a retired gentleman, not as an actor. He resisted the entreaties of the managers in Pittsburgh and Cincinnati, then softened in St. Louis and performed during the month of November. In Cleveland he agreed to give manager John Ellsler six nights. Everything went well until December 21, when the gout again forced him to cancel the final performance.

The theatrical strain could not be blamed for the collapse. At seven o'clock that morning Forrest and Ellsler had walked some eight miles out Euclid Avenue and back along the lake, battling the violent winds. At one point, according to Ellsler, Forrest climbed on a rock, looked out over the foaming water and shouted: "If there are any infidels in Cleveland, let them come here, and look upon this magnificent element of creation, and let them go home and pray." Forrest went home to his hotel bed and remained there for the next month.

He was not able to return to Philadelphia until late January; not until March was he able to move about and take an occasional drive in the country. Even then he did not feel as kindly toward the Deity as he had, standing on the shore of

Lake Erie. Early that spring (1858) Philadelphia had been swept with a religious revival. Someone had spread a rumor that the great Edwin Forrest had "gone forward." No doubt a zealous lieutenant hoped to promote the campaign by listing the name of the famous actor on the roster of the "saved." Incredible as the report of Forrest's conversion may have seemed to some, the believers found convincing explanations for his religious rebirth. His illness had driven him to God. He sought relief from his domestic distress. Others insisted that he was repenting for a life spent in the work of the devil.

Neither the explanations nor the rumor was true. Forrest's conscience compelled him to set the record straight, awkward as it was to disappoint some of his devout friends. A congratulatory letter from Reverend E. L. Magoon was particularly painful to answer. He advised the Reverend that "as in most matters which pertain to me, the rumor was most pitifully in error." His spirits had never been "so tranquil and serene"; not because they had been rejuvenated in the tabernacle, he assured the Reverend, simply because the rheumatism had been subdued.

He admitted that his lengthened illness had given him a chance "to review the past and carefully to consider the future, both for time and for eternity." Much as he might regret some of his past deeds, he was sustained by the conviction that he had always "been actuated solely by an honest desire to adhere strictly to the rule of right." He had always lived by the Divine precept: "As ye would that men should do to you, do ye also to them likewise."

Unwittingly, Magoon showed Forrest's letter to some of his colleagues. He must have thought that the high moral tone of Forrest's disquisition would enlighten his associates who categorically condemned the theatre. If this was his motive, it misfired. From their pulpits they charged at Forrest as if he himself had initiated the rumor of his salvation. One labeled Forrest's letter "as melancholy a picture of the hardihood of the unbelieving and impenitent heart as can well be drawn." "What Christian," another asked, "is so perfect yet as to be able to review a single year of his life, in the light of the Divine holiness, with any such complacency as this proud and violent man bestows upon his whole sad career?"

Forrest may not have been unduly disturbed by this clerical abuse—"the bite of a mosquito is not fatal," he observed to Oakes—still he was incapable of ignoring the attack. In a letter to his friend William W. Clapp, the chronicler of the Boston stage, he gave his view of these "anti-christian bigots" and their hypocritical mish-mash. "If this be their mode of showing their love for their enemies, may God help their friends!" This was a sore point with Forrest. "I love my friends and hate my enemies," he wrote, "and no man who knows me will doubt my sincerity in this—and no man on earth will believe the hypocrite who says he loves his enemies."

Unlike other controversies revolving around the actor, the tempest over his immortal soul blew out after this first flurry. Forrest returned to the serious business of his retirement: cultivating his mind and improving his surroundings.

The walls, the tables, and the floor-to-ceiling shelves in his library became crowded with his new acquisitions. He studied the paintings and kept the books on a constant journey from shelf to desk and back to shelf. According to one observer, there was "little worth reading in the English language that he did not study." He was naturally endowed for this scholarly enterprise because he had a "will of iron, a mind susceptible to impression as new fallen snow and a memory retentive as marble." Forrest did not limit himself to great literature. Three volumes that fascinated him during this period were: *The History of the Female Sex; The Philosophy of Marriage*; and *Prostitution, the Greatest of our Social Evils.*

For more than ten years he had anticipated the simple joys of living in quiet seclusion. He had lost the chance at Fonthill. He was not going to lose it at Broad and Master. Judging from the reports of two visitors who penetrated his privacy, he was happily absorbed in his daily chores. A Southerner observed that Forrest was an early riser. Through the daylight hours he cultivated the grounds and in the evenings retired to his library. An air of cleanliness pervaded the house. A visitor from New York was impressed by the homey atmosphere, by Forrest's courtesy, and, most of all, by his generosity in sharing a bowl of fruit.

The brownstone mansion on Broad Street lacked the exotic grandeur of Fonthill Castle. In its somber elegance, general size, and arrangement it was very similar to the Twenty-second Street house. The main entrance, eight stone steps above the street level, opened into an entrance hall that ran the length of the building. A reception parlor and dining room occupied the right half of the main floor; a drawing room stretched the entire length on the left side. Each room had floor-to-ceiling windows, and, at the rear of the drawing room, French doors opened into the garden. Although the garden was filled with flowers, Forrest was more interested in the grape arbors and trees. As he remarked to one visitor: "I prefer the trees; I love to hear the wind whistling through their branches. When alone in my library, it sounds like a voice from another world." In later years Forrest added an art gallery along the south wall of the drawing room and a little theatre in the basement below the gallery. Two bedrooms and the library were on the second floor. As in all of Forrest's establishments, the library became the sacred center of the house.

Many people were perplexed by Forrest's new life. How could a man who had been constantly on the move, continually in the public eye, hem himself into this tiny corner? How could a brawny giant who loved to perch himself on a windy cliff above the Hudson, or listen to the wild music of Niagara, settle for the small world of garden and library? Yet, he did, and for two years seemed to relish his seclusion.

The pleasures of his retirement were disrupted only twice. On December 1, 1859, Bradley announced that on the basis of his calculations of Forrest's fortune, the alimony should be boosted to $4,000 per year. Worse than that, he instructed the actor to pay $35,593 in arrears. Three weeks after this unhappy decision, Forrest was sent to bed for a month-long "sweating tussle with the old devil," the gout. He escaped the first calamity momentarily by transferring it to Van Buren, advising him to start the legal machinery again. The second he finally vanquished with warm blankets and a blazing fire.

CHAPTER XX

Gout, Rheumatism, and Sciatica

During the spring of 1860 Forrest became depressed about his chances for preserving his happy solitude. Van Buren reported that in spite of a new appeal that had been thrown into the legal mill, he might be forced to pay the alimony. If Van Buren was right, Forrest would have to return to work. Whatever evil demands the courts might make on him, he was determined that they would not dig into his fortune.

By June Van Buren's letters had become so gloomy that Forrest decided to resist no longer. He asked his Philadelphia newspaper friend James Rees to tease the public with a tentative announcement. Rees happily obliged, informing his readers that relief from the "present sickened state of the drama" was finally in sight. Mr. Forrest was contemplating a return to the stage.

As soon as the word was out, the managers besieged him with offers. To all of them he gave the same reply: "I have not yet determined to act during the coming season, but should I do so my professional services are already pledged to another." Actually, Forrest had already signed up with a relative newcomer, James N. Nixon. Fully aware of the dubious professional qualifications of this former equestrian director of the Castle Garden Circus, Forrest had succumbed to Nixon's unorthodox terms because he knew that no other manager could match them: half the gross for one hundred nights on a schedule of not more than three performances per week.

Forrest began with a two-week trial run in Baltimore and

on September 17 opened in New York at Niblo's Garden, a theatre that previously had offered opera, ballet, and variety entertainments. Simple economy had dictated the choice. The Broadway had been torn down; Niblo's was the largest establishment available. At capacity the house held 3,500, the treasurer's drawer, $1,750, and money was the principal object in the present venture.

Business considerations did not, however, dictate Forrest's schedule. He had another motive in choosing one of his weakest roles for opening night. A new American star had stepped into the vacuum left by his retirement, his twenty-seven-year-old namesake, Edwin Booth. Had Junius Brutus's son shown the good grace to be content with a supporting, or even a second-player billing, Forrest would have encouraged the boy. He could not tolerate him as a star. During the previous two seasons Booth had been extravagantly praised for his Hamlet. Forrest would now show them a real Hamlet.

After his three-year absence, the audience was less interested in making a comparison than in welcoming back their old favorite. Forrest acknowledged their warm cheers with one of his flowery curtain speeches, assuring them that whether he continued to trod the boards or retreated to the simple solitude of his library, he could never forget this heartwarming reminder of their enduring affection.

Nixon had gone overboard to give the engagement a strong beginning. The first volume of a new "Edwin Forrest Edition of Shakespearean Plays" was on sale in the lobby for fifteen cents. *Hamlet* was now available; the other plays would be published as Forrest added them to his schedule.

Playing an entertainment palace was not the only innovation in the new season. Not for some time had Forrest enjoyed the luxury of a three-nights-a-week program, rarely had he held to one play for so long: *Hamlet* for the first three weeks; *Lear* for the next three; and then *Othello* for two. More than that, he kept one foot on Broad Street. Each week after the Friday night performance, he rushed off to Philadelphia, not returning until early afternoon the following Monday.

341

When Booth began his season at the Winter Garden Theatre in mid-November (he had been in Boston in September), Forrest returned to *Hamlet*. The audiences must be given an opportunity to make a direct comparison. The contest was futile. Forrest's devotees simply could not tolerate the young actor's casual manners; Booth's coterie urged the bombastic Hercules to crawl back into retirement. Every actor since Thespis has had to contend with the rising generation. In his first triumphant years, the young actor is invariably hailed for his naturalness, his honest image of life. In his declining years, he finds that some fresh youngster with a new realism has replaced him. Except to those who have grown old with him, he has become a stagey old fool. Forrest had not reached this sad turning point, yet he was dangerously near it.

On one of his off nights, Forrest took a box at the Winter Garden to see Booth's *Macbeth*. When the young actor ambled onto the stage looking "excessively natural," with his head bowed, Forrest was reported to have remarked to his companion: "What's the damned fool doing: he looks like a super hunting for a sixpence." Forrest was distressed to find his namesake so deluded in his notions about acting.

Forrest remained at Niblo's throughout the year—the first time in his career he had stayed in New York, or any one place, for an entire season. He had his weekends in Philadelphia, interspersed with occasional visits with Oakes and, apparently, with a Miss "Nahmeokee" in Boston. Against his better judgment Forrest had slipped into a mild flirtation with a young Boston lady, simply identified as "Nahmeokee," the character name of his loving wife in *Metamora*. For the next few years his letters to Oakes invariably included some kind greetings to "Nahmeokee."

Romance was not, however, on Forrest's mind during the 1860-1 season. He was too concerned over the fate of his country. With secession fever running high after the fateful December 17 meeting of the People's Convention in the Baptist Church in Columbia, South Carolina, Forrest feared that "the States might tremble into ruin." "Great God, in what a melancholy condition is our country now!" he lamented to Oakes. "An ineradicable curse begins at the very root of the heart that harbors the single thought that favors disunion. May God in his wisdom and strength avert the overwhelming evil."

Even with the country falling apart Forrest held to his engagement. He was laid up with a rheumatic attack on April 12, 1861, the day the guns fired on Fort Sumter; on the 15th he returned for his final week.

During the summer in Philadelphia, Forrest struggled to keep up his spirits. "The political aspect of our country is ominous indeed," he wrote to a friend in Cincinnati, "yet I hope with you that in the Divine Providence that there will be some great good brought out of this evil state of affairs and by September next all our difficulties will be adjusted." If they were not, "we must gird up our loins and put on our armor." Now is the time to proclaim to the world that "we HAVE a Government stronger and more enduring than that of kings and potentates, because it is founded on equal and exact justice."

Forrest's faith in his country could not be shaken; he wished he had a comparable faith in "exact justice" in his personal battle. On June 2, 1860, the courts had handed down another judgment against him. Van Buren appealed to the Court of General Term and on December 7, they reaffirmed the ruling of their predecessors. Forrest still refused to concede. He advised Van Buren to petition the Court of Appeals. If he had lost his hope of winning, he could at least get some revenge by delay. Delay was all he won. On December 31, 1862, the Court of Appeals threw themselves in line with the others. Forrest ignored their decision. He would rely on the verdict of the people and on his own stubbornness.

How puny this legalistic battling seemed in comparison with the struggle between the States and even with the struggle against his own infirmity. He spent much of the summer of 1862 in bed, fighting another rheumatic attack. In September he was back at Niblo's for his third season, and, judging from the report of Artemus Ward, apparently going strong:

The awjince was all-fired large and the boxes was full of the elitty of New York. Sevral opery glasses was leveld at me by Gothum's fairest darters, but I didn't let on as tho I noticed it, tho mebby I did take out my sixteen-dollar silver watch and brandish it round more than was necessary. But the best of us has our weaknesses and if a man has gewelry let him show it. . . .

Edwin Forrest is a grate acter. I thot I saw Otheller before me all the time he was actin, and when the curtain fell, I found my spectacles was still mistened with salt-water, which has run from my eyes while poor Desdemony was dyin. Betsy Jane—Betsy Jane! let us pray that our domestic bliss may never be busted up by a Iago!

Mr. Forrest makes money acting out on the stage. He gits five hundred dollars a nite and his board and washin. I wish I had such a Forrest in my Garding!

Ward did not greatly exaggerate Forrest's profits. It was a good season, in spite of Booth's strong competition. One night Forrest sent a spy to count Booth's house at the Winter Garden. He was delighted with the report: $550, if all paid, which he doubted, compared to his own $676.75. In twelve weeks Forrest added over $12,000 to his cushion against the alimony.

In December he went to Boston for a Christmas-season engagement and a reunion with his old friend James "Acorn" Oakes. For both men this was the high spot of any season, the opportunity to enjoy the crowning friendship of their lives. Undoubtedly the two men had been drawn together by their many similarities. Both were strong and vigorous, impatient with human frailty in themselves and in others. They cherished simple virtues, abhorred sham, and loved their country. They were both shouters, blunt and direct in word and deed, downright and forthright. Above all, they both loved the theatre. Oakes was not professionally attached to the theatre—he ran the Old Salt Store at 49 Long Wharf, but he had a passion for the stage and for stage people.

A psychoanalytically disposed observer could build a case for homosexuality in their relationship. Certainly in the mid-twentieth century two men would shy from expressing their affection so openly. Some of their letters sound like love letters: "For I am, from top to bottom, inside and out, and all through, forever yours," Oakes wrote on one occasion. Reverend Alger, Forrest's official biographer, reported that "whenever they met after a long separation, as soon as they were alone together they threw their arms around each other in fond embrace with mutual kisses after the manner of lovers in our land or of friends in more tropical and demonstrative climes."

The collapse of his marriage and his growing distrust of the female sex had led Forrest to center his affection on Oakes. He once wrote in his notebook: "Something of the cat enters into the feminine composition which cannot be eradicated, a trifle of treachery, *a dash of deceit*, a flavoring of inconstancy." Women occasionally made good wives, sisters, and mothers, yet they were incapable of a true Damon and Pythias devotion.

It would be unfair to strain the evidence. Except for the extravagant expressions of their affection, there are no grounds for believing that their relationship was unnatural. Their letters are filled with virile observations on the sexual proficiency of various females. Forrest simply needed the genuine and enduring friendship that he found with a man like Oakes.

Their Christmas holiday this year was particularly pleasant. Oakes had a new project to talk over with Forrest. He and a group of friends proposed to commission Thomas Ball to create a life-size statue of the actor. However much Forrest protested against the tiresome hours of sitting that would be demanded, he had a lively interest in having his image captured for posterity. Mathew B. Brady, the famous Civil War photographer, had recently executed a series of "imperial photographs" of him in his principal roles. A statue by the Boston sculptor would be a distinct honor. Ball had modeled the bas-reliefs "Signing of the Declaration of Independence" and "Signing of the Peace Treaty of Paris" for the pedestal of Franklin's monument in front of the Boston City Hall and had just completed an equestrian statute of Washington for the Public Gardens.

On January 26, 1863, Oakes and Ball signed the contract. The sculptor was "to make and finish to the best of his ability and to the satisfaction of the said Oakes, a marble statute six feet six inches in height of Mr. Edwin Forest [*sic*], tragedian, in the character of Virginius; to be delivered when finished in Boston or New York," and was to receive $3,000 for his labors. In February, Ball began, catching Forrest with his calipers between scenes at the Chestnut Street Theatre. He reported that he found him a most willing subject, "a most amiable great bear, at some moments as tender as a woman." In two weeks Ball returned to Boston with the measurements and began the modeling.

During the next two years he changed his mind about the actor's amiability. When Forrest played *Coriolanus* in Boston in February 1864, he decided that Ball should remodel the statue to represent him as Coriolanus instead of Virginius. In September Forrest complained that the whiskers were not right. Annoyed by the suggestion, Ball proposed to shave the face clean. Forrest wrote again. He merely wanted the imperial and mustache modified. The present mustache swelled the upper lip and made the nose too small. It would be wrong to represent him devoid of whiskers. The Romans did not shave their faces until a half-century after the death of Coriolanus. The argument continued throughout the fall; in December, Ball finally agreed to Forrest's tonsorial demands and happily left for Florence to transform the model into the marble statue that now stands at the end of the main corridor in the Forrest Home.

When Forrest first saw the gigantic figure at A. A. Child's Gallery in Boston in mid-October 1867, he was amazed that cold marble could transmit such power. Ball had captured the dynamic strength in the character that Forrest had exhibited on the stage. Like most actors, Forrest was perpetually distressed with the nightly mortality of his art. "What a pity," he had once written to Oakes after a particularly inspired Lear, "that it could not have been photographed! I mean the entire representation of the character with all its changeful passions— with all its unspeakable subtleties." Forrest immediately offered the committee $10,000 for the statue, cautioning Oakes not to reveal the price. Some might question such extravagant narcissism. It was not only extravagant in cost; including the pedestal, the figure stood eleven feet and weighed three tons.

Through the spring and summer of 1863, after his sittings for Ball, the war was perpetually on Forrest's mind. He and Oakes kept up a steady exchange of observations on the daily battle reports. In July Forrest wrote: "I should not be at all surprised to hear that Lee is captured and if so they have lost their tower of strength." Two weeks later he was chiding the Northern Generals for their mishandling of the Battle of Gettysburg. If Lee had trapped Meade as Meade had trapped Lee, the Northern General would not have escaped. The quick end that Forrest had hoped for seemed to be hidden in the cloudy future.

He became skeptical about other aspects of his country's future. He was distressed when the Democrats nominated General George B. McClellan, though he would vote for anyone in preference to the incumbent. Another four years of Lincoln's misrule and the country would be "sunk below Heaven's reaching mercy." When the President was re-elected in November 1864, Forrest challenged Oakes to explain how the people could be so blinded "to their true interests, or is it, that those whom the Gods would surely destroy, they first make mad."

Forrest's successive legal battles manifested a similarly gloomy aspect. O'Conor brought the case back into court in October 1863. The original judgment was affirmed. Forrest refused to pay and instructed Van Buren to file another appeal. On November 30, 1864, just two days after the election calamity, the General Term Court denied his appeal.

In the early summer of 1863 Forrest tried to divert his attention from the general dreariness of the world. He sent Miss Minnie Lehman money to pay her train fare to Philadelphia. Forrest had met Miss Lehman in Boston and thought her friendship worthy of cultivation. He quickly changed his mind when she requested additional funds. "She is a damned humbug," he lamented to Oakes, "another of that large class of female swindlers who practice their arts on such easy fools as have more good nature than good sense." The more he thought about her the more he fumed: "Miss Lehman is a whore as well as a liar and a cheat. Thank God, we just found her out in good time."

His romance with "Nahmeokee," whatever its true nature, progressed more smoothly. He always spoke kindly of her, sent her pictures of himself, visited her whenever he was in Boston, and once brought her to New York and Philadelphia for a few weeks. With Forrest's perpetual trouble with Caucasian females, it would add an exotic touch to report that he finally found true love with a noble red woman. Unfortunately, only the pet name supports this possibility. And however strong the attachment, he never considered marriage. When a Boston newspaper made this proposal, Forrest said that he would not be surprised to read next of his own execution for some horrendous criminal offense. "When that marriage takes place," he explained to Oakes, "you may order the new suit for the wedding, which I will pay for and give you besides a yearly income of twenty thousand dollars. No, we will have no more marriages, no more legal prostitution."

As usual, Forrest found his escape from the miseries of the world in the theatre. He began his season at Niblo's on August 31, 1863. "It was a triumph!" he cheerfully reported to Oakes. "You my dear would have enjoyed it. There is no theatrical enthusiasm in the country like that which manifests itself in a New York audience. Hearty—inspiring—and discriminating." He moved along in grand style for seven weeks; then, on October 23, he was struck by another calamity: his sister Henrietta died.

After his mother's death, he had depended on Henrietta to maintain the Philadelphia household. Now the responsibility must be shared by Caroline and Eleanora, neither of whom had Henrietta's solid grasp of domestic affairs. It was a painful loss. Her wisdom had been "a lamp to my feet," he mourned to Oakes, "her love a joy to my heart."

When Forrest returned to New York after the funeral, someone handed him a newspaper dated Saturday, October 24. It read: "Mr. Forrest repeated his great character of Spartacus last evening before one of the most brilliant and enthusiastic audiences of the season. His acting was grand throughout and at the end of the last act he received a perfect ovation from the audience." What heartless and careless knaves! On the night of this reported ovation, he had been in Philadelphia mourning over Henrietta's death.

Again he sought his peace in the theatre, playing the full season in New York, Boston, Washington, Philadelphia, and Baltimore.

In the summer he was back on Broad Street with two new projects to keep him busy: installing three new furnaces and building his picture gallery. Normally he would have stayed at home until September; this year the August heat drove him to the seashore. He regarded such a retreat as a sign of weakness. Perhaps it could be tolerated in a man who was approaching sixty. He enjoyed his month at Long Branch (New Jersey), and when he checked in at the Metropolitan Hotel in New York on Saturday, September 3, 1864, he was glowing with anticipation for the new season.

Monday was a dreary, sultry day. The clouds drooped low over the city; just before curtain time the rains came pouring down; yet, when Forrest stepped on the stage at Niblo's, only a few scattered gaps could be detected among the 3,000 seats. It was a happy evening, and the public rejoicing continued long after Forrest had walked across the stage in his final call. "What a thrill," he wrote to Oakes the next day, "to know that the people do not forget me." In spite of the continuing rain, the second night was even better: $1,745.85 in the treasury, just $4.15 under absolute capacity.

What a beautiful seven weeks! After the first two stormy nights, the weather cleared. New York caught a long run of those bright fall days that have always seemed so special to the city. Forrest had never seen Central Park more glorious; he had never encountered more lively strangers sampling the pleasures of the metropolis. Niblo's was crowded nightly, giving him a profit of $17,000 for his twenty-eight performances.

Albany greeted him with comparable enthusiasm. According to Forrest, the people "crowded in like pigs" every night of the week. The *Times and Courier* estimated that his sentences were worth as much as telegraphic sentences: "First ten words forty cents, and three cents for each additional word."

On November 21 he began a six-week engagement at the Academy of Music in Philadelphia and on January 2 five weeks at Ford's Theatre in Washington.

The private boxes and orchestra chairs at Ford's were regularly ornamented with members of the Cabinet, Foreign Ministers, Senators, and Representatives. Even the President came. In fact, Forrest barely missed getting his name into the history books along with John Wilkes Booth. On Wednesday, January 18, when the President's office announced that Lincoln and two friends would attend *Jack Cade* that evening, Booth and his band of conspirators decided to "capture" the President while he watched the play. During the afternoon, manager Ford removed the partition between boxes seven and eight and installed the President's rocker. Early in the evening, Booth arrived at the theatre and rehearsed his plan. Everything was in order, yet he was thwarted by the one detail over which he had no control. The President did not appear. Forrest went on as scheduled; Booth had to cancel.

Forrest's luck finally ran out during the Washington engagement. He was ravaged by an attack of sciatica. Throughout the final three weeks the pain raced up and down his legs whenever he moved. Each day he remained in bed; each night he struggled to the theatre, never missing a performance. No other man in the profession could have done it; in fact, he admitted to Oakes, "there is no one who under such pain and anguish would be fool enough even to try."

Even though he had not completely recovered by the end of the engagement, he moved on to Baltimore. John Ford promised him that the Holliday Street Theatre would be well heated and everything arranged for his comfort. He found neither heat nor comfort. According to Forrest, the theatre was so chilly that "his limbs were paralyzed and the words froze on his lips." As a result, he had another attack; yet, he kept to his schedule, even adding another week in Washington. This second attack on his sciatic nerve left him with a permanent drag in his right leg.

In the middle of March Forrest retreated to Philadelphia to get warm. The days were bright. In the early afternoons he stretched out on a bench in the garden, soaking up the warm sun and filling his lungs with fresh air. As devoted as he was to pills and ointments, Forrest had an enduring faith in the therapeutic powers of fresh air and sunshine. By the first of April he was certain that his old strength was returning. The slight twinge he still felt in his right hip should be cured by a few vigorous strides across the stage. At any rate, he intended to keep his April engagement at Niblo's.

The first two nights went well. On Thursday he noticed that his right leg was swelling. By Saturday it had become "a sight to make demons shudder." He had escaped one infection to be poisoned by another; nor was he comforted to discover that it resulted from the stupidity of the apothecary who had mixed sixty drops of croton oil, instead of three, into the lotion prescribed for his leg.

In spite of his asymmetrical lower limbs, Forrest returned to the theatre on Monday. It was not a happy week for him or for the world around. Richmond had fallen; Grant and Lee met at Appomattox on Sunday. The bells were ringing. To some they sounded merry; to Forrest they were sad funeral dirges for the bereaved hearts in desolated homes across the country.

On Friday he struggled through *Othello;* the same night Lincoln relaxed in his rocker at Ford's Theatre in Washington to watch Laura Keene in *Our American Cousin.* The next morning Forrest was in his room at the Metropolitan Hotel, bathing his leg, when John McCullough burst in shouting that Lincoln had been shot by Wilkes Booth. According to his own account, McCullough paced the room muttering: "I don't believe it. I can't believe it." Whereupon Forrest snarled: "Well, I do. All those God damned Booths are crazy."

Forrest went home to Broad Street at the end of April. He was certain that if he resigned himself to his infirmities, they would disappear in a week. It was a mistaken prognostication. The tired machine began to break down in other places. His arms and shoulders tightened up with rheumatism. His hands became so stiff that he could not hold a pen. Forrest gave up and settled into bed for a lonely and miserable summer.

When he turned the corner into September, his spirits brightened. Each day he stretched his muscles a bit more and with less pain. By the end of the month he spent half the day in the garden. How exciting, he wrote to Oakes, "watching the sunbeams stream through the golden veil of autumn with a softened radiance. How gratefully I receive these benedictions from the Universal Cause!" In early October he signed with William Wheatley, the Niblo's impresario; and as if challenging his rheumatic tormentors to the final battle, he agreed to start the season as a strolling player. The opening night, October 23, 1865, was scheduled for New Haven.

During the lowest days of the summer Forrest could not escape the gloomy thought that he might be approaching his last days. He had resolved that if he got back on his feet, he would arrange his affairs for posterity. Aside from his sisters, no one had a claim on his fortune, no one except the profession that had rewarded him so richly. He loved the theatre, hated the managers, and though he had little affection for the host of incompetents who cluttered the stage, he grieved for any actor who was impoverished when he reached the end of his career. If Forrest could, as he later wrote in his will, "smooth the pillow of the unfortunate in sickness or other disability, or the decay of the declining years," he would serve his profession long after his death.

Day after day in September, Forrest rode through the countryside looking for a house that might eventually become an actors' home and that, during his lifetime, would make an appropriate country seat. He finally chose "Springbrook," an old house some eight miles northeast of the center of Philadelphia and less than a mile from the Holmesburg railroad stop.

Forrest knew the estate from his childhood when it had belonged to an Englishman named Caleb Cope, a dealer in silk and Biddle's second-in-command at the United States Bank. George H. Stuart, the Philadelphia merchant and Y. M. C. A. leader, now owned the place. Much of it stood just as Forrest remembered it: the massive wall of Trenton stone in front of the house, along the Bristol Turnpike—Washington had ridden along this route on his way to his inauguration in New York—the brownstone posts with their heavy iron gates, and the three-story mansion of roughcast yellow stone.

Forrest was impressed by the improvements: the serpentine walks, the lake, the grape arbors, and, most of all, the conservatories. He counted seventeen glass houses, protecting the most exotic tropical plants that he had ever seen. Cope was said to have had the finest collection of orchids and camellias in the country.

The negotiations were simple. "Springbrook" was up for auction; Forrest outbid all the competitors and on October 19, 1865, transferred $40,000 of public securities to Stuart as a down payment. The full price for the 111 acres was to be $91,000.

With his domestic affairs in order, he was ready for the theatre. Forrest had set a rough schedule for the initial three weeks: two split-weeks in New Haven, Hartford, Springfield, and Worcester, a long weekend's rest with Oakes in Boston, then four nights in Providence and one in New Bedford. He made only one concession to ease the strain; he limited himself to two plays, *Richelieu* and *King Lear*.

Through the first week his legs held up remarkably, then just before he finished in Worcester his shoulder stiffened. In Boston an application of Bishop Soule's liniment seemed to ease the pain. Oakes insisted that he also be checked over by a Dr. Streeter. Apparently the doctor believed that a general purgative would eliminate both the rheumatism and the sciatica. Forrest took the prescribed dose just before leaving New Bedford for New York. He reported to Oakes that when he arrived he had "such an outpouring as I never had before." In another week the sciatica had improved, though not because of the purgative. Forrest had discovered a new treatment: sitting in a hot bath with electricity from a galvanic battery applied to his sciatic nerve. Forrest had always advocated Turkish baths. They equalized the circulation of the body and purified the blood more effectually than any medicine. Now he had found a superior treatment. After a single electrified bath, he had pranced through a performance of *Virginius* without pain and with his lameness barely perceptible.

Three big nights during his six weeks in New York reassured him that however feeble he might sometimes appear he was still the idol of the American stage. On December 7 *Metamora* drew $2,168.65, giving Forrest a single night's profit of $937.64. On November 20 seventy-nine firemen attended en masse. On Thursday, November 16, General Grant was in the audience, along with his wife and two little boys, and accompanied by General Burnside, Commodore Warden, and a retinue of staff officers. They arrived, after the play had begun, with good timing. The trumpets sounded; Gloucester announced: "The King is coming!" Someone in the foyer shouted: "Three cheers for General Grant." As he came down the aisle, "the ladies leveled a thousand lorgnettes, loaded with two thousand beautiful eyes at the hero of the great American conflict," the *New York World* reported. Forrest gladly allowed the General a proper entrance. This was Grant's first public appearance in New York prior to the official reception scheduled for the following Monday at the Fifth Avenue Hotel. Forrest was flattered by the honor. He was also encouraged for the future of the democracy when he saw the General climb in with the crowd in the parquet, instead of perch himself in a stage box.

Forrest was always delighted to see a public figure shun aristocratic airs. Forrest himself admitted that his own casual street costume—a loose black coat, a carelessly tied string tie hanging out of a broad collar, a wide black ribbon stretched across his chest to his watch—was designed to tell the world that he was not a "society" man. Fancy and fashionable manners were not his meat. Once, when an ill-advised *grande dame* invited him to a formal reception, Forrest was said to have exclaimed: "What! I pirouette in a swallow-tailed coat and hang over a piano! I'd sooner go to my execution."

Forrest continued at Niblo's until the Friday before Christmas. On Saturday he went home to his sisters for a hasty holiday. The excitement he had stirred up on his barnstorming tour of New England had whetted his appetite; he was going to try a two months' whirl through the Midwest beginning at Turner's Opera House in Dayton on New Year's Day. He had even tentatively agreed to risk a late-spring engagement in San Francisco. Forrest had said nothing to anyone about his California plans, yet they were reported in the press. He insisted to Oakes that undoubtedly Tom Maguire's wife had told someone, for "women are notoriously leaky about their secrets."

His Midwest venture was to be unlike any previous tour. Instead of entrusting the supporting roles to the local stock company, he was going to carry his own entourage. In addition to Joseph McArdle, a young Philadelphian who had failed as an actor and who was now to be given a chance as a manager, Forrest had hired Mme. Ponisi, a British actress who had first attracted attention in Boker's *Francesca da Rimini* and with whom Forrest had performed in Boston in 1863; John McCullough, a young Irish-born actor who had first appeared at the Arch Street Theatre in 1857 and who had been with Forrest at Niblo's in 1862; and a nineteen-year-old newcomer, Miss Lillie, better known to her Boston schoolmates as Lillie Swindlehurst. Forrest had not abandoned his search for a protégé. In the middle of December Forrest had sent Oakes a contract to be signed by Lillie's father. Apparently, Swindlehurst agreed immediately; the contract was returned before Forrest concluded his New York engagement. Miss Lillie was on the roster for Dayton.

C H A P T E R *x x i*

From Maine to California

O n his first barnstorming adventure forty-three years earlier, Forrest had appeared in an improvised theatre in Dayton. Now he returned as the star attraction in the gala New Year's Day opening of the quarter-of-a-million-dollar Turner's Opera House, the biggest social event in Dayton's history.

Forrest could not have asked for a more encouraging beginning. For two weeks the Opera House was packed every night; the press was extravagant in its praise; his health improved daily; and he was delighted with his gamble on Miss Lillie. She had made a favorable impression with her "charming naturalness," and off stage she behaved like a "good pure child."

From Dayton the company went to Columbus, Chicago, St. Louis, and Cincinnati. Everywhere they were received by wild cheers. His Chicago engagement at Crosby's Opera House was the greatest professional triumph of his life, not only in pecuniary terms (a gross of $11,385 for the first five nights), nor in the assurance that the "veteran does not lag superfluous on the stage," as he explained to Oakes, but also because he had never found audiences of "higher intelligence and culture."

A few fussy reviewers complained that Forrest moaned and whined; the *Chicago Tribune* announced *The Gladiator* under the laconic heading:

> Ah-h-h-h-h-h-h!
> Ugh-gh-gh-gh-h!
> Oyeow-w-w—w-wh!

A St. Louis critic reported that in the dying scenes Forrest laid down, got up, groaned like a sick tiger, and then collapsed with such finality that some in the pit thought that he was actually defunct. These "pert scribblers," the *Chicago Railroad Gazette* declared, were so many "chickens pecking at a Colossus," a view to which Forrest readily subscribed as long as the theatres were full, and they were.

Forrest boasted that it was the most satisfactory engagement of his life. For the nine weeks, his half-share of the proceeds came to almost $30,000. Not all was clear profit. He paid the traveling and hotel expenses of his troupe, plus their salaries: McCullough received $100 per week; Mme. Ponisi, $80; and Miss Lillie $75. It seems surprising that a novice like Miss Lillie received almost as much as the well-seasoned Ponisi; perhaps Lillie was recompensed for additional duties.

Forrest was pleased with his $25,000 profit and still more pleased with his health report. He had had a momentary setback in St. Louis when the temperature dropped to twelve below and the manager failed to provide a stove in his dressing room, yet he hung on by sheer nerve, never missing a performance. When he had finally thawed out in Cincinnati, he was convinced that his will power still held a slight edge over his rheumatism.

Back in Philadelphia, Forrest settled down to a hectic month of taking inventory of his personal affairs. If he were going to expose himself to the unknown hazards of the Far West, he must be prepared for the most disastrous eventuality. He set to work on his will.

Forrest had never labored so carefully over anything in his life. Creating a memorial out of money and words that would have a reasonable chance at perpetuity was not easy.

First of all, he provided for his sisters. They were to live at Springbrook with all taxes and expenses borne by the estate, and each was to receive a yearly annuity of six thousand dollars. When one of them married or died—Forrest regarded both states equally abhorrent—the annuity would pass to the other until she died or married. Within twenty-one years—sooner "if judiciously practicable"—after the last submitted to death or marriage, the Edwin Forrest Home for Decayed Actors was to be established at Springbrook. The Rules and Regulations governing its operation were meticulously spelled out. The executors, James Oakes, James Lawson, and Daniel Dougherty, could use their best judgment in liquidating his holdings, other than Springbrook, to establish the trust fund. They could not revise or modify his "educational, self-sustaining, and eleemosynary" plans for the Home.

They must arrange for regular lectures on science, literature, and the arts that would be open to everyone in the profession; lectures that would "prepare the American citizen for a more creditable and effective discharge of his public duties," that would raise "the intellectual and moral tone and character of actors, that thereby they may elevate the drama to subserve its true and great mission, as the profoundest teacher of virtue and morality." No one could misconstrue his noble purpose; it was reiterated throughout the two-thousand-word document.

Every morning during the month of March Forrest labored over the will. Finally, on March 29, he called in his old friend and legal consultant Daniel Dougherty, to give it the lawyer's eye, an unnecessary precaution. Forrest had been so steeped in legal lingo for fifteen years that he had mastered the style. Dougherty had only to send in one of his clerks to make the official copies. On Thursday morning, April 5, the will was signed and witnessed, and at noon Forrest took the train for New York where he was to meet Oakes and Lillie.

Forrest had urged Oakes to go with him to California, offering to pay all his expenses; Oakes had regretfully declined, insisting that he could not leave the store. He had, however, persuaded the Swindlehursts to let Lillie go. Two weeks before their scheduled departure, Forrest had had some misgivings about taking her when Miss Lillie had written asking if she and Forrest were to be married. Oakes straightened her out on this matter, and Forrest forgave her womanly indiscretion.

Oakes came down from Boston with Lillie and for the three

days prior to their sailing tried to cheer Forrest. According to Oakes, Forrest was oppressed with the morbid conviction that his doomsday was just around the corner. He was certain that his poor rheumatic body would be wrapped in a sheet and tossed over the side of the ship long before they reached California.

When they went aboard on Wednesday morning, April 11, Forrest was still muttering about his sad fate and wondering if the gloomy fog would ever lift. It finally did. The sea air, the long sweet hours of sleep, and the cheering mixture of childish and womanly attentions from Miss Lillie revived his spirits. The sailing was smooth until they were heading north along the coast of Mexico, after the overland journey across the Isthmus of Panama. When they struck the heavier weather, Forrest had completely recovered his fighting spirit. He wrote to Oakes about the night that he had tramped the deck during a particularly vicious squall, challenging the elements with an oath every time that he was pitched off balance. He was unaware that his lone companion was a clergyman. The Reverend finally introduced himself and asked if Forrest knew that "our Saviour went to sea in a vessel and a great storm arose. . . ." Before he concluded his rebuke, a wave thundered over the prow. When the ship righted, Forrest reminded his questioner: "Yes, so He did but when He got tired of the storm He got out and went on foot. We can't."

They docked in San Francisco on May 3 1866 and on Monday, May 14 he opened his engagement. Forrest had heard of the wild manners of the Western audiences; still, he was not prepared for the savage swarm at the theatre. Even though the prices had been doubled, the demand was so great that the final batch of opening-night tickets was sold at auction; one seat actually brought $500. The New York reporter who had said that Forrest would get "as much gold as he wants without digging" was right. In seven weeks he played to some 60,000 spectators and to a profit of $20,000. He was tripping along so well that he contemplated a tour of Australia in July; he even spoke of returning to New York by way of England. At the end of June, his plans collapsed. The gout caught him again, and he was forced to quit.

After trying futilely to shake the attack, he accepted the advice of a local doctor and went north to test the therapeutic powers of the hot and cold mountain springs. Even though his lameness disappeared in a month, he decided to stay until fall. He enjoyed the baths and living in the out-of-doors.

Not for years had he really indulged his passion for natural wonders, and California offered spectacular opportunities. The giant redwoods ran a close second to Niagara in stirring a man's soul. Sheer size always impressed Forrest. One tremendous tree, some 450 feet long and over 100 feet in circumference, had crashed down some years before and the trunk had been hollowed out. One day at sunset, Forrest rode through the tree on horseback, and when he came out, the level beams of the sun illuminated the columns of the grove and turned it into a golden cathedral. Forrest reported that he was overawed by the spectacle. By the end of the summer, he was spending most of his days in the saddle, sometimes as long as eight hours at a stretch, riding over the trackless mountains and breathing the wonderful air. He had never found a better therapy for mind and body.

Forrest was scheduled to return to Maguire in October and then go to Sacramento and Los Angeles. After sampling the tropical climate of southern California, he would return to San Francisco instead of risking the rigorous midwinter voyage home. Again his plans were thwarted. Just before the opening of his re-engagement, he received word that his sister Caroline was ill. Family duty still outranked all other obligations. On October 20 he sailed for home.

When he arrived in Philadelphia, he was relieved to find that Caroline had almost recovered. He was not so happy with his own health. The California sunshine that he thought had been stored up in his body could not combat the bitterly cold Philadelphia winter. He bundled up in front of the fire in the library and rejoiced that he was not out on the road frosting his limbs in drafty dressing rooms. When the New York managers tried to entice him back to the theatre, he refused. For the moment he would limit his activity to the library. His Springbrook tenant came in for long talks about spring planting. Forrest proposed to put the fields into wheat, corn, and oats and to abandon the flower cultivation in the conservatories. He wanted them transformed into graperies. The floriculture was much too expensive: $2,429.75 for the three bouquets he had seen on the table during the past year. "Far better to expend this sum in clothing the poor," he explained to Oakes, "and leave unto God to clothe the lily."

During the winter he kept up a steady correspondence with Oakes. Some shyster had swindled Oakes, and he seemed in danger of losing the "Old Salt House." Forrest saved him with a loan of $10,000. In January Oakes invited him to a wedding in Boston. Forrest answered him with a disquisition on marriage. What had it done for him: tie him to a woman who was "vain, trifling, lying, a drunkard, and by consequence a whore." For these "good wifely qualities, dear Oakes, she is to be rewarded with the yearly sum of four thousand a year out of my pocket." Since the distasteful subject had been brought up, he sent Oakes a copy of the published account of the Forrest Divorce Case, advising him to read it *after* church. His soul would need the consolation of religion when he read of the "damned outrages imposed in the name of the law." Forrest wondered how their wicked tribe had survived. "Our Saviour's personal denunciation of them" should have ruined their trade, and "His experience of the Judges was even worse than mine." The world was full of unfathomable evils.

In early February, Forrest announced to Oakes that he had become impatient with his invalid's existence; he needed "the excitement of the theatre to fill the vacuum." He decided to test his strength with a trial engagement: two weeks in Washington and one in Baltimore. To conserve his strength, he assigned the rehearsal drudgery to Joe McArdle. The system worked so well that in April he undertook a series of one-week stands in Cincinnati, Louisville, Mobile, and Memphis.

When he returned to Philadelphia, his health was still intact. He spent the summer tending his agricultural projects, planning a fall engagement in New York, and consulting with Van Buren. Forrest explained to Oakes that they were going to appeal to the Supreme Court of the United States to seek relief from the vile scheme to rob him and to lavish his hard-earned profits on "a drunken female whose prostitutions and shameless acts have circled the world." He was convinced that the previous iniquitous decision had done more "to insult virtue and to commend vice and immorality than all the pimps, panders, bawds, and brothels in the state."

When Forrest began his New York engagement the first week in September at the Broadway Theatre (formerly Brougham's Lyceum), he wondered if anyone who had been in the audience at his first appearance forty years earlier would be there now. If someone were, he wrote to Oakes, "I would like to meet that man and hear from his own lips if the promises of springtime have been entirely fulfilled by the fruits of the autumn of life." Forrest was preoccupied with his age and his precarious tenure. He took every precaution to preserve his health. Before going to Boston he asked Oakes to be certain that his room at the Tremont House was equipped with a hard mattress and two good blankets. Someone had told him that the actor Charles Macklin, who was still vigorous at ninety-three, had always slept between blankets on a hard bed. The electricity imparted by the blankets injected vitality into the system.

During two solid months of playing in New York, Boston, and Philadelphia Forrest never tried to husband his strength. He did, however, solicit the latest medical information everywhere he went. In Philadelphia he visited a Dr. Newton who boasted of having cured a lady from paralysis. In Boston he saw a Dr. Wyseman Marshall who had some theories about positive and negative women. Although the doctor's prescription was not exactly clear, Forrest interpreted him to mean that at his time of life he ought to have "a woman who could be satisfied with a little horizontal refreshments once a week and be a right faithful nurse all the rest of the time." He also consulted a Dr. Windship in Boston who advised him to wear flannel nightgowns and to buy a vibrating contraption that would pummel him with India rubber balls. This machine was supposed to "prove efficacious in promoting a complete circulation of all the fluids." When he returned to Philadelphia, Forrest asked Oakes to buy the gowns and the rubber balls. "It would be most pleasant," he thought, "to be patted all over so." He also asked Oakes to inquire of Windship, "how much was *too much* pounding with the other balls." Perhaps it was best, at his age "to give mine a perpetual jubilee, in consideration of the labour already done—the labour we delight in—and which physics pain." Forrest was not always gloomy about his ailments.

His health campaign was not his sole preoccupation during this season (1867-8). In the theatre, particularly in New York, he was forced to combat the new sensational melodramas that had caught the public's fancy. *The Black Crook*, which had pre-empted Niblo's, forcing Forrest into the Broadway, had been packing the theatre for fourteen months. One reporter declared that it would probably continue until the "crack of doom." This astonishing combination of melodrama and spectacle had evolved quite by accident. A troupe of ballet dancers had been imported from London to appear at the Academy of Music. The Academy burned down. William Wheatley, manager of Niblo's, who was about to present Charles M. Barras's *The Black Crook*, was suddenly struck by one of those ridiculous notions that have so frequently proved profitable in the theatre. He hired the dancers and worked them into the melodrama. The resulting hodgepodge, which took five hours to perform on opening night, completely captivated the audience. Chills alternated with thrills. At one moment the spectators were fascinated by the evil exploits of the alchemist (the black crook) who had sold his soul to the devil. The next moment they were dazzled by a daring and massive display of female pulchritude. Never had so many beautiful girls appeared in so little: they wore flesh-colored tights and abbreviated diaphanous skirts. In the grotto scene they tripped about among the stalactites. In the finale they "lolled about in negligent grace" on silver couches or descended from the clouds in gilded chariots. The stage had never been filled with such sheer barbaric splendor.

Under the Gaslight, another kind of melodramatic thriller, had opened in August 1867. Augustin Daly's play was packed with nerve-tingling scenes: the heroine thrown into the North River by the villain; the hero tied to the railroad tracks. In the latter scene the audience hears the train approaching; the beam of its headlight flashes across the stage; the heroine, who has been locked in the near-by station, finally breaks down the door, races for the tracks, unties her lover, "takes his head from the track and the train of cars rushes past with a roar and whistle."

The demand for thrills and sensational spectacles had been growing furiously during the preceding five years. Adah Isaacs Menken in *Mazeppa* had been charging up a rocky mountain trail, her beautiful, almost naked body lashed to a wild horse; *East Lynne* had begun its long career of tear-jerking; Hawkshaw, the detective in *The Ticket of Leave Man,* had electrified the audiences with his exciting adventures.

Forrest might suppress his infirmities with new health machines. He had no new defensive weapons to throw against the public's changing taste. He must rely on his old repertoire and his own powers to stir up a bit of wonderment. Fortunately, his combination still worked in Boston and Philadelphia, if not in New York. Forrest boasted to Oakes that his November engagement in Philadelphia was "the greatest ever known within the walls of the Walnut Street Theatre."

His month in Philadelphia was, however, marred by a series of articles in the *Dispatch,* which purported to be interviews with the great actor. Forrest might have overlooked the reflections on his eccentricities: the reporter noted that when the callboy summoned Forrest for *Metamora,* the actor pounded his chest and shouted: "Look me heap big Injun!" He might even have tolerated the aspersions on his physique:

a practical joker was said to have once pricked his leg with a pin and let out a mound of sawdust. He could not ignore the libelous suggestion that he depended on the bottle to carry him through a performance. Forrest was not a teetotaler; he had, however, seen too much of the evil effects of liquor in the dressing room, particularly with his old friend J. B. Booth, to take a drink in the theatre.

Forrest filed a suit against the *Dispatch,* claiming $50,000 damages "in loss of popularity." The legal sparring went on for years, until the *Dispatch* finally settled out of court for an unrevealed sum and on March 27, 1871, published an apology: since Mr. Forrest had generously consented to withdraw the case, they were delighted "to express regret at the publication of articles which went beyond the limits of dramatic criticism."

After his Philadelphia engagement Forrest played a week each in Baltimore and Washington before departing for the Western circuit. He undertook the journey expecting to enjoy two month of southern sunshine and then to savor the first sweet delights of the budding spring as he moved north. He was disappointed everywhere. New Orleans was cold and damp; Mobile and Memphis soaked with rain; and on the journey from Chicago to Detroit, he battled the worst snow storm of the winter. When he finally returned to Philadelphia on May 1, he desperately needed the repose of Springbrook and Broad Street. As he observed to Oakes, he had not only been living his own life, "but the lives of Macbeth, Othello, Lear, and Hamlet into the bargain," and their vicissitudes surpassed his own. However, after three weeks of bathing his legs with an old Indian mixture that he had procured from a frontier specialist in rheumatism, he recovered sufficient strength to play a week at the Philadelphia Academy of Music.

Toward the end of July he was aroused by another flutter of activity in the divorce business. Oakes reported that the Confederate General Jeff Thompson knew a Mr. Walcot in New Orleans who claimed that he had seen Jamieson "in the act" with Mrs. Sinclair in the hotel in Cincinnati and that he still had a letter and diamond ring that Mrs. Sinclair had sent to him at the time of the trial to keep him quiet. Forrest went to New York to report the story to his lawyers. James Brady (Van Buren's assistant) was unimpressed and very discouraged about Forrest's prospects. The Supreme Court was unwilling to hear their petition; they must struggle again with the Court of Appeals.

Forrest hated to accept Brady's gloomy outlook, yet he had no choice. He returned to Philadelphia and, in another attempt to defend himself against the inevitable calamity, deeded Springbrook to his sisters. It was not a wise move. When his sisters died and the Broad Street mansion and Springbrook reverted to him, he had to pay over $40,000 in state inheritance tax.

During the summer Forrest turned his attention to a new project. He began searching for a likely candidate to write his biography. Among the prospects were his friend James Rees, the "Colley Cibber" of the *Sunday Mercury* and James Parton (grandfather of the present publisher of *American Heritage* and *Horizon*), the biographer of Greeley, Burr, Jackson, Franklin, and John Jacob Astor. Forrest rejected both of them: Rees, for lack of experience in the biographical art; Parton, because he had "prostituted his great talents by making silk purses out of pigs ears." Forrest did not explain in his letter to Oakes which of Parton's biographies he found objectionable, nor did he indicate that he might have ruled out Parton on other grounds. The biographer was married to N. P. Willis's sister.

Forrest mulled over the problem while he was at Long Branch for his customary pre-season rejuvenation. When he returned to Philadelphia, he had the solution. Oakes must do the biography. Forrest advised him of his decision and, assuming that the matter was settled, turned his attention to the theatre.

Again Forrest attacked the new season in a spirit of desperation, imposing an unnecessarily heavy burden on his limping leg. Instead of beginning in New York, he launched his fall campaign in upstate New York: Rochester, Buffalo, Syracuse, and Utica. It was a treacherous and unrewarding prelude: playing every night and rehearsing every day, battling his bad leg and a painful attack of gout in his right hand, and everywhere encountering the most unsympathetic weather—a cold rain seemed to be following the same circuit. Although the daily chore of reviving himself for the evening occupied his full attention, he did not miss the small newspaper item on October 5, 1868, which reported that George W. Jamieson had been killed by a railroad train near Yonkers. "God is great," he wrote to Oakes, "and Justice, though slow, is sure—another scoundrel has gone to Hell, I trust forever."

Back in New York Forrest struggled vainly against the spectacles and melodramas. "Tragedy receives the cold shoulder" from the audiences and "old and worn scenery" from the managers, the *Daily Star* observed. Another reporter insisted that the shabby scenery resulted from manager Henry Palmer's conviction "that while he had to pay $500 a night for his acting, Forrest ought to have painted his own scenery."

On November 6 Forrest closed his engagement at Niblo's. The next week he appeared at the Court of Appeals for the fearful final-act denouement of his real-life drama. Brady's prognostication had been correct. Forrest was directed to pay Catherine $68,000 alimony in arrears and $4,000 a year thereafter. This was the "premium for prostitution." He was so "sad and disheartened," he lamented to Oakes, that he could "willingly die with an utter contempt for this world and with perfect indifference to his fate in the world to come." So many facts would now never be publicly revealed. Did Oakes know, for example, that the foreman of the jury had admitted on his deathbed that the jury was packed and that "he could die happy but for the wrong he had done me by his verdict."

Even Catherine found little satisfaction in the final settlement. After sixteen years of legal warfare, she received just over $15,000. O'Conor took $38,850.71 and his assistant, Nelson Chase, who had handled the case since 1865, pocketed $15,975.32. Not all of this was for legal fees; some $12,000 was in repayment of loans they had made to Mrs. Sinclair. For the next eight years Catherine protested that O'Conor had agreed to take the case for nothing. Her final futile plea appeared in the *New York Times* on April 18, 1875: a five-column letter from Henry Sedley, Catherine's brother-in-law, summarizing the case. Sedley maintained that O'Conor had been widely applauded for his charity and that he had never denied that he had donated his services until he received Forrest's check. Like all of his tribe, he could not bear to see the money go where it rightfully belonged.

After the miserable business was settled, Forrest returned to the theatre: a two-week engagement in Philadelphia, a week in Troy, and, for the Christmas season, three weeks in Boston. As usual, he was happy to spend the holiday with Oakes. Immediately after Christmas, Forrest struck out on the back-country circuit and for the next six weeks ranged through New England in a mad rush of one- and two-night stands. He had never been quite so far off the main track and was astonished at his popularity in the small towns of Maine, Vermont, and New Hampshire. In Woonsocket, Rhode Island, he drew an incredible $600 for one night of *Jack Cade*. Considering the size of the town (11,000), Forrest insisted that it was the best night of the season. On the home stretch he stopped in Springfield, Hartford, and New Haven, concluding with a one-night stand at the Brooklyn Academy of Music on February 8.

Forrest had refused an invitation to appear as Othello, with Booth as Iago, at the opening of the new Booth Theatre on February 3. He would never consent to share the stage with this young upstart. In fact, the previous fall he had refused to use the same scenery as Booth had used. When the Walnut Street Theatre stage manager had set up Booth's *Hamlet* scenery, Forrest forced him to tear it down, insisting that he and Edwin's father had played Hamlet countless times without the aid of any damned steps and arches. In Forrest's opinion there had been too much scenery and very little Hamlet in Booth's production.

After the most strenuous six weeks of touring that he had ever attempted, Forrest faced a disheartening homecoming.

He was cold and exhausted after a night on the train; his gout and rheumatism were coming back. He found his sister Caroline moaning on her bed, hot with fever, and Eleanora with her ankles so badly swollen that she was barely able to move. The entire Forrest family seemed to be disintegrating at once.

The more calamities thrown his way, the more desperately Forrest hung on. After a week at home he went off to perform in Newark, came back for the weekend, and was then off again to Paterson and Trenton. When he returned on Sunday, February 28, he knew he should never have left. Caroline was delirious and Eleanora was hobbling in and out of the room with cold compresses. For two days he watched Caroline suffer; the doctors said that nothing could be done, and on Tuesday night she died. "Why has not God given us souls comforting reasonable hope under such bereavements?" he asked Oakes. True, man's vanity and self-love "have betrayed him into such a belief, but who knows the fact to substantiate it."

Forrest could not dredge up any facts strong enough to support a hope for the hereafter. In the theatre he trusted magic and self-hypnosis; off-stage he wanted facts. For the next month and a half he wallowed in his sadness, not leaving the house. The gout and rheumatism were in full command, and the new "pneumatic treatment" that someone in New York had recommended proved utterly useless. Even the weather failed to produce any of the bright signs of hope that one expected at this time of the year. It was damp and changeable, "not from hot to cold, but from cold to colder to coldest." Even the house was collapsing. A spring under his "little theatre" had rotted the beams and the flooring.

Not until the middle of May was he able to shake off the spell. Gradually the weather brightened, his hip began to loosen, his fingers straightened out. Eleanora was getting around the house with the help of a cane. The chores at Springbrook and on Broad Street seemed more inviting. He started digging a well in the garden, hoping to drain off the water that had rotted the theatre. He even thought of attending the "Jubilee Week" [1] in Boston if Oakes could procure reasonable accommodations at the Tremont House. The past winter they had charged him as much for a single room as he usually paid at the Metropolitan Hotel in New York for a parlor, bedroom, bath, water closet, and board. He was not blaming Oakes for their prices; he merely resented paying so much for so little.

One morning in early June he packed his traveling trunk and set out for Boston, the first time he had been away from Philadelphia in three months. The Tremont gave him a nice room at a cut rate and filled the room with flowers to celebrate his arrival. Once again life seemed worth living.

One object of the visit was to get acquainted with the Reverend William Rounseville Alger. Oakes had refused to undertake the biography and had recommended the Reverend as a likely candidate. Throughout the spring Oakes had been building up the case for Alger. At first Forrest had thought that the proposal was preposterous; he softened when he read some of the sermons Alger had delivered to the Bullfinch Street Society. They were so different from the run-of-the-mill homilies "which people the earth with demons, heaven with slaves, and hell with men." When Forrest met the Reverend, he was amazed by Alger's knowledge of his career and his extraordinary sympathy for the stage. He agreed with Oakes that Alger was the man for the job.

At the end of June Forrest came home fired with enthusiasm for his collaborator; on July 22 Alger came to Philadelphia for a preliminary conference. For the next two days, from early morning until late at night, Forrest recited the story of his life. On dates and places his memory would have to be checked against the notebooks and scrapbooks. Alger must understand his passion for money. He had never sought wealth for its own sake, only for the sake of his mother and sisters. The Reverend must be wary of the stories about his sour disposition and vile temper; many of these were grossly exaggerated. Those that

[1] Jubilee Week was a celebration to commemorate the restoration of peace and harmony throughout the land.

were true could be easily explained. He hated falsehood, injustice, and wickedness of any description, and, contrary as it might be to Christian doctrine, he hated his enemies. Above all, Alger must tell the blunt truth in every particular.

When Forrest put Alger on the train for Boston, he was convinced that Oakes had picked the right man. For the remainder of the summer, Forrest busily bundled up scrapbooks, notebooks, and account books and shipped them off to Alger. Forrest must have been convinced of the Reverend's liberality. In one carton he included six bottles of whisky for Oakes.

In October Forrest began a month of split-week and one-night stands, starting in Troy and ending in Elmira. The first half of the tour went smoothly; the second half was a nightmare. When he opened in Buffalo on November 2, the theatre had not been heated for a week and the manager started a fire just an hour before the performance. Forrest's right leg became paralyzed, and he would happily have closed the curtain, could he have brought himself to disappoint the crowd that was bundled up out front. A week later, his rheumatic pains forced him to spend the days in bed and to drag himself to the theatre in the evening by sheer force of will; however, when he closed in Elmira on Friday night, November 13, he had not missed a performance. On the following Monday he opened in Philadelphia.

After two weeks at home he was on the move again, headed for Cincinnati and the Midwestern circuit. He was driven to this desperate schedule, he explained in a letter to Lawson, because he needed the excitement of the stage to "drive away the canker care and avert the progress of decay."

Except for the hazardous weather, the tour was exciting and profitable. In Frankfort he battled a hailstorm that made so much racket on the roof that the actors could not be heard. In Lexington he had a happy morning ride around the countryside with General Breckinridge. January was a treacherous month in Ohio and Michigan; yet he maintained his schedule. As he explained to Oakes, "the professional call comes with a monarch's voice and must be obeyed." From Detroit he went to Pittsburgh, then to Canton, Fort Wayne, Cleveland, and Meadville, Pennsylvania. He was blanketing the country; no town was too small. When he arrived in Decatur, Illinois, at the end of March and detected the first signs of spring pushing through the gloomy winter, his thoughts turned toward home. He sent Eleanora a list of instructions: some bright evergreens from Springbrook should be transplanted in front of the Broad Street house; the fruit trees in the garden were to be well dressed with stable manure; the fence must be painted and the front door rubbed down with linseed oil. She should be able to hire a good painter for "$3.00 per day, $3.50 at the most."

From Illinois he went to Iowa: Keokuk, Des Moines, Davenport, Dubuque; and finally to Milwaukee, Grand Rapids, and Kalamazoo, Michigan. Forrest was amazed at his endurance. Since he began in Troy, he had played 156 nights and covered over 5,000 miles. He was even more astonished that he was still able to walk when he arrived in Philadelphia at noon on Monday, May 30, after being imprisoned in the railroad cars for two days.

It had been a lucky season. He was an old man of sixty-four who had ducked in and out of half the theatres in the Midwest, had sat up all night in cold and dreary coaches; yet he felt stronger now than he had six months before. A year ago he was certain that he was circling the brink of his grave. Now he had driven off the gloomy thoughts; he hoped permanently.

For most of the summer he played the Lord of Broad Street and the Squire of Springbrook. No big projects were underway, still the days were filled with "thousands of little businesses." In the morning he remained in town, wandering in the garden or sitting at his desk in the library, writing to Oakes, and then "off to Springbrook with abounding joy." One of the "little businesses at hand," he reported to Oakes, was a letter from a Miss Anna Potter in Toledo, who wanted him to build a "house for fifty orphan girls to be called the Edwin Forest Home. There's some fame for you, and the lady not know how to spell my name. What shall I be called upon to do next? Perhaps Miss Potter means maternity: she would like to help me in peopling my house with babies—the world is *so* unselfish."

On the first of August he went to Boston. He had given Alger a $1,000 advance on the biography, and he wanted to check on his progress. For two weeks they sat in the Tremont lobby or walked in the Common, Alger asking questions, Oakes prodding, and Forrest reminiscing. It was a happy time.

With all his memories still churning around in his brain, Forrest could not sleep the night he went back to New York. Fortunately, he had taken an outside stateroom on the steamer, though it cost an extra dollar, and at 2:00 a.m. he got up, "walked out on the deck in *puris naturalitus,* enjoyed the salt air for twenty minutes, went back to bed and slept soundly until morning." Forrest had never given up his passion for fresh air, and the more epidermis that could be exposed, the better. It never occurred to him that some of his pet therapies might be dangerous. No one could have convinced him that his matutinal nudist frolic had brought on the sciatica that struck him when he got home. It was the sudden cold change in the weather, he explained to Oakes, and he had quickly subdued the attack with a "turkish at 215°."

For the new season (1870-1), Forrest again took to the road. He had a three-year plan for saturating the country: New England; the Midwest; and now, the South. Before beginning the journey, he warmed-up with a week at the Walnut Street Theatre and a week at the Brooklyn Academy of Music.

Oakes and Alger came down to join him for the week in Brooklyn: Alger with more questions and Oakes to talk of his retirement. Oakes was going to abandon the "Old Salt House" and move in with his sister in Arlington. Knowing that his old friend did not have the means to give him the "perpetual sunshine" he so richly deserved, Forrest advised Alger that he planned to provide Oakes with an annuity: $2,500 per year beginning on July 5, 1871. Oakes was not told of the plan until later when Forrest wrote to him from Macon, Georgia, explaining that the settlement was "no more than I owe you for the innumerable kindnesses I have experienced at your hands." Let us hope that it "will make the residue of your life glide on in ceaseless ease."

The Southern expedition began badly. Richmond was flooded. In Raleigh Forrest tripped on the stairs coming out of the theatre and tumbled into the street. Had it not been for his professional skill in falling, he would probably have ended with a cracked skull or a broken hip. He escaped with a few bruises and continued without interruption to Wilmington (North Carolina), Columbus (South Carolina), Augusta, and Charleston. On November 14, he settled in Savannah for two weeks.

Savannah was wonderful. The theatre was crowded nightly and the "heaven sent days filled the world with gladness." His letters to Oakes were ecstatic. "The skies are bright," he wrote; "the air is filled with fragrance drawn by the warm sun from the balsamic trees, while the autumnal wild-flowers waft their incense to the glorious day." Lest Oakes think he had lost all touch with reality, he added: "All these, though they may meliorate in a degree the sadness of one's life, cannot bind up the broken heart, heal the wounded spirit, nor even, as Falstaff has it, 'set a leg.' "

Forrest was sorry to leave Savannah, but the "monarch's voice" called. The next stop was Macon, three days, and then Atlanta for a week. Atlanta gave him a roaring welcome. Forrest was amazed to find how his fame had spread; occasionally, just as amazed to find a spectator who had never been in a theatre before. During a performance of *Virginius,* he spied a green-looking chap who was obviously taking the play too seriously. When Virginius was dragged into the Forum, the character fumbled at his belt and pulled out an enormous seven-shooter. Fortunately, his more enlightened neighbor grabbed his arm before he could fire. One night in Charleston Forrest saw the Indian chief Osceola and a half-dozen braves in the audience. He greeted them with a blood-curdling war-whoop; the Indians jumped to their feet and answered with another whoop. Three ladies fainted and the audience nearly panicked before they realized what was going on.

After Atlanta the tour became rougher. The twice-a-week jumps were longer and harder. The theatres and hotels in Montgomery and Selma (Alabama) were cold and dreary. Rome (Georgia) was not an ideal spot for Christmas, nor the rough road from Chattanooga to Knoxville for New Year's. He caught a cold that remained with him to Lynchburg, and, every day or two, he had a twinge of gout in his right hand. Forrest was relieved when he finally arrived in Baltimore on January 9, 1871. Just two weeks to go, one in Baltimore and one in Washington; then he would be home.

CHAPTER *xxii*

The Final Exit

After three months on the road Forrest knew that his poor body needed a complete rest. He feared, however, that if he were too lenient with his frailties they would demand more time than he could spare. He compromised on a week's respite from his labors before going to New York.

Except for his few days in Brooklyn the previous September, Forrest had not tried a New York engagement for over two years. In the old days such a long absence would have assured him a triumphant welcome; not now. He came in as a second-rater into the second-class Fourteenth Street Theatre. Booth was riding the crest at his new theatre. Niblo's had a re-engagement of the ubiquitous *Black Crook*. Even the old Olympic ignored him, offering a burlesque of Booth's *Richelieu*.

Forrest made one considerate gesture to his crumbling legs: he limited himself to Lear and Richelieu, two roles in which his infirmities would be least conspicuous. It was a useless precaution. His opening night, February 6, was the coldest and most cheerless night he had ever spent in the theatre. Never had he seen so many gaping holes of empty seats, or heard such puny applause. The brutal blow struck him full in the face. No longer was it just a matter of screwing up his strength for the painful last steps from dressing room to stage, knowing that once he passed the wings, he entered his own special nirvana. His old friends were not there to work the magic. Some had died; many, he feared, had succumbed to newer fancies. In

their place was a small assembly of brash, sharp-eyed young-
sters who had come to check the myths about the old man.
Surely this slow staggering figure was not the legendary Forrest. As one sprig of young America was reported to have
summed it up: "I'll tell you what it is, Pop, the people ain't got
time to think as much of Washington these days as you old
men did when you were boys. Steam, the telegraph, and speculation has driven most of the old ideas out of our heads. We are
fast men and live fast. We have no lesson to learn from these
broken-down heroes from the past."

After the performance Forrest plodded back to his dressing
room tired and disheartened. He had known that some sad
day the halo that he had worn for forty-four years would fade.
He had not expected it to vanish so suddenly. Yet, it never occurred to him to give up even when a severe nosebleed forced
him to cancel a performance. He came back the next night,
assured by his doctor that the bleeding had saved him from
a fit of apoplexy.

With all his dogged determination, he was relieved when
he passed the second week and substituted *Richelieu* for *Lear*.
He was certain that another night of the mad old man would
have killed him. Throughout the whole sad month Forrest
found pitifully few bright moments. He was pleased that the
Courier thought the city had treated him shamefully, and that
William Winter, the great khan of the critics, found his Lear
"beautiful and irresistible." Belated praise from Winter moved
him less than the simple letter from the boy in Waltham, Massachusetts, who wrote: "Being one of the small army of boys
called after you, I should feel happy to receive some token
from my illustrious namesake, if nothing more than his auto-
graph." At least this "small army" would keep his name alive.

Forrest was glad to retreat; the city had passed him by. A
few years earlier, if they had turned their backs on him so
brutally he would have been crushed; now he knew that fifty
theatres across the country would take him in and pay handsomely for the privilege. Leave New York to her fancy trash;
he would find shelter elsewhere.

In a way, the rebuff had its compensations. For the moment it subdued his compulsion to keep moving. He returned to Philadelphia for a quiet, if gloomy, month. Eleanora was again troubled with her ankles; the sharp March winds made the excursions to Springbrook a painful chore; and he was obliged to write one of the most dismal letters that he had ever written.

Three years earlier Oakes had borrowed $10,000. Every half-year he had faithfully sent a $365 check for the interest. Now he was four months overdue. Again and again Forrest had lent money to poor actors without expecting repayment, certainly without expecting interest; with Oakes it was different. If he lost faith in his lifelong friend, no faith was left in the world. Finally, on March 10, he outlined the situation to Alger. "While we profess to love our friends," he wrote, "let us not be blinded to their faults nor blind to our own faults for that would be gross negligence of ourself and them. Mr. Oakes has never said a word to me of his failure to pay the half yearly interest. He knows full well how sensitive I am, and how averse for years I have been to have any money dealings with a friend." Forrest did not need the money, nor had he gone back on his promise of an annuity for Oakes. He simply did not want to endanger their friendship: "True friendship while never jealous of the objects of its regard is most exacting in all its friendly dues." Forrest had postponed the wretched task as long as he could. He knew that Oakes and Alger were about to leave the country for a time. "It may be for all time, and in this hour of my much wounded spirit I have written this letter without set phrase or varnished sentence but even as the thoughts have bubbled from my heart. So what is writ is writ."

If Forrest's letter to Alger eventually shamed Oakes into paying the interest, the account was apparently not settled before they sailed at the end of March. Forrest did not go to New York to see them off, and his *bon voyage* note was cool and perfunctory.

A week later Forrest embarked on another sally into the

West: a quick split-week series in Illinois, Iowa, and Wisconsin, just enough to fill out the season. In June and for the remainder of the summer he was back in Philadelphia. It was a sad summer.

Just after he had returned, his sister Eleanora died. "My heart is desolate," he wrote to Alger; "there is no one now on earth whose veins bear blood like mine." One after another, all the Forrests had joined the mournful parade. Had any man ever reached his peak in such a climactic climb and then been driven down the melancholy slope on the other side so relentlessly: by the death of his mother, the cruel loss of his wife's love and then of his wife, the loss of two sisters, the collapse of his health, and, finally, scorned and tumbled out of his command in New York, to have his only remaining sister snatched away?

In his gloomy desolation he could not brood over a default on a mere $365, principle or no principle. In mid-June he wrote to Oakes, welcoming him back and urging him to come to Philadelphia. He needed the comfort of the only true friend he had left in the world. Oakes came, stayed for the summer, and together the two old men plucked away at the few remaining joys left in the world. They talked over their daily complaints, shared their remedies, and gloated over each encouraging sign of their indestructibility. They spent long hot days at Springbrook, sitting in back of the house, watching the river, and tramping through the greenhouses. When the summer passed and Forrest knew the theatres were lighting up in New York and Philadelphia and Boston, he automatically began flexing his legs, painful as they were, and rummaged through his wardrobe.

He decided to concentrate on *Lear* and *Richelieu* for the new season with the other plays on call, the only concession he made to his comfort. He began with a two-week warm-up engagement in Philadelphia, concluding on Friday, October 20. The following Monday he opened in Columbus and a week later in Cincinnati.

By keeping on the move constantly he kept his joints limber.

His spirits, however, did not ride the crest as they usually did on the road. The taste for theatrical sensations had begun to infect the hinterland, and only at the new stops, where he himself was a new sensation, did he pack the theatres and hear the old-time roar. In Houston the entire audience rose en masse when the play concluded. In Kansas City the Forrest name "acted as a magnet upon the prairies of Kansas and the woods of Missouri." The Fort Scott Railroad brought in a trainload of spectators, including three brass bands. Leavenworth, St. Joseph, and Omaha gave him a full-scale holiday welcome.

After the first two weeks the gout and rheumatism had been gnawing at him almost constantly. In Galveston a doctor prescribed a new remedy which, Forrest explained to Oakes, was as "pleasant to the taste as a mint julep in 'fly time'" and which "reproduced all the excessive paroxysms of the gout" before working its cure. He could not stop long enough to give it a fair trial. The most he could do was to try to keep warm, not an easy task as he circled back through the snow belt of Cleveland, Detroit, and Buffalo. Even in Houston, he insisted on having a fire blazing in the cast-iron stove in the greenroom. The rest of the actors were backed against the wall, while Forrest sat with his legs propped up on either side of the stove. He hated to acknowledge his infirmities, and any actor who treated him as a cripple would be rebuked for his sympathy. John B. Wright, his stage manager, set the ground rules at the first rehearsal in each town. No actor must come in contact with Forrest's feet nor touch his right thumb. There were many sadly humiliating moments. Some evenings his right hand was so paralyzed that his sword had to be strapped to his arm just before he went into combat. One night in Albany he had to be carried downstairs from his dressing room and held up in the wings before his entrance. He was grieved to give up *Damon and Pythias;* a single try in Cincinnati had convinced him that he must. The final scene demanded that he leap to the scaffold to rescue Pythias. In his prime, the platform had always been three feet high; during the past few years it had been gradually whittled down to three inches. When he came on in Cincinnati and found that the stage carpenter had laid down two boards for his big jump, he knew that he was through with *Damon and Pythias.*

After his final night, March 22, in Albany, Forrest took the 2:00 a.m. train for Boston. Oakes met him at the station at 11:00, and, at Forrest's insistence, drove him immediately to a Russian bath. The operator apparently did not recondition his body for the sharp breezes of Boston Common. When Forrest arrived at the St. James Hotel, he was seized with a violent chill. He appeared near complete collapse as he struggled into bed, still he assured Oakes that with the weekend's rest he would be ready to begin at the Globe Theatre on Monday.

He was, and by sheer determination carried through six successive nights of *Lear.* Every morning Forrest began from scratch. His first touchy step sent a flame of pain through his body; by evening he had loosened his joints, fired up his will, and was ready to go. The newspapers helped. Every day they were filled with words of encouragement. One reporter noted that Garrick had never played more than 138 nights in a season, and, during the last five years of his professional life, had never acted more than fifty-four. Both Kemble and Garrick had quit in their sixtieth year. Forrest had passed his sixty-sixth birthday, had just completed an 8,000-mile tour, had never missed a night except on two occasions when his baggage had been misrouted, and had played some 125 performances in fifty-two different places. No actor alive, or dead, could match his record. And in spite of his continuing battle to stay on his feet, the reporter had Forrest's own words for it—"he parted with more vitality in one performance of Lear than would keep an Alderman alive for a lustrum."

One observer insisted that the old passion was still there, even if it did not show in the theatre; he had evidence to prove it. He had once written some unfavorable notices and had now called on Forrest to apologize. "Forrest was bent over like a wounded lion about to spring," he recalled; "his disabled arm was held up like a massive paw ready to strike, his dark seamed face became purple, the veins in his gladiatorial neck were tied in knots. Some kind of premonitory hissing as of coming lava, issued from his lips, followed by volcanic rumblings deep down. 'You damned whippersnapper,' he shouted, 'have you come here to bark at my heels or to lick my boots?' When he reached the theatric climax he drew himself up in a final violent and blasphemous explosion and then dropped back into his chair."

By the end of the first week, Forrest's voice was so hoarse that he could hardly speak above a whisper. Again, he was certain that with a full day's rest on Sunday, he could give Richelieu full voice on Monday. Everything on stage had been arranged for his comfort. The stiles across the doorways had been removed; an arm chair was placed off stage next to his entrance. Every night Oakes took him from the hotel to the theatre, helped him dress, and stayed with him every moment he was not on stage.

On Monday night some thought they detected a slight improvement in his voice. On Tuesday afternoon he was too feeble to talk. Still he refused to give up. The doctor had given Oakes a phial of whisky to relieve his suffering. Forrest refused to take it. He whispered to Oakes that if he were to die on the stage, he would not have rum on his breath. Oakes helped him from his chair and he tottered on stage. The first burst of applause seemed to revive him for a moment, but for the remainder of the evening he walked in a daze.

The next morning his doctor solemnly announced that if he went to the theatre again, he would die. Oakes reported that even then "he disputed for a moment before bursting into tears like a child and hiding his head in the pillow." He had played his last regular performance.

For the next three weeks the billboard in the vestibule of the Globe carried daily bulletins on his condition: "the cold has driven into his lungs"; "for two days his body has been tortured with fits of violent coughing"; "pneumonia has brought him to the verge of the grave." The first note of encouragement appeared on April 19: "His health is returning." Two days later the *Sunday Herald* announced that "the native strength of his constitution and the faithful and loving hand of James Oakes have pulled him through."

On Saturday night, April 27, Forrest took the sleeping car to New York, and in spite of a two-hour wait for the connection to Philadelphia, arrived home with no sign of a relapse. He wrote immediately to Oakes thanking him for "his watchful care and tender solicitude." How marvelous it was to have been "spared from death's effacing fingers and permitted for a little longer to worship God in the glad sunshine of his eternal Temple." Forrest went to his bedroom, opened the window to the soft friendly breezes, and lay back on his bed. What a happy relief from the tortuous seven months; yet he had no regrets. He had kept going; he had given a new generation of Americans a taste of what the theatre was like before it succumbed to cheap thrillers. Certainly this was worth the drain on his feeble body, to say nothing of the $39,675 added to his bank account.

Forrest did not relish the prospect of spending the summer alone in Philadelphia with his right leg propped on a stool and his right hand nesting in a pillow. What desolate loneliness, gluing himself to one spot from morning to night. In the past he had trusted his will power to work miracles when everything else failed; now the more he willed himself out of his gloom, the heavier the gloom became. His poor body had built up an immunity and stubbornly rebelled at any further submission. To get through the summer, he had to shout for help. Oakes came, and for the rest of the season the two old men sat together at Springbrook, peacefully resigned to their immobility, dreaming of the past, yet still scheming for the future.

Forrest might not be able to ride a full circuit in the fall as he had the year before. He might have to limit himself to quick jaunts into New England or down the Coast. He had no thought of resigning. Late in August he began a daily routine of testing his legs, forcing them to carry him a bit farther each day. In spite of the three-month rest he had given them, they refused to obey. After a few days it became painfully clear that they had finally given out. As soon as he moved, the demons began their relentless hammering, and each step called a few more to their devilish duty.

If Forrest had to admit defeat, he did not intend to admit total defeat. His mind was clear, his voice was strong; they would have to take over the burden. Propped behind a pulpit in the center of the stage, he could still give a performance that would put the new darlings, even Booth, into the shade.

To ease into his new career, he set up his reading stand at the Philadelphia Academy of Music on October 15. He felt strangely alone on the bare stage, as if he were a minister exhorting his flock. And like many preachers he had to search through row after row of empty seats before he pieced together a congregation; it was a dismal beginning. The newspapers noted that he had given an "inspired reading of *Hamlet*" (the first three acts), that his health was restored, that they sincerely hoped he would attempt other roles. Polite praise for a native son, nothing more. Forrest himself agreed with the reporter who thought that comparing Shakespeare from the pulpit with Shakespeare from the stage was like "comparing the light of a bedroom lamp with the glare of the noon-day sun." A few more seats were filled for the repeat readings on the 18th and 22nd, still no great swell of enthusiasm. This was enough for Philadelphia.

Had there been an alternative, Forrest might have abandoned the project. Perhaps after he and the audiences adjusted to the new style, they both might feel more comfortable. To give himself an extra night's practice, he stopped in Wilmington on his way to New York.

Recalling his New York fiasco a year-and-a-half earlier, Forrest was happy to appear on the platform of Steinway Hall rather than in a theatre, though it seemed strange to submit himself for comparison with Charles Dickens, who had appeared in the same hall four years before. On his first night, November 19, four hundred curious souls gave him a warm welcome. The next day the *New York Times* reminded the new generation that if Forrest's melancholy Dane were less controlled and introspective than the Prince (Booth's) that was currently favored, certainly Shakespeare's magnificent lines had never been read more "trippingly on the tongue." Forrest thought that he was catching his stride in the new enterprise. However, on the 22nd, only 250 turned out for *Othello*.

He would try once more, in Boston. He began with *Othello* at the Tremont Temple on Monday evening, December 2; on Wednesday he read *Hamlet,* and on Saturday afternoon repeated *Othello.* As usual, Oakes was with him constantly during the Boston week, escorting him to the Temple and helping him into his reading clothes: striped trousers and a swallow-tail coat that Forrest insisted made him look ridiculous. "He never wore it," Oakes explained, "except when compelled to do so, and absolutely refused to wear it into the public dining room of the hotel." After the final matinee, he asked Oakes to pack the black suit in the bottom of the trunk.

The readings had not gone well. When he went back to New York on Saturday night, he was resolved to abandon the silly exercise. He would wait patiently in the library on Broad Street until his strength returned; then he would undertake a regular tour.

He arrived in New York at 6:00 a.m., went directly to the Metropolitan Hotel, ordered a fire, and went to bed. Monday was the coldest morning of the season. When he went to the train, he was happy to bundle his neck in the scarf which Oakes's daughter had knitted for him. The only comfort he could find was in the happy thought that he was not headed for Quincy, Illinois, or Omaha, Nebraska, with an evening's performance at the end of the journey. He went home to the warm fires that the servants (Lizzie and Kate) had laid in the library and in his bedroom.

When he got up on Tuesday morning after a long night's rest, he was certain that within a couple of weeks he would be ready. To play it safe, he would wait until after the New Year. On Wednesday morning he was even more optimistic. He wrote to McArdle asking him to alert the managers, and to

Oakes, reporting on his rapid rejuvenation. His happy letter was filled with odd bits of domestic news: the gigantic breakfast that Lizzie had fixed for him on the first morning, the lovely fresh bouquet that someone had put on his dressing table. If Oakes would please remember to get his smallpox vaccination, they could have another reunion in a month or two: "God bless you ever, my dear and much valued friend."

In the afternoon the weather was brisk but bright. He ordered the carriage. Springbrook was not a cheerful sight at this time of the year, still a landowner had his duties even in the dreary seasons. When he came back to Broad Street in the evening, he read for an hour in the library and at eleven went to bed.

The next morning Katie had the breakfast ready early and rang for Mr. Forrest. She waited ten minutes, then rang again. After another five minutes she knocked on his door. She could hear him breathing heavily and groaning. She called through the door, asking if he was sick. There was no answer. She tried the door, thinking it was locked. It opened. Forrest was stretched out on the bed, moaning and twisting. She raced downstairs and called her sister from the kitchen. Lizzie opened his collar; Katie ran for a pan of cold water and then for the doctor. Lizzie kept sponging his head with cold water, trying to wipe away the "red streak" on the side of his neck He tried to speak to her. All he could command, according to Lizzie, "was a look of unutterable despair." When Katie came back with Dr. Gross, Forrest was dead.

Apparently he had followed his usual morning habit. He was fully dressed, except for his coat and tie, which hung on a chair in the corner. The movable mirror was at the foot of the bed and beside him the eight-pound dumbbells with which he exercised every morning. On the bedside table was a copy of *Hamlet,* face down at the page he had been reading.

Oakes received the news by telegram in the afternoon and took the train immediately, arriving in Philadelphia at four the next morning. "I went directly to his bedchamber," he wrote to Alger. "There he lay, white and pulseless as a man of marble. For a few minutes it seemed my body was as cold as his and my heart as still. No language can express the agony of that hour."

The body was laid out in the room in which he had died, and on Monday morning, December 16, 1872, Oakes dressed him in the black swallow-tail coat he had worn on the platform. "No human mind can conceive the agony of my heart at that dreadful hour."

At nine o'clock the front doors were opened, and some 2,000 Philadelphians marched past the coffin. The room was so densely packed with flowers that it looked as if the mourning parade were passing through a tropical paradise. A wreath of white japonicas, Forrest's favorite flower, rested above his head.

Just after noon, the house was taken over by the special friends who had received the simple black-bordered command:

> You are requested to attend the funeral of the late
> Edwin Forrest
> which will take place on Monday next, December 16, at
> 1:00 P.M. from his late residence 1346 North Broad Street.

There were few intimate friends in the group, for few could claim that honor.

The brief service was spoken by Rev. Joseph D. Newlin of the Church of the Incarnation. Just before the casket was closed, Mrs. Sinclair, who had been sitting in a corner with her head resting on her hand, her fingers working nervously, rose and went to the coffin. She drew her veil aside, placed her hand on the cold forehead, passing it gently down to the hand, which she held firmly for several minutes. She took a sprig from the japonica wreath and returned to her seat.

The sixty carriages in the cortege moved slowly down Broad Street to Walnut and then to St. Paul's. The streets were lined with bowed heads all the way. At the churchyard the Reverend S. H. Boyer of St. Paul's said a short prayer as the coffin was lowered into the Forrests' vault. Edwin's name had already been entered in the final space on the granite slab.

. . .

Actors have never had an easy time holding a place in memory after their final bow. One spin around the seasons, and most of them are forgotten. The actor may roar up a nightly storm to make the painter or writer sick with envy, yet he pays a heavy price for his power.

Forrest held on longer than most of his tribe. He had cut his way into the theatre with such tornado force that the image faded more slowly, just as the light of the sun on the horizon outlasts the moon. Almost everyone had seen him at some theatre or other, sometime or other. No American actor, no actor in America, had ever had his name on more lips.

Although time chipped away at the memory of his Lear, Jack Cade, and Metamora, it made slower progress with the name of Forrest. Every year or so, another monument or memento gave his name new life. An Edwin Forrest Club was established in New York on March 9, 1874, Forrest's birthday. For the next sixty years the club held an annual banquet on the sacred day. Another Edwin Forrest Club was founded in Boston in 1892.

On February 13, 1883, his costumes, swords, and jewels were sold at auction. Anyone with a few dollars in his pocket could purchase his own private remembrance. If he wanted one of Forrest's diamonds, he had to bid up to $400. If he was satisfied with a bit of stage paraphernalia, the price was ridiculously small. The Metamora tomahawk, $12.50; the bloody Virginius knife, $3.50; the Macbeth armor, $9.50; three Roman togas, $1.75 each; the magnificent Othello robe in rich green velvet trimmed with gold and lined with yellow satin, $14.00. Someone bought a "well worn bone toothpick" for forty-five cents.

More enduring monuments appeared later. On November 27, 1906, a crowd watched the laying of the cornerstone of the Edwin Forrest Theatre in Philadelphia. Fritzi Scheff, then the rage of New York for her singing of "Kiss Me Again" in Victor Herbert's *Mlle Modiste,* spread on the first trowel of mortar. Ethel Barrymore, David Warfield, John Barrymore, and W. C. Fields took their turns after her. On March 9, 1923, a "monster benefit" for the Edwin Forrest Home held at the Forrest Theatre included Leopold Stokowski's Philadelphia Orchestra, John Philip Sousa conducting the combined pit bands of all the Philadelphia theatres, and "the greatest array of stars ever assembled": E. H. Sothern, Julia Marlowe, O. P. Heggie, Helen Hayes, Ernest Truex, Helen Gahagan, Beth Merrill, and William Seymour, among others.

On November 24, 1925, the Shuberts opened their Forrest Theatre (now the Coronet) and the adjoining Forrest Hotel on Forty-ninth Street in New York.

During the years immediately after his death, Forrest's name appeared, as it had so frequently during his lifetime, in the courts. Dougherty, Lawson, and Oakes, the three executors, tried to make a quick settlement. Forrest could have told them that once they were trapped by the courts, they might as well be patient.

They had their problems even before the will was filed. At 3:30 a.m. on Wednesday, January 15, just a month after the funeral, a defective flue started a fire in the southeast corner of the library. Although Oakes and McArdle, who were still staying in the Broad Street house, immediately called the firemen, $30,000 worth of books were destroyed and the first folio Shakespeare was badly charred.

As might have been expected, a disgraceful scramble began when the will was filed on January 16. Forrest had not provided for his two servants, Katie and Lizzie. When Dougherty offered them a week's salary, they moved out in a huff. Joseph McArdle, who had arranged Forrest's recent tours, was not mentioned in the will, though the executors found a note among Forrest's papers advising them that McArdle had lost a purse containing $3,000 during their last trip and that he should make restitution for his carelessness. McArdle did not adopt the servants' course. He stayed on in his room on Broad Street and refused to budge.

A Miss Lillie Ballard from Boston wrote, asking about a diamond cross that Mr. Forrest once let her wear at a party. He had told her that "once she broke herself of the habit of biting her finger nails" he was going to give it to her. She assured the executors that she had broken the habit. In case they did not believe her story, could they please keep the cross until she had funds to buy it?

An enterprising lawyer advertised in the *New York Herald*: "Wanted! The heirs of Edwin Forrest. They will hear something to their advantage by calling on John Townsend." Forrest could have warned the executors that the shysters would be busy. Townsend found one prospect, a William B. Forrest from Nova Scotia, who claimed to be a second cousin. However incredible his story, Oakes remembered that Forrest had spoken of an uncle in Scotland and rather than risk a protracted court battle the executors settled for $16,000.

Alger's unfinished biography had to be dealt with. In January, 1874, Oakes urged Lippincott to make an advance announcement of the publication to "clip the wings of James Rees in the bud." They were not successful in nipping the buds of Rees's wings. His unofficial biography appeared later that year; and in spite of Oakes's continual needling, Alger did not deliver his manuscript and receive his check for $2,000 until April 26, 1877.

The most troublesome maneuvering involved the dower for Mrs. Sinclair. In early January, 1874, Oakes heard that some of her rich friends were prepared to support her case in court. The executors wished to avoid a legal battle. As Oakes remarked in a letter to Dougherty, "those coming after us would care little about Forrest's wishes for his Home; they would prolong the adjudication just to feed on the fees." In May they settled with Mrs. Sinclair, giving her the $75,000 mortgage on Fonthill Castle plus $25,000 in cash.

On June 12, 1875, the executors made their first accounting to the Orphan's Court in Philadelphia. With Mrs. Sinclair taken care of and all outstanding debts paid, the estate was valued at $297,539.83.

In the two-and-a-half years since Forrest's death many people had begun to wonder about the plans for the Home. One reporter had commented that it seemed doubtful if any old actor would ever "enjoy a meal, frugal or otherwise, under his sheltering roof." Forrest's old friends could never have broken faith with his fondest dream. In the summer of 1876, as soon as they completed the sale of the Broad Street mansion —to a J. Travis Quigg for $20,000 cash and a $78,000 mortgage— they prepared Springbrook for its new tenants. The executors followed Forrest's instructions to the letter, including his wish that the "enclosure around the grounds shall be such as to permit persons five feet in height to look into them from the sidewalk outside." Perhaps Forrest thought that keeping the actors under the surveillance of the public would restrain them from misbehaving.

Even after the Home was opened on November 7, 1876, and after twelve old actors had taken up residence, occasional complaints appeared in the newspapers. On January 3, 1878, the *Philadelphia Transcript* reported that the estate was being mismanaged: "The figures wobble out of line like drunken soldiers." No evidence was offered to support the charge.

Lawson died in the spring of 1878, and Oakes on June 4 of the same year. Dougherty had to prepare the final accounting. This would have been simple had not Quigg reneged on his purchase of the Broad Street house. Apparently it was not an easy property to sell. For two years the gallery and grounds were rented out for art exhibitions and fairs, and during the summers Theodore Thomas's Symphony Orchestra gave concerts in the garden.

In 1880 Dougherty finally found a buyer, the Philadelphia School of Design for Women (now the Moore Institute of Art). Although the school offered only $45,000, Dougherty was happy to get the property off his hands. Finally, on March 30, 1882, he had completed his task, filed his account with the court, and put $300,000 in trust for upkeep of the Home.

When the School of Design ladies moved in on Broad Street, Forrest must have shuddered in his grave. His castle had already been taken over by the Catholic Sisters; now his mansion was to be cluttered with giggling female painters. As one reporter commented, "thus it is that violets and roses of womankind have sprung up to sweeten and beautify all the spots intimately associated with the memory of a man who is supposed to have died with an implacable animosity toward the fair sex."

For fifty years the actors lived on his bounty amid the idyllic charm of his country estate. In 1925, when manufacturing establishments began to invade the Holmesburg area, the Managers decided to seek another location. Times had changed in other respects. Two bathrooms for twelve guests had seemed luxurious in 1876, not in 1925. Fortunately, $242,000 still remained in the trust fund to say nothing of the value of the Springbrook property; the Managers could select freely. To bring the actors closer to the center of the city, they decided to build on South Washington Square. However, when they discovered that the building code would not permit such a structure in the Independence Hall region, they bought a tract of land on Parkside, overlooking Fairmount Park. The transaction was profitable. Springbrook sold for $600,000; the new Elizabethan manor house cost $142,300; thus the actors acquired an elegant new home and the trust was increased by over $450,000.

The new Home was dedicated on Friday, September 28, 1928. Dr. Horace Howard Furness, the Shakespearean scholar, then vice-president of the Board of Managers, made the presentation, and Walter Hampden, the Shakespearean actor, accepted on behalf of the theatrical profession.

The move to Parkside Avenue was not the last stroke of good fortune for Forrest's heirs. When John Frederick Zimmerman died in December, 1924, he left his estate in trust, the income to be available to his son. When his son died, it was to be divided equally between the Actors' Fund Home, West New Brighton, Staten Island, and the Edwin Forrest Home. Zimmerman had owned most of the theatres in Pennsylvania and was a member of the Theatrical Syndicate that for eighteen years prior to 1914 had held a despotic control over the American theatre. Zimmerman had squeezed his fortune out of helpless actors who had to do his bidding or starve; now he finally returned what he had taken. When his son died in 1949, the Edwin Forrest Home received $650,000. With this substantial sum added to what was left of Forrest's fortune, the Home has carried on without financial hardship. The $50,000 annual income from investments is more than enough to provide for the actors.

The story of the Home cannot be told with a financial statement, phenomenal as it is that the life savings of an actor should have survived so long. The real story of Forrest's munificent monument rests with the hundred old actors who have enjoyed his hospitality during the past eighty-four years. As James A. Herne, the playwright, once remarked, "One need but go through that Home to know the soul of the man who once lived there."

Most of the "decayed" actors have found peace and comfort, which they rarely knew during their precarious days in the profession. Only two or three have been unable to respond to the refined environment. In July 1886 James Ward O'Brien was dismissed for "want of improved cleanliness and respect"; two others were sent packing for drunkenness. The rest have waited quietly for their final departure. One old lady wanted to be certain her demise was not announced prematurely. She wrote in the register on May 14, 1894: "Mrs. Rachel Cantor wishes a lighted candle held to the soles of her feet as a test of life. Should it raise a blister, hold off!" Some enjoyed only a few brief months before the end. Signor Perugini, Lillian Russell's ex-husband, entered in January 1914, and died the following December. Some have sadly ended the journey in a hospital. For most the light has dimmed slowly and gently. The story has frequently been told of one old lady who sat by the window in the evenings looking across the field. One night she thought that she recognized Forrest coming up the slope to Springbrook. She rose to greet him. The figure stopped outside the window, raised its hat and spoke: "Madame, I shall soon have the honor to welcome you to a sweeter home than this." At breakfast the next morning she reported the visitation; before evening she died.

A present-day visitor to the Home is immediately struck by the relaxed and easy manner of the guests. Whatever hardships they may have endured during their days in the theatre, they have quickly adjusted to the new luxury. Recently, Mrs. Cavanna, the resident supervisor, volunteered the services of the Home's chauffeur to drive me back to the railroad station. Since the driver was off duty, she asked if I would mind if he did not wear his uniform, explaining that some of the actors refused to ride with him unless he wore his full livery.

They give a commanding performance in their new roles. As these words are written, on a bright Sunday afternoon, the dinner gong has just rung at the Edwin Forrest Home; the twelve old actors are shuffling along the corridor under the gaze of Coriolanus. Perhaps they appear a bit more eager to reach the dining room than on weekdays, for they know that the sumptuous feast will be augmented with the extra added attraction for Sunday, a glass of wine, compliments of Mr. Forrest.

His Mobile Magic

The main road of Forrest's career is relatively easy to track. Occasionally, on sudden side excursions, he gets out of sight, though only for a moment. He was too big a man, too much in the public eye, and the broad swath he cut through new territory was too fresh and clear to be hidden. Temperamentally, he was incapable of hiding himself from the world. He may have been stung at times to see his private affairs appropriated by the public; even this, he recognized, was a price he paid for his fame. He willingly acknowledged the public's rights to his stage creations. They belonged to them as much as to him, and that their true nature is now so elusive cannot be blamed on Forrest.

One could just as well hope to jump a hundred feet in the air, catch a bird on the wing, and capture the grace and beauty of its flight as it streaked across the sky, as to comprehend the magic of yesterday's actor. The real essence of the player's art evaporates into the night air as soon as he disappears into the wings on his final exit. Even the critic who races to his writing table while still under the spell flounders when he tries to transfer the actor's mobile magic to the printed page.

One hundred years later one must sadly admit that the original image is irretrievable. The eyes of the writer who saw him may have been feeble or badly focused, or his pen may have been unable to follow his heart and mind. The perversions, prejudices, and inadequacies of those who wrote of

Forrest cannot be known completely. In a way, the image of his acting can only be pieced together from the comments that seem most common and persistent and from the few peripheral and indisputable facts.

His compelling power on the stage—and even his sharpest critics recognized this power—was derived from his commanding physique, his booming and penetrating voice, and from that indefinable "x" quality, that personal magnetism which has served so many actors. There was more than that. The second order of magnitude of his powers would include his carefully studied readings of the text, his strenuous realism, and his choice of characters whose driving passions paralleled his own. Give him a hero fired with democratic passions who slashed out at a tyrant, and he could rouse an audience to shouting. Even those who were reluctant to bestow the mantle of "great tragedian," willingly granted him the title, "greatest American tragedian."

Forrest unconsciously embodied and represented in himself "the vital, burly, aggressive Americanism of his age." The *Spirit of the Times* (July 14, 1877) said that his acting "was as directly opposed to the creamy smoothness and prancing propriety of Macready's art as Walt Whitman's virile lines are opposed to the dainty and supersensuous dialectics of Mr. Tennyson."

Forrest may have stood a mere five feet ten; on stage his bulky, muscular frame seemed to tower like a giant over the puny actors around him. The vibrancy of the figure rather than its size was overpowering. Anyone who had seen him as Spartacus in *The Gladiator* could never forget the tense muscles, the distended neck, the swollen arteries and veins, the rigid jaws, "the orbs now rolling like the dilated and blazing eyes of a leopard, now white and set like the ferocious deathly eyes of a bull, while smothered passion seemed to threaten an actual explosion of the whole frame." He was a "magnificent animal," as William Winter once called him. His extravagant muscularity, particularly his chunky lower limbs, were often ridiculed. One actor burlesqued Spartacus, playing the part with bulbously padded calves, and even after his fellow actors made a pin cushion of his legs with their daggers, he continued to prance about, until someone finally pointed out the knives, whereupon he dropped to the floor and "writhed with anguish" all over the stage. Poking fun at Forrest's physique was easy, yet no one denied its power. His muscles were always tuned up for action, even on the thirtieth or fortieth night of an engagement. As *Harpers* once observed: "There he is—the neck, the immemorial legs, the ah-h-h-h-h in the same hopeless depth of guttural gloom. We may call it the muscular school; the brawny art; the biceps aesthetics; the tragic calves; the bovine drama, pant, roar, and rigamarole; but when then; but what then? Metamora holds his mighty arms and plants his mighty legs, and with his mighty voice sneers at us 'Look there!' until the very ground thrills and trembles beneath our feet."

The audience might tremble when he unleashed his power; his fellow actors shook in their boots. No one could predict what havoc might result when he was on a rampage. One of his favorite tricks on an exit was to drive his sword into the wooden column behind the proscenium and leave it quivering as a warning to anyone who might cross him. One night in Boston an Englishman sitting in the front box ran out of the theatre screaming that the "damned brute was going to cut down the theatre." Actors often explained a black eye or bump on the head by saying that they had played Lucullus to Forrest's Damon. One night Forrest's opponent in *Oralloossa* lost two front teeth. The wags in the greenroom reported afterward that this was only to enable him to pronounce the name of the play properly: "Oh-they-are-loose-sir." The local stage managers always had difficulty in hiring supers who were brave enough to stand up to Forrest. One manager, annoyed by Forrest's repeated complaints about weak warriors, hired six strong-arm men and instructed them to maul the braggart actor. Forrest caught on to the trick and charged into the bruisers, knocked their heads together, and pitched one of them into the bass drum in the orchestra pit.

Admittedly, some of the less rugged souls in the audiences

preferred gentler acting. As one critic commented, stretching the point a bit: "Some admire the painful Pre-Raphaelite style in painting, every leaf finely shaded, every flower distinctly drawn, a kind of ladies' work, others like the broad and vigorous execution that reveals immediately the workings of a genius." Moreover, it took a man with a solid frame and with quivering muscles to support Forrest's democratic and revolutionary principles. If a common man was to be his own sovereign, each man a king, he had to be a man of uncommon strength. If a Tell was to stand up to Gessler, a Spartacus confront the praetor, a Cade defy Lord Say, or a Metamora challenge the English, he must be an extraordinarily endowed hero. If the glitter of the titular monarchs was to fade in the presence of such lowly born adversaries, the virtue, power, and nobility of the rebellious heroes must be clearly and immediately apparent.

With all his rugged Gargantuan strength, Forrest was not heavy-footed. He covered the stage with a firm and graceful stride. His actresses often insisted that no man ever bowed and kissed a hand more gently.

There was charm and power in the massive torso, in the Roman head "set on a neck like the trunk of a tree," in the strong and manly features of his face. Alone they could capture an audience. They might not have subdued them had they not been supported by an equally commanding voice. None of Forrest's contemporaries could shake the walls of the theatre as he could. Only Henry Ward Beecher, shouting from the pulpit, came near to matching him. Forrest possessed a voice "such as God never put into any other man," the *Dramatic Mirror* noted. "He could sigh like a zephyr or roar like a hurricane." When, as Richelieu, he threatened to launch the ecclesiastical curse, Forrest's bellow made the theatre walls tremble. Lear's delirious prayer to nature reverberated like a thunderstorm. A Bowery B'hoy once commented that Forrest had to keep his voice down to a whisper; "if he spoke out loud he'd be heard down to the battery." When he stood in the wings of the Pittsburgh theatre one evening chastising the dresser for not adjusting his costume properly, his whispered off-stage curses carried to the top gallery. The audience gave him a round of applause before he entered.

Forrest was blessed with more than sheer savage power. His articulation was always sharp. He could range from piano to forte, from lowest bass to highest treble with ease, and his vocal chords could withstand the most severe strain. One critic reported that he could play through two tragedies in one evening and still deliver his final dying words as clear as a bell. Nor was his voice all roar. In the delicate and tender passages he could sing in a soft tremulo that would move the hardest heart. When Virginius says to his motherless daughter: "I never saw you look so like your mother in all my life," the sweet pathetic tones never failed to start the tears rolling.

Much as Forrest gloried in his God-given powers, and much as he cultivated them, he took greater pride in the fruits of his study in the library. Nothing delighted him more than to dig a new meaning out of Shakespeare's text, test the elocutionary modeling that might carry it across the footlights, and then watch the audience to see if it caught hold. Certainly none of his contemporaries had Forrest's passion for constant study. Although he played Lear for forty years, he never went on without spending the day with the text; still he could recall only one evening when he had left the theatre satisfied with his performance. Even if an actor never reached his ideal, he was lost if he stopped trying.

The critics who thought that Forrest's emotional outbursts were all rant and roar, that he lacked the imaginative power to see the dagger, or Banquo's ghost, admitted that he grasped and disclosed the meaning of a passage with greater precision and lucidity than any of his contemporaries. Anything that could be understood logically, he got. He was a demon for sticking to the text, utterly impatient with the actor who improvised. Some reporters occasionally objected to his elaborate elocution; yet all in all, as one critic commented, "the world has probably never seen a more effective speaker of words."

His efforts to underline new meanings and invent natural

399

readings frequently led Forrest to linger too long over a word or phrase or elongate a pause. The *Washington Post* once observed that they had never seen a Richard take so long in getting ready to go to bed. Another reporter noted that after the final slaughter in *Hamlet,* some gallery boy invariably called out: "Wake me up when Forrest dies." One spectator wrote that Forrest sometimes sounded as if he intended to take up an everlasting rest on a period, go to sleep over a semicolon, or spend the evening with a comma: "If his pauses got much longer, the audience would have time to stroll in the lobbies between his sentences." Senator Robert Stockton, the old naval commander, reported that he once met a man coming out of the Broadway Theatre and asked him what was going on inside. "Oh, nothing," the man replied, "just Forrest in one of his pauses!" His fascination with pauses was to be expected; Kean had been similarly inclined.

How much Forrest copied Kean cannot be determined precisely. In his early days he undoubtedly imitated his readings and postures, as he also imitated those of Cooper, but Forrest was never a mere copier. From the beginning, he rebelled at the notion that an actor should merely carry on the traditions of his predecessors. As much as he might learn from Kean and Cooper, the solid sinew of his acting had to come from himself. In fact, he became distinguished as a new breed of American actor, out of the main stream of the established schools, precisely because he disregarded the stage manners of the past, looked freshly at himself and life around him, stocked his characters with the homely virtues that he himself cherished, and insisted that the audience must be persuaded to believe in the reality of the stage hero just as strongly as he himself believed.

More than any actor before him and more than any of his colleagues, he spoke "with such a closeness to nature as to convey the impression of spontaneous utterance rather than recitation from memory." Two stories are told of his touching reading of the lines, "Virginia, Virginia!" Virginius has just murdered his daughter and returns to his home pathetically calling for her. Catherine M. Reignolds-Winslow, the actress who played Virginia on many occasions, reported that when she returned to her dressing room after being killed, she regularly felt that Forrest was actually calling for her to come back on stage. At one performance a man in the pit became so completely absorbed that when he heard the cry, he stood up and shouted: "You killed her in the market house, you damned villain!"

Forrest's compulsion to capture natural renderings was not, however, centered on such simple lines as the "Virginia, Virginia." He was more fascinated with being faithful to nature in Lear's madness or in the death throes demanded in most of his roles. Henry W. Longfellow once remarked that he thought Forrest's Lear was a noble conception, as fine and close to nature as any performance he had ever seen. When Forrest had an audience trapped in the spell of his Lear, he held them to the final curtain. On one occasion he became so excited that he tore the white wig from his head and threw it across the stage; no one laughed. The audience was just as engrossed in the part as Forrest.

Although his fidelity to nature in *Lear* was regarded as a supreme achievement, many found the painfully clinical death rattles in other roles unbearable: for example, hanging out his tongue, contorting his features, and writhing on the stage floor. In defense of his fierce exhibition, Forrest maintained that a man of his massive physique could not die without a show of extreme agony. Some insisted that his eclectically composed demonstrations of love, hate, terror, and anger, though nerve-shattering in their authenticity, were Forrest's rather than Hamlet's, Othello's, or Macbeth's. Others objected to the stage trickery he employed for realistic effect: the rattling saber, the whetstone on which Shylock made such a to-do of sharpening his knife, and more particularly the hollow-bladed dagger filled with red paint that he used in *Virginius*. On the pressure of a spring it would release a spurt of blood. After a lady in Providence fainted dead away, Forrest himself decided this was artifice and not art and abandoned it.

The extravagances in Forrest's back-to-nature policy may appear grotesque to a twentieth-century playgoer accustomed to Marlon Brando's mumbling or Gary Cooper's polite whispers. For most of the audience of his time he had caught a persuasive mixture of heroics and naturalness. And he wisely stuck to his own tested brand of true-to-life acting when Edwin Booth and the new school took over with their substitution of attitude for passion, languor for power, and effeminacy for manliness, as one critic described it.

Forrest's biceptual gymnastics and lion's roar would undoubtedly drive a present-day audience out of the theatre; however, a Booth, Henry Irving, or E. H. Sothern could probably empty the theatre just as quickly. An actor is always *persona non grata* to the next generation.

The meticulous stage directions and marginal notes in Forrest's prompt books reveal that his concept and intent were revolutionary for their time and yet remarkably appropriate to our own time. An actor could follow his *Hamlet* book, for example, and create a thoroughly acceptable twentieth-century performance. He abandoned the conventional flowing wig for the part; he cut out the crawling around the stage floor in the "players scene." The stage direction "terrible, *tearful* grief" for the lines: "Remorseless, treacherous, lecherous villain!" could have been written by John Barrymore or Maurice Evans. Hamlet's touching scene with Gertrude in her chamber was carefully annotated with realistic stage business that could serve a Gielgud or an Olivier. Forrest may have seemed a "bull in a china shop" in *Hamlet,* or "painfully unfit, temperamentally and physically," as Winter observed. Certainly his careful conception of the part, as he himself recorded it, was not bombastic nor grotesque. Even the dying, as he described it, slipping into Horatio's arms, easing to the floor as Horatio kneels to support him, a "sudden convulsive movement" as he catches his last choking breath, seems fairly standard for this final tragic scene.

Forrest worked up a part with the greatest care. No other

nineteenth-century American actor could match his diligence and devotion to his profession. He insisted on absolute punctuality at rehearsals. One stage chronicler wrote that if an actor was late, Forrest would sit with his heavy gold watch open in his hand. When the offender arrived, he snapped the watch shut, rose in his best King Lear manner, and withered the culprit: "Sir! You have taken from these ladies and gentlemen that which Almighty God himself cannot restore to them— their time!" He demanded strict attention to all the minutiae of stage business and absolute quiet in the wings during rehearsal and performance; and although he took only passing interest in the scenic backgrounds, let a stagehand slide in the wrong wing or fail to get the drop in on time and he had better run for his life. He was equally impatient with the audience. Once at Niblo's he refused to proceed with the play until Nixon had driven a particularly obstreperous party out of their private box. Ellen Terry reported that she once saw him go down to the footlights and gravely and sincerely admonish the audience: "If you don't applaud, I can't act."

Careless and incompetent actors drove him to distraction. "You are a butcher by trade, are you not?" he was reported to have shouted at an actor who had stumbled through his lines. "No, sir; I am an actor," the poor fellow replied. Forrest grabbed him by the collar and dangled him at arms length. "An actor! You are not, sir; you are a butcher. Go resume your calling, kill sheep, kill oxen, kill asses, if you must, but never kill Shakespeare more."

The stories of his fierce impatience circulated widely among the profession. Every actor who ever played with him had a favorite story. In fairness to Forrest, the coin must be turned over. One youngster reported that when he forgot his lines and ran crying to his dressing room, Forrest assured him that such a lapse of memory could strike anyone, that it had often happened to him in his early days. He rearranged the boy's costume, dried his eyes, and led him back to the stage. Frequently he would give an actor a "reading" for a line, and then say: "That is my idea, but you do it as you like." James O'Neill (Eugene O'Neill's father) began his acting career in support of Forrest. He recalled the occasion when, exceedingly flurried and nervous, he forgot his lines. Forrest fed them to him "in a way that no one in the audience knew he was doing it." When O'Neill tried to apologize after the performance, Forrest assured him that no apology was required. "You are young, my boy," he said, "and if you are worth anything, those fits will overtake you; I wouldn't give a peanut for the professional prospects of an actor who is not nervous."

Mrs. John Drew once wrote that though some found Forrest morose and churlish at rehearsals, she thought that he was the handsomest man and the fairest actor she ever played with. "If you had anything good, he let you show it." What was more astonishing in a star actor, he would drop a little below you on the stage, turning his back to the audience, so that the attention would be on you. An endless stream of actors testified to his generosity; though he might drive them beyond their capacities in the theatre, if he heard of a hardship in their personal lives, he quickly offered a ten-, fifty-, or hundred-dollar "loan" to relieve their distress.

Unlike most actors who traded on physique and passion, Forrest did not ride the high-wire one night and plod in the dust the next, rage through the dressing rooms drunk and demented before the curtain, and return sad, sober, and pathetic when the play was done. He was steady and predictable; managers, actors, and audiences knew what to expect. If Forrest was in the theatre, a strong performance was guaranteed.

Of all his roles, Lear was clearly the greatest. Most agreed, they had never seen a better Lear; a sizable group concurred with the reviewer who wrote, that "no actor of ancient or modern times had rendered the role like Forrest." Some thought his Coriolanus would have run a close second had the play been more popular. The flag-wavers, though admitting he had less to work with, cheered the native plays. Richard Penn Smith, author of *Caius Marius*, one of the unsuccessful prize plays, once wrote:

His Mobile Magic

Let no one question his transcendant art;
The tragic muse to him should yield the throne
Who to Bird's muse new beauties can impart
And cast a veil e'en o'er the faults of Stone.

One of the few critics who pulled together his thoughts on Forrest's acting was "Weeping Willie" Winter—he was called "Weeping Willie" because he outlived so many of his contemporaries and was repeatedly asked to write their obituaries. Winter had never really liked Forrest. He was too much of an Anglophile to believe a home-trained actor could reach the top. Even he admitted that Forrest was no mere ranter. He might be lacking in imagination and spirituality, be obsessed with an unfortunate and colossal animal selfishness, yet he had passion and tenderness. He was like a rugged old tower that stood out on the landscape: "The architecture may not be admired, but the building is distinctly seen and known. He was tremendously real. He had a grand body and a glorious voice, and in moments of simple passion he affected the senses like the blare of trumpets and clash of cymbals, or like the ponderous, slow-moving, crashing, and thundering surges of the sea."

The only trustworthy measure of Forrest's greatness rests with a few indisputable facts. In the middle fifty years of the past century no native-born, native-trained actor climbed so high, summoned American writers to the drama with such fervor, spread the enduring glories of the mighty Shakespeare so widely, and carried the raging democratic fever to the stage with such fierce passion. And no actor compelled so many Americans to pay so much for a tempestuous evening in the theatre.

☞ **First Appearance of the celebrated**

Mr. EDWIN FORREST,

THE EMINENT AMERICAN TRAGEDIAN.

Theatre Royal, Drury Lane.

This Evening. MONDAY, October 17th, 1836.

Their Majesties' Servants will perform (1st Time on the English Stage) a Tragedy in Five Acts, entitled

THE GLADIATOR

With New Scenery (by the Messrs. GRIEVE*). New Dresses, and Decorations.*

Marcus Crassus, (*Urban Prætor*) Mr. WARDE.

Gellius, (*Consul*) Mr. F. COOKE.   Lentulus, Mr. HOOPER.

Jovius, (*a Centurion*) Mr. BARTLEY.

Braechius, Mr. MATHEWS,   Florus, Mr. BRINDAL.

Spartacus, - - - - Mr. EDWIN FORREST,

Who will have the honor, on this occasion, of making his First Appearance on the British Stage

Phasarius, (*Brother to Spartacus*) Mr. COOPER,

Œnemaus, Mr. BAKER,   Crixus, Mr. DURUSET.

Mummius, Mr. MEARS,   Scropha, Mr. HONNER,

Boy, Miss MARSHALL,   Centurion, Mr. T. MATTHEWS,

Julia, (*Niece to Crassus*) Mrs. HOOPER,—*her 1st Appearance,*

Senona, (*Wife of Spartacus*) Miss HUDDART,—*1st Appearance these 5 Years*

☞ *The Principal Scenery will consist of*

A ROMAN STREET.   THE HOUSE OF CRASSUS.

A ROMAN AMPHITHEATRE!

The Plain of Pæstum after the Battle

THE TENT OF CRASSUS.   CAMP OF SPARTACUS.

STREET LEADING TO THE PRÆTORIUM.

Retreat of Spartacus, near Rhegium!

☞ In order that the Public may judge of the effects of the New Orchestra, previous to the Tragedy.

THE BAND WILL PLAY THE OVERTURE TO "ANACREON."

The Evening's Performances will terminate with (**2nd Time at this Theatre**) the Farce of

SCAN. MAG.

Mr. Theodore Singleton, Mr. BARTLEY, Edward Singleton, Mr. HOOPER, Capt. Tinderly, Mr. BAKER

Tommy Caudle, Mr. MEADOWS,   John Grub, Mr. BEDFORD,   Bendle, Mr. T. MATTHEWS,

Emily Singleton, Mrs. VINING,   Fanny, Mrs. HUMBY,   Julia, Miss LEE,   Mrs. Caudle, Mrs. C. JONES.

To-morrow, Shakspeare's Comedy of **AS YOU LIKE IT.** Orlando, Mr. Cooper, Jaques, Mr. Warde,

Amiens, Mr. Wilson,   Adam, Mr. Bartley,   Touchstone, Mr. Meadows,   Rosalind, Miss Taylor,

(*her First Appearance these Two Years*) Audrey, Mrs. Humby. After which, (**First Time**

at Half-Price) Balfe's Grand Original Opera of

THE SIEGE OF ROCHELLE!

On Wednesday, a Tragedy in which Mr. EDWIN FORREST will appear.

On Thursday, will be produced (*for the First Time*) a Drama, in Three Acts, to be entitled

The Duchess ? Ormond.

The Duchess of Ormond, - Miss HUDDART,

After which will be revived, **WITH ALL ITS ORIGINAL SPLENDOUR,**

THE JEWESS!

On Friday, a Tragedy in which Mr. EDWIN FORREST will appear.

Mr. BALFE

will appear in his own Opera of *The Siege of Rochelle,* To-morrow Evening, and will immediately afterwards appear **IN A NEW GRAND OPERA!**

*Playbill for Forrest's first appearance on the London stage.
His performance was wildly cheered.*

CHESNUT STREET THEATRE.

ACTING AND STAGE MANAGER, • • MR. FREDERICKS.

PRICES OF ADMISSION.

Dress Circle and Parquet, • • Fifty Cents Second Tier and Family Circle, Twenty-Five Cents
Third Tier, • • • Twenty-Five Cents Boxes for Colored Persons, • Twenty-Five Cents
Two Large and Commodious Private Boxes have been added on the Second Tier; also, Two Proscenium Boxes on a level with the First.

Proscenium Boxes, • • • • • • • • • • • • $5 00.
Private Boxes, holding Twelve Persons, • • • • • • • 12 00.

The Box Office will be open from 10 o'clock, A. M. until 3 o'clock, P. M.

DOORS OPEN AT 7 O'CLOCK.   PERFORMANCE COMMENCE AT HALF-PAST 7 O'CLOCK

BENEFIT

OF

Mrs. C. N. Sinclair,

LATE

MRS. FORREST

AND

HER LAST APPEARANCE BUT ONE!

WHEN SHE WILL PERSONATE

MARGARET ELMORE AND LADY TEAZLE!

In the Third and Fourth Acts of

THE SCHOOL FOR SCANDAL!

Mr. George Vandenhoff in Two Characters

WEDNESDAY EVENING, March 31, 1852

Will be acted Shakspeare's Admirable Comedy of

MUCH ADO ABOUT NOTHING!

BEATRICE, - - - - - Mrs. C. N. SINCLAIR
BENEDICK, - - - - - Mr. GEORGE VANDENHOFF

Don Pedro..............Mr. DAWSON	Dogberry..............Mr. JOHN GILBERT
Don John..............Mr. MANNE	Seaton..............Mr. BRADLEY
Count Claudio..............Mr. TAYLOR	Steacole..............Mr. GEORGE
Leonato..............Mr. FREDERICKS	Oatcake..............Mr. HALL
Antonio..............Mr. PARDEY	Vergis..............Mr. SCHARF
Friar..............Mr. LOMAS	
Borachio..............Mr. BRIGGS	Hero..............Miss G. KINLOCK
Conrad..............Mr. DAVENPORT	Ursula..............Miss DAVIDGE
Balthazar..............Mr. WENTWORTH	Margaret..............Miss PARKER

DANCE, - - - - - BY MISS M. A. DENHAM

OVERTURE BY THE ORCHESTRA.

To conclude with, first time here, the Elegant Comedietta of

THE QUEEN'S HUSBAND!

Or, Where there's a Will, there's a Way.

DON MANUEL, - - - Mr. GEORGE VANDENHOFF
DONNA FRANCESCA, - (Her First Appearance in Place) - Mrs. SINCLAIR

Don Scipio de Pumpolino..............Mr. DAWSON	Officer..............Mr. WENTWORTH
Don Lopez..............Mr. EYTINGE	Servant..............Mr. HALL
Secretary..............Mr. GEORGE	Donna Blanche..............Miss KINLOCK

Thursday, will be produced the Beautiful Play of

THE PATRICIAN'S DAUGHTER.

FRIDAY, Mrs. SINCLAIR'S BENEFIT AND LAST APPEARANCE BUT ONE.

Requests being constantly made at the Box Office for a repetition of the

SCHOOL FOR SCANDAL

Due Notice will be given of its next representation.

Scott's Steam-Press Job Printing Establishment, 12 Hudson's Alley, below Chesnut, above Third Street, Philada.

Playbill for Mrs. Forrest's performance. She went on the stage immediately after the divorce, though she had never acted before.

NOTES ON SOURCES

Although the story has not been interrupted to ask the reader to dive for footnote documentation, the details of Forrest's life have been drawn from many sources. Few readers will want to shuffle through the writer's entire pack of dog-eared notes. Some may wish to glance at the "face" cards. Even those unblessed with bibliophilistic curiosity will, I hope, allow the writer a few lines to ease his conscience and acknowledge the generosity of his behind-the-scenes collaborators.

The Board of Managers of the Edwin Forrest Home, their lawyer John Hippel, and the resident supervisor Mrs. Walter Cavanna granted me easy access to Forrest's books, papers, and miscellaneous memorabilia and gave me the same hospitality as that accorded to the retired actors.

The Theatre Collections of Harvard College and of the New York Public Library have been invaluable and their staffs most helpful at every stage: George Freedley, Elizabeth P. Barrett, Paul Myers, and Seymour Quinn at the New York Public; Dr. William Van Lennep and Mary Reardon Keating at Harvard. Sources of particular importance at Harvard were Forrest's diary of his first trip abroad, a scrapbook of items relating to Edwin and Catherine labeled "Collection Dramatique" assembled by someone in Philadelphia in 1857, some forty Forrest letters, countless playbills, nine published accounts of the divorce trial, and the magnificently extra-illustrated volumes of *Actors and Actresses* by Brander Matthews and Laurence Hutton (New York, 1886). Particularly helpful at the New York Public Library were the prompt copies of plays in which Forrest appeared and the rich mine of scrapbooks and playbills. The full facilities of both of these great libraries were used, especially the files of the New York Public Library's

Newspaper Collection on West Twenty-fifth Street, just a few blocks from Forrest's New York home.

The Princeton Library kindly allowed me to copy their collection of letters from Forrest to Oakes (just under two hundred of them). May Davenport Seymour, Curator of the Theatre Collection at the Museum of the City of New York, was, as usual, most helpful in turning up a few items unavailable elsewhere. The Players Club Library yielded some Forrest letters, and, of course, playbills and clippings relating to Edwin Booth's and Catherine Sinclair's California venture. The late Messmore Kendall permitted me to use his rich library (recently acquired by the University of Texas). Particularly rewarding here was the extra-illustrated *Edwin Forrest* by Lawrence Barrett.

Forrest letters and memorabilia have been widely scattered. The Cooper Union Library, the Pierpont Morgan Library, the New York Historical Society, the Howard University Library (the Channing Pollock Collection), and the Boston Public Library contributed small, yet vital, bits of information. The University of Pennsylvania Library gave me access to the Robert Montgomery Bird papers. The Moore Institute of Art was helpful with information regarding the Broad Street Mansion.

For the story of Forrest's adventures away from the theatrical centers I am indebted to the Ohio Historical and Philosophical Society in Cincinnati, the Cincinnati Public Library, the Lexington Public Library, the Kentucky Historical Society in Frankfort, the Western Reserve Historical Society in Cleveland, the Chicago Historical Society, the Missouri Historical Society in St. Louis, the San Francisco Public Library, and the Sacramento City Library.

One of the pleasantest periods in the Forrest exploration was spent in England enjoying the superb services and facilities of the British Museum and the Victoria and Albert Museum. I was, of course, disappointed to discover that the theatrical periodicals covering Forrest's intervals in England: *The Dramatic and Musical Review*, the *Theatrical Observer*, the *The-*

atrical *Examiner,* the *Edinburgh Dramatic Spectator, Tallis's Dramatic Magazine,* and the *Theatrical Journal* had been destroyed in the bombing of the British Museum. The first of these was, however, located at the Royal College of Music and the last at the Finsbury Public Library. The curators of the British Museum Newspaper Library at Colindale seemed capable of responding quickly to any request, whether for an old newspaper from London, or from Manchester, Sheffield, or Bath. The collection of playbills and clippings in the Enthoven Collection at the Victoria and Albert Museum and the guidance of the Curator, George Nash, and his assistant, Miss Johnson, were most helpful. The public libraries of Finsbury, Holburn, Marylebone, and Westminster willingly produced pertinent documents from their collections of theatre memorabilia. The public libraries in Manchester, Liverpool, and Bristol were extremely co-operative as were the national libraries in Edinburgh and Dublin. Commander E. S. Satterthwaite, Secretary of the Garrick Club in London, kindly opened their clubrooms and library to me.

Any biographer, I presume, is impelled to his task by the biographers who have preceded him, not only by what they have written, but also by what they have left unwritten. Five major biographies (only one in this century) and three minor accounts of Forrest's life have appeared:

> Alger, William Rounseville: *Life of Edwin Forrest.* 2 Vols. Philadelphia, 1877.
> Barrett, Lawrence: *Edwin Forrest.* Boston, 1881.
> Harrison, Gabriel: *Edwin Forrest.* Brooklyn, 1889.
> Moses, Montrose: *The Fabulous Forrest.* Boston, 1929.
> Rees, James ("Colley Cibber"): *The Life of Edwin Forrest.* Philadelphia, 1874.

> Durang, Charles: "Life of Edwin Forrest." (Thirty-seven manuscript pages in Durang's hand in the Harvard Library, presumably written sometime between 1864 and 1869.)

Notes on Sources

E. T. W. [*sic*]: *The Biography of Edwin Forrest.* Philadelphia, 1835. (In the Harvard Library.)
*The History of Edwin Forrest, the Celebrated American
Tragedian, from His Childhood to His Present Elevated Station as a Performer.* "Written by an individual who has known him from his boyhood." New
York, 1837. (In the Harvard Library.)

All of the biographies have been helpful, for some information indispensable; yet the inadequacy of each prompted the
present undertaking. Fact and accuracy were given short
shrift in all of them. Even Alger, the official biographer, who
had more first-hand material available than the others, reports
many events incorrectly. For example, he has Forrest married
in the wrong church, by the wrong minister, and describes the
wedding as a large affair when, in fact, it was meagerly attended. Forrest had admonished Alger to report his life truth-
fully: he wanted "no exemptions from the infirmities of my
temper or my disposition." Perhaps the fact that Alger wrote
most of his voluminous account after Forrest's death explains
his easy disregard for Forrest's advice. He chose the path common to most nineteenth-century biographers, sheltering his
hero under a cover of romantic and sentimental apology. Rees,
like Alger, had access to Forrest's scrapbooks and account books
—he looked after the Broad Street house during Forrest's last
tours. However, Rees was too eager to get his reminiscences
into the bookstores before the official biography to take time to
study the documents at hand.

Barrett, an actor who had played with Forrest and who in
the late eighties became Booth's right-hand man, arranging
his tours and appearing with him as a co-star, gave a straight-
forward quick sketch of Forrest's life. He touches only the high
points. Harrison, an actor, writer, painter, and a friend of Forrest, devoted himself almost exclusively to a description of
Forrest's interpretation of his various roles. In the only recent
biography, Moses created the most vivid image of the man
and his times. His picture is incomplete and misleading, partly

411

because he used only those sources that were readily available, but more especially because he clearly did not like Forrest. How Moses managed to live, as a biographer must, with a man he found so disagreeable is difficult to understand.

In addition to the biographies, many specific sources of information regarding various aspects of Forrest's life were helpful. The following are selected samples:

Eaton, Walter Prichard: "Edwin Forrest." *Atlantic Monthly,* Vol. 162 (August 1938), pp. 238–47.

"Forrest's Second Reception in England." *Democratic Review,* Vol. XVI (April 1845), pp. 385–7.

"Mr. Forrest's Petition to the Legislature of Pennsylvania for a Divorce." (In the New York Public Library.)

Newton, A. Edward: "Edwin Forrest and His Noble Creation." Published by the Managers of the Edwin Forrest Home, 1928.

O'Conor, Charles: "Address to the Bar Association of the City of New York." April 11, 1876. (In the Princeton Library.)

Randall, Mr. [Josiah?]: "On the Forrest Divorce and the Right of the Pennsylvania Legislature to Grant It." (In the New York Historical Society.)

Records of the Orphan's Court of Philadelphia. April 1882. Philadelphia City Hall.

Sabin, Joseph: *Catalogue of the Library of Edwin Forrest.* Philadelphia, 1863.

Wikoff, Henry: *The Reminiscences of an Idler.* New York, 1850.

Wilson, Garff: "American Styles and Theories of Acting from Edwin Forrest to David Belasco." Unpublished Ph.D. Dissertation, Cornell University, Ithaca, New York, 1950.

Winter, William: *The Wallet of Time.* 2 Vols. New York, 1913.

Any student of the American theatre is dependent on
George C. D. Odell's monumental *Annals of the
New York Stage* (15 Vols. New York, 1927–49), and
on Arthur Hobson Quinn's two volumes: *History of
the American Drama from the Beginning to the
Civil War* and *History of the American Drama from
the Civil War to the Present Day* (New York, 1943);
and, also, if to a somewhat lesser degree, on the
following:

Brown, Thomas Allston: *A History of the New York Stage
from 1732 to 1901.* 3 Vols. New York, 1903.

Coad, Oral Sumner and Edwin Mims, Jr.: *The American
Stage.* New Haven, 1929.

Dunlap, William: *History of the American Theatre.* 2 Vols.
New York, 1832.

Hornblow, Arthur: *History of the Theatre in America from
Its Beginning to the Present Time.* 2 Vols. New
York, 1919.

Hughes, Glenn: *A History of the American Theatre 1700–
1950.* New York, 1951.

Ireland, Joseph N.: *Records of the New York Stage from
1750 to 1860.* 2 Vols. New York, 1866.

Morris, Lloyd: *Curtain Time.* New York, 1953.

Seilhamer, G. O.: *History of the American Theatre.* 3 Vols.
Philadelphia, 1888.

Two other general sources of information have been particularly valuable: the biographies, autobiographies, and chronicles of actors and managers; and the local and regional theatre
histories. Many of the histories have been written as theses in
theatre departments in various universities and have been
made available through the courtesy of their libraries. The
following are again selected items:

ACTORS AND MANAGERS

Barnes, Eric Wollencott: *The Lady of Fashion*. New York, 1954.

Bunn, Alfred: *The Stage: Both Before and Behind the Curtain*. 3 Vols. London, 1840.

Hackett, James Henry: *Notes and Comments upon Certain Plays and Actors of Shakespeare*. New York, 1864.

Lawrence, W. J.: *The Life of Gustavus Vaughan Brooke*. Belfast, 1892.

Logan, Olive: *Before the Footlights and Behind the Scenes*. Philadelphia, 1870.

Ruggles, Eleanor: *Prince of Players*. New York, 1953.

Stebbins, Emma, ed.: *Charlotte Cushman: Her Letters and Memories of Her Life*. Boston, 1878.

Stone, Henry Dickinson: *Personal Recollections of the Drama; or, Theatrical Reminiscences*. Albany, 1873.

Toynbee, William, ed.: *The Diaries of William Charles Macready*. 2 Vols. New York, 1912.

Vandenhoff, George: *Leaves from an Actor's Note-book*. New York, 1860.

Wemyss, Francis Courtney: *Twenty-six Years of the Life of an Actor and Manager*. New York, 1847.

Wood, William B.: *Personal Recollections of the Stage*. Philadelphia, 1855.

REGIONAL AND LOCAL HISTORIES

Bailey, Frances Margaret: "A History of the Stage in Mobile, Alabama, from 1824–1850." Unpublished M.A. Thesis, State University of Iowa, 1934.

Blake, Charles: *Historical Account of the Providence Stage, 1762–1891*. Providence, 1868.

Carson, William G. B.: *Managers in Distress*. St. Louis, 1949.

—— *The Theatre on the Frontier*. Chicago, 1932.

Clapp, W. W., Jr.: *A Record of the Boston Stage*. Boston, 1853.

Fletcher, Edward Garland: *Records and History of Theatrical Activities in Pittsburgh from their Beginning to 1861.* Cambridge, Mass., 1931.

James, Reese D.: *Old Drury of Philadelphia, a History of the Philadelphia Stage 1800–1835.* Philadelphia, 1932.

Kendall, John S.: *The Golden Age of the New Orleans Theater.* Baton Rouge, La., 1952.

Langworthy, Helen: "The Theatre in the Frontier Cities of Lexington, Kentucky, and Cincinnati. Ohio, 1797–1835." Unpublished Ph.D. Dissertation, State University of Iowa, 1952.

Ludlow, Noah: *Dramatic Life as I Found It.* St. Louis, 1880.

MacMinn, George R.: *The Theater of the Golden Era in California.* Caldwell, Idaho, 1941.

McGlinchee, Claire: *The First Decade of the Boston Museum.* Boston, 1940.

Morrow, Marguerite: "A History of the English Stage in New Orleans from 1817 to 1837." Unpublished M.A. Thesis, State University of Iowa, 1926.

Pelby, William: *Letters on the Tremont Theatre.* Boston, 1830.

Phelps, Henry Pitt: *Players of a Century, a Record of the Albany Stage.* New York, 1890.

Roppolo, Joseph P.: "A History of the English Language Theatre in New Orleans, 1845 to 1861." Unpublished Ph.D. Dissertation, Tulane University, 1950.

Sherman, Robert L.: *Chicago Stage: Its Records and Achievements.* Chicago, 1947.

Smith, Sol: *Theatrical Management in the South and West.* New York, 1868.

Tompkins, Eugene and Quincy Kilby: *The History of the Boston Theatre 1854–1901.* Boston, 1908.

Turner, Vivian: "The Stage in New Orleans, Louisiana, after 1837." Unpublished M.A. Thesis, State University of Iowa, 1929.

Willard, George: *History of the Providence Stage, 1762–1891*. Providence, 1891.

Wilson, Arthur H.: *History of the Philadelphia Theatre 1835–1855*. Philadelphia, 1935.

Finally, I am happy to express my thanks to the Graduate School and the Research Committee of Indiana University for their assistance, and to Harold Strauss for his patient and astute editorial guidance.

Index

Index

Index

Index

Index

Index

Index

A Note about the Author

RICHARD MOODY's interest in theatrical history stems from an active and varied career in the dramatic arts. He was born in Des Moines, Iowa, in 1911, and was educated at Drake University (B.A. and M.A.), Cornell University (Ph.D.), and Yale, where he spent two years in the Department of Drama with George P. Baker of 47 Workshop fame and with Allardyce Nicoll. He held a National Theatre Conference Fellowship at Cornell and a Guggenheim Fellowship for theatre research in England in 1959–60.

He acquired practical experience as a free-lance radio actor and announcer and acted with the Forty-Niners summer theatre in New Hampshire. He taught drama courses and produced plays at Cornell, Northwestern, the University of Illinois, and the University of Hawaii. In 1942 he joined the Department of Speech and Theatre at Indiana University, became a full professor in 1955, and Director of the Indiana University Theatre in 1958.

He has contributed articles on the theatre to *American Heritage*, the *Enciclopedia dello Spettacolo*, the *Quarterly Journal of Speech*, and the *Educational Theatre Journal*. *Edwin Forrest* is his third book; the others were *America Takes the Stage* (1955) and *The Astor Place Riot* (1958). He lives with his wife and two children in Bloomington, Indiana.

A NOTE ON THE TYPE

The text of this book is set in Caledonia, a Linotype face designed by W. A. Dwiggins (1880–1956), who was responsible for so much that is good in contemporary book design. Though much of his early work was in advertising and he was the author of the standard volume Layout in Advertising, *Mr. Dwiggins later devoted his prolific talents to book typography and type design, and worked with great distinction in both fields. In addition to his designs for Caledonia, he created the Metro, Electra, and Eldorado series of type faces, as well as a number of experimental cuttings that have never been issued commercially.*

Caledonia belongs to the family of printing types called "modern face" by printers—a term used to mark the change in style of type-letters that occurred at the end of the eighteenth century. It is best evidenced in the letter shapes designed by Baskerville, Martin, Bodoni, and the Didots.

This book was composed, printed, and bound by The Plimpton Press, Norwood, Mass. The paper was manufactured by S. D. Warren Company, Boston. Typography and binding based on designs by W. A. Dwiggins.